STRATEGIC ASIA 2021–22

STRATEGIC ASIA 2021–22

NAVIGATING TUMULTUOUS TIMES
in the Indo-Pacific

Edited by

Ashley J. Tellis, Alison Szalwinski, and Michael Wills

With contributions from

Michael J. Green, Marcin Kaczmarski, Huong Le Thu, Rohan Mukherjee, Rebecca Strating, Ashley J. Tellis, Joanne Wallis, and Suisheng Zhao

THE NATIONAL BUREAU *of* ASIAN RESEARCH
Seattle and Washington, D.C.

THE NATIONAL BUREAU of ASIAN RESEARCH

Published in the United States of America by
The National Bureau of Asian Research, Seattle, WA, and Washington, D.C.
www.nbr.org

Copyright © 2022 by The National Bureau of Asian Research

All rights reserved. No part of this publication may be reproduced, stored in a retrieval system, or transmitted in any form or by any means, electronic, mechanical, photocopying, recording, or otherwise, without prior permission of the publisher.

ISBN (print): 978-1-939131-69-0
ISBN (electronic): 978-1-939131-70-6

Cover images
  Front: Lightning over Lake Overholser in Oklahoma City, Oklahoma ⓒ Raychel Sanner
  Back (left to right): U.S. Navy Petty Officer 3rd Class James Vazquez; Office of the Maryland Governor; Joseph Liu; and Government of South Korea

Design and publishing services by The National Bureau of Asian Research.

Cover design by Stefanie Choi.

Publisher's Cataloging-In-Publication Data
(Prepared by The Donohue Group, Inc.)

Names: Tellis, Ashley J., editor. | Szalwinski, Alison, editor. | Wills, Michael, 1970- editor. | Green, Michael J., contributor. | National Bureau of Asian Research (U.S.), publisher, sponsoring body.

Title: Navigating tumultuous times in the Indo-Pacific / edited by Ashley J. Tellis, Alison Szalwinski, and Michael Wills ; with contributions from Michael J. Green [and 7 others].

Other Titles: Strategic Asia ; 2021-22.

Description: Seattle ; Washington, D.C. : The National Bureau of Asian Research, [2022] | Includes bibliographical references and index.

Identifiers: ISBN 9781939131690 (print) | ISBN 9781939131706 (electronic)

Subjects: LCSH: Indo-Pacific Region--Strategic aspects. | United States--Strategic aspects. | Globalization--Indo-Pacific Region. | COVID-19 Pandemic, 2020---Indo-Pacific Region. | China--Foreign relations--United States. | United States--Foreign relations--China.

Classification: LCC DS341 .N38 2022 (print) | LCC DS341 (ebook) | DDC 327.091824--dc23

Printed in the United States.

The paper used in this publication meets the minimum requirement of
the American National Standard for Information Sciences—Permanence
of Paper for Printed Library Materials, ANSI Z39.48-1992.

Contents

Preface ix
Alison Szalwinski and Michael Wills

A Tempestuous Hegemon in a Tumultuous Era 3
Ashley J. Tellis
    An examination of the genesis of the disorder in the Indo-Pacific that became manifest during the Trump years and how U.S. policy has managed U.S.-China competition, the risks to globalization, and the Covid-19 pandemic.

China's Big-Power Diplomacy: Strategic Rivalry and Geopolitical Expansion in the Indo-Pacific 37
Suisheng Zhao
    An study of China's foreign policy under Xi Jinping in the context of heightened U.S.-China rivalry, deglobalization, and the Covid-19 pandemic.

Northeast Asia: Alignment Despite Anxiety 63
Michael J. Green
    An examination of the impact of anti-globalization populism and the Covid-19 pandemic on the resilience and strategic trajectories of Japan, South Korea, and Taiwan.

Russian Foreign Policy in a Time of Rising U.S.-China Competition ... 95
Marcin Kaczmarski
    An assessment of Russia's response to the challenges of U.S.-China competition, deglobalization, and the Covid-19 pandemic.

Leveraging Uncertainty: India's Response
to U.S.-China Competition 127
Rohan Mukherjee
> A study of how India has taken intensified U.S.-China competition as an opportunity to push forward in its quest to become a leading power in Asian and global affairs.

Southeast Asia in Great-Power Competition:
Between Asserting Agency and Muddling Through 161
Huong Le Thu
> An examination of the impact of great-power competition, the Covid-19 pandemic, and economic decoupling on Southeast Asia, with a focus on Indonesia, the Philippines, and Vietnam.

Strategic Competition in Oceania 187
Rebecca Strating and Joanne Wallis
> An assessment of the effects of strategic competition, primarily between the United States and China, on the national trajectories and economic and security policies of states in Oceania.

About the Contributors 223

About Strategic Asia 229

Index 233

Preface

Alison Szalwinski and Michael Wills

The twenty-year period from 1917 to 1937 was hugely consequential to shaping the global order that exists today. The intervention of the United States in World War I in April 1917 was decisive in bringing an end to a violent conflict that pitted the old order of European empires against one another on the battlefields of Europe and marked the beginning of the end of that imperial order. Six months later, the Bolshevik Revolution in Russia in October 1917 and the subsequent creation of the Soviet Union provided both an ideological and a material example of an alternative political-economic model to the prevailing order of liberal democracies and constitutional monarchies. Often overlooked as a post–World War I footnote until recent events have brought it back to the fore, the great influenza pandemic of 1918–19 circled the globe in successive waves, infecting one-third of the world's population and leaving more than 50 million people dead. And ten years later, the stock market crash of October 1929 led to the Great Depression and sparked a desperate, decade-long search for policies to revitalize economic growth and alleviate poverty. By the end of the 1930s, the different responses adopted—militaristic nationalism in Germany, Italy, and Japan; revolutionary Communism in Russia and, in nascent form, in China and elsewhere in Asia; and a spectrum of laissez-faire approaches and social welfare programs in weary democracies—had brought the world to the brink of a second global conflict.

For those attuned to history's rhymes, a century later the echoes of these tumultuous forces are reverberating once again. The end of the Cold War starting in 1989 and the collapse of the Soviet Union in December 1991 marked the conclusion of a period of intense geopolitical competition but relative stability in international relations. And like the emergence of the Soviet Union, Nazi Germany, and imperial Japan, the rise of the People's Republic of China (PRC) as both a major global power and, more importantly, an alternative model for governance and economic growth is a major challenge to the liberal international order that was established after 1945. Add to the mix the Covid-19 pandemic, which since February 2020 has caused major shocks to the global economy and an unprecedented suspension of international travel and commerce. The pandemic has the potential to bring significant change to the global balance of power in the medium to long term, based on the varied recovery trajectories of different states. Further destabilizing the international order is the crisis of confidence in many democracies, beset by intense polarization, political and electoral dysfunction, and rising nationalism. Once again, all the ingredients are present for another profound experiment in international politics.

This book, the twentieth volume in the National Bureau of Asian Research's *Strategic Asia* series, begins from this baseline of potential epochal change. It assesses the impact of three major trends on the geopolitical environment of the Indo-Pacific region. The first is the intensifying strategic competition between China and the United States.[1] The second is growing pushback against globalization, which is marked by a rise in economic nationalism and an increased interest in reshoring the production of critical technologies and securing supply chains.[2] And the third trend is the still unfolding Covid-19 pandemic, which has engendered massive spending programs and interventions by governments on a scale not often seen outside wartime, the economic, social, and political reverberations of which will mark the decade to come.[3]

These three trends are colliding with and amplifying underlying changes in the relative balance of power in the Indo-Pacific that we have been examining in this series for two decades. Most notable among these, of course, is the growth of China as a major global power, pulling away from other regional powers in Asia and emerging as an almost peer competitor to the United States. China's rise would have been unsettling for the United States under any circumstances, as Washington began to grapple with the realities that its fleeting post–Cold War unipolar moment was already passing. But the particular nature of China's Communist party-state regime, its domestic repression and human rights violations, its increasingly assertive international behavior, and its massive military modernization

---

[1] U.S.-China strategic competition is examined in detail in Ashley J. Tellis, Alison Szalwinski, and Michael Wills, eds., *Strategic Asia 2019: China's Expanding Strategic Ambitions* (Seattle: NBR, 2019); and Ashley J. Tellis, Alison Szalwinski, and Michael Wills, eds., *Strategic Asia 2020: U.S.-China Competition for Global Influence* (Seattle: NBR, 2020).

[2] Thomas Wright, "Stretching the International Order to Its Braking Point," *Atlantic*, April 4, 2020.

[3] Hanns W. Maull, "The Coronavirus Pandemic and the Future of International Order," *Survival* 63, no. 1 (2021): 77–101.

program and the specific capabilities and weapons systems that it has developed over the past two decades have caused growing trepidation among China's neighbors in the Indo-Pacific region and all but guaranteed a strong U.S. response.

A second significant feature of the Indo-Pacific strategic landscape is the series of increasingly clear choices that other major, middle, and small powers in the region are making. Japan, a major power still beset with economic and demographic challenges, is doubling down on its alliance with the United States as part of its strategic reorientation to face the China challenge. India, an emerging major power whose relations with China have worsened, is also leaning more clearly toward the United States even while striving to maintain its autonomy. And middle powers such as Australia and Taiwan are, like Japan, making a clear decision to align more fully with the United States—exemplified in the rapid evolution of the Quad, the formation of Quad-Plus arrangements, and the announcement in September 2021 of the AUKUS security partnership between Australia, the United Kingdom, and the United States. Among the exceptions to this trend are South Korea, which is still held back by the challenge from North Korea and opting for a strategic nondecision, and Indonesia, which insists on nonalignment even as the pressures on Southeast Asia and the Association of Southeast Asian Nations (ASEAN) are increasing.[4] Meanwhile, the smaller powers in Southeast Asia, Central Asia, and across the Indian and Pacific Oceans, despite desperately preferring not to choose sides in the U.S.-China competition, have nonetheless begun to lean toward one or the other. In the process, many of these states have continued to show a remarkable degree of agency and, in some cases, have successfully worked to maximize their opportunities in this more competitive strategic environment by adroitly playing off China and the United States.

The interplay between the three trends and these changes in the relative balance of power have, as Ashley Tellis describes in his introductory chapter to this book, raised deep concerns among governments struggling to make good strategic choices in an environment where it seems that the established international order might be giving way. Increasing hesitancy about globalization and a loss of faith in free market frameworks following the 2008–9 financial crisis, coupled with the Trump administration's withdrawal from the Trans-Pacific Partnership and willingness to adopt tariffs as part of the competition with China, are all challenging the liberalized global

---

[4] See Ji-Young Lee, "South Korea's Strategic Nondecision and Sino-U.S. Competition," in Tellis, Szalwinski, and Wills, *Strategic Asia 2020*; Joseph Chinyong Liow, "Southeast Asia and Sino-U.S. Competition: Between a Rock and a Hard Place," Tellis, Szalwinski, and Wills, *Strategic Asia 2020*; and Ja Ian Chong, "Shifting Winds in Southeast Asia: Chinese Prominence and the Future of the Regional Order," Tellis, Szalwinski, and Wills, *Strategic Asia 2019*.

market approach that has dominated international business and politics for four decades.

Beginning in the spring of 2020, the reaction of many governments to the Covid-19 pandemic only intensified this pressure. Closed borders, restricted international travel, and the lockdown of economic and social life for more than a year have dramatically disrupted global manufacturing and trade. The pandemic revealed the fragility of just-in-time global supply chains and led governments of all ideological persuasions to seek ways to secure their access to critical resources and technologies. As a result, policy choices that until recently were shunned in liberal economies, such as favoring specific domestic industries with subsidies and pursuing comprehensive economic statecraft, have shifted from the wings to the center stage of policymaking. There is now a remarkable acceptance of massive state intervention in economic policy, the development of sectors deemed critical for national security, and the reshoring of supply chains for technologies on which future economic growth, innovation, and the creation of national economic and military power will depend.

The net effect of these changes is twofold. There is a much greater willingness to resort to government intervention in the pursuit of national objectives, which for free-market democracies complicates the established political and business environment that has existed since the 1980s. In addition, various forms of nationalism—the economic nationalism described above, plus ethnic nationalism—are noticeably on the rise in a growing number of countries. A level of uncertainty and anxiety now underpins political debate, electoral politics, and strategic thinking around the world, including in the Indo-Pacific region.

In this environment, effective policymaking and good strategic thinking will depend on three conditions. The first is a clear-eyed approach to the strategic competition with China that prioritizes a whole-of-government and society-wide response. It is now evident that the U.S.-China relationship is, and for the foreseeable future will be, defined by competition, irrespective of the academic debate about whether such competition is appropriate or desirable. This has long been understood in Beijing but is now widely acknowledged in Washington and other democratic capitals. It is critical for the United States to craft policies from this baseline. As principals in both the Trump and Biden administrations have been at pains to make clear, competition does not mean confrontation in all instances, and it does not need to result in conflict. But the competition between China and the United States will be enduring in nature, and Washington needs to devote serious attention to its strategic preparations.

Second, the development of this approach should be done in a bipartisan manner that will survive the inevitable election cycles and transitions in democratic politics. Such a consensus is emerging on Capitol Hill, where an increasing number of senators and representatives from all corners of the country within both parties are clear about the challenges and are working to craft policies toward a shared objective. For the United States to prevail, it will need to recreate the broad strategic consensus that existed during the early years of the Cold War with the Soviet Union, where the adoption by the political establishment of George Kennan's containment strategy led to a consistent strategic approach over decades.

Third, even with this consensus achieved, the United States must make smart, effective strategic choices. Drawing historical parallels, the early years of the Cold War era took place at a time when the United States was the preponderant global power, alone comprising more than 45% of the global economy. This position of strength allowed Washington to create a multilateral alliance system to counter the Soviet Union in Europe and a bilateral hub-and-spoke alliance system to counter Soviet and Chinese Communism in Asia, as well as to offer generous aid and development programs to U.S. allies and partners across the world that helped create the conditions for the emergence of democracies and open economies in the decades that followed. Domestically, Washington provided significant public support for basic and applied research into scientific and technological solutions that would ensure the United States remained ahead of the Soviet Union, as well as investments in education and language training to cultivate generations of specialists with expertise in countries critical to strategic competition.[5]

The situation is much more challenging today now that the United States' relative economic power has fallen to around 20% of total world output (and while China has grown to the same level). In these more difficult circumstances, Washington has much less room to make strategic missteps, and so must ensure that all aspects of U.S. national power are effectively and appropriately trained on the most critical challenges and opportunities. Beyond their human cost, the two-decade counterinsurgency operations spanning North Africa, the Middle East, and Afghanistan since the September 11 attacks have distracted from efforts to counter rising Chinese power. Three successive administrations sought various forms of rebalancing toward the Asia-Pacific, and all were set back by the prosecution of the war on terrorism. The Biden administration and those that follow will need to ensure that the focus on the Indo-Pacific is truly implemented and sustained

---

[5] Richard J. Ellings and Robert M. Hathaway, "The Need for Policy-Relevant Asia Studies," *Asia Policy*, no. 9 (2010): 2–11.

in the face of all the challenges of the decade ahead. During this period, if China's window for opportunistic actions narrows, a bold leader who has consolidated power might be willing to take risky actions before the onset of deep-rooted demographic and economic constraints.[6]

Finally, the United States needs to focus on four specific priorities in the years ahead to maximize the chances of dissuading China from taking aggressive actions against the liberal international order. First, Washington must consistently develop and implement national security and national defense strategies that ensure that the U.S. security presence, alliance system, and new partnerships are priorities for successive administrations. The elevation of the Quad during the past few years, the AUKUS announcement in September 2021, and the growing support for ensuring Taiwan's defense against Chinese aggression are all encouraging trends in this regard.

Second, Washington should step up the diplomatic activities that underpin U.S. engagement—not just with existing allies and partners but with potential new partners—to ensure that the United States is centrally involved in regional diplomatic efforts. This will require the expansion of aid and public diplomacy activities, the rapid assignment of experienced diplomats, and the encouragement of public-private partnerships and private sector investment in critical sectors and economies across the Indo-Pacific.

Third, U.S. policymakers need to articulate a set of trade and economic policies that will continue to keep the United States actively engaged in the region and find a way to make those policies as beneficial and palatable as possible for the domestic electorate so that they endure. After four years of intense ambivalence and uncertainty during the Trump administration, and now a further year of no clear trade policy signals from the Biden administration, the risks to U.S. interests are rising. Regional trade arrangements such as the Comprehensive and Progressive Agreement for Trans-Pacific Partnership (CPTPP) and Regional Comprehensive Economic Partnership (RCEP) are rapidly evolving without U.S. participation. Washington cannot assume that it has the luxury of time to figure out what it wants and then re-engage with a regional trade environment that has moved on.

Fourth, Washington needs to find a way to ensure that the values that underpin the liberal democratic order remain at the forefront, in contrast with the state-led control and censorship of the Chinese model. Those values continue to be attractive to many governments and peoples across

---

[6] Michael Beckley and Hal Brands, "Competition with China Could Be Short and Sharp," *Foreign Affairs*, December 17, 2020.

the Indo-Pacific and beyond. They are evident in many Asian countries' own formulations of their free and open Indo-Pacific strategies and are a natural glue that encourages alignment among like-minded nations. In foreign policy, this requires crafting a values-based dimension of U.S. strategy that encourages countries to align with free and open frameworks as soon as they are ready to do so. And in domestic politics the values-based approach will need to be managed and messaged with nuance, particularly given unfortunate examples throughout U.S. history of a tendency to demonize the other within. At its core, the competition is one between democratic values and an authoritarian Communist party-state, not a struggle against China as a culture or society.

Acknowledgments

The publication of this twentieth book in the *Strategic Asia* series affords an opportunity to reflect on and acknowledge the contributions of the more than 150 authors whose deep expertise and insightful analysis have helped track and explain the significant changes in the balance of power in Asia since 2000. The collective wisdom of these scholars from around the world has shaped our understanding of this complex, rapidly changing region. Looking back over the twenty volumes of the series provides a detailed explanation of developments at specific points of time, as well as the underlying forces and shifts in relative power over the past two decades.

For this year's volume, we offer our thanks to the seven authors, based in Australia, Singapore, the United Kingdom, and the United States, for their analysis and findings. We are also grateful to twelve anonymous reviewers—both scholars and government officials—whose comments have helped sharpen the conclusions in each chapter.

To our colleagues at NBR, we offer sincere thanks once again to the publications team led by Joshua Ziemkowski, with assistance from Jessica Keough, Dylan Plung, Robin Huang, and Ian Smith, whose editing ensures the high quality of another volume in the series. Thanks also to our colleagues Audrey Mossberger, Joshua Nezam, and Sandra Ward for all their efforts in promoting the volume. Special thanks are owed as well to Jonathon Marek, Joanna Nawrotkiewicz, Darlene Onuorah, Jeremy Rausch, Eliot Roberts, and Alura Winfrey for their research assistance and indexing, and especially to Olivia Truesdale for her tireless and enthusiastic research and program support, without which this book would not have been possible.

Last, but not least, thank you again to our co-editor Ashley Tellis, who contributed as an author to the first volume twenty years ago and has served as research director of the Strategic Asia Program for the past seventeen years. Ashley's keen strategic insights, collegial approach, and wonderful style have become hallmarks of the program, and it has been a personal and professional privilege for us to work with him on *Strategic Asia 2021–22: Navigating Tumultuous Times in the Indo-Pacific*.

Alison Szalwinski
Vice President of Research
NBR

Michael Wills
Executive Vice President
NBR

STRATEGIC ASIA 2021–22

EXECUTIVE SUMMARY

This chapter examines the genesis of the disorder in the Indo-Pacific that became manifest during the Trump years and how the U.S. has managed U.S.-China competition, the challenges of globalization, and the Covid-19 pandemic.

MAIN ARGUMENT

The tumultuousness of Trump's presidency was rooted in developments that long predated him. China's integration into the international trading system provided significant benefits for the U.S., but also imposed considerable burdens on key segments of its population. These hardships were compounded by sharply rising inequality domestically, failed U.S. military campaigns abroad, and the global financial crisis, which together stimulated a destabilizing nationalism and increased isolationism at just the time when China had become a potent strategic competitor. The Covid-19 pandemic only magnified the turmoil. Although Trump's response to these crises failed to dismantle the liberal international order, his nationalistic trade policies, transactional approach to alliances, and ragged response to the pandemic damaged trust in the U.S. globally. That these behaviors did not destroy the U.S.-led order demonstrates its resilience while also doing credit to Trump administration officials who protected it despite the president's disinterest.

POLICY IMPLICATIONS

- The U.S. must couple economic rebuilding at home with a sensible foreign policy to protect democracy domestically and preserve U.S. leadership of the liberal international order.

- The U.S. should maintain healthy economic ties with China to increase U.S. welfare gains, which are also necessary to effectively compete with China. In its competition with China, the U.S. should focus on preserving its military advantages, technological dominance, and ideational attractiveness globally.

- The U.S. should recommit to expanding international trade both to limit China's growing influence and to increase U.S. competitiveness and innovation, thereby strengthening its own economic power.

Overview

A Tempestuous Hegemon in a Tumultuous Era

Ashley J. Tellis

There is little doubt that Donald Trump's presidency was tumultuous not only for the United States but also for the international system. By elevating a self-consciously nationalist politician to the highest office, Trump's election challenged the long-established expectation that Washington would continue to unflinchingly bear the burdens of hegemony, uphold the open trading system, and promote liberal democracy as the normative standard of governance around the globe. Trump's views on each of these issues—partly reflecting those of his support base—ran counter to standing U.S. policies since at least the end of the Cold War, if not the beginning of the postwar period itself.

Reflecting a particular brand of "populist American nationalism,"[1] Trump disparaged U.S. alliances and demanded greater financial contributions from allies on the assumption that collective defense arrangements did not contribute toward the maintenance of American primacy and were little other than a favor to the United States' protégées. He also denigrated international institutions that he perceived as unfavorable to U.S. interests, while misunderstanding the value of the U.S.-led and -protected global order for the

---

Ashley J. Tellis is the Tata Chair for Strategic Affairs and a Senior Fellow at the Carnegie Endowment for International Peace. He is also Research Director of the Strategic Asia Program at the National Bureau of Asian Research. He can be reached at <atellis@ceip.org>.

The author is deeply grateful to Caroline Duckworth for research assistance and to Arthur C. Tellis for his helpful critique of this chapter.

[1] Colin Dueck, "American Nationalism and the Future of the Trump Doctrine," in *The Trump Doctrine and the Emerging International System*, ed. Stanley A. Renshon and Peter Suedfeld (Cham: Palgrave Macmillan, 2021), 366.

United States' own security.² Utilizing nationalist idioms, Trump furthermore trained his guns on international economic interdependence. Because of a long-standing belief that all U.S. economic partners were unfair traders, he responded by seeking to entrench new forms of protectionism, stimulate the comprehensive reshoring of manufacturing, and gut the many multilateral and plurilateral trading agreements that the United States had previously signed.³ Finally, at the ideational level—and in the sharpest departure from the past— Trump rejected the liberal vision entirely, conflating liberal internationalism with a "globalism" that he believed not only undermined the integrity of the nation-state but also justified endless interference in the internal affairs of other countries, which then produced ruinous wars, foolish attempts at nation-building abroad, and unlimited expenditures on protecting the international order over concrete U.S. interests.⁴ All these actions together— rooted in a seemingly atavistic nationalism, not to mention Trump's own personal rambunctiousness—shocked the international community, which had long viewed the United States as a sturdy bastion of stability even though some U.S. foreign policy decisions were occasionally damaging.⁵

The conclusive end of the post–Cold War period signaled by the Trump administration's decision to finally call out China as a strategic competitor of the United States only added to the sense of tumult. For almost 40 years, the United States had championed peaceful relations with China, encouraged its economic integration with the global system, and overlooked the more odious aspects of its autocratic governance as long as the Chinese Communist Party did not behave in especially egregious ways at home and abroad.⁶ By the time Trump entered office, however, Deng Xiaoping's counsel that China should "maintain a low profile" and "never seek leadership" had been

---

² For an excellent analysis of the issues involved here, see Doug Stokes, "Trump, American Hegemony and the Future of the Liberal International Order," *International Affairs* 94, no. 1 (2018): 133–150.

³ A useful survey of Trump's vision of trade and its consequences can be found in Adam S. Posen, "The Post-American World Economy: Globalization in the Trump Era," *Foreign Affairs*, March/April 2018, 28–38.

⁴ A helpful attempt to contextualize Trump's nationalism against the multiple notions of globalism can be found in Michael A. Peters, "Trump's Nationalism, 'the End of Globalism', and 'the Age of Patriotism': 'The Future Does Not Belong to Globalists. The Future Belongs to Patriots,'" *Educational Philosophy and Theory* 52, no. 13 (2020): 1341–46. The connections between Trump's attacks on globalism and the failures of recent U.S. foreign policy are examined in Jason A. Edwards, "Make America Great Again: Donald Trump and Redefining the U.S. Role in the World," *Communication Quarterly* 66, no. 2 (2018): 176–95.

⁵ Richard Wike, "The Trump Era Has Seen a Decline in America's Global Reputation," Pew Research Center, November 19, 2020, https://www.pewresearch.org/fact-tank/2020/11/19/the-trump-era-has-seen-a-decline-in-americas-global-reputation.

⁶ For an overview that assesses the wisdom of this approach, see Kurt M. Campbell and Ely Ratner, "The China Reckoning: How Beijing Defied American Expectations," *Foreign Affairs*, March/April 2018, 60–70. The debate that followed can be found in Wang Jisi et al., "Did America Get China Wrong? The Engagement Debate," *Foreign Affairs*, July/August 2018, 183–95.

decisively consigned by Xi Jinping to the dustheap of history. What replaced it was a renewed desire to cement China's centrality in the international system—an objective that only made the "trade shock" produced by China's integration into the global economy even more painful.[7] This burden was now complemented by both rising Chinese assertiveness in Asia and a comprehensive Chinese military transformation that threatened U.S. regional allies, sought to neutralize Washington's extended-deterrence guarantees, and ultimately constituted the foundations for China to challenge the United States as the hegemonic power in world politics.[8]

As if these structural shocks were not enough, the international community was roiled by the worst pandemic—apart from the AIDS crisis—since 1918. The origin of Covid-19 quickly became an object of controversy amid Chinese attempts to cover up the initial outbreak of the disease in Wuhan. The pandemic has to date officially cost over five million lives worldwide, though the actual toll is estimated to be much higher.[9] It has produced the worst economic crash since the Great Depression, and has generated serious supply chain disruptions, labor market dislocations, and increasing inflation (in part due to the heavy financial mitigation undertaken by various central banks around the world).[10] Although a series of vaccines capable of either providing immunity to the virus or mitigating its worst effects have been successfully brought to market with unprecedented rapidity, their production has still not reached the levels required to universally inoculate all humanity.[11] Even when the vaccine manufacturing limits are overcome, however, it is likely that vaccine hesitancy and resource constraints (both among and within countries) will prevent the goal of universal inoculation

---

[7] David H. Autor, David Dorn, and Gordon H. Hanson, "The China Shock: Learning from Labor Market Adjustment to Large Changes in Trade," *Annual Review of Economics* 8, no. 1 (2016): 205–40.

[8] For a summary of how China's strategic orientation changed over time and how U.S. policy in turn changed toward China, see Ashley J. Tellis, "Pursuing Global Reach: China's Not So Long March toward Preeminence," in *Strategic Asia 2019: China's Expanding Strategic Ambitions*, ed. Ashley J. Tellis, Alison Szalwinski, and Michael Wills (Seattle: National Bureau of Asian Research [NBR], 2019), 3–46; and Ashley J. Tellis, "The Return of U.S.-China Strategic Competition," in *Strategic Asia 2020: U.S.-China Competition*, ed. Ashley J. Tellis, Alison Szalwinski, and Michael Wills (Seattle: NBR, 2020), 3–43.

[9] For estimates of the actual death toll, see "The Pandemic's True Death Toll," *Economist*, November 2, 2021, https://www.economist.com/graphic-detail/coronavirus-excess-deaths-estimates.

[10] A useful, even if early, overview of the impact of the Covid-19 pandemic on the global economy can be found in Richard Baldwin and Beatrice Weder di Mauro, eds., *Economics in the Time of COVID-19* (London: CEPR Press, 2020). A good more recent survey is T. Ibn-Mohammed et al., "A Critical Analysis of the Impacts of COVID-19 on the Global Economy and Ecosystems and Opportunities for Circular Economy Strategies," *Resources, Conservation and Recycling* 164 (2021): 1–22.

[11] Chad P. Bown and Thomas J. Bollyky, "How COVID-19 Vaccine Supply Chains Emerged in the Midst of a Pandemic," Peterson Institute for International Economics, August 2021, https://www.piie.com/publications/working-papers/how-covid-19-vaccine-supply-chains-emerged-midst-pandemic.

from being reached speedily, thus resulting in persisting public health and economic distress in many parts of the world.

More pertinent to the tumult that has characterized recent history, however, is the fact that coping with the pandemic proved beyond the reach of the U.S.-led international order. At the beginning of the crisis, when global leadership was most required, the United States under Trump legitimized a nationalist approach to what was the most significant international public health calamity in generations.[12] Although this approach has shifted under President Joe Biden, fears that the earlier "America first" attitude still survives are prevalent within the wider international community.

This volume in the *Strategic Asia* series focuses on the impact of the tumult of the last several years on key states and subregions in the Indo-Pacific. Each chapter assesses how the new uncertainties about U.S. global leadership and the onset of U.S.-China competition, the threatened trade "decoupling" arising from that competition and the possible risks to globalization, and the devastation caused by the Covid-19 pandemic, whose long-term effects are still uncertain, have shaped the attitudes and policies of important Asian states. Each study explores the impact of these three intersecting developments on the grand strategy of the country concerned, or the impact on a specific region—in particular, focusing on how the challenges have affected the capacity to generate national power and what their consequences have been for the regional security environment and the United States.

This overview chapter is divided into two main sections. The first section explores the genesis of the disorder that became manifest during the Trump years. The second section then examines how U.S. policy under Trump affected the three issues described above, flagging key insights from the regional responses that are detailed in the chapters that follow. The brief conclusion highlights the challenges still facing the United States in the context of the remediation now being undertaken by the Biden administration.

The Structural Roots of a Convulsion

Although the challenges posed by China as a strategic competitor and the discontent with globalization reached their high point during the Trump presidency, the undercurrents driving both developments had been slowly intensifying long before the American people voted Trump into office. These pressures arose because of strategic decisions made in Washington after the

---

[12] Colin Kahl and Thomas Wright, *Aftershocks: Pandemic Politics and the End of the Old International Order* (New York: St. Martin's Press, 2021).

Cold War ended, but these choices too were rooted in the broader policies pursued by the United States early in the postwar period itself.

The Evolution of the U.S.-Led International Order

    The United States emerged from World War II triumphant and largely untouched by its physical devastation. Appreciating that the extended roots of the conflict were nourished by a combination of troublesome economic realities—the Great Depression, beggar-thy-neighbor trade policies, closed trading blocs, and predatory imperialism—the victorious United States sought to create an open international economic system as the centerpiece of the postwar political order. The idea that a global free-trade system could produce both increased prosperity and lasting peace became increasingly influential in the United States after World War I. But the negotiations during both the interwar years and World War II suggested that the postwar dream of free trade would have to be subordinated to mainly institutionalizing freer trade through bilateral reciprocity.[13] The newly designed International Trade Organization (ITO) was intended to be the institutional vehicle for managing this process, through which various individual trade agreements could be steadily generalized to create a progressively larger network of gradually liberalizing trade. The ITO would be supplemented by other Bretton Woods institutions such as the International Monetary Fund (IMF) and the International Bank for Reconstruction and Development (the World Bank). With the IMF managing the international monetary system, and the World Bank providing finance for capital projects in the developing world, the postwar international economic order was thus conceived as an integrated enterprise that would help avert the recurrence of major systemwide war by increasing prosperity through the institution of free markets within countries and freer trade between them.[14]

    Consistent with this vision, the United States itself slowly reduced its previously high tariffs and, to make this the new global norm, invited all nations to join the proposed ITO. However, its emerging rival, the Soviet Union, with its command economy and suspicions about free trade, spurned the U.S. overture, only indicating a willingness to join—for propaganda purposes—long after President Harry Truman's administration ultimately gave up on the ITO because of its inability to assuage domestic fears about

---

[13] For an excellent history of this shift, see Thomas W. Zeiler, *Free Trade, Free World: The Advent of GATT* (Chapel Hill: University of North Carolina Press, 1999).

[14] For a brief overview of these convictions, see Aaron Cavin, "Trade Wars: The Collapse of America's Free Trade Consensus," *Origins* 10, no. 4 (2017). For a more detailed history, see Susan Ariel Aaronson, *Trade and the American Dream: A Social History of Postwar Trade Policy* (Lexington: University Press of Kentucky, 2021).

the new supranational organization's power to intervene in Washington's management of the national economy.[15] This failure, which roughly coincided with the beginning of the Cold War and the resulting competition between the United States and the Soviet Union, finally undermined the American vision of unifying the entire postwar global order on the foundations of free markets domestically and freer trade internationally.

Cognizant of the need to rebuild the war-torn economies of its Western European and East Asian allies to contain Soviet and Chinese Communism, the United States constructed an asymmetrically open trading system that would bind its partners and enable their speedy reconstruction in the face of the looming Communist threat. This arrangement, which was integrated into the reciprocal tariff reductions negotiated under the auspices of the General Agreement on Tariffs and Trade (GATT)—the successor to the ITO—gave the United States' formal allies as well as its friends, especially in the developing world, preferential access to the wealthy U.S. market in order to bolster their economic growth and, thereby, their resilience against Communism.[16] The importance of this goal also prodded Washington to tolerate the rise of various state-managed economies around the world, but especially in Asia, against its own preference for free market solutions. Accordingly, the United States reconciled itself to significant deviations from its own liberal orthodoxy by accepting many state-led economies that were significantly protectionist while still providing them with preferential access to the U.S. market for their exports.

This strategy of allowing U.S. allies and friends to benefit from Washington's elevated trade openness made sense at a time when the United States was truly an economic colossus internationally and when defeating the Soviet threat was the overriding geopolitical imperative. Consequently, the United States complemented its strategy of deep, yet asymmetric, economic integration among its friends with many formal alliances, wherein Washington also bore the primary burden for ensuring common security in the face of the various continental and maritime threats emanating from its Communist rivals. These economic arrangements and the extended security guarantees together typified the hegemonic power of the United States. Washington bestowed on its partners more economic and security benefits than it received from them not only because it could afford to do so but also because doing so ultimately enhanced its own structural power in the

---

[15] See Harold Karan Jacobson, "The Soviet Union, the UN and World Trade," *Western Political Quarterly* 11, no. 3 (1958): 673–88; and Alan Renouf, "The Abortive Charter for an International Trade Organization," *Canadian Bar Review* 53 (1951): 87.

[16] For an insightful early history, see Robert A. Pollard, *Economic Security and the Origins of the Cold War, 1945–1950* (New York: Columbia University Press, 1985).

international system. That is, it created systemwide ordering arrangements that benefited U.S. interests disproportionately in that the United States, as the strongest power, had the most to lose were its adversaries able to gain any fundamental advantages in the intense and multifaceted competitions that came to characterize the Cold War.[17]

The progressive rise of the United States' allies encouraged by this hegemonic strategy undoubtedly produced a relative decline in U.S. power over time. But that erosion was acceptable because it generated greater collective capabilities across alliances, which contributed to the ultimate defeat of the Soviet Union. Moreover, the steady growth of allied capabilities was not particularly alarming—in fact, it was exactly what Washington intended—because it buttressed the ability of U.S. partners to build the warfighting capabilities that were necessary to contain the Communist threat. Neutralizing this danger was essential to preserving the United States' global primacy, which, in turn, rested on the assumption that a liberal hegemony was the best antidote against the emergence of new great-power rivals, other disorderly forms of multipolarity, and any desires on the part of subordinate states to revise the U.S.-led international order to Washington's disadvantage. Thus, the United States continued to bear the asymmetrically higher costs of collective defense long after its allies had grown rich and were arguably more capable of bearing a larger share of these burdens.[18] Although Washington regularly appealed for greater financial contributions from the allies for much of the Cold War and after, it acquiesced to their inclinations on burden shifting because, when all was said and done, the United States was still the strongest power internationally. A U.S.-dominated world provided Washington with far greater strategic leverage, as well as structural and positional advantages, that made it worth the costs of defending those protected.[19]

With the decisive U.S. victory in the Cold War, marked by the collapse of Soviet power, Washington went a step further: it sought to more deeply integrate countries that were not its allies into the open trading system. In effect, this represented continuity with the vision that had animated U.S. policy soon after World War II ended, when the idea of the ITO was first mooted. This process gathered steam during the last decades of the Cold

---

[17] Ashley J. Tellis et al., "Sources of Conflict in Asia," in *Sources of Conflict in the 21st Century: Regional Futures and U.S. Strategy*, ed. Zalmay Khalilzad and Ian O. Lesser (Santa Monica: RAND Corporation, 1998), 43–170.

[18] The "fundamentalist" versus "Atlanticist" elements of this issue in the NATO context are usefully analyzed in Charles A. Cooper and Benjamin Zycher, *Perceptions of NATO Burden-Sharing* (Santa Monica: RAND Corporation, 1989).

[19] Carla Norrlof, *America's Global Advantage: U.S. Hegemony and International Cooperation* (Cambridge: Cambridge University Press, 2010); and Michael Mastanduno, "System Maker and Privilege Taker," *World Politics* 61, no. 1 (2008): 121–54.

War itself when the economic transformations occurring in the diverse states of Southeast Asia, such as Hong Kong, Singapore, Thailand, Malaysia, and Indonesia, acquired a great boost thanks to regional integration; preferential access to wealthier markets in the United States, the newly formed European Union, and Japan; and even the opportunities offered by regional wars.[20] While these later success stories too would exemplify state-guided economic development, these gains were valued by the United States because they opened opportunities for American investors while increasing local resilience against the challenges posed by domestic threats, external subversion, and foreign aggression. Again, the steady growth of Southeast Asia through trade over time increased the absolute gains accruing to the United States, its global partners, and the regional states themselves, even though Southeast Asian successes then masked some serious internal structural weaknesses. The economic costs imposed on Washington by increased Southeast Asian prosperity were minimal, and these at any rate were sought to be corrected by more energetic efforts to secure greater "market access" and "market-opening," which "became the keywords of U.S. policy in the region."[21] This approach, in turn, focused largely on expanding trade opportunities by supporting the institutionalization of the Asia-Pacific Economic Cooperation forum (APEC).

The Integration of China into the International Order

The idea that state-directed economic growth was beneficial was poised to change in dramatic ways with the next evolution of U.S. policy, even though these shifts were far from visible at the time. After the end of the Cold War and thanks to the rapprochement in Sino-U.S. relations that had steadily gathered steam since Jimmy Carter's presidency, Washington was faced with the question of whether to integrate China, which had begun its own domestic economic reforms under Deng Xiaoping, into the wider international trading system. After bruising domestic battles yearly over whether China should be afforded access to the U.S. market, President Bill Clinton finally persuaded

---

[20] Angkeara Bong and Gamini Premaratne, "Regional Integration and Economic Growth in Southeast Asia," *Global Business Review* 19, no. 6 (2018): 1403–15; Belay Seyoum, "A Comparative Study of U.S. and Japanese Generalized System of Preferences," *Multinational Business Review* 13, no. 2 (2005): 63–87; Adnan Seric and Yee Siong Tong, "'East Asian Miracle' through Industrial Production and Trade Lenses," Industrial Analytics Platform and UNIDO, September 2019, https://iap.unido.org/articles/east-asian-miracle-through-industrial-production-and-trade-lenses; and Richard Stubbs, "War and Economic Development: Export-Oriented Industrialization in East and Southeast Asia," *Comparative Politics* 31, no. 3 (1999): 337–55.

[21] Ronald Palmer, "U.S. Policy Towards Southeast Asia," *American Diplomacy*, December 2001, https://americandiplomacy.web.unc.edu/2001/12/u-s-policy-towards-southeast-asia.

Congress to grant Beijing permanent normal trade relations.[22] This action eased the way for China to join the World Trade Organization (WTO)—the successor institution to the GATT—and for U.S. companies to benefit from the commitments that China had made to secure its membership.[23] Unlike previous expansions of the liberal trading order, however, China's entry into the WTO was potentially consequential because of its huge size and future strategic ambitions, which may not have been entirely convergent with the vision of the United States. China's large population obviously made it extremely appealing for U.S. and international businesses, which saw an enormous market and a vast pool of skilled labor that could be used to transform manufacturing on a global scale. The uncertainties about China's long-term strategic ambitions did not seem to matter much because the country's still significant material weaknesses made it an insignificant threat to the United States at a time when Sino-U.S. ties were relatively amicable, and Beijing was able to astutely—and consciously—obscure its competitive aims where Washington was concerned.[24]

However, the U.S. decision to integrate China into the liberal trading order, through both the offer of "most-favored-nation status" bilaterally and support for its WTO membership multilaterally, was not solely a product of state agency, even though Washington played a pivotal role. Rather, the far-reaching consequences of building a liberal economic order in the aftermath of World War II were causally coequal in importance. What the emphasis on encouraging open markets domestically and freer trade internationally produced was a gradual but transformative efflorescence of capitalism itself. Although initially nourished within the United States and in Europe, capitalism quickly moved abroad as the trading system brought more and more countries into the common Western network. Many developing states, especially in East Asia—and China was merely a later, albeit a more consequential, example—nurtured domestic private firms with state support. In time, these entities, just like their U.S. and European counterparts, crossed their national borders in search of resources and markets and developed trading and production networks abroad.[25]

---

[22] Bill Clinton, "Letter to Congress Advocating Granting China Permanent Normal Trade Relations," March 8, 2000, available at https://china.usc.edu/bill-clinton-%E2%80%9Cletter-congress-advocating-granting-china-permanent-normal-trade-relations%E2%80%9D-march-8.

[23] Nicholas R. Lardy, "Permanent Normal Trade Relations for China," Brookings Institution, Policy Brief, no. 48, May 2000.

[24] Oriana Skylar Mastro, "The Stealth Superpower—How China Hid Its Global Ambitions," *Foreign Affairs*, January/February 2019, 31–39.

[25] A succinct history can be found in B. Kogut, "Multinational Corporations," in *International Encyclopedia of the Social and Behavioral Sciences*, ed. Neil J. Smelser and Paul B. Baltes (Amsterdam: Elsevier, 2001), 10197–204.

Before long, the commercial interactions between U.S. and various international (to include Asian) companies produced the increasingly dense and integrated economic system that exemplifies global capitalism today. As other exogenous developments such as the revolutions in transportation and in information and communications technologies materialized, what initially began as discrete two-way trade transactions in finished goods gradually morphed into a complex mesh involving intricate global supply chains. Now the production of components was distributed across national boundaries based on both cost and coordination advantages, and trade consisted of multiple movements of millions of elements that represent "flows of goods, investment, services, know-how and people in novel ways."[26] The tangible artifacts themselves are integrated at varying levels and into finished goods in different national locations, potentially far from their source of origin, only to be exported to still other countries possibly even farther away.[27]

The critical upshot of this evolution is that the multinational production system has gradually escaped the easy control of the state. The state alone still exercises legitimate command over the instruments of coercion and can under conditions of emergency exert powerful influence on economic entities that either operate on its territory or need access to it. However, it cannot pervasively discipline the logic of commercial activity without arresting its fecundity—and thereby limiting the resources that the state itself garners in order to carry out its order maintenance and other welfare functions. The state and private economic activity, especially that operating across national boundaries, are thus bound dialectically: private capital pursues its productive activities driven by a search for profit wherever that may be found—within national boundaries to be sure, but increasingly even in the territories of a nation's rivals; and the state, which private capital relies on for effective rule enforcement, cannot simply constrain these endeavors if they are to generate the resources required by the state to maintain order and satisfactorily compete with its international competitors.[28]

The United States' decision to integrate China into the international economic order was thus shaped by both the preferences of politics and the imperatives of economics—by both choice and necessity. The political drivers were anchored in a desire to support China's political evolution in the hope that increased prosperity would accelerate democratization and

---

[26] Richard Baldwin, "Global Supply Chains: Why They Emerged, Why They Matter, and Where They Are Going," Center for Economic Policy Research, Discussion Papers, 2012.

[27] For a useful overview of the mechanics of global supply chains, see Panos Kouvelis and Ping Su, *The Structure of Global Supply Chains* (Hanover: Now Publishers, 2008).

[28] For an interesting exploration of different dimensions of this issue, see Ellen Meiksins Wood, "Global Capital, National States," in *Historical Materialism and Globalization*, ed. Mark Rupert and Hazel Smith (London: Routledge, 2002), 17–39.

that democratization, in turn, would strengthen cosmopolitanism over nationalism, thus mitigating the dangers of future geopolitical rivalry both regionally and with the United States. The economic drivers were manifested in the cravings of U.S. businesses for access to the Chinese market and to China's large pool of skilled lower-cost labor, which could be utilized to produce goods for domestic consumption within China but more importantly for export to wealthier markets globally, thereby increasing their profitability and competitiveness against other commercial rivals.[29]

Because U.S. policymakers necessarily had to protect the economic opportunities available to U.S. companies in China—since their success in principle promised increased welfare gains for the United States as a whole, not to mention generating resources for Washington to use in support of its larger foreign policies—midwifing China's entry into the global economic system could not have been avoided as readily as is sometimes supposed today.[30] China's domestic economic liberalization had already primed the country for integration with other regional and global partners. Consequently, the only choice before the United States was whether it would forgo the absolute gains from trade with China that the other Asian (and European) states were poised to enjoy, just as Beijing too readied itself to incur such benefits reciprocally. These ties would expand dramatically after China joined the WTO. As Duncan Snidal demonstrated in a pathbreaking analysis around 30 years ago, the relative gains derived from abstaining from economic cooperation in a multi-actor environment can be meager, if they are at all positive, and may not provide enough justification for forgoing trade integration with any given partner when that entity has a variety of other commercial collaborators to choose from.[31] In such circumstances, the state that renounces trading with another effectively relinquishes the absolute gains that may advantage it in its competition with its rivals, including the very partners it trades with.

This tension within the intertwined logic of state rivalry and economic interdependence was penetratingly discerned by Karl Marx almost two centuries ago when he argued that global capitalism would end up threatening the nation-state.[32] While the latter requires the former for its material viability and competitive success in an antagonistic interstate system, global capitalism

---

[29] Campbell and Ratner, "The China Reckoning."

[30] See John J. Mearsheimer, "The Inevitable Rivalry: America, China, and the Tragedy of Great-Power Politics," *Foreign Affairs*, November/December 2021, 48–58.

[31] Duncan Snidal, "Relative Gains and the Pattern of International Cooperation," *American Political Science Review* 85, no. 3 (1991): 701–26.

[32] See the discussion in Andrew Linklater, "Marxism," in *Theories of International Relations*, 5th edition, ed. Scott Burchill and Andrew Linklater (New York: Palgrave Macmillan, 2013), 113–37.

also ends up potentially empowering new state rivals while simultaneously constraining all of them in inescapable ways. This outcome is amply illustrated by Sino-U.S. economic "codependency" today.[33] The rise of China as a new great power through, among other things, trade integration was thus inherently baked into the logic of the expanding liberal international economic order that Washington has sought to institutionalize since the end of World War II. This process would inevitably escape U.S. state control once private agents—American and foreign—began to conduct economic transactions across national boundaries, which could not be drastically curtailed in any way short of war without the United States itself incurring high costs in the first instance.

The Economic and Political Consequences for the United States

China's deep economic integration with the United States after its entry into the WTO produced two outcomes, one internal and one external, which would eventually contribute to the tumult witnessed in recent years. The internal consequence was the accelerated deindustrialization of the United States. Although this deindustrialization has complex causes, including the rise of labor-saving technology, there is little doubt that the "China trade shock" contributed significantly as U.S. companies, freed from the uncertainties about stable and predictable access to the Chinese market, moved manufacturing previously resident in the United States into China.[34] Such shifts in the global division of labor are exactly what open international trade engenders. While its consequences include increased prosperity overall, these gains may not be shared equally between nations, even as they impose different distributional costs within the economies of the trading partners.

Within the United States, the demographic segments most affected by the intensifying trade with China "were whiter, less educated, older and poorer than most of the rest of America,"[35] a group that would in time play an important role in propelling Trump to the presidency. The losses borne by this population could have been ameliorated in principle in three ways. First, China's comparative advantage might have been reduced by holding Beijing exactly to its WTO commitments, thereby leveling the playing field in China and thus reducing the perverse incentives for U.S.

---

[33] Stephen Roach, *Unbalanced: The Codependency of America and China* (New Haven: Yale University Press, 2014).

[34] Autor, Dorn, and Hanson, "The China Shock."

[35] China Trade Shock, https://chinashock.info.

companies to continuously shift their investments abroad.[36] Second, and as a complement to the first way, the U.S. domestic social safety net could have been enhanced in order to lower the adjustment costs borne by those Americans otherwise harmed by economic intercourse with China.[37] Third, the global trading system itself could have been expanded in order to permit U.S. companies greater access to other markets beyond China, or it could have been supplemented by plurilateral agreements incorporating higher standards that would have permitted other U.S. comparative advantages to pay off in the face of China's lower-cost labor edge.[38]

As it turned out, the United States faltered on all three counts. Despite interminable economic dialogues with China, Washington proved unable to change Beijing's predatory economic behaviors multilaterally and, until the advent of Trump, chose not to resolutely use bilateral instruments to force any fundamental change in Beijing's traditional strategy of maintaining a state-controlled domestic market. Washington's failure on this count was linked in part to the close ties between U.S. private capital and U.S. governing elites. Deriving an excess of satisfaction from the overall trade gains, both neglected the importance of correcting China's trade distortions expeditiously and protecting the social classes in the United States that had lost out geographically, demographically, or sectorally. Washington also did not invest in reinforcing the domestic social safety net to deliberately redress these trade losses, in part because of the deep divides between Republicans and Democrats that are visible to this day. Nor did the United States succeed in creating compensating trade opportunities to recover the relative gains lost to China. Reform at the WTO proved elusive because the consensus rule prevented any meaningful agreement in the face of the deep international divisions over trade. Similarly, the remarkably high-quality workarounds that the United States did support, such as the Trans-Pacific Partnership (TPP) and the Transatlantic Trade and Investment Partnership, ultimately became victim to other domestic and international vicissitudes.

Despite the overall benefits accruing from trade with China, the specific economic costs—including the loss of intellectual property and the diversion of U.S. technology to Beijing's military projects—were compounded by other

---

[36] Stephen Ezell, "False Promises II: The Continuing Gap Between China's WTO Commitments and Its Practices," Information Technology and Innovation Foundation, July 26, 2021.

[37] Edward Alden, *Failure to Adjust: How Americans Got Left Behind in the Global Economy* (Lanham: Rowman and Littlefield, 2017).

[38] Ashley J. Tellis, "The Geopolitics of the TTIP and the TTP," in *Power Shifts and New Blocs in the Global Trading System*, Adelphi Series, no. 450, ed. Sanjaya Baru and Suvri Doga (London: Routledge, 2015), 93–120.

unfavorable developments within the United States.[39] To begin, the United States has experienced striking increases in inequality since about 1980 at levels greater than in other peer countries. The data suggests that since 1970 the share of U.S. aggregate income accruing to upper-income families has been steadily increasing to the point where this segment now enjoys almost half the total national income.[40] By contrast, middle-income families, which once enjoyed 62% of aggregate U.S. income, now enjoy only 43% of it. Lower-income families have had their share reduced as well, though the deterioration in this case has been more marginal. The wealth gaps are even more striking. Since the early 1980s, upper-income families have rapidly increased their share of U.S. aggregate wealth from 60% to 79% in 2016—the year Trump was elected president. During the same period, the share of wealth enjoyed by middle-income families dropped from 32% to 17%, with lower-income families facing a reduced share from 7% to 4%. The stark increases in inequality during the post–Cold War period thus contributed to a growing sense within the U.S. population that although the country may have been doing well in general, in part due to expanded trade, the resulting prosperity was not shared equitably.

The problems of inequality were complemented by growing domestic disenchantment with U.S. military interventionism in the post–Cold War period—especially after military interventions in Afghanistan and Iraq evolved into ineffective and protracted campaigns of uncertain purpose—which also imposed high financial and social costs on the U.S. polity.[41] In part, the absence of a superpower competitor freed Washington to use military force around the world much more readily than it might have done had it been constrained as it was during the Cold War. The record in Afghanistan and Iraq demonstrated, however, that military success was not assured even against technologically unsophisticated opponents. In fact, despite expending what could have been as much as $8 trillion on its wars since the al Qaeda attacks in the United States, successive administrations ultimately failed to achieve their objectives in Afghanistan and may have

---

[39] James Andrew Lewis, "How Much Have the Chinese Actually Taken?" Center for Strategic and International Studies, Commentary, March 22, 2018, https://www.csis.org/analysis/how-much-have-chinese-actually-taken.

[40] Juliana Menasce Horowitz, Ruth Igielnik, and Rakesh Kochhar, "Trends in Income and Wealth Inequality," Pew Research Center, January 9, 2020, https://www.pewresearch.org/social-trends/2020/01/09/trends-in-income-and-wealth-inequality.

[41] See, for example, Hannah Hartig and Carroll Doherty, "Two Decades Later, the Enduring Legacy of 9/11," Pew Research Center, September 2, 2021, https://www.pewresearch.org/politics/2021/09/02/two-decades-later-the-enduring-legacy-of-9-11; and Christopher Gelpi, Jason Reifler, and Peter Feaver, "Iraq the Vote: Retrospective and Prospective Foreign Policy Judgments on Candidate Choice and Casualty Tolerance," *Political Behavior* 29, no. 2 (2007): 151–74.

chalked up at best ambiguous success in Iraq.[42] One scholar concluded that "twenty years from now, we'll still be reckoning with the high societal costs of the Afghanistan and Iraq wars—long after U.S. forces are gone."[43] Thus, it should not have been surprising that Trump was able to persuade a large segment of disaffected Americans that maintaining the liberal international order through hegemonic strategies that overused military instruments only brought high costs without any perceptible benefits for the United States.

Finally, the global financial crisis that began in 2008 and ran its course during President Barack Obama's first term in office further exacerbated the growing inequality in American society. Thanks to a dramatic injection of liquidity into national and international markets, the worst consequences of the financial crisis were immediately averted. These remedies undoubtedly prevented a new "great depression." They came with extreme moral hazards, however, insofar as the financial bailouts protected those who were responsible for the crisis while leaving the larger populace to bear the burden. Although the economy made a surprisingly quick comeback, the pecuniary consequences of the financial crisis still endure.[44] Thus, for example, although the average U.S. household wealth in 2019 finally exceeded the average in 2007, the median wealth declined by 19% over the same period. In other words, more families had still not made up the losses suffered during the crisis. The evidence suggests that white, wealthier, and more educated households recouped faster, whereas others struggled in what has been described as a "wealthless recovery." These problems would unfortunately soon be exacerbated by the Covid-19 pandemic beginning in early 2020.[45]

Beyond the material costs—lost growth, uneven recovery, and deepening inequality—the financial crisis in the United States and internationally had equally startling political consequences: a deepening polarization within society, the rise of populism (together with suspicion about governing institutions), intensifying racial divisions, and growing antagonism

---

[42] Neta C. Crawford, "The U.S. Budgetary Costs of the Post-9/11 Wars," Watson Institute, Brown University, September 1, 2021, https://watson.brown.edu/costsofwar/files/cow/imce/papers/2021/Costs%20of%20War_U.S.%20Budgetary%20Costs%20of%20Post-9%2011%20Wars_9.1.21.pdf.

[43] Stephanie Savell, quoted in "Costs of the 20-Year War on Terror: $8 Trillion and 900,000 Deaths," Brown University, September 1, 2021, https://www.brown.edu/news/2021-09-01/costsofwar.

[44] Regis Barnichon, Christian Matthes, and Alexander Ziegenbein, "The Financial Crisis at 10: Will We Ever Recover?" Federal Reserve Bank of San Francisco, FRBSF Economic Letter, August 13, 2018, https://www.frbsf.org/economic-research/files/el2018-19.pdf; and Gautam Mukunda, "The Social and Political Costs of the Financial Crisis, 10 Years Later," Harvard Business Review, September 25, 2018.

[45] Austin Clemens, "New Wealth Data Show That the Economic Expansion after the Great Recession Was a Wealthless Recovery for Many U.S. Households," Washington Center for Equitable Growth, October 2020, https://equitablegrowth.org/wp-content/uploads/2020/10/100520-SCF-racial-disagg-ib.pdf.

toward immigrants.[46] These social stresses were on stark display in Europe, but, as Trump's election in 2016 would indicate, the United States was not immune to these pressures. While the precise causality that connects the financial crisis to the resurgence of populist nationalism in the United States is hard to discern, it is difficult to escape the conclusion that the reactionary upsurge that brought Trump to power was precipitated by a "legitimacy crisis" that had been steadily building up over the previous decade.[47] This crisis was fueled by accumulating domestic economic losses (irrespective of their sources), rising racial and class differences, and the failure of traditional politics to address the concerns of diverse social segments, especially the beleaguered middle class. The 2016 election thus brought diverse constituencies together to propel Trump into office in a race that finally hinged on a few pivotal states.[48]

Even as these wrenching internal developments were unfolding in American society, there was a consequential external transformation as well: China's gradual manifestation as a genuine great-power rival of the United States. The processes that produced this outcome were long and slow and were obviously rooted partly in the benefits that China gained from economic integration globally. Because China never intended to become a post-modern "trading state" like Germany and Japan—states that had also benefited from external trade ties—its emergence as a military rival to the United States was all but assured over time as long as China continued to possess an ambitious national leadership and sustained its internal political cohesion and broad economic success.[49] The United States alone stood between China and its long-standing aspiration of restoring its geopolitical centrality in Asia. This aim implicitly entailed the political subordination of the other major Asian powers, such as Japan and India. Because U.S. security guarantees bound many states on China's periphery, such as Japan, South Korea, Taiwan, and the Philippines, Beijing's desire to reconstruct a new hierarchy in Asia inevitably

---

[46] Manuel Funke, Moritz Schularick, and Christoph Trebesch, "The Financial Crisis Is Still Empowering Far-Right Populists," *Foreign Affairs*, September 13, 2018, https://www.foreignaffairs.com/articles/2018-09-13/financial-crisis-still-empowering-far-right-populists.

[47] Inderjeet Parmar, "The Legitimacy Crisis of the U.S. Elite and the Rise of Donald Trump," *Insight Turkey* 19, no. 3 (2017): 9–22.

[48] See "An Examination of the 2016 Electorate, Based on Validated Voters," Pew Research Center, August 9, 2018, https://www.pewresearch.org/politics/2018/08/09/an-examination-of-the-2016-electorate-based-on-validated-voters; and Rob Griffin, Ruy Teixeira, and John Halpin, "Voter Trends in 2016," Center for American Progress, November 1, 2017, https://www.americanprogress.org/issues/democracy/reports/2017/11/01/441926/voter-trends-in-2016.

[49] Aaron L. Friedberg, "Globalisation and Chinese Grand Strategy," *Survival* 60, no. 1 (2018): 7–40.

forced it to contend with the United States as the principal obstacle to this larger aim.[50]

The domestic developments in China only accelerated this process, which acquired a decisive fillip with Xi Jinping's rise to power. Casting aside Deng Xiaoping's advice to lie low, Xi dramatically expanded the ambitions more quietly laid out by his predecessor, Hu Jintao. In particular, he accelerated China's military transformation (whose anti-access and area-denial components are aimed at decoupling the Asian periphery from U.S. protection); militarized many island reefs in the South China Sea, while levying new ambiguous territorial claims therein; increased China's intimidation of Taiwan, Japan, India, and maritime Southeast Asia; and more significantly, charged the Chinese armed forces to prepare for multidimensional military conflicts with the United States. Even as China steadily consolidated this course, it has consciously sought to wrest domination of the global technology frontier from the United States through huge state-directed national investments. Simultaneously, it has appropriated key technologies, including those developed abroad, for defense applications that are intended to enable China to project its military power globally just like the United States.[51]

While both the George W. Bush and Obama administrations attempted to avert a confrontation with China, by the time Trump arrived in office the United States could no longer pretend that this prospect could be staved off in perpetuity. Consequently, Trump's declaration of China as a strategic competitor only confirmed what many nations in the Indo-Pacific had long sensed was an emerging reality. Yet even that denouement did little to clarify how the return to a new and possibly intensified bipolar rivalry might play out in the years to come.

Wayward Nationalism in Power and Its Consequences

The domestic stresses within the United States described above combined in complex ways to bring Trump to office in January 2017. His election signified the emerging power of nationalist elements within American politics and signaled the fracturing of the internationalist-nationalist coalition that, by marginalizing isolationism, sustained the hegemonic role that the United States had assumed since the end of World War II. The internationalists believed that preserving U.S. global dominance and maintaining the

---

[50] Aaron L. Friedberg, *A Contest for Supremacy: China, America and the Struggle for Mastery in Asia* (New York: W.W. Norton, 2011).

[51] Tellis, "Pursuing Global Reach."

international institutions that manifested it both served Washington's interests and were good in themselves—and hence were worth the costs. The nationalists had no particular affection for international institutions per se but supported them to the degree that they served to achieve the objective of defeating the Soviet Union.[52] The isolationists, who had been discredited by the war, remained on the sidelines until the economic crises and the political reversals of the post–Cold War period gave them a new lease on life on both the right and the left. On the right, these neo-isolationists grew intensely critical of what they perceived to be Washington's imperial behavior abroad. On the left, the failure to invest in domestic reconstruction because of expensive foreign entanglements became the new foundation for political mobilization in the face of growing national inequality and losses to foreign trade. These grievances also increased the disenchantment among the nationalists. Seeing little inherent value in international institutions at a time when their specific costs to the United States seemed to exceed the benefits they provided, and when U.S. allies were perceived as not paying their fair share, the nationalists effectively joined ranks with the neo-isolationists to question the benefits of these external commitments for Washington.[53]

Riding the support offered by such critics, Trump came into office suspicious of the United States' external engagements and in particular the benefits of alliances and international institutions. His determination to revoke these foreign commitments was complemented by a consequential domestic shift as well: instead of promoting a civic nationalism that debated how "a more perfect union" of peoples drawn from diverse backgrounds and beliefs could be constructed, Trump championed an ethnic nationalism that, returning to earlier traditions in American politics, effectively painted nonwhites and immigrants (especially Hispanic immigrants) as threats to his nativist vision of the United States.[54] Accentuating the grievances of his nationalist base, he displayed little regard for the country's constitutional ideals and deepened the polarization in American politics through, among other things, his disrespect for governing norms when in office. This contempt reached its nadir on January 6, 2021, when Trump encouraged armed

---

[52] This framing is owed greatly to the insights found in Colin Dueck, *Age of Iron: On Conservative Nationalism* (New York: Oxford University, 2019); and Colin Dueck, "U.S. Strategic Culture: Liberalism with Limited Liability," in *Strategic Asia 2016–17: Understanding Strategic Cultures in the Asia-Pacific*, ed. Ashley J. Tellis, Alison Szalwinski, and Michael Wills (Seattle: NBR, 2016).

[53] The steady growth of isolationist sentiments, as reflected in recent U.S. national elections, is insightfully detailed in Kyle Dodson and Clem Brooks, "All by Himself? Trump, Isolationism, and the American Electorate," *Sociological Quarterly* (September 20, 2021).

[54] Hilde Eliassen Restad, "What Makes America Great? Donald Trump, National Identity, and U.S. Foreign Policy," *Global Affairs* 6, no. 1 (2020): 21–36.

protestors to storm the U.S. Capitol in an effort to overturn his November 2020 electoral defeat.

While the Trump years were destructive of democracy at home, his presidency only underscored for international audiences that the United States was a deeply divided society; that its long-standing effort to escape the Old World's struggles with ethnicity, class, and race had by no means been as successful as it previously seemed; and that, given the rising discontent about the burdens associated with preserving external order, Washington could no longer be counted on to act as the guardian of the international system as it was throughout the postwar era. For all of Trump's actions that confirmed these doubts, however, his policies while in office were more substantively erratic than ideologically consistent. Neither his domestic nor his foreign policies exhibited a coherence that advanced his nationalist foreign policy goals or even dependably benefited his larger nationalist base. Consequently, there was no successful "displacement strategy" that permitted him to durably replace inherited policies with his new populist approach.[55] The attacks on trade, economic interdependence, and globalization; the assault on U.S. alliances and the liberal international order as well as the confrontation with China; and U.S. management of the Covid-19 pandemic thus demonstrated Trump's disjointedness in myriad ways but also simultaneously reflected the limits of his wayward nationalism.

The U.S. War on Trade

Trump entered office intent on exiting as many multilateral trading arrangements as he could because of his belief that only bilateral engagements protect U.S. interests. Consequently, he pulled the United States out of the long-negotiated TPP—the one agreement that might have not only enlarged U.S. gains from trade in Asia, while limiting China's advantages simultaneously, but also cemented U.S. leadership in developing new trading rules that would have benefited the United States in the emerging global economy.[56] Trump sought to similarly exit the North American Free Trade Agreement (NAFTA) and other previously negotiated bilateral pacts, but his more temperate subordinates persuaded him to negotiate revisions that only marginally improved the agreements—as became evident in the Korea-U.S.

---

[55] For an argument relating to how this applied to foreign policy, see Daniel W. Drezner, "Present at the Destruction: The Trump Administration and the Foreign Policy Bureaucracy," *Journal of Politics* 81, no. 2 (2019): 723–30.

[56] Jefferey J. Schott, "TPP Redux: Why the United States Is the Biggest Loser," Peterson Institute for International Economics, January 23, 2018, https://www.piie.com/blogs/trade-and-investment-policy-watch/tpp-redux-why-united-states-biggest-loser.

Free Trade Agreement and the U.S.-Mexico-Canada Agreement (USMCA) that replaced NAFTA.

Trump further attempted to rectify what he perceived to be the burdens imposed by free trade by seeking to reduce the bilateral trade deficits with key states. This included sharply raising tariffs on spurious national security grounds, compelling additional purchases of U.S. products, and attempting to reshore manufacturing so as to reverse the job losses that were intensified by the China trade shock. None of these solutions delivered on his ostensible goal: forcing the decoupling of the U.S. and Chinese economies.[57] In fact, the only arguably successful example of decoupling was provided by China in the digital realm, where the powerful Chinese state was able to constrict both U.S. companies and its own society to maintain a largely Chinese ecosystem. In contrast, the relatively weaker U.S. state could not compel its own private companies to leave the Chinese market. By the time Trump left office, the U.S. trade deficit was larger than before and the reshoring effort petered out because, in the absence of macroeconomic, trade, currency, and tax reforms, the logic of the global marketplace kept manufacturing where it was most efficient—primarily in China, with some modest displacement to other low-cost Asian countries. The gains at home, however, were meager. As one authoritative study concluded, the United States had "not reclaimed manufacturing jobs in any material way."[58]

Trump's efforts at undoing international economic interdependence thus failed because they butted up against the much stronger imperatives that were driving globalization.[59] These forces could not be arrested by Trump's piecemeal attacks, although his rhetorical aggression against trade did create consternation in the minds of many Asian leaders whose nations' economic fortunes depended on the survival of the international trading system. The Trump administration's economic war with China, however, induced many Asian states to consider supplemental insurance strategies. For the most part, these included diversifying their investments beyond China and creating greater redundancy in their supply chains. These measures had already been contemplated prior to Trump's arrival in office because of the fears provoked by China's previous economic coercion and the shifts in comparative

---

[57] "Trump Again Raises Idea of Decoupling Economy from China," Reuters, September 15, 2020, https://www.reuters.com/article/usa-trump-china/trump-again-raises-idea-of-decoupling-economy-from-china-idUSKBN25Z08U.

[58] "Global Pandemic Roils 2020 Reshoring Index, Shifting Focus from Reshoring to Right-Shoring," Kearney, 2021, 1, https://www.kearney.com/documents/20152/107419246/Global+pandemic+roils+2020+Reshoring+Index%2C+shifting+focus+from+reshoring+to+right-shoring.pdf/11177804-6baf-7906-d07d-5f5a419c122a?t=1619648328000.

[59] Pol Antràs, "De-Globalisation? Global Value Chains in the Post-COVID-19 Age," National Bureau of Economic Research, Working Paper, November 2020, http://www.nber.org/papers/w28115.

advantage produced by the rising cost of Chinese labor. Trump's policies, therefore, altered the patterns of regional investment on the margins, but they could not undo the dense webs of globalization. On this count, the structural factors that animate global capitalism proved to be far more resilient in the face of state agency, even if that agency was exercised by the world's most powerful leader.

The chapters in this volume corroborate this conclusion from other perspectives. Suisheng Zhao's chapter on China suggests that even though the fundamental patterns of globalization remain resilient, Beijing has begun to double down on statist control of the economy, partly because of its fears that the changing U.S. attitudes to trade might deny it access to international technology and markets in the years ahead. But China's new strategy of "dual circulation," which attempts to expand the domestic market as a complement to export-driven growth, is motivated as much by internal concerns about rising inequality and Xi Jinping's desire to enforce greater party control over the economy. China's centrality in the global manufacturing system—which shows no signs of diminishing—therefore suggests that any genuine restructuring of the global value chains is still a long time away. Michael Green's chapter on Northeast Asia also confirms this point. Japan, South Korea, and Taiwan are indeed seeking to diversify their economic ties beyond China, especially in the technology arena, for both strategic and economic reasons. But for the foreseeable future the extant links promise to remain prominent. As a state seeking to become an industrial power, India represents an interesting case. Rohan Mukherjee points out that the threat of deglobalization heralded by Trump's rhetoric has opened opportunities for New Delhi to entice those businesses looking for options outside China. India's record in attracting this shift on a significant scale, however, has faltered largely because of internal failings, even as its own trade dependence on China remains remarkably robust.

Given the centrality of trade to the Southeast Asian economies, it is not surprising that Trump's war on economic interdependence and the U.S. exit from the TPP have been disconcerting. Huong Le Thu's chapter indicates that despite their significant strategic concerns about Beijing, most nations within this region view the threat of U.S.-China economic decoupling with alarm, even though its specific impacts are still incomplete and ambiguous. The conspicuous exception is Vietnam, which has benefited from business diversification from China. A similar situation exists in Oceania. Although Australia has moved perceptibly closer to the United States in recent years thanks to Beijing's aggressive attitude toward Canberra (with New Zealand following), Rebecca Strating and Joanne Wallis's chapter highlights the reality that all the regional states (including Australia and New Zealand) are still deeply intertwined with China economically. Many of the small Pacific Island states seek to benefit from both the United States and China. While their larger neighbors contemplate bolder strategies of economic diversification, the kind of decoupling from China that the Trump administration sought to engineer has proved beyond reach even where major U.S. allies are concerned.

Russia, as Marcin Kaczmarski points out, is a remarkable outlier with respect to the threat of deglobalization. Outside of energy exports and the arms trade, it is a marginal participant in the international economic system. Moreover, Russia's troubles with the West, which have resulted in more stringent U.S. sanctions, have led to deepened cooperation with China that is unlikely to disappear anytime soon.

On balance, therefore, Trump's campaign against multilateral trade, and in particular bilateral trade with China, though startling, did not produce any transformative reversal of globalization—as was to be expected given the power of capitalism operating across state boundaries. As Barry Eichengreen summarized, "if by globalization we mean an era when flows of merchandise, capital and labor across borders grow several times faster than GDP, then we can say that this phase in global affairs is already over" because of the overall slowdown in international economic growth since the financial crisis. But if globalization implies "a state where national economies are linked together by those flows—subject to adjustments as different countries see fit—then globalization remains firmly in place."[60]

The International Order and U.S. Alliances during the Trump Years

The evidence also suggests that Trump did not do much better when it came to restructuring the United States' engagement with the world, including reforming its alliances. The failure to understand the intimate relationship that exists between a world order that benefits the United States and global institutions and alliances underwritten by U.S. power prompted Trump's attacks on these institutions and alliances. Consequently, he withdrew the United States from membership in the UN Educational, Scientific and Cultural Organization (UNESCO), the UN Human Rights Council, the Paris Agreement, and the Joint Comprehensive Plan of Action with Iran. He also pulled the United States out of negotiations pertaining to the United Nations' Global Compact for Migration, ended funding for the UN Relief and Works Agency, and exited the Open Skies and Intermediate-Range

---

[60] Barry Eichengreen, "Will Globalisation Go into Reverse?" *Prospect*, November 2016, https://www.prospectmagazine.co.uk/magazine/will-globalisation-go-into-reverse-brexit-donald-trump.

Nuclear Forces (INF) treaties with Russia.[61] While Trump's protests about some of these institutions and agreements were amply justified, his pique did not always produce results favorable to the United States. Barring the decision to exit the INF Treaty, the impact of his other withdrawals ranged from questionable to unfavorable. For one thing, most of the international organizations affected by the United States' departure have survived—often with the support of others—thus leaving Washington without opportunities to shape their direction.[62]

Mistreating allies, at any rate, had potentially more serious consequences. Because of his belief that alliances were merely a one-way street, with Washington offering protection without getting anything in return, Trump repeatedly insinuated that the United States might not be bound by its strategic obligations in extremis if the allies did not pay more. His more responsible subordinates, however, worked to protect U.S. alliances in both Europe and Asia because of their importance for protecting both U.S. security and primacy. Exploiting Trump's obsession with more equitable burden sharing, they utilized the additional resources gained from Trump's negotiations to actually reinvigorate the alliances to meet new emerging threats. On this score, allied leaders in Asia often helped their own cause greatly. Recognizing, for example, the importance of the U.S.-Japan alliance for Japanese security, or the import of Trump's iconoclastic outreach to North Korea for peace on the Korean Peninsula, or the value of the U.S.-India partnership for New Delhi's own interests, Shinzo Abe, Moon Jae-in, and Narendra Modi, respectively, artfully engaged Trump in ways that disarmed him and deflected his more egregious demands, arguably to the advantage of both sides.[63]

Between the extraordinary efforts made by Trump's national security officials and the adroit handling of a mercurial U.S. president by various foreign leaders, the United States miraculously found itself at the end of Trump's term with sharply improved relations with most of its Asian partners. Although the same could not be said generally of Washington's ties with Europe, the fact that the Asian affiliations were strengthened despite Trump's own instincts was critical in the context of the evolving U.S. competition with China. The imperative of constraining both China's geopolitical aggressiveness and its economic misdeeds should have induced Trump to treat the United States' European allies with greater consideration. Defeating China's statist

---

[61] Srijan Shukla, "Paris Deal to WHO, the 11 Organisations Donald Trump's U.S. Has Pulled Out Of, Weakened," *Print*, May 30, 2020, https://theprint.in/world/paris-deal-to-who-the-11-organisations-donald-trumps-us-has-pulled-out-of-weakened/432486.

[62] Jack Goldsmith and Shannon Togawa Mercer, "International Law and Institutions in the Trump Era," *German Yearbook of International Law* 61, no. 1 (2019): 11–39.

[63] Edward Luce, "Tickling Trump: World leaders Use Flattery to Influence America," *Financial Times*, May 4, 2018.

globalization certainly required European collaboration, especially given Beijing's efforts to cleave Europe from the United States.[64] By failing to appreciate that Washington's grievances toward its European alliance partners on both economic and security issues were insignificant in contrast to its problems with Beijing, Trump lost the opportunity to consolidate a common transatlantic front against China just when the Sino-U.S. rivalry was finally shifting into high gear.[65]

On this count, Trump himself proved to be curiously uninterested. Although his administration was articulating and implementing a major change in U.S. national strategy toward China—shifting from the previously optimistic approach that emphasized cooperation to a more realistic posture that accepted the realities of geopolitical competition—Trump personally focused first on flattering Xi Jinping and later on prosecuting a confusing trade war with China that attempted to reduce its trade surpluses rather than correct its trade malpractices. The "phase two" agreement that was intended to address these problems never materialized because of Trump's 2020 electoral defeat. All the same, it was remarkable how his national security aides were able to stitch together, albeit uncomfortably, an intellectual framework—exemplified most clearly by the 2017 National Security Strategy—which married the president's America-first rhetoric to a strategy that nonetheless discharged U.S. global security obligations in the face of Trump's disinterest. Consistent with the vision articulated in that document, his national security team focused sensibly on the challenges posed by China's threat to U.S. technological domination, its expanding global influence through the Belt and Road Initiative, and the dangers to U.S. power projection in Asia and globally.

Even if the instruments used to counter these challenges were not always effective (or appropriate), the Trump administration deserves credit for reorienting U.S. policy toward China. The elevation of the Indo-Pacific as the centerpiece of U.S. regional strategy; the resuscitation of the Quad with Australia, India, and Japan; the enhanced strategic cooperation with Japan and Taiwan; the renewed focus on Oceania; the gradual shift in U.S. strategic investments away from Southwest Asia (along with the new realignments in the Middle East); the vigorous assertion of freedom of navigation and overflight throughout the Asian rimland (and especially in Southeast Asia);

---

[64] Erik Brattberg and Philippe Le Corre, "The Case for Transatlantic Cooperation in the Indo-Pacific," Carnegie Endowment for International Peace, Working Paper, December 2019, https://carnegieendowment.org/files/WP_BrattbergLeCorre_FINAL1.pdf.

[65] See Wendy Cutler, "Strength in Numbers," Asia Society Policy Institute, Issue Paper, April 2019, https://asiasociety.org/sites/default/files/2019-04/Strength%20in%20Numbers.pdf. For a sensible assessment of the possibilities of U.S.-European cooperation vis-à-vis China, see Paul Gewirtz et al., "A Roadmap for U.S.-Europe Cooperation on China," Yale Law School, Paul Tsai China Center, February 2021, https://law.yale.edu/sites/default/files/area/center/china/document/roadmap_for_us-eu_cooperation_on_china.pdf.

and the emphasis on revitalizing U.S. defense capabilities to project military power more effectively to service U.S. extended-deterrence obligations in Asia must all be counted as strategic successes in the larger effort at balancing China.[66] This beneficial outcome highlights a reality that was last witnessed clearly during the Cold War: rising international political competition that embodies dangers to critical U.S. interests tends to obliterate the distinctions between nationalist and internationalist solutions to U.S. security predicaments. Although their conceptual underpinnings may diverge, these solutions end up looking very similar in practice.

The imperative of protecting these interests is highlighted by Zhao's chapter in this volume, which illuminatingly documents how Xi's arrival at the helm of Chinese politics set the nation on a more confrontational course. Clearly, the shift in the underlying material balance of power created the preconditions for this metamorphosis. But Xi has distinguished himself from his predecessors by transparently declaring his ambition to take a strong China to the center stage of global politics. He envisions a China that will protect its core interests, if necessary by resisting the United States, over and above the priority previously placed on assuring the international community that it was indeed intent only on rising peacefully. The emergence of this powerful and unyielding China represents a structural transformation in the international system—a gradual return to bipolarity on current trends. Hence, it is not surprising that this incipient shift in systemic polarity—and the resulting upsurge in competition with the United States—remains, as the chapters in this volume clarify, the single most important aspect of the era of tumult affecting all the states in the broader Indo-Pacific.

Only Russia on this count has been exceptional again, as Kaczmarski's discussion indicates. Yet this is only because Moscow had already embarked upon a strategic partnership with China to counter the United States as a common threat long before the Trump administration declared Beijing to be a strategic rival. For all other states, this declaration and the actions surrounding it were catalyzing not because the confrontation itself came as a surprise but because Washington's transparent acknowledgment of its reality put them into a situation where they could now be faced with hard choices—depending on where Trump and his successors might take the United States. As Mukherjee notes, the upsurge in U.S.-China rivalry provided new opportunities for India because Sino-Indian ties happened to fray at roughly the same time. Washington's strong support for New Delhi during its own crises with Beijing opened the door for a deeper U.S.-India partnership.

---

[66] For an assessment of Trump's overall strategy vis-à-vis China in the Indo-Pacific, see Ashley J. Tellis, "Waylaid by Contradictions: Evaluating Trump's Indo-Pacific Strategy," *Washington Quarterly* 43, no. 4 (2021): 123–54.

However, India's enduring interest in rising as an independent great power, in a manner analogous to China on this count, implies that India and the United States will have convergent but not necessarily congruent interests over the long term—depending on what happens to India's own internal revitalization and Beijing's behavior toward New Delhi in the interim.

Such concerns are less pressing where U.S. allies are concerned. Green's and Strating and Wallis's discussions in their chapters on Northeast Asia and Oceania, respectively, confirm that Japan, South Korea, Taiwan, Australia, and New Zealand have only intensified their alliance relationships with the United States because of the rising Chinese threat. These states dexterously managed Trump's idiosyncrasies and, given their inability to neutralize the dangers posed by Beijing independently, have expanded their contributions to collective defense at a time when Chinese assertiveness appears to be unrelenting. Strating and Wallis observe that the smaller island states in Oceania have actually benefited from the U.S.-China rivalry insofar as it has created space for them to profit from the attention of both big powers. In Southeast Asia, where fears of China are widespread but closeted, Le Thu highlights Vietnam's exceptionalism in resisting China openly. This contrasts with other countries in the region, including formal U.S. allies such as Thailand and the Philippines, which have been more circumspect, although for different reasons in each case. The continuing economic dependence of the Southeast Asian states on China, combined with their military weaknesses and proximity, has altogether pushed them to hope that the U.S.-China competition simply goes away. The fear that it might not, and could even become more unmanageable, only fills them with great trepidation.

On balance, then, many key U.S. bilateral relationships in the Indo-Pacific region have been deepened in the face of the United States' rising competition with China. That these ties have improved despite Trump's personal skepticism about alliances testifies both to the power of structural pressures produced by intensifying Chinese threats and to the resilience of old affiliations, not to mention the energetic efforts of Trump administration officials in protecting U.S. security partnerships with the most important countries along the Asian rimland.

The U.S. Response to the Covid-19 Pandemic

Although the Trump administration chalked up important gains on strategic issues, especially in Asia, its catastrophic shortcomings with respect to managing the Covid-19 pandemic irreparably harmed the United States' international reputation. The outbreak of the pandemic was clearly a surprise, but Trump's response only made a bad situation worse. Obviously, this tragedy, which has to date cost the United States over 800,000 lives and counting, was produced by multiple intersecting factors. The decentralized public health administration in the United States, the striking missteps of the premier federal agencies responsible for public health, the limitations of a medical system that prioritizes efficiency over resilience, the corrosive domestic politics that catalyzed resistance to public health measures, and the sheer lack of knowledge about how to manage a novel pathogen all contributed to the early difficulties that the United States had in responding to the pandemic. Tragically, Trump's attitude and behavior amplified these problems, which were only compounded by the unwillingness to mobilize the international community in developing a cooperative response to what was the most acute collective action problem (besides climate change) to confront humanity in recent years.[67]

Investing in an enlightened internationalism in the face of the pandemic would not have required the administration to subordinate the interests of Americans to other nations. The United States understandably would have prioritized the provision of personal protective equipment and medicines (and eventually vaccines) for its own citizens. But by failing to rope in the international community in a coordinated plan of action—because defeating the pandemic is ultimately a coordination problem, not a prisoner's dilemma—the United States lost an opportunity to develop effective solutions to the problems posed by divergent international travel restrictions, global inadequacies relating to the production of medical (and eventually vaccine) supplies, and the need for heightened financial assistance, especially to highly indebted countries. In sharp contrast to the efforts of Bush and Obama during the global financial crisis, when the United States led the global effort to manage the calamity, Trump did little to strengthen the international order even when that might have directly benefited the United States.

Against the larger tale of woe, however, the Trump administration did register two significant achievements. To begin with, Operation Warp Speed helped accelerate the development of Covid-19 vaccines and bring them to market in record time. The huge anticipatory orders placed with multiple manufacturers positioned the United States to inoculate its citizens faster than any comparably sized country could have. Given these successes amid all the tribulations, it is particularly tragic that the United States still has not conclusively defeated the Covid-19 pandemic in large measure because of vaccine resistance, which arguably derives from a self-regarding culture that

---

[67] Ashley J. Tellis, "COVID-19 Knocks on American Hegemony," NBR, May 4, 2020, https://www.nbr.org/publication/covid-19-knocks-on-american-hegemony.

both prizes personal freedom over collective responsibility and is distrustful of elites to the point of disregarding science at its own peril.[68]

Another important accomplishment, which is directly owed to the U.S. Federal Reserve Bank but must nevertheless be acknowledged as possibly arising from Trump's public pressure, was the continued sustenance of global liquidity in much the same way that Washington did earlier during the global financial crisis. By providing decisive leadership through domestic interest rate management and emergency assistance to central banks abroad, the United States stabilized asset markets worldwide, as well as foreign currencies, thus affording the global economy breathing room to manage what would have otherwise been a catastrophic meltdown. The massive domestic stimulus also provided the supporting effective demand for export-reliant countries as well. The costs of underwriting global stabilization in this way obviously still have to be repaid, but if the United States can emerge stronger after the pandemic—something that domestic vaccine hesitancy still undermines—it will have been well worth the burdens where protecting American hegemony is concerned.[69]

The long-term costs of the Covid-19 pandemic are obviously still unclear. One authoritative study has suggested that the deleterious macroeconomic consequences of pandemics appear to persist for around 40 years.[70] The IMF has already estimated that the pandemic will cost the global economy close to $30 trillion in lost output.[71] And the International Institute of Finance has estimated that governmental rescue plans worldwide have added $24 trillion to global debt, pushing the overall total to a record $281 trillion.[72] These realities should temper any undue optimism that the economic recovery now visible in many countries, including the United States and countries in Asia, implies an inexorable return to normalcy. As the IMF concluded in June 2020, "the extent of the recent rebound in financial market sentiment

---

[68] Jennifer Kates, Jennifer Tolbert, and Kendal Orgera, "The Red/Blue Divide in COVID-19 Vaccination Rates," Kaiser Family Foundation, September 14, 2021, https://www.kff.org/policy-watch/the-red-blue-divide-in-covid-19-vaccination-rates. See also Samuel Bazzi, Martin Fiszbein, and Mesay Gebresilasse, "Rugged Individualism and Collective (In)action during the COVID-19 Pandemic," National Bureau of Economic Research, Working Paper, September 2020, https://www.nber.org/system/files/working_papers/w27776/w27776.pdf.

[69] This paragraph is based on Carla Norrlöf, "Is COVID-19 the End of U.S. Hegemony? Public Bads, Leadership Failures and Monetary Hegemony," *International Affairs* 96, no. 5 (2020): 1281–1303.

[70] Òscar Jordà, Sanjay R. Singh, and Alan M. Taylor, "Longer-Run Economic Consequences of Pandemics," Federal Reserve Bank of San Francisco, Working Paper, March 2020.

[71] Larry Elliott, "IMF Estimates Global Covid Cost at $28tn in Lost Output," *Guardian*, October 13, 2020.

[72] Marc Jones, "COVID Response Drives $24 Trillion Surge in Global Debt: IIF," Reuters, February 17, 2021, https://www.reuters.com/article/us-global-debt-iif/covid-response-drives-24-trillion-surge-in-global-debt-iif-iduskbn2ah285.

appears disconnected from shifts in underlying economic prospects…raising the possibility that financial conditions may tighten more than assumed."[73]

The chapters in this volume highlight the fact that national performance in managing the Covid-19 pandemic varies considerably. Zhao notes that China, from whence the virus emerged, has been most successful in containing its spread domestically. Its resolute authoritarianism has made the country far more effective in managing the pandemic than some of its democratic counterparts. Beijing has also made a faster economic recovery than most other regional states, despite the fact that its zero-tolerance policy is now impeding a return to full normalcy. However, the early success of China's mask and vaccine diplomacy is unlikely to be as enduring as Beijing would have hoped, because its highly dramatized vaccine and personal protective equipment exports were eventually found to be marred by many shortcomings.

Green's discussion of Northeast Asia notes that Japan, South Korea, and Taiwan mismanaged their vaccine rollouts after early successes at containment. As a result, in contrast with the impact on Xi Jinping, the pandemic has partly discredited their national leaders at a time when the competence of democracies worldwide in managing the public health crisis has been questionable. Green, nonetheless, concludes that the pandemic has not fundamentally transformed any of the long-term trends already underway in the region, but that in itself is not automatically reassuring. Although Northeast Asia survived Trump's turbulence better than one would have expected, the secular trends pertaining to economic and population growth, technological innovation, and the military balances vis-à-vis China still remain issues of concern.

A similar set of challenges afflict both India and Southeast Asia. Mukherjee's assessment of India suggests that the country, which was terribly hard hit by the Delta variant, will make a comeback where economic growth is concerned but that its medium-term prospects will depend heavily on whether the Modi government can move doggedly on resuscitating domestic economic reforms. In particular, the weaknesses in private consumption and investment must be bridged by public investments and trade if India is to recover the domestic growth needed to sustain both Modi's burgeoning welfare programs and the rising defense expenditures necessary to balance a more aggressive China. Le Thu's chapter on Southeast Asia emphasizes that the Covid-19 pandemic has taken a toll on public health while producing a crisis in both governance and defense modernization. At a time when coping with rising Chinese power is the ubiquitous challenge throughout

---

[73] IMF, "World Economic Outlook Update: A Crisis Like No Other, an Uncertain Recovery," June 2020, 1, https://www.imf.org/en/Publications/WEO/Issues/2020/06/24/WEOUpdateJune2020.

the Indo-Pacific, vaccination disparities within the region, coupled with the enticements of China's vaccine diplomacy, threaten to produce both an uneven recovery and increased Chinese influence in an already unsettled, but critical, area of the Asian rimland.

The states in Oceania appear to have managed the pandemic better than most, but, as Strating and Wallis note, they too have not been immune to its external consequences. The collapse of tourism and foreign remittances have had particularly deleterious impacts on the Pacific Island states. The impact of the pandemic on Russia seems less clear. Kaczmarski observes that the economic effects have been unexpectedly mild so far—with the initial collapse of energy demand having more serious consequences. But he also flags the uncertainties associated with the absence of good information and argues that the demographic costs could be especially high. The Covid-19 pandemic, he emphasizes, has undermined Russia's efforts to reverse its demographic decline, with the decrease in national population showing the sharpest drop since 2005.

Whatever the various national stories about the pandemic's impact may be, the bottom line seems clear: Covid-19 has set back economic growth throughout the Indo-Pacific. China's ability to come out of the pandemic faster than most other countries suggests that it will have outsized advantages, at least in the short term, in the quest to restore its geopolitical centrality. The United States' efforts to strengthen its primacy unfortunately have not accrued similar advantages in part because of the tumultuous legacy of the Trump years.

Repairing the Damage

Biden came into office after Trump's turbulent presidency vowing to repair the damage done to the United States at home as well as to the liberal international order abroad. His first year as president focused almost entirely on domestic concerns: protecting democracy, revitalizing the middle class, and accelerating the recovery from Covid-19. These three goals are deeply intertwined, and Biden's strategy has consisted fundamentally of increasing governmental expenditures to advance them simultaneously. The $1.9 trillion American Rescue Plan Act focused on providing additional direct financial assistance to Americans to help cope with the pandemic, while extending unemployment and healthcare benefits. As a complement to financial support, he has also aggressively promoted Covid-19 vaccination, including through diverse mandates and incentives, in an effort to sustain the momentum of the economic recovery. More expansive governmental funding has also been unleashed. The Infrastructure Investment and Jobs Act committed more than

$1 trillion over a decade to fund physical infrastructure, public transit, and broadband expansion. And a third vehicle, the roughly $2 trillion Build Back Better Act, whose final size and scope are still being negotiated in Congress at the time of writing, is intended to shore up social welfare programs while also targeting climate change.

These initiatives, which could top out at beyond $4 trillion eventually, are intended to bolster the middle class through focused government spending that seeks to remedy the losses suffered in the marketplace due to the economic transformations of the last few decades. If these spending plans deliver as intended, Biden will have succeeded not only in alleviating some of the economic grievances that partly drove Trump's ascent to power but also in credibly demonstrating that democracy can work for ordinary citizens who consequently do not have to rely on either a populist mobilization or a divisive politics that destroys existing institutions in order to protect their political, economic, and social interests. While Biden's aims obviously include weaning back many of Trump's nationalist supporters to the Democratic Party, securing their renewed allegiance is also important if the United States is to successfully reclaim its global leadership and return to its traditional role as the guardian of the liberal international order.[74] After all, if the domestic support for this ambition is lacking, no president—regardless of vision or zeal—will be able to sustain this mission. The best device, accordingly, for mustering such support is to demonstrate that protecting the hegemonic order actually pays off in terms of material benefits for the citizenry.

Securing these gains, therefore, requires greater investments at home to begin with. But they must be complemented by wise policies abroad. On the latter count, Biden has signaled his determination to work closely with allies; to protect U.S. interests by force if necessary, but without indulging in reckless wars; and to strengthen international institutions (sometimes by simply rejoining them) in order to sustain a favorable normative order that economizes on the active use of U.S. power to produce beneficial outcomes. Given the convulsive legacy of the Trump years, it will be a while, however, before the international community can be persuaded either about Biden's ability to make good on his intentions or that the domestic support for sustaining hegemonic responsibilities has been rebuilt within the United States. Biden's emphasis on global coordination to combat the Covid-19 pandemic, his increased commitment to sharing vaccines abroad, and his ambition to create a global partnership to detect and respond to emerging public health threats augurs well for restoring confidence in U.S. leadership, although much more remains to be done.

---

[74] Salman Ahmed et al., "Making U.S. Foreign Policy Work Better for the Middle Class," Carnegie Endowment for International Peace, September 2020.

Two pronounced elements of continuity with Trump's foreign policy persist on Biden's watch. First, the Biden administration has accepted the reality that China is a great-power competitor of the United States. Although that reaffirmation is reassuring for many critical Asian states, the administration's inability to define the contours of competition clearly thus far amid the resilient backdrop of economic interdependence—a task that also eluded Trump—will complicate ties with U.S. allies and others both in Asia and especially in Europe. Achieving a balance between competition and cooperation with China is undoubtedly a complicated matter. U.S. interests would be best served if the elements of rivalry are restricted primarily to protecting the United States' military superiority, technological dominance, and ideational attractiveness. Still, the policy predicates of even these restricted goals and their internal tradeoffs are numerous and complex. But limiting the antagonism to what is most important for preserving U.S. primacy and allied security at least allows for cooperation in other areas that mitigates conflicts, while permitting the United States to maintain those absolute gains from continued economic ties with China that are essential for both increased welfare benefits and successful competition with Beijing.[75]

Implementing such an approach necessarily requires the United States to make investments in its own domestic economic revitalization, something the Biden administration appears to have clearly grasped even if many other aspects of the solution remain a work in progress. It also requires the administration to focus on correcting the unfair sources of China's current trade advantages—forced technology transfer, the theft of intellectual property (including through cyberattacks), the subsidies to state owned-enterprises (and other private entities), and the pervasive industrial policies, among others—if the bilateral trade relationship is to be sustained in ways that provide mutual benefit. Unfortunately, during its first year the administration appears to have been more interested in implementing Trump's phase-one agreement with Beijing than in addressing these fundamental structural distortions. Countering these challenges, as well as the security threats posed by China, will ultimately require dominance of the global innovation cycle as well as deepened collaboration within the transatlantic community and with the United States' Asian allies, tasks that require renewed focus both at home and abroad.

Second, the Biden administration appears to have—again unfortunately— persisted with its predecessor's animus toward international trade. Partly scarred by the distributional costs of past trade openness, especially with

---

[75] An extended elaboration of this idea can be found in Ashley J. Tellis, *Balancing without Containment— An American Strategy for Managing China* (Washington, D.C.: Carnegie Endowment for International Peace, 2014).

China, the administration has doubled down on its "buy American" agenda. This decision not only exemplifies a pernicious mercantilism but also sustains an undesirable continuity with Trump's economic policies. The retention of many of the tariffs (especially on allies), the desire to pursue an amorphous "worker-centric" trade policy, and the deep reluctance to consider even plurilateral trade agreements that are highly favorable to U.S. geopolitical and economic interests, such as the TPP, suggest that the political benefits of avoiding leadership on trade take precedence over an economic strategy centered on sensible international integration. The importance of resuscitating international trade should be rooted not merely in the symbolic imperatives of signaling returning U.S. leadership in an open international economic order. Rather, the pursuit of this goal should be driven fundamentally by the material imperatives of securing those efficiencies that are essential to successfully competing with China across the board and warding off the rising international drift toward localization, autarky, and trade barriers in both goods and services. China's political assertiveness has undoubtedly increased the incentives for many countries to pursue various import substitution strategies as a means of mitigating risk. While some such insurance is necessary, the United States should not as a rule cast its lot with protectionism, however disguised, if it is to preserve market access abroad and sustain the competitiveness that makes it the world's most innovative economy.

EXECUTIVE SUMMARY

This chapter examines China's foreign policy under Xi Jinping in the context of heightened U.S.-China rivalry, deglobalization, and the Covid-19 pandemic.

MAIN ARGUMENT

Xi Jinping has abandoned Deng Xiaoping's low-profile diplomacy and instead adopted big-power diplomacy to restore China's historical centrality on the world stage. Competing from a perceived position of strength, China has increasingly challenged the U.S.-led liberal international order and promoted the superiority of the China model of authoritarianism. Xi's big-power diplomacy has also expanded China's geopolitical reach in the Indo-Pacific by launching new initiatives and forging partnerships with emerging countries. But this projection of power and confidence has covered up the reality that China still is a fragile superpower facing serious domestic economic and political challenges. Externally, China's ambition continues to be checked by U.S. power. As the two rivals are incapable of dominating each other, they must find ways to prevent their competition from escalating into a cold war or even a hot war in which everyone would lose.

POLICY IMPLICATIONS

- The U.S. must coordinate with its allies and partners on important issues in the competition with China and push back against the fantasies of Chinese nationalists. Yet Washington should not force countries to take a side and make the alliances and partnerships exclusively confrontational against China in a zero-sum game.

- Cooperation between rivals may be uncomfortable but is necessary. The U.S. cannot make progress on global challenges such as climate change, the pandemic, and nuclear proliferation without working together with China.

- The world is in danger of moving toward a power vacuum, where it is every country for itself, which could be more dangerous than power hegemony. The U.S. must welcome China to take on more global responsibility and join the U.S. and others in making rules for global governance.

China

China's Big-Power Diplomacy: Strategic Rivalry and Geopolitical Expansion in the Indo-Pacific

Suisheng Zhao

Conditioned by circumscribed capabilities and geostrategic isolation after the end of the Cold War, Jiang Zemin and Hu Jintao followed Deng Xiaoping's "low-profile diplomacy" to live with a hegemon and adapt Chinese foreign policy to the reality of U.S. dominance in the international system. As China has become a power with interests spanning its own region and beyond and acquired the capacity to act on them, Xi Jinping has used China's newly gained might and singlehandedly committed to a change in direction from a low-profile foreign policy to big-power diplomacy to achieve the "China dream of great rejuvenation," which aims to return China to the position of global centrality it once enjoyed when the Chinese empire incorporated vast areas into its territory. Calling on Chinese diplomats to demonstrate their "fighting spirit" (*douzheng jingshen*) and "show their swords" (*ganyu liangjian*) to win diplomatic battles, Xi has set boundaries that other countries cannot cross.

Big-power diplomacy has intensified China's rivalry with what Beijing perceives as a declining United States that will do whatever it takes to maintain its primacy by holding China down. Competing from a perceived position of strength, China has challenged U.S. dominance in the world order and U.S.-led liberal globalization and promoted the superiority of the China model of authoritarianism. This big-power diplomacy has also expanded China's geopolitical reach in the Indo-Pacific. China has launched new initiatives and forged partnerships with the so-called emerging big powers to establish

---

Suisheng Zhao is Professor and Director of the Center for China-U.S. Cooperation in the Josef Korbel School of International Studies at the University of Denver. He can be reached at <suisheng.zhao@du.edu>.

its dominance in the region and beyond. It has also modernized the People's Liberation Army (PLA) Navy to establish itself as a great maritime power capable of taking back Taiwan by force if necessary and resolving the maritime disputes in the East and South China Seas on Beijing's terms.

Xi's big-power diplomacy has important policy implications. Advocating state-centered globalization and regarding the U.S.-led liberal world order as hostile to China's interests as a rising power, China has become a revisionist power that demands the reform of the world order and advances national interests and statist values. For this purpose, China has competed with the United States for dominance in global governance institutions and led initiatives to create new international economic institutions. The devastation caused by the Covid-19 pandemic has not slowed down these efforts. Taking advantage of its early success in containing Covid-19, Beijing launched a diplomatic offensive to promote the superiority of its authoritarian system during the crisis and boost the image of China as a generous and responsible power through mask and vaccine diplomacy.

The domestic support for Xi's big-power diplomacy has been delicate. On the one hand, as China has built advanced, broad-based technology and a globally competitive, dynamic economy, Xi has gained support, particularly among nationalistic youth. On the other hand, China's projected power and confidence tends to conceal its domestic economic and political constraints and insecurity as a fragile superpower. Additionally, its ambition is checked by the United States and other powers. Although a new bipolarity has emerged as China significantly narrows its power gap with the United States and widens the gap with the rest of the world, multiple big powers, such as the European Union, Russia, India, and Japan, remain independent and can upset the central balance of power. Neither the United States nor China has dominated the other, and they must find ways to prevent their competition from escalating into a new cold war, or even a hot war.

This chapter starts with an examination of China's new foreign policy under Xi and moves on to explore the U.S.-China rivalry, mask and vaccine diplomacy during the Covid-19 pandemic, and geopolitical expansion in the Indo-Pacific under the banner of big-power diplomacy. It then analyzes the delicate domestic support for big-power diplomacy. The chapter concludes by drawing policy implications for the emerging U.S.-China great-power competition, the backlash against liberal globalization, and the ongoing Covid-19 pandemic.

The New Direction of Chinese Foreign Policy

The term "big-power diplomacy" started to appear in Chinese foreign policy discourse in the 1990s, but Presidents Jiang Zemin and Hu Jintao were reluctant to endorse the concept. Instead, they emphasized that China was a developing country because its level of economic development and technological prowess still lagged far behind Western countries and even some of its Asian neighbors.[1] Declaring the arrival of a new era, Xi Jinping has predicted profound changes unseen in hundreds of years as the East rises and the West declines. Just days after becoming the general secretary of the Chinese Communist Party (CCP), he delivered his famous "China dream" speech in which he presented his vision for the Chinese people to reclaim their place on the stage of world history and make China great again.

The dream of a strong China has been the central theme of the political and strategic discourse of every CCP leader, but Xi has distinguished himself from his predecessors. He has declared that "while China stood up under Mao and became rich under Deng, China will become powerful in the new era. China has never been closer to the center of the global stage."[2] In other words, China has gone from building the state to making it rich and strong.[3] Big-power diplomacy is therefore known as "rejuvenation diplomacy" (*fuxing waijiao*) to make China strong and respected.[4]

This big-power diplomacy has changed the direction of Chinese foreign policy. Xi highlighted the new direction at the Central Conference on Peripheral Diplomacy in October 2013, stating that "the primary theme of China's foreign policy should be the striving for achievements, moving forward along with time changes, and acting more proactively."[5] Foreign Minister Wang Yi, in his inaugural press conference in March 2014, characterized the new diplomacy as "proactively striving for achievements

---

[1] Wu Xinbo, "Four Contradictions Constraining China's Foreign Policy Behavior," *Journal of Contemporary China* 10, no. 27 (2001): 293–302.

[2] Xi Jinping, "Juesheng quanmian jiancheng xiaokang shehui, duoqu xinshidai Zhongguo tese shehuizhuyi weida shengli" [Secure a Decisive Victory in Building a Moderately Prosperous Society in All Respects and Strive for the Great Success of Socialism with Chinese Characteristics for a New Era], Xinhua, October 27, 2017, http://www.gov.cn/zhuanti/2017-10/27/content_5234876.htm.

[3] Zhao Kejin, "Zhongguo waijiao 70 nian, lishi luoji yu jiben jingyan" [Chinese Diplomacy in 70 years: Historical Logic and Basic Experiences], Northeast Asia Forum, 2019, 3–20.

[4] Ibid.

[5] Xi Jinping, "Rang mingyun gongtongti yishi zai zhoubian guojia luodi shenggen" [Let the Concept of the Community of Common Destiny to Take a Root Among China's Peripheral Countries] Xinhua, October 25, 2013, http://news.xinhuanet.com/politics/2013-10/25/c_117878944.htm.

to let the world hear Chinese solutions and Chinese voices."[6] Xi's speech at the 4th Central Foreign Affairs Work Conference in 2014 elaborated on big-power diplomacy as "a distinctive diplomatic approach befitting its [China's] role as a big power to show Chinese features, Chinese style, and Chinese confidence" and effectively use China's strength to achieve the two centenary objectives of the China dream.[7] When meeting with French president Emmanuel Macron, Xi stated that "the contemporary world is facing increasing instabilities and uncertainties, which calls for more responsibilities of major countries," a role China is willing to assume.[8]

In taking a new direction as a big power, Xi's commitment to a peaceful rise is conditioned by external accommodation to China's core national interests and premised on reciprocity. Forcefully protecting China's core interests is given greater importance than a peaceful rise. China used to prefer to state what it hoped other countries would do but has moved toward "baseline thinking," whereby it seeks to safeguard its interests by setting a red line that other countries cannot cross.[9] This baseline thinking has required Chinese diplomats to exhibit a "fighting spirit" and "dare to attack and dare to win."[10] The emphasis on fighting spirit highlights how big-power diplomacy conceives diplomacy as a war against enemies that must be defeated. Chinese diplomats, who had been known for courtesy, are now known as "wolf warriors," a term derived from the Chinese movie *Wolf Warrior* in which a Chinese special-operations soldier defeats Western-led mercenaries by defending China's overseas interests. Chinese ambassador to France Lu Shaye described wolf-warrior diplomacy as a change in China's diplomatic style resulting from a rise in national strength and changes in the external environment. From this perspective, China has grown to become

---

[6] "Waijiao buzhang Wang Yi jiu Zhongguo waijiao zhengce he duiwai guanxi huida zhongwai jizhe tiwen" [Foreign Minister Wang Yi Meets the Press], Ministry of Foreign Affairs of the People's Republic China (PRC), March 8, 2014, http://www.fmprc.gov.cn/mfa_chn/wjb_602314/wjbz_602318/xghds/t1135388.shtml.

[7] Xi defined two centennial objectives to achieve the China dream. First, by the CCP's centenary in 2021, China should have built a moderately prosperous society in all respects. Xi declared the achievement of this first objective in his speech to celebrate the one-hundredth birthday of the CCP on July 1, 2021. Second, by the PRC's centenary in 2049, China should have become a global power in all aspects. "Xi Jinping chuxi zhongyang waishi gongzuo huiyi bing fabiao zhongyao jianghua" [Xi Jinping Attended the Central Foreign Affairs Work Conference and Made an Important Speech], Xinhua, November 29, 2014, http://news.xinhuanet.com/politics/2014-11/29/c_1113457723.htm.

[8] "Xi Jinping tong Faguo zhongtong Makelong tong dianhua, liangguo yuanshou jiu xiajieduan Zhongfa hezuo dacheng zhongyao gongshi" [Xi Jinping Speaks with French President Macron on the Phone: The Two Leaders Reach Important Consensus on China-France Cooperation in the Next Stage], Xinhua, December 9, 2020, http://www.xinhuanet.com/politics/leaders/2020-12/09/c_1126842434.htm.

[9] Zhao, "Zhongguo waijiao 70 nian, lishi luoji yu jiben jingyan."

[10] Wang Zhihui, "Douzheng! Xi Jinping zhenbian jianghua dayou shengyi" [Struggle! Xi Jinping's Speech Is Very Meaningful], Xinhua, September 4, 2019, http://www.xinhuanet.com/politics/leaders/xijinping/index.htm.

a giant and can no longer hide its ability. Faced with containment efforts by the United States and other Western countries, China must safeguard its sovereignty, security, and developmental interests by shifting from "lamb diplomacy" to wolf-warrior diplomacy.[11]

Wolf-warrior diplomacy has made headlines around the world amid the Covid-19 pandemic. As the world watched the outbreak in China, Beijing raised the stakes of its foreign relations and proposed that countries were either with it or against it. When China stabilized the situation within its borders and the pandemic went on a rampage through Europe and the United States, Chinese diplomats stationed all over the world waged an all-out "discourse" war in international newspapers to respond to critics of China and highlight the failure of the United States and other Western countries to contain the virus.[12] Justifying this strident and combative diplomacy, a *Global Times* editorial declared that "the days when China can be put in a submissive position are long gone…. As Western diplomats fall into disgrace, they are getting a taste of China's 'wolf warrior' diplomacy."[13]

Rivalry with the United States from a Perceived Position of Strength

One conceptual building block undergirding Xi's big-power diplomacy is the "new model of great-power relations." Although the model includes China's ties with traditional and emerging powers, none of these relationships is as important as the Sino-U.S. relationship.[14] Only the United States and China, as the two largest economies in the world, qualify as great powers, and they must work together to build a new model to manage the bilateral relationship and resolve global issues. Beijing has described three essential features of the new model: no conflict or confrontation, mutual respect,

---

[11] "Zhongguo zhufa dashi: Women xianzai waijiao fengge bianle, nimen yao shiying" [Chinese Ambassador to France: Our Diplomatic Style Has Changed, You Must Adapt], Guancha, June 16, 2021, https://www.wenxuecity.com/news/2021/06/16/10649308.html.

[12] Gerry Shih, "China's Bid to Repair Its Coronavirus-Hit Image Is Backfiring in the West," *Washington Post*, April 14, 2020, https://www.washingtonpost.com/world/asia_pacific/chinas-bid-to-repair-its-coronavirus-hit-image-is-backfiring-in-the-west/2020/04/14/8611bbba-7978-11ea-a311-adb1344719a9_story.html.

[13] "West Feels Challenged by China's New 'Wolf Warrior' Diplomacy," *Global Times*, April 16, 2020, https://www.globaltimes.cn/content/1185776.shtml.

[14] "Goujian xinxing daoguo guanxi" [Construction of a New Model of Major-Country Relations], *People's Daily*, June 4, 2013, 7.

and win-win cooperation.[15] Mutual respect of core national interests is the most important feature because great powers can coexist only if they do not challenge each other and make their strategic aspirations incompatible.[16]

During the initial decades of reform and opening, China reluctantly acceded to U.S. demands because it was relatively weak. The primary objective of its foreign policy was to create, sustain, and exploit external conditions to facilitate rapid and sustained economic development. As China has grown and gained more freedom to maneuver over the past three decades, Chinese diplomats have perceived a shift in the balance of power in China's favor. Although sustained growth remains a priority, it has been supplanted by the need to counter the perceived threat of U.S.-led efforts to forestall the West's decline by thwarting China's rise. Beijing no longer bends to Washington's pressure or unilaterally accommodates U.S. interests without conditions. Instead, the United States must accede to China's core interests in exchange for collaboration to manage a range of challenges confronting the United States and the world, such as North Korea and Iran.

The prospect of an increasingly powerful China rivaling the United States has alarmed U.S. leaders and spurred them to redefine the relationship. While the tipping point came much earlier, the Trump administration declared great-power competition as the focus of the U.S. National Security Strategy released in December 2017 and launched a trade war against China. The Biden administration has continued many of Donald Trump's policies, countered Chinese adventures in the Taiwan Strait and the South China Sea, and increased public criticism of China's human rights violations in Xinjiang, Tibet, and Hong Kong. The Chinese government has criticized the United States for adopting a cold war mentality based on a zero-sum mindset and ideological prejudice.[17] Just days after Joe Biden's inauguration, Xi warned that "to build small circles or start a new cold war…will only push the world into division and even confrontation."[18]

---

[15] "Wang Yi Bulujinsi Xuehui yanjiang: Zhongmei goujian xinxing guanxi" [Speech by Foreign Minister Wang Yi at the Brookings Institution, toward a New Model of Major-Country Relations between China and the United States)], Ifeng, September 20, 2013, http://news.ifeng.com/mainland/special/wangyifangmei2013/content-2/detail_2013_09/21/29769744_0.shtml. An English version is available at http://www.china.org.cn/world/2013-09/21/content_30086631.htm.

[16] Li Jingtian, "Building on the Bottom Line," *China Daily*, July 1, 2013, http://www.chinadaily.com.cn/cndy/2013-07/01/content_16694116.htm.

[17] Zhong Sheng, "Lengzhan siwei dang xiuyi" [The Cold War Mentality Should Stop], *People's Daily*, July 10, 2020, http://theory.people.com.cn/n1/2020/0710/c40531-31778024.html; and "China Urges U.S. to Discard Cold War Mentality," Xinhua, July 21,2020, http://www.xinhuanet.com/english/2020-07/21/c_139227316.htm.

[18] "Xi Jinping's Speech at the Virtual Davos Agenda Event," CGTN, January 26, 2021, https://news.cgtn.com/news/2021-01-25/Full-text-Xi-Jinping-s-speech-at-the-virtual-Davos-Agenda-event-Xln4hwjO2Q/index.html.

In response to the Trump administration's trade war and the Biden administration's continued tough policies, the Chinese media has been filled with emotional stories of China being forced to fight back in defense of its national interests. Mao Zedong is once again celebrated for having boldly gone to war against the United States in Korea and fighting to a truce. People critical of China's assertive stance toward the United States are criticized as having "soft bone disease" and "worshiping" or "kneeling to" the United States. "A self-reliant China is the best medicine for this kind of rickets," stated a Xinhua article.[19]

Confident in the shift of the power balance in Beijing's favor and mindful of China's own historical experience with cycles of growth and collapse, Chinese leaders anticipate the decline of the United States. The very ascent of Trump to the presidency was seen as a symptom of a profound systemic crisis, and the United States' poor management of the Covid-19 pandemic reinforced this perception of decline. The U.S. withdrawal from Afghanistan and the indelible images of the chaotic exit only strengthened these beliefs.

Chinese leaders believe that the United States will not accept its fall from grace but will do whatever it takes to protect its global hegemony, including taking reflexive actions to undermine China's rise. A hegemon can be even more dangerous in decline than when it was an unchallenged superpower. The perception in China, therefore, is that bilateral relations will remain rocky until China overtakes the United States. Though preparing for a long-term struggle, Beijing believes that Washington's containment strategy will eventually prove futile and self-defeating.

Reflecting this perception of a changing balance of power, China's top diplomat Yang Jiechi told his counterparts in the Biden administration at their first in-person meeting in March 2021 that "the United States does not have the qualification to say that it wants to speak to China from a position of strength" and "must stop advancing its own democracy in the rest of the world" while dealing with discontent among its own population. Foreign Minister Yi added that "it is time for the U.S. to correct the longstanding bad practice" of willfully interfering in China's internal affairs.[20] These comments circulated widely on Chinese social media, resonating with the belief that

---

[19] Xin Shiping, "Chongmei, guimei de ruangubing dezhi" [The Soft Bone Disease of Worshiping America and Kneeling to America Must Be Cured], Xinhua, December 16, 2020, http://www.xinhuanet.com/2020-12/16/c_1126869721.htm.

[20] "How It Happened: Transcript of the U.S.-China Opening Remarks in Alaska," *Nikkei Asia*, March 19, 2021, https://asia.nikkei.com/Politics/International-relations/US-China-tensions/How-it-happened-Transcript-of-the-US-China-opening-remarks-in-Alaska.

China's "rise to great-power status entitles it to a new role in world affairs—one that cannot be reconciled with unquestioned U.S. dominance."[21]

Beijing demonstrated its position of strength again when U.S. deputy secretary of state Wendy Sherman visited China in July 2021. Although the U.S. State Department did not agree with China arranging for one of its four vice foreign ministers, Xie Feng, to serve as her counterpart in the meetings, Sherman still made the trip. According to Chinese media, Xie expressed anger at Washington and rejected the Biden administration's strategy of simultaneously pursuing confrontation and cooperation because the "collaborative aspect is just an expediency, and the competitive aspect is a narrative trap." Foreign Minister Yi met Sherman briefly and defined three red lines that the United States could not cross: challenging China's political system, disrupting its development, and interfering in sovereignty issues, especially in Hong Kong, Tibet, Xinjiang, and Taiwan.[22]

Following Sherman's visit, the U.S. special presidential envoy for climate, John Kerry, made a trip to China the next month. Chinese leaders met only virtually with Kerry and gave no ground on his appeal for cooperation on climate change. They also reiterated that the United States should attach importance and actively respond to the "two lists" and "three bottom lines" put forward by China.[23] The chilly treatment of both Sherman and Kerry reflected Beijing's increasingly assertive approach to diplomacy with Washington and was a stark departure from the long-standing conservative, restrained style of diplomacy. Once scorned by the Chinese public for being weak, wolf-warrior diplomats demonstrated their new and aggressive tone.

Challenging U.S. Dominance in the World Order and Liberal Globalization

The post–World War II order was constructed under U.S. leadership and reflected American values. Prospering in the U.S.-led order and benefiting from liberal globalization during Deng Xiaoping's market-oriented reform and opening years, Chinese leaders welcomed U.S. deputy secretary of state Robert Zoellick's invitation to become a "responsible stakeholder" in the

---

[21] Yan Xuetong, "Becoming Strong: The New Chinese Foreign Policy," *Foreign Affairs*, July/August 2021, https://www.foreignaffairs.com/articles/united-states/2021-06-22/becoming-strong.

[22] Catherine Wong, "U.S.-China Relations: Beijing Takes Pointers from Mao in Protracted Power Struggle with U.S.," *South China Morning Post*, August 2, 2021, https://www.scmp.com/news/china/diplomacy/article/3143505/us-china-relations-beijing-takes-pointers-mao-protracted-power.

[23] "Wang Yi Meets with U.S. Special Presidential Envoy for Climate John Kerry via Video Link at Request," Ministry of Foreign Affairs (PRC), September 1, 2021, https://www.fmprc.gov.cn/mfa_eng/zxxx_662805/t1904000.shtml.

international system. A rising China, however, has regarded the order as unfair and unreasonable, not reflecting the interests and values of emerging powers. Instead, China has become a revisionist power seeking to advance its status as a rulemaker, expand its influence in the international hierarchy, and change aspects of the order that it views as undermining its values and interests.[24]

China's position has been enhanced because the United States' promotion of liberal values has not produced global peace and prosperity and has often led to disruption and chaos worldwide. The result of using force to spread democracy, exemplified by the wars in Iraq and Afghanistan, has undermined support for democracy and generated anti-Americanism. Chinese scholars have blamed the United States for the fragmentation, disorder, and dysfunction of the international order, "leading to a global trust deficit, governance deficit, peace deficit, and development deficit."[25] According to one Chinese observer, "the post–World War II order has quickly become a disorder and is in danger of failing. World conflicts and contradictions have approached new thresholds, leading to an unpredictable and turbulent future."[26]

Xi Jinping, therefore, has vowed to supply Chinese characteristics, style, wisdom, and ambition to help reform the world order. He put forward "two guidances" in 2017: China should guide the international community to build a more just and reasonable new world order and to safeguard international security. A commentary from the CCP Central Party School held that Xi's two guidances were profound, coming as the Western-dominated world order was nearing its end.[27]

Presenting the Chinese vision for the reform of the world order, Xi proposed the "community of shared future for mankind" (*renlie mingyun gongtongti*) in 2013, rejecting Western values as universal and calling for all sociopolitical systems to be respected as equally valid (democracy as well as authoritarianism). All should peacefully coexist and not attempt to

---

[24] Suisheng Zhao, "A Revisionist Stakeholder: China and the Post–World War II World Order," *Journal of Contemporary China* 27, no. 113 (2018): 643–58.

[25] Han Zhu, "Guoji zhixu yu shijie zhixu de boyi yu Zhongguo de weizhi" [The Game between International Order and World Order and China's Position], China Research Center, Fudan University, November 26, 2019, http://www.cifu.fudan.edu.cn/24/91/c12233a205969/page.htm.

[26] Zhou Xinmin, "Dabianju shidai huhuan shiji zhengzhi lingxiu" [The Era of Great Changes Calls for World Political Leaders], Military Net, June 9, 2020, https://club.6parkbbs.com/military/index.php?app=forum&act=threadview&tid=15782581.

[27] "Xi Jinping shouti liangge yindao you shenyi" [It Is Profound That Xi Jinping Stated the Two Guides for the First Time], Learning China, February 21, 2017, http://www.ccln.gov.cn/hotnews/230779.shtml. Foreign Minister Wang Yi used the term "leading goat" to describe China's role in "guiding the reform of global governance." See "Wang Yi tan 2021 nian Zhongguo waijiao gongzuo zhongdian" [Wang Yi on the Priorities of Chinese Diplomatic Works], *China Daily*, January 4, 2020, https://language.chinadaily.com.cn/a/202101/04/WS5ff27c44a31024ad0baa03fc_1.html.

transform others.[28] Beijing also has rejected the concept of the rules-based order as defined by the United States and other Western countries. For Beijing, the United States cannot represent the international community and is not qualified to define the international order, let alone impose its own standards on others. China should "safeguard the international order and the international system to the purposes and principles of the UN Charter as the core and defend the international order underpinned by international law."[29] Claiming that state sovereignty and nonintervention in the internal affairs of other states should be based on UN Charter principles rather than Western values, China has demanded reforms so that it can exert control as a rulemaker, expand its influence in the power hierarchy, adjust rules in its favor, and change aspects of the international order that it views as undermining its values and interests.[30]

Beijing's objective is, in Xi's words, "to position China in the commanding heights of the international competition."[31] For this purpose, it has sent its best and most talented diplomats to compete for an increasing number of leadership positions in UN institutions, including taking the helm in four of fifteen UN specialized agencies since 2015: the Food and Agriculture Organization, International Telecommunication Union, UN Industrial Development Organization, and International Civil Aviation Organization (ICAO). A Chinese delegation also chairs the UNAIDS Program Coordinating Board. These are all elected posts, which Beijing won after heavily lobbying member states.

While officials in UN organizations are meant to be politically neutral, Chinese diplomats have used these positions to advance China's economic interests and political ends. The ICAO, for example, has denied Taiwan's participation as an observer ever since a Chinese official became secretary-general in 2015. Headed in 2006–17 by Margaret Chan, a Chinese national from Hong Kong, the World Health Organization (WHO) allowed Taiwan to participate as an observer as "Chinese Taipei" during Ma Ying-jeou's presidency (2008–16). But the WHO suspended Taiwan's observer position after Tsai Ing-wen was elected president in 2016 because Beijing was concerned about her pro-independence tendency. A Taiwan diplomat

---

[28] Xiang Bo, "China Keywords: Community with Shared Future for Mankind," Xinhua, January 24, 2018, http://www.xinhuanet.com/english/2018-01/24/c_136921370.htm.

[29] "Xi Jinping Delivers an Important Speech at the High-Level Meeting to Commemorate the 75th Anniversary of the United Nations (UN)," Ministry of Foreign Affairs (PRC), September 21, 2020, https://www.fmprc.gov.cn/mfa_eng/zxxx_662805/t1817250.shtml.

[30] Zhao, "A Revisionist Stakeholder."

[31] Xi Jinping, "Tuidong quanqiu zhili tizhi gengjia gongzheng heli" [Pushing for a More Just and Reasonable Global Governance], Xinhua, October 13, 2015, http://news.xinhuanet.com/politics/2015-10/13/c_1116812159.htm.

complained that the WHO had delegated decisions concerning Taiwan to Beijing.[32]

China's demand for reform of the world order has been guided by sovereignty-centered statist values that leave ample leeway for authoritarian states to conduct themselves without intrusive liberal values dictating governance. These statist values have been enhanced amid mounting backlash against liberal globalization that creates disparity in income distribution and regional development, resulting in the unprecedented concentration of wealth in a few rich countries and multinational corporations.[33] In 2016, rich countries accounted for only 20% of the global population but consumed more than 70% of global resources, whereas people in the poorest countries struggled on less than $2 per day.[34] Liberal globalization has exacerbated the widening income gap. Although China has also grappled with stark income inequality, Chinese publications have cited the United States as an extreme example of internal inequality as multinational companies, financial institutions, and senior management on Wall Street thrive, but wage increases for blue-collar workers are very limited.[35]

China has thus emerged as a champion for statist globalization, which is fundamentally different from the liberal globalization promoted by the West. According to one Chinese scholar, each country must choose which style of globalization is best for itself. China promotes economic globalization supported by political multipolarity and multiculturalism, whereas liberal globalization emphasizes political democratization, economic privatization, and universalization of liberal values.[36]

China's statist values gained ground during the Covid-19 pandemic because the liberal globalization that had created so many opportunities for economic growth also made the world vulnerable. Global interconnectedness "meant that when things go bad in one place, that trouble can be transmitted

---

[32] Vincent Yi-hsiang Chao, "Why Taiwan Belongs in the World Health Organization (WHO)," *National Interest*, April 20, 2020, https://nationalinterest.org/feature/why-taiwan-belongs-world-health-organization-who-146172.

[33] Thomas Piketty, *Capital in the Twenty-First Century* (Cambridge: Harvard University Press, 2014), 15, 21.

[34] World Bank, *Poverty and Shared Prosperity 2016, Taking on Inequality* (Washington, D.C.: World Bank, 2016) https://www.worldbank.org/en/publication/poverty-and-shared-prosperity-2016.

[35] Mei Xinyu, "Facing Up to Anti-Globalization," *Beijing Review*, September 8, 2016, http://www.bjreview.com/Current_Issue/Editor_Choice/201609/t20160905_800066884.html.

[36] Huang Renwei, "Cong quanqiuhua, ni quanqiuhua de youxuanze de quanqiuhua" [From Globalization and Anti-Globalization to Selective Globalization], *Exploration and Contention*, March 21, 2017, https://www.yicai.com/news/5251702.html.

farther, faster, deeper and cheaper than ever before."[37] As a result, many countries, including liberal democracies, began to enhance state authority to fight the virus by closing borders, imposing stringent quarantines, and limiting the movement of people. National borders tightened and protectionism became the norm rather than the exception. While China has been criticized for its contact-tracing system that facilitates increased surveillance, some democratic countries have used surveillance technologies to enforce quarantines and track people's contacts with the virus, exchanging privacy for safety. Although adopting invasive health surveillance systems can have astounding consequences, including vastly increasing state authority and opportunities for serious abuse, more intrusive contact-tracing models have become increasingly attractive as countries struggled to balance concerns about public health and the economy.

Some democracies have also used state capitalism as part of their own industrial policies. The Trump administration slapped tariffs on foreign products, enhanced the state's role to rebuild a national economy instead of a global one, and increased the levels of redundancy in manufacturing systems regardless of cost or rationality. The first executive orders issued by Biden included a directive to "buy American provisions" and a review of gaps in domestic manufacturing and supply chains dominated by "nations that are or are likely to become unfriendly or unstable."[38] A report released by the White House in June 2021, "Building Resilient Supply Chains and Revitalizing American Manufacturing," recommended increasing the levels of redundancy in production chains.

From China's perspective, as liberal globalization has intensified economic, informational, technological, and other forms of competition, what used to be a self-regulating economic process has turned into a political instrument for suppressing business competitors, with unreasonable restrictions in the name of national security.[39] The U.S. government has tightened restrictions by barring U.S. companies from supplying Chinese competitors with products manufactured with U.S. technology, using national security justifications that Beijing views as specious. Wary of China's acquisition of critical technology, the United States, Australia, and Japan have tightened screening of FDI. By using such measures to protect U.S. companies

---

[37] Thomas L. Friedman, "Our New Historical Divide: B.C. and A.C.—the World Before Corona and the World After," *New York Times*, March 17, 2020, https://www.nytimes.com/2020/03/17/opinion/coronavirus-trends.html.

[38] Thomas Franck and Kayla Tausche, "Biden to Order Review of U.S. Reliance on Overseas Supply Chains for Semiconductors, Rare Earths," CNBC, February 18, 2021, https://www.cnbc.com/2021/02/18/biden-to-order-supply-chain-review-to-assess-us-reliance-on-overseas-semiconductors.html.

[39] Zhu Yunhan, *Quanqiuhua de liejie yu zaironghe* [The Fragmentation and Integration of Globalization] (Taipei: Tianxi Wenhua, 2020), 35–71.

against global competition, the United States in Beijing's eyes has become as much of a proponent of state-led growth as China.

The backlash against liberal globalization and the increased interest in reshoring supply chains in the United States and Europe was a wake-up call to a China that retained a high dependency on the U.S. market and its technologies.[40] In response, Xi announced his domestic and international dual circulation strategy in 2020. Leveraging nearly 1.4 billion consumers and emphasizing domestic production for home consumption, he has pushed hard for indigenous innovation and basic science and technology investment. Recalling the Maoist slogan of "self-reliance," Xi also has encouraged Chinese firms to localize key industrial products and systems because "there is no way that China can ask for or rely on buying the key and core technology from foreign countries."[41]

Strengthening the relative integrity and autonomy of the domestic industrial chain, particularly in chokepoint areas and strategic links,[42] China has become the only country in the world that owns all industrial categories listed in the UN Industrial Classification. It can independently produce all industrial products from clothing to aerospace and from raw materials to industrial motherboards.[43]

Yet, even as the pushback against liberal globalization has hastened a trend toward diversification in production chains, "Made in China" has created a lucrative option for most investors because of China's enormous market and strong business ecosystem. It is tough for any country to match, at least initially, China as a manufacturing hub, making any exodus from the country not just cost-intensive but also heavily unfavorable because companies lose China's manufacturing skillsets.[44] As the center of the world economy and consumer market has shifted to Asia, China is not

---

[40] The following discussion draws on the author's article "The U.S.-China Rivalry in the Emerging Bipolar World: Hostility, Alignment, and Power Balance," *Journal of Contemporary China* 31, no. 134 (2022): https://doi.org/10.1080/10670564.2021.1945733.

[41] "Xi Jinping zai Zhongguo Kexueyuan di shijiu ci yuanshi dahui, Zhongguo Gongchengyuan di shisi ci yuanshi dahui shang de jianghua" [Xi Speech at the China Academy of Sciences], Xinhua, May 28, 2018, http://www.xinhuanet.com/politics/2018-05/28/c_1122901308.htm.

[42] Li Xiaohua, "Tuijin chanyelian xiandaihua yao jianchi dulizizhu he kaifa hezuo xiang cujing" [The Modernization of the Industrial Chain Must Adhere to the Promotion of Independence and Development Cooperation], *Guangmin Daily*, April 10, 2020, https://rmh.pdnews.cn/Pc/ArtInfoApi/article?id=12669528.

[43] Some technologies have progressed from "running to follow" to "running parallel" and to "running to lead." "Woguo shi quanshijie weiyi yongyou quanbu gongye menlie de guojia" [China Is the Only Country in the World with All Industrial Categories], Xinhua, September 20, 2019, http://www.xinhuanet.com/politics/2019-09/20/c_1125020250.htm.

[44] Amrita Jash, "Will Covid-19 Cost China its 'World's Factory' Title?" Pacific Forum, October 6, 2020, https://mailchi.mp/pacforum/pacnet-55-will-covid19-cost-china-its-worlds-factory-title-1170474?e=19e05c85a8.

only a supplier but the largest non-U.S. market for many U.S. companies and organizations. Prominent U.S. companies have embedded themselves more deeply than ever in the country.[45] The Chinese economy has recovered more quickly from the pandemic than any other major country and was the only major economy to post positive GDP growth in 2020 (2.3%). The export sector continued to exceed expectations, despite the trade war with the United States and disruptions caused by the pandemic, testifying to "China's robustness as a manufacturing base, the breadth of goods that it can produce, and the skill of its exporters in navigating tough times."[46]

Mask and Vaccine Diplomacy during the Covid-19 Pandemic

China's success in containing the Covid-19 outbreak by strict confinement measures provided an opportunity to boost its credentials as a generous and responsible big power.[47] The outbreak was initially described as China's "Chernobyl moment," a mishandled disaster that could cause the Chinese leadership to lose political legitimacy, with geopolitical consequences.[48] Although the government got off to a slow start and discouraged early and transparent recognition, the state quickly entered crisis mode once it realized the scale of the threat. Declaring a "people's war" against the virus, Xi Jinping deployed an arsenal of propaganda and used previously unseen, harsh control measures, a testament to the state's ability to mobilize vast resources and restrict citizens' rights in times of crisis. These stringent actions delivered results. China announced zero new domestic cases on March 18 and reported no coronavirus deaths on April 7. The 76-day Wuhan lockdown was lifted on April 8.

The leadership highlighted its success in containing the virus through social control, harsh confinement, and surveillance as buttressing claims of the China model's superiority, in contrast with the Western democracies' incapacity to handle the crisis. Covid-19 tallies became a metric for the state. China began with a relatively high number of cases and fatalities but was

---

[45] Thomas Hale et al., "Wall Street's New Love Affair with China," *Financial Times*, May 28, 2021, https://www.ft.com/content/d5e09db3-549e-4a0b-8dbf-e499d0606df4.

[46] Arthur Kroeber, "Don't Bet Against China's Investment-Led Growth Model," *Financial Times*, May 20, 2021, https://www.ft.com/content/1e71be2e-0e6e-4af8-a703-1c92066065c7.

[47] This section draws on the author's article "Rhetoric and Reality of China's Global Leadership in the Context of COVID-19: Implications for the U.S.-Led World Order and Liberal Globalization," *Journal of Contemporary China* 30, no. 128 (2021): 233–48.

[48] Adam O'Neal, "Coronavirus and the Chernobyl Analogy," *Wall Street Journal*, May 22, 2020, https://www.wsj.com/articles/coronavirus-and-the-chernobyl-analogy-11590167999.

soon overtaken by the United States and European countries. Owning most of the global medical supply chain, the Chinese government then launched mask diplomacy by sending medical equipment and sometimes doctors to many pandemic-ravaged countries. Chinese media dutifully reported every delivery.[49]

While mask diplomacy was the buzzword in 2020, vaccine diplomacy became a buzzword in 2021. Chinese vaccine makers were among the earliest in the world to begin clinical trials and self-report key results. They have not, however, published any underlying data in peer-reviewed journals, producing skepticism about safety and effectiveness. Yet after approaching Western vaccine makers and not receiving the requested supplies, many countries were desperate and jumped at the opportunity to receive Chinese vaccines. Despite the criticism by the West for the lack of complete data and other deficiencies, China quickly rolled out its Covid-19 vaccines to developing countries in need amid a global shortage.

Framing itself as the solution rather than the cause of the pandemic, China advanced vaccine diplomacy primarily because the United States and the EU countries prioritized distribution of vaccines to their own citizens. Leaders in Western democracies faced high infection rates at home and the imperative to meet their voters' demand to inoculate domestic populations first. China faced neither problem. Its own infection rates were low enough that it could afford to send vaccines abroad, and Chinese leaders do not have to worry as much about public opinion in an authoritarian state. Just by showing up and plugging the colossal gaps in the global supply of vaccines in spring 2021, China gained ground in vaccine diplomacy.[50] As with mask diplomacy, Chinese media covered every delivery of the vaccine shipments.

From this vantage point, Xi called on Chinese officials "to take initiative and effectively influence international public opinion by telling stories of China's fight against the epidemic and showing the spirit of the Chinese people united and working together."[51] The Chinese government published a white paper to rebut accusations that it covered up the initial outbreak and to document the information-sharing between China and both the WHO

---

[49] Anne Applebaum, "The Rest of the World Is Laughing at Trump," *Atlantic*, May 3, 2020, https://www.theatlantic.com/ideas/archive/2020/05/time-americans-are-doing-nothing/611056.

[50] Kareem Fahim and Karen DeYoung, "China Has Made Big Vaccine Promises. When They Come Up Short, Nations Struggle," *Washington Post*, April 7, 2021, https://www.washingtonpost.com/world/middle_east/china-sinovac-turkey-coronavirus-vaccine/2021/04/06/f87bc1bc-93cd-11eb-aadc-af78701a30ca_story.html.

[51] "Xi Jinping: Zai Zhongyang Zhengzhiju Changweihui huiyi yanjiu yingdui xinxing guanzhuang bingdu feiyan yiqing gongzuo shi de jianghua" [Speech at the Politburo Standing Committee on the Response to the Coronavirus], Central Government of the PRC, February 15, 2020, http://www.gov.cn/xinwen/2020-02/15/content_5479271.htm.

and other governments.⁵² Many Chinese scholars joined the propaganda campaign and supported China's one-party rule. One Chinese scholar argued that it did not matter if a state was democratic or authoritarian; what mattered was governance. By winning the battle to contain Covid-19, China had demonstrated its outstanding governance ability.⁵³ Taking a victory lap to celebrate China's success in comparison with other countries' failure, another Chinese scholar concluded that this "control group experiment" confirmed the superiority of China's system and that the Western model of limited government could not cope with a crisis like a pandemic. Instead, a strong and decisive state was necessary: "Because abnormality and normality are a pair of blurred concepts, a system that cannot deal with abnormal crisis is not a good system."⁵⁴

Claiming that the pandemic had marginalized the United States from the center of the world stage, one Chinese scholar asserted that "in the past, people regarded the U.S. economy, political system, ideas, and popular culture as the benchmark of the world. Through this pandemic, the world has a clearer understanding of the real situation in America. The United States is no longer a model for the future of the world."⁵⁵ With the United States' reputation tarnished, and the U.S. model faltering, Chinese people altered their perceptions and increased their confidence in the CCP regime, making Beijing less concerned about the implications of its repression in Hong Kong and the damage done by its wolf-warrior diplomacy.

A survey by the China Data Lab at the University of California, San Diego, revealed that the average level of Chinese trust in the government on a scale of 1 to 10, with 10 being the highest, increased from 8.23 in June 2019 to 8.65 in February 2020 and 8.87 in May 2020 when the government controlled the spread of Covid-19. Similarly, on a 1 to 5 Likert scale, responses to the question of whether Chinese prefer living under China's political system increased from an average of 3.89 in June 2019 to 4.14 in February 2020 and 4.28 in May 2020. In contrast, Chinese favorability toward the United States on a scale of 1 to 10 dropped from 5.77 in June 2019 to 4.77 in May 2020.

---

⁵² "Kangji Xinguan feiyan yiqing de Zhongguo xingdong" [Fighting Covid-19 China in Action], State Council Information Office (PRC), June 2020, http://www.gov.cn/zhengce/2020-06/07/content_5517737.htm.

⁵³ Wu Xinbo, "Yiqing jiasu shijie hou banquan shidai de daolai" [Covid-19 Has Accelerated the Advent of the Post-Hegemony Era], Reference News, June 16, 2020, http://www.cankaoxiaoxi.com/china/20200616/2412828.shtml.

⁵⁴ Fan Yongpeng, "Zhongyang jiquan zhi shiyongyu jiduan zhuangtai? Zhezhong guandian hulue le yige wentim" [The Centralization of Power Only Applies to Extreme Conditions? This View Ignores a Problem], Guangcha-net, April 7, 2010, https://www.guancha.cn/FanYongPeng/2020_04_07_545745.shtml.

⁵⁵ Wang Yong, "Yiqing xia de Zhongmei guanxi yu guoji dabianju" [Sino-U.S. Relations and Global Great Changes under the Pandemic], Pangoal, April 16, 2020, https://ishare.ifeng.com/c/s/v002gWw9LSxl9U-_xlbAYfxgjdOsRPZf3Nj6m1AK3GLLM2JY.

Although the reliability of such surveys could be questioned because the Chinese government exercised extensive control over the information available to its citizens, China's relative success in controlling the spread of Covid-19 and the dismal performance of the United States during the pandemic contributed to these results.[56]

Geopolitical Expansion in the Indo-Pacific

Big-power diplomacy has expanded China's reach in the Indo-Pacific, or the greater periphery in Beijing's terminology. This includes Northeast Asia, Southeast Asia, South Asia, Central Asia, the South Pacific, and West Asia (Eurasia).[57] The importance of China expanding its traditional periphery beyond adjacent areas for its big-power aspirations is described by various phrases, such as the indispensable path (*bijing zhilu*), the compulsory course (*buxiu zhike*), the foothold (*lizhudian*) and basis (*gengjudi*), and the starting point and big rear area (*da houfang*).[58]

Because regional primacy is a precondition to be a global power, Chinese leadership has worked assiduously on its greater periphery. This is the same path that the United States followed in the western hemisphere in building global primacy under the Monroe Doctrine. China cannot achieve regional primacy if it remains surrounded by U.S. allies and partners. Xi first demonstrated his intention to drive the United States out at the 2014 Shanghai summit of the Conference on Interaction and Confidence Building Measures in Asia by announcing the "new Asian security concept": "It is for the people of Asia to run the affairs of Asia, solve the problems of Asia, and uphold the security of Asia."[59] This vision of "Asia for Asians" implies that the region can take care of its own security without U.S. meddling.[60]

China has launched new initiatives to help pursue its greater periphery strategy. The Belt and Road Initiative (BRI) is the most important one,

---

[56] Lei Guang et al., "Pandemic Sees Increase in Chinese Support for Regime, Decrease in Views towards the U.S.," China Data Lab, July, 2020, http://chinadatalab.ucsd.edu/viz-blog/pandemic-sees-increase-in-chinese-support-for-regime-decrease-in-views-towards-us.

[57] "Zhongguo de zhoubian anquan tiaozhan yu dazhoubian waijiao zhanlue" [China's Peripheral Security Challenges and Greater Periphery Diplomatic Strategy], *World Economics and Politics*, no. 3 (2013): 25.

[58] Cheng Xiangyang, "Zhongguo tuijin da zhoubian zhanlue zhengdangshi" [It Is Time for China to Advance the Greater Periphery Strategy], Fisnet, January 16, 2015, http://comment.cfisnet.com/2015/0116/1300445.html.

[59] Xi Jinping, "New Asian Security Concept for New Progress in Security Cooperation" (remarks at the Fourth Summit of the Conference on Interaction and Confidence Building Measures in Asia, Shanghai, May 21, 2014), https://www.fmprc.gov.cn/mfa_eng/wjdt_665385/zyjh_665391/201405/t20140527_678163.html.

[60] Rory Medcalf, "China's Premature Power Play Goes Very Wrong," *National Interest*, June 3, 2014, http://nationalinterest.org/feature/chinas-premature-power-play-goes-very-wrong-10587.

establishing a China-led network of more than one hundred countries and international organizations. Spending billions of dollars on the construction of infrastructure projects in partner countries, BRI will cover two-thirds of the world's population by building six economic corridors across Eurasia, the Indian Ocean, and the Pacific. Although BRI is framed by China as a global public good and an example of its benevolence that offers other countries developmental opportunities, the initiative is but an expression of newly found pride in the nation's power wrapped in globalist terminology. Advancing China's geoeconomic and geopolitical interests, Xi aims to restore China's past greatness by dominating the greater periphery just as he dominates his own country.

The greater periphery strategy has targeted "developing and newly emerging powers," which include a handful of large, rapidly emerging, and politically influential non-Western states. Most belong to the Emerging 7 (E-7)—China, India, Russia, Indonesia, Turkey, Mexico, and Brazil—a list of countries that have challenged the dominance of the G-7. While the aggregate economic size of the E-7 was only half that of the G-7 in 1995, it reached the same level in 2015 and could double the size of the G-7 by 2040.[61] China has also developed strategic relations with emerging economies through groupings such as BRICS (Brazil, Russia, India, China, and South Africa) and engaged subsets of them through multilateral forums such as the G-20. In addition, China has concluded bilateral "strategic partnership" agreements with several emerging states. Among them, its partnerships with Russia and Iran have gained global significance and become an "'antihegemonic' coalition united not by ideology but by complementary grievances."[62]

China's emergence as a maritime power is a significant milestone in its expansion in the Indo-Pacific. Paying special attention to maritime interests, Xi stated in 2013 that "the oceans and seas have an increasingly important strategic calculus concerning global competition in the spheres of politics, economic development, military, and technology."[63] China's 2015 defense white paper—the first one released by the Xi administration—placed unprecedented emphasis on the maritime domain. Stating that "the traditional mentality that land outweighs sea must be abandoned," it required the PLA Navy to move from "near-seas defense" to "a combination of 'near-

---

[61] John Hawksworth, Hannah Audino, and Rob Clarry, "The Long View: How Will the Global Economic Order Change by 2050," PwC, February 2017.

[62] Zbigniew Brzezinski, *The Grand Chessboard: American Primacy and Its Geostrategic Imperatives* (New York: Basic Books, 1998), 54.

[63] Xi Jinping, "Jinyibu guanxin haiyang, renshi haiyang, jinglue haiyang, tuidong haiyang qiangguo jianshe buduan qude xin chengjiu" [Further Care about the Oceans, Understand the Oceans and Manage the Oceans, Building a Maritime Power and Make New Achievements], Xinhua, July 31, 2013, http://www.xinhuanet.com//politics/2013-07/31/c_116762285.htm.

seas defense' and 'far-seas protection.'"[64] The 2019 defense white paper went further: "One of the missions of China's armed forces is to effectively protect the security and legitimate rights and interests of overseas Chinese people, organizations, and institutions."[65] Xi has presided over a major overhaul of the PLA Navy, which overtook the U.S. Navy in both number and total tonnage of vessels annually launched and became the world's largest navy in 2019.[66]

An ongoing theme in Chinese maritime strategy is breaking through the three island chains for access to the Pacific. The first chain stretches from Japan to Taiwan to the Philippines; the second chain extends through the Mariana Islands, including Guam; and the third is in the central Pacific. The PLA Navy began regularly sailing through the first island chain in 2009. With China's first aircraft carrier, the *Liaoning*, entering the fleet in 2012 and the second carrier, the *Shandong*, in 2019, the Chinese fleet has developed the capability to operate far beyond the first island chain.

The Taiwan contingency is the main planning scenario for China's maritime power development. As an integral part of the first island chain, Taiwan is not just a "lost territory" needing to be recovered; it is of critical geostrategic value and a key forward defensive position for the PLA to defend China's maritime interests and highly industrialized and urbanized eastern seaboard. Becoming increasingly impatient with the prospect of peaceful unification, Xi is confident that he can resolve the Taiwan issue during his term because the military balance has shifted firmly in China's favor. Although Beijing has never abandoned using force for national unification, Chinese leaders have become increasingly impatient because of their concerns that Taiwan is drifting away from China alongside increased U.S support. Beijing has made no secret that it is building up the military capabilities necessary to subjugate Taiwan. It is hard to know whether China can easily take Taiwan by force. Beijing's intensified pressure may remain part of the strategy to undermine confidence in Taiwan's ability to hold out against China. Xi wants the fear and threat of invasion to be reinforced to stop or at least slow Taiwan's drift toward independence. In addition, he wants to warn the United States, which has increased the scale and frequency of arms sales to Taiwan and warship transits through the Taiwan Strait and has sent senior officials to visit the island.

China's fast-growing maritime capabilities also have important implications for territorial disputes in the East and South China Seas.

---

[64] State Council Information Office (PRC), *China's Military Strategy* (Beijing, May 2015).

[65] State Council Information Office (PRC), *China's National Defense in the New Era* (Beijing, July 2019).

[66] U.S. Department of Defense, *Annual Report to Congress: Military and Security Development Involving the People's Republic of China* (Washington, D.C., 2020), https://media.defense.gov/2020/Sep/01/2002488689/-1/-1/1/2020-DOD-CHINA-MILITARY-POWER-REPORT-FINAL.PDF.

Believing that some of its neighbors in the past capitalized on China's relative weakness to assume control of disputed islands, Beijing has now taken a tougher position as a big power. "Comply with China's demands or suffer the consequences" is the unequivocal message. For example, China passed the Maritime Police Law in early 2021, empowering the China Coast Guard to use weapons when sovereign rights or jurisdiction are infringed on or threatened. In the South China Sea, Beijing for a long time employed a strategy of strategic ambiguity to avoid officially stating the extent, meaning, nature, and legal basis of its claims in order to prevent other claimants from making counterclaims and starting the process of clarification and negotiation. Xi has switched from a strategy of ambiguity to one of clarity. Expanding maritime law enforcement and sending combat-ready patrol ships regularly to escort fishing fleets, China scaled up land reclamation on and around disputed islands and turned small islets into man-made islands with giant dredging ships, adding a total of 290,000 square meters of landmass between 2014 and 2017. After an arbitral tribunal ruled in favor of the Philippines in July 2016 that China has no legal basis to claim historic rights in the area within its nine-dash line, the Chinese government rejected the ruling by declaring "four no's": nonparticipation, nonrecognition, nonacceptance, and nonenforcement.[67]

China's coercive actions to exert its claims over disputed territories are widely seen as a litmus test of its big-power aspirations. Although using its wealth to establish a strong posture to dominate the region may help restore China's historical centrality, this willingness to back up its interests through coercion has raised questions about whether China wants a neo-tributary system.

The Delicate Domestic Support for Big-Power Diplomacy

Although China's relative global position is important for the success of Xi Jinping's big-power diplomacy, domestic support is also fundamental. Domestic support, however, is delicate.

On the one hand, Xi has built strong economic and political support to develop broad-based technology and a globally competitive, dynamic economy. Presenting himself as a strong, shrewd, visionary, and purposeful leader, Xi dramatically consolidated his personal power with the consent of the ruling elite who had complained that the Hu leadership was too weak and the factional makeup of collective leadership was too divisive to curb massive corruption and ineffectiveness of governance and establish civilian authority

---

[67] Suisheng Zhao, "China and the South China Sea Arbitration: Geopolitics versus International Law," *Journal of Contemporary China* 27, no. 109 (2018): 1–15.

over the military.⁶⁸ There had been important power balances in CCP elite politics historically: for example, between Mao Zedong and Liu Shaoqi and between Deng Xiaoping and Chen Yun. But by sidelining his rivals, Xi as a supreme leader has run the country without interference from elders or rivals, or any credible political challengers.

Turning U.S. pressure to a political advantage, Xi used the trade war to blame the United States for the slowdown in China's economy and other problems. External hostile pressure has historically helped mobilize Chinese nationalism against any concessions that could be regarded as surrendering to foreign powers. At a time when suspicion of the United States is at an all-time high, standing up to U.S. pressure has supercharged Xi's and the CCP's popularity. One Harvard University survey published in 2020 confirmed that satisfaction with the government had increased across the board since 2003 and that Chinese citizens rated the government as more capable and effective than ever before because of the real, measurable changes in their material well-being.⁶⁹

Xi has been especially successful in getting his message across to younger generations. Chinese youth are more fiercely patriotic and loyal to the party-state than older generations because they have grown up witnessing China's rising living standards and rapid modernization with no memory of anything other than steady growth and increasing opportunities. One survey in September 2020 found that over 90% of teenagers used terms such as "lucky and satisfied" to describe how they felt about growing up in China. Many who had admired the United States were now convinced that they lived in a country that others looked on with admiration because of the advantages of the Chinese system in advancing the people's welfare.⁷⁰

This performance-based legitimacy is reinforced by the regime's overwhelming control of information. By expanding surveillance efforts, ratcheting up the pressure for journalists to speak with one voice to support party policies, and cracking down on the internet, Xi has blocked channels through which people could encounter perspectives different from official party narratives. The internet, which many in the West thought would ultimately bring democracy to China, is no longer an open channel for thinking about, learning from, or debating China's historical

---

⁶⁸ Sangkuk Lee, "An Institutional Analysis of Xi Jinping's Centralization of Power," *Journal of Contemporary China* 26, no. 105 (2017): 325–36.

⁶⁹ Edward Cunningham, Tony Saich, and Jesse Turiel, "Understanding CCP Resilience: Surveying Chinese Public Opinion through Time," Ash Center for Democratic Governance and Innovation, Harvard Kennedy School, July 2020, https://ash.harvard.edu/files/ash/files/final_policy_brief_7.6.2020.pdf.

⁷⁰ Liza Lin, "Xi's China Crafts Campaign to Boost Youth Patriotism," *Wall Street Journal*, December 30, 2020, https://www.wsj.com/articles/xi-china-campaign-youth-patriotism-propaganda-11609343255?mod=hp_lead_pos10.

mistakes and political system. Ruthlessly censoring alternative versions of history, suppressing dissenting voices, and closing alternative sources of information, government propaganda has become more believable and changed the public conversation.

Most Chinese people, for example, know little about what has happened in Hong Kong, and to the extent that they do know, most have accepted the official story that the island's people were unpatriotic, un-Chinese, ungrateful for Chinese support, and pawns of foreign meddling and incitement. A survey in 2020 found that the majority of respondents thought that most Hong Kong residents had a positive view of the CCP despite massive protests. Likewise, one survey in 2017 revealed that a majority of urban residents supported the government using force to take back the disputed Diaoyu Islands from Japan, even though such an action would risk war with the United States.[71]

On the other hand, the powerful and confident image that China projects tends to cover up the reality of its domestic challenges.[72] Besides environmental pollution, corruption, and other problems, China's one-child policy has hastened and exacerbated the slowdown in birthrate, leading to a demographic crisis. The level of inequality is also worrying. China stopped publicizing its Gini coefficient in 2014, but Premier Li Keqiang admitted in 2020 that over 600 million people still live on a monthly income of less than 1,000 yuan ($140).[73] Still a fragile rising power, China faces questions about whether it can become the first authoritarian regime to avoid the middle-income trap that has kept many emerging economies from entering the club of high-income countries. No large economy has made the transition without liberalizing. Riding the waves of economic globalization without political liberalization, Xi's policy of maximizing political control over society and the economy may eventually limit market efficiency. The most acute internal challenge, however, is the possible succession crisis. Making himself president for life and thus far refusing to nominate a successor, Xi has weakened the institutionalized mechanism for power succession. In doing so, he has created a potentially destabilizing succession crisis and possible political turmoil if anything were to happen to him before a successor is identified.

Although interest in democracy is under relentless attack in China, its basic ideas still have inspired Chinese liberal intellectuals. Xi was stung

---

[71] Yang Zhong and Wonjae Hwang, "Why Do Chinese Democrats Tend to Be More Nationalistic? Explaining Popular Nationalism in Urban China," *Journal of Contemporary China* 29, no. 121 (2020).

[72] The following discussion draws on the author's article "Rhetoric and Reality of China's Global Leadership in the Context of COVID-19."

[73] Zhou Xin, "Is China Rich or Poor? Nation's Wealth Debate Muddied by Conflicting Government Data," *South China Morning Post*, May 29, 2020, https://www.scmp.com/economy/china-economy/article/3086678/china-rich-or-poor-nations-wealth-debate-muddied-conflicting.

by widespread criticism of his initial handling of the Covid-19 pandemic. The government's mismanagement provided an opportunity for liberals, such as Tsinghua University professor Xu Zhangrun, private entrepreneur Ren Zhiqiang, and activist Xu Zhiyong, to publicly denounce Xi's personal autocracy and demand freedom of speech. The state placed blame squarely on local officials and fired the party chief in Hubei Province and the mayor of Wuhan, along with some health officials. But Chinese social media was still overflowing with messages demanding accountability and transparency. Informed by social media, many saw the initial coverup by Wuhan and Hubei officials not just as bad performance by local officials but also as symptomatic of the weakness of the Chinese system: bureaucrats' fear of revealing bad news. Li Wenliang in Wuhan became a martyr for this cause of free speech.

In response to the unease in a society where nobody under 40 has experienced national economic setbacks, the Chinese government called on young people to make "long-term preparations for hardship," which "may mean higher prices, no expected salary increases, and to withstand temporary unemployment." Warning that "young people cannot take the fast track of national development for granted," the government further called on each individual to take on the responsibility of facing the hardship.[74] These warnings underscored the insecurity of the regime, which saw itself as a besieged fortress. Recognizing the formidable and daunting internal and external challenges, one strategist in Beijing has long warned about "the risk of strategic overdraft"—making international promises and setting strategic objectives beyond the reach of China's national strength.[75] In this case, Xi must fight an uphill battle to mobilize resources to assure the success of big-power diplomacy.

Conclusion

As the post–Cold War unipolar moment and multipolarity have given away to the emerging U.S.-China competition, Xi Jinping has identified China as a big power and advocated big-power diplomacy to gain the high ground in the competition. Amid the new uncertainties about U.S. global leadership as a result of Trump's worldview and policies, as well as the continuing domestic political transformations within the United States, Beijing has positioned itself as a challenger to U.S.-led liberal globalization and the international order.

---

[74] Central Political and Law Commission (PRC), "Zuohao jianku fendou de changqi zhunbei, buyao zhangjia jiu maniang" [Make Long-Term Preparations for Hard Work], Tacent News, June 1, 2020, https://xw.qq.com/cmsid/20190601A0HLM600?from=groupmessage&isappinstalled=0.

[75] Shi Yinhong, "Amid Western Uncertainties, China Mustn't Spread Too Thin," Global Times, October 26, 2016, http://www.globaltimes.cn/content/1013884.shtml.

China's early success in containing the outbreak of Covid-19, in contrast with the incapacity of Western democracies during the pandemic, has enhanced the confidence of Xi to return China to the center of the global stage and achieve the China dream of great national rejuvenation.

China's big-power diplomacy and geopolitical expansion across the Indo-Pacific have alarmed the United States and generated a heightened level of insecurity among China's neighbors. Without simply submitting to China's big-power ambitions, the United States and some other countries have pushed back to protect their interests. Although China's domestic economic and political constraints may check its ambitions, the most important external check is U.S. power. China may dominate the world, making rules and subordinating others to its rule, if the United States is overtaken by China in their power rivalry. This scenario cannot be ruled out. China's rise in recent decades has been faster than that of any nation in history, and Washington has never faced a rival that is competitive in so many realms. More importantly, U.S. power has been in relative decline, and U.S. resilience has been seriously tested. For perspective, as Graham Allison has noted, the United States produced nearly half the world's GDP after World Ward II, one-quarter at the end of the Cold War, and only one-seventh in 2021.[76] What was once almost universal admiration for U.S. democracy has given way to disappointment over displays of racial tensions, political polarization, socioeconomic inequality, and xenophobia.

This scenario, however, is not inevitable. Observers have claimed the decline of the United States for decades but been proved wrong many times. Although the United States has gone through many crises in its history, it has shown a formidable ability to overcome challenges, often through electing new leaders to correct course. In this case, U.S. policy toward China must be extremely measured to check any aggressive behavior while avoiding overextension.

First, the United States should stand firm and work with its allies and partners to collectively (and unilaterally if necessary) defend liberal values and democracy, push back against Chinese coercion and predation, balance China's big-power ambitions, and shape its policy choices. But the focus should be on the revival of domestic competitiveness and addressing domestic challenges, such as crumbling infrastructure, a divided society, dysfunctional democracy, and overextended foreign policy, rather than waging a new cold war. While Biden has used the challenges posed by China to spur his domestic economic and political agenda, the United States should take steps to put its own house in order rather than use China as a scapegoat

---

[76] Graham Allison, "Grave New World," *Foreign Policy*, January 15, 2021, https://foreignpolicy.com/2021/01/15/biden-10-challenges-foreign-policy-economy-united-states-china.

for U.S. failures. Washington can no longer take its dominance and global leadership for granted.

Second, Biden has portrayed the competition with China as a battle between democracy and autocracy, but Beijing cannot expect the United States to accept its governance system and values, nor can Washington alter China's intrinsic values, change its regime, and stop its rise. A bipolar world of two-system competition and coexistence is the new normal. The United States should accept this reality and avoid overly ideological policies that limit its own flexibility.

Third, the United States must coordinate with its allies and partners on important issues such as transferring technology, deepening trade integration, and ensuring that countries in the Indo-Pacific are both willing and able to counter potential Chinese military actions. Washington should not force countries to take a side and make U.S. alliances and partnerships a zero-sum game. It must be flexible in its competitive coexistence with Beijing for advantage and influence. In this context, the United States should stop pushing China and Russia together and exploit their divisions to its advantage.

Fourth, while a major improvement in the relationship is unlikely in the short term because of China's increasingly provocative behavior and the U.S. domestic consensus to be tough on China, a full-scale confrontation would be extremely costly. Cooperation between rivals may be uncomfortable but is necessary. Because of the durability of the emerging bipolarity, both countries will lose if they pursue power dominance. The United States must be willing and ready to pursue joint and shared responsibilities to address global challenges such as climate change, nuclear proliferation, and the pandemic.

Fifth, the United States must welcome China to take on more global responsibility and leadership roles. While U.S. global leadership has been seriously damaged, China has not stepped up to assume global leadership for the better. The world is in danger of moving toward disorder and a power vacuum, which could be a more dangerous scenario than the emergence of a new hegemon.

EXECUTIVE SUMMARY

This chapter examines the impact of anti-globalization populism and the Covid-19 pandemic on the resilience and strategic trajectories of Japan, South Korea, and Taiwan.

MAIN ARGUMENT

The rise of Chinese power and Beijing's increasing use of coercion against neighboring states have driven closer alignment by Japan and Taiwan with the U.S. and each other, while South Korea maintains strong security ties with the U.S. to deter North Korea. The election of Donald Trump shook Northeast Asian allies much less than it did U.S. allies in Europe, in part because the U.S. national security establishment generally protected those strategic relationships as U.S. competition with China intensified. Nevertheless, the Trump administration's retreat from the Trans-Pacific Partnership undermined U.S. leadership in the region and left a gap in economic statecraft that the Biden administration so far has chosen not to fill. The Covid-19 pandemic damaged the political standing of leaders in Japan, South Korea, and Taiwan—permanently in the case of Japan—but it did not fundamentally change geopolitical and geoeconomic trends. The precipitous and poorly planned U.S. exit from Afghanistan was perhaps a greater shock to those alliances.

POLICY IMPLICATIONS

- The U.S. approach to issues such as trade, export controls, and democracy promotion remains too unilateral and too transatlantic, despite more careful legal and international framing of the policies under President Biden.
- U.S. allies in Northeast Asia must do more to close the crisis-management and capability gaps in their national security systems and deterrence postures.
- Close coordination among U.S. allies must be at the center of any new international approach to managing future pandemics.
- After the pandemic weakened political leadership, limited diplomatic flexibility, and made personal diplomacy in the region more difficult, the new leaders of Japan and South Korea will need to begin rebuilding mutual trust.

Northeast Asia: Alignment Despite Anxiety

Michael J. Green

The back-to-back shocks of the Trump presidency and the Covid-19 pandemic were jarring for Japan, South Korea, and Taiwan, yet these disruptions did more to accelerate and illuminate emerging strategic trends in Northeast Asia than cause discontinuity. The larger tectonic shift for Tokyo, Seoul, and Taipei had already occurred with the emergence of a revisionist China under Xi Jinping. Donald Trump's victory in the 2016 presidential election and the Covid-19 pandemic did little to resolve that challenge or fundamentally alter the three democracies' approaches to China. Surveys of strategic elites in the region since 2014 have shown that the Northeast Asian democracies unambiguously prefer a U.S.-led order in Asia. At the same time, distrust of China has reached unprecedented levels in all three democracies, even as each continues to work to maintain productive economic ties with Beijing.[1]

Despite closer bilateral alignment with Washington, however, Tokyo, Seoul, and Taipei have not moved in lockstep with each other. Japan has doubled down on a maritime strategy of alignment with its Quad partners (the United States, Australia, and India) while stepping up to replace a recalcitrant United States as the regional leader on trade, diplomacy, and

---

Michael J. Green is Director of Asian Studies and Chair in Modern and Contemporary Japanese Politics and Foreign Policy at the School of Foreign Service at Georgetown University and Senior Vice President for Asia and Japan Chair at the Center for Strategic and International Studies. He can be reached at <mjg73@georgetown.edu>.

---

[1] Michael J. Green and Nicholas Szechenyi, *Power and Order in Asia: A Survey of Regional Expectations* (Lanham: Rowman and Littlefield, 2014); and Laura Silver, "China's International Image Remains Broadly Negative as Views of the U.S. Rebound," Pew Research Center, June 30, 2021, https://www.pewresearch.org/fact-tank/2021/06/30/chinas-international-image-remains-broadly-negative-as-views-of-the-u-s-rebound.

development under Tokyo's "free and open Indo-Pacific" vision. The Republic of Korea (ROK), in contrast, has embraced "strategic ambiguity" in the larger competition with China—opting out of the Quad and other plurilateral groupings of democracies designed to counterbalance China, but clinging closely to bilateral deterrence and diplomatic coordination with the United States on the Korean Peninsula. Taiwan, meanwhile, has shifted from an obsession with cross-strait relations under the Ma Ying-jeou administration to an ardent pursuit of closer cooperation with Japan and other maritime powers, fueled by the damning example of what Beijing's "one country, two systems" has meant for Hong Kong.

This variation in Northeast Asian responses to Xi's China probably has more to do with geography and identity than Trump, the Covid-19 pandemic, or even economics. South Korea is more dependent on China for trade than Japan is, but not more so than Taiwan, for example. Yet Beijing's assault on Hong Kong's autonomy triggered a much deeper crisis of security and identity in Taiwan than Beijing's economic embargo on Korean companies to punish Seoul for enabling the deployment of U.S. Terminal High Altitude Area Defense (THAAD) missile defense did in South Korea (though the boycott did some damage to Korean views of China). Meanwhile, China's increasing deployment of military and paramilitary ships around the Senkaku Islands (known as the Diaoyu Islands in China) in the East China Sea did far more to intensify Japan's debate about long-range strike capabilities and defense of Taiwan than the THAAD boycott did to change Korean defense policies vis-à-vis China—despite the far larger economic impact (over $6.8 billion in damages) imposed on South Korea by China's actions.[2]

For reasons of geography, the Korean Peninsula has always been more vulnerable to continental China's influence. Japan, by contrast, has used its surrounding seas to defy Chinese hegemony since the mythical god Izanagi dipped his jeweled spear in the Pacific and formed the Japanese archipelago, imbuing Japan's imperial line with equal divine status to China's. Meanwhile, Taiwan has long suffered from polarized identity politics between pro-independence "green" and pro-unification "blue" camps. With China's growing coercive pressure, however, Taiwan's strategic identity has shifted away from the mainland and toward a maritime outlook more aligned with Japan—much to Beijing's alarm. Geography and history explain more than a few years of human and microbiological disruption.

As we shall see in this chapter's examination of the structural impact of U.S.-China strategic competition and the intervening shocks of the

---

[2] Echo Huang, "China Inflicted a World of Pain on South Korea in 2017," Quartz, December 21, 2017, https://qz.com/1149663/china-south-korea-relations-in-2017-thaad-backlash-and-the-effect-on-tourism.

Trump presidency and Covid-19 pandemic, the U.S. security relationships in Northeast Asia are remarkably resilient. However, Beijing's stubborn determination to weaken those alliances and partnerships remains undiminished as the United States, Japan, South Korea, and Taiwan have exposed some capacity and resilience problems of their own. This chapter examines the variables that lead to this conclusion, isolating the primary structural impact of China's hegemonic expansion and the intervening variables of the Trump administration and Covid-19 pandemic on the strategic trajectories of Japan, South Korea, and Taiwan.

Northeast Asia's Democracies after Trump and the Covid-19 Pandemic

Initial projections by well-established scholars were that the Trump presidency and later the Covid-19 pandemic would transform geopolitics in Asia. For example, the *Economist* and several U.S. scholars predicted that Trump's election would spell disaster for U.S. alliances in the region.[3] Similarly, Kurt Campbell and Rush Doshi argued in March 2020 that Covid-19 would fundamentally transform geopolitics by undermining U.S. leadership and vaulting China to a stronger position in the region.[4] Both sets of preliminary predictions appear overblown in retrospect. While Trump tested U.S. alliances and partnerships in Asia by withdrawing from the Trans-Pacific Partnership (TPP), demanding massive increases in payments for U.S. bases, and swinging wildly from threats of war to talk of love with North Korea's Kim Jong-un, the reality is that the U.S. military relationships with Japan, South Korea, and Taiwan all deepened in the same period. Tokyo and Taipei were not displeased with the Trump administration's intense focus on strategic competition with China, and Seoul was relieved at Trump's eventual pursuit of summitry over military confrontation with Pyongyang. All three governments quietly urged the incoming Biden administration to continue many of those basic policies, and Joe Biden agreed.

But like the impact of a joy ride through cornfields on the suspension of a car, the Trump years also did damage to the undercarriage of American credibility in Northeast Asia. While the Trump administration made some

---

[3] For example, see "Farewell to Asia," *Economist*, December 8, 2016, https://www.economist.com/united-states/2016/12/08/farewell-to-asia; and Thomas Wright, "Donald Trump Wants America to Withdraw from the World," Brookings Institution, March 24, 2016, https://www.brookings.edu/blog/order-from-chaos/2016/03/24/donald-trump-wants-america-to-withdraw-from-the-world.

[4] Kurt M. Campbell and Rush Doshi, "The Coronavirus Could Reshape Global Order," *Foreign Affairs*, March 18, 2020, https://www.foreignaffairs.com/articles/china/2020-03-18/coronavirus-could-reshape-global-order.

gains in bilateral security relations, there was a marked lack of leadership on regional networking of alliances beyond the elevation of the Quad to a foreign ministers' meeting, and Japan-ROK relations suffered as a result. Meanwhile, Trump's disinterest in defending democratic norms created a permissive environment for what Freedom House has deemed the most significant degradation of democracy in the region and at home in a generation.[5] This has meant the United States squandered one of its most important advantages in the Indo-Pacific, where surveys show that large majorities across the region prefer democratic norms to China's system of authoritarian development.[6] Trump's reckless flirtations with Xi, Putin, and especially Kim also unsettled many pro-U.S. officials in the region. Finally, the lack of effective U.S. economic statecraft for the region has left a void in which Europe and Japan are now considered more important leaders on regional economic rulemaking than the United States.[7] This lack of U.S. leadership explains why trust in the United States declined precipitously in Japan and South Korea during the Trump years, even as polls showed increased support for the alliance relationship.[8]

Covid-19 caused a similar degradation of alignment and trust—not only with China but among Northeast Asian democracies as well. President Trump's inability to manage the crisis at home as he demonized China through frequent references to the "China virus" undercut confidence in U.S. crisis management while filling the pages of Japanese and Korean newspapers with images of racist attacks on Asian Americans who share their own heritage. In contrast, Japan, South Korea, and Taiwan handled the initial outbreak with various degrees of calm professionalism, reflecting the degree to which each government had already learned from the earlier SARS and MERS outbreaks in the region. But in the second phase of the pandemic, it was the United States that demonstrated relative competence in rolling out vaccines, while Japan, South Korea, and Taiwan bungled their

---

[5] Sarah Repucci and Amy Slipowitz, "Freedom in the World 2021: Democracy Under Siege," Freedom House, 2021, https://freedomhouse.org/report/freedom-world/2021/democracy-under-siege.

[6] Sharon Seah et al., *The State of Southeast Asia: 2021 Survey Report* (Singapore: ISEAS–Yusof Ishak Institute, 2021).

[7] Ibid. This self-damaging aspect of Trump's approach to the region has been largely continued by Biden.

[8] For example, see Richard Wike, Janell Fetterolf, and Mara Mordecai, "U.S. Image Plummets Internationally as Most Say Country Has Handled Coronavirus Badly," Pew Research Center, September 15, 2020, https://www.pewresearch.org/global/2020/09/15/us-image-plummets-internationally-as-most-say-country-has-handled-coronavirus-badly; Aizawa Yuko, "Survey Suggests Growing Concern among Japanese at Prospect of Trump Re-election," NHK World, May 19, 2020, https://www3.nhk.or.jp/nhkworld/en/news/backstories/1096; and Karl Friedhoff, "While Positive Toward U.S. Alliance, South Koreans Want to Counter Trump's Demands for Support," Chicago Council on Global Affairs, December 16, 2019, https://www.thechicagocouncil.org/research/public-opinion-survey/while-positive-toward-us-alliance-south-koreans-want-counter-trumps.

own vaccination policies because of varying combinations of complacency, bureaucratic intransigence, and misguided economic nationalism. In 2021, it was Prime Minister Yoshihide Suga, President Moon Jae-in, and President Tsai Ing-wen who were appealing to the United States to help them accelerate the delivery of vaccines to their own people.

The Covid-19 pandemic did not fundamentally transform geopolitics in Northeast Asia any more than the Trump administration did, but the pandemic's stress test did reveal weaknesses in crisis management and the vulnerability of elected leaders—if not the democratic system of government—to performance legitimacy shortfalls. To the extent that Covid-19 affected geopolitics at the systemic level, however, Beijing's hubris during the pandemic probably accelerated the alignment of U.S. Northeast Asian allies and partners with Washington. This was true in terms of not only security policies but also the reshoring of supply chains for all the economies involved. The fastest to respond was Japan.

Japan: The Quiet Shaper

Japan's Strategic Trajectory before the Pandemic

Japan entered the turbulent years of Trump and Covid-19 with the most established framework for strategic competition with China of any middle or major power. While other countries like the United States were distracted from the China challenge by the lingering political effects of the 2008 financial crisis and displacement caused by globalization, Japan passed through these travails in fairly quick order. Before Brexit and "Make America Great Again," Japan experienced its own anti-establishment regime change in the 2009 election of the Democratic Party of Japan (DPJ) under Yukio Hatoyama. Within a few years, however, the fundamentally conservative Japanese voters punished the DPJ for bungling the 2011 Great Tohoku Earthquake and mismanaging the U.S.-Japan alliance, as China surged into the East China Sea to press its claims to the Japan-administered Senkaku Islands. Japan had already weathered the most disruptive economic impact of globalization with its own offshoring and restructuring that occurred with the appreciation of the yen in the 1980s.[9] Rather than turning against international trade and opening, the Japanese people were finally ready to embrace economic internationalism as a source of growth and influence, in contrast to American or British voters still reeling from the 2008 financial crisis. And the Liberal Democratic Party (LDP) was ready to resume governing on a pledge to counter Chinese coercion.

---

[9] Yoichi Funabashi, "Japan, Where Populism Fails," *New York Times*, February 8, 2017; and Mireya Solis, "The Underappreciated Power: Japan After Abe," *Foreign Affairs*, November/December 2020.

As a result, Shinzo Abe returned to power at the end of 2012 with far more national consensus behind his deliberate competition strategy with China than the world press recognized at the time.[10] Having failed as prime minister in 2006–7, Abe was careful to impose more discipline and structure on his new government. He moved away from the heavy and divisive emphasis on ideology of his first term and was careful to coordinate policies with the pacifist-leaning Komeito party in his ruling coalition. At the same time, he appointed career diplomats rather than ideologues to a newly established National Security Council (NSC) staff in the Prime Minister's Office. In 2013 that staff produced Japan's first National Security Strategy, outlining a framework for competition with China through strengthened alliances and partnerships and investments in resilience and rulemaking in Asia. Four years before the Trump administration's own somewhat hyperbolic embrace of strategic competition with China, Abe's government put forward a durable strategy for managed competition toward which the most powerful democracies have since gravitated.[11]

The cornerstone of this strategy involved strengthening the bilateral security alliance with the United States. After ham-handed efforts at increasing Japan's autonomy from the United States, an imploding DPJ government moved by its third year and third prime minister in 2011 to tighten defense relations in the face of growing Chinese gray-zone coercion. Abe then put the bulk of his newfound political capital into completing that task, passing in 2015 comprehensive security policy legislation premised on the use of collective self-defense—essentially joint operations with U.S. forces if they come under attack outside of Japan's narrow defense—that previous Japanese governments had avoided for decades lest they become entrapped in U.S. conflicts elsewhere in Asia. The new legislation was a clear indication that the risks of abandonment in the face of Chinese threats were seen in Tokyo as far more serious than any risk of entrapment, particularly since China's maritime expansion around Japan meant Tokyo could no longer enjoy the comfort of being in the "rear area" of regional conflicts. Stuck on the front line, Japan now needed both the domestic legislative changes and concurrent renegotiated Guidelines for Defense Cooperation with the United States to ensure what the legislation called "seamless" operations among the defense

---

[10] In 2012, Japanese views of China hit an all-time low, with unfavorability up to 84.3% from 78.3% the previous year. See "Genron NPO dai hachi-kai nitchu kyodo yoron chosa no kekka kohyo" [Genron NPO Announces the Results of the 8th Japan-China Joint Public Opinion Survey], Genron NPO, June 20, 2012, https://www.genron-npo.net/press/2012/06/npo-10.html.

[11] White House, *National Security Strategy of the United States of America* (Washington, D.C., December 2017), 2–3, https://trumpwhitehouse.archives.gov/wp-content/uploads/2017/12/NSS-Final-12-18-2017-0905.pdf; and Prime Minister of Japan and His Cabinet, *National Security Strategy* (Tokyo, December 2013)

forces and with U.S. and other allied forces (such as Australia) in crises—even outside Japan—that had a direct impact on Japan's security.[12]

This external balancing strategy was complemented by the return of Abe's earlier proposal for a U.S.-Japan-Australia-India Quad, which the Trump administration agreed to elevate to a ministerial in 2017.[13] Abe's bilateral and plurilateral strategies for external balancing were further supplemented with the announcement in 2015 of a "free and open Indo-Pacific" concept focused on providing "quality infrastructure" for developing Asia based on a more reliable alternative to China's newly branded Belt and Road Initiative.[14] Indeed, Japan's financing quickly surpassed China's in the region. Abe also ensured that Japan led on the establishment of broader economic rulemaking for the Indo-Pacific, increasing the amount of Japanese trade covered under economic partnerships and trade agreements from less than one-fifth to more than three-fourths of Japan's overall trade during his tenure.[15] Japan convinced the TPP countries to complete the renamed Comprehensive and Progressive Agreement for Trans-Pacific Partnership with a place at the table left for the United States. It also negotiated a bilateral agreement with the European Union in 2019 and led the Regional Comprehensive Economic Partnership (RCEP) to completion in 2020, despite India's exit and the challenges of negotiating virtually under Covid-19 restrictions.[16]

Experts at Australia's Lowy Institute concluded in 2019 that Japan had become "the leader of the liberal order in Asia," while public opinion polls in Southeast Asia consistently showed Japan to be the most trusted country in that subregion.[17] The Trump administration also embraced key aspects of Abe's strategy, announcing its own "free and open Indo-Pacific" strategy in 2017 and joining with Japan on infrastructure financing and

---

[12] Ministry of Foreign Affairs (Japan), "Cabinet Decision on Development of Seamless Security Legislation to Ensure Japan's Survival and Protect Its People," July 1, 2014.

[13] Ankit Panda, "U.S., Japan, India, and Australia Hold Working-Level Quadrilateral Meeting on Regional Cooperation," *Diplomat*, November 13, 2017, https://thediplomat.com/2017/11/us-japan-india-and-australia-hold-working-level-quadrilateral-meeting-on-regional-cooperation.

[14] Ministry of Foreign Affairs (Japan), "Jiyude aka reta indotaiheiyo senryaku" [Free and Open Indo-Pacific Strategy], in Ministry of Foreign Affairs (Japan), *Diplomatic Bluebook 2017* (Tokyo, September 2017).

[15] Peter Landers, "Japan, the Original Trade Villain, Now Casts Itself as the Hero," *Wall Street Journal*, March 9, 2018, https://www.wsj.com/articles/japan-the-original-trade-villain-now-casts-itself-as-the-hero-1520591404.

[16] Ministry of Foreign Affairs (Japan), "The 4th Regional Comprehensive Economic Partnership (RCEP) Summit and RCEP Agreement Signing Ceremony," November 15, 2020, https://www.mofa.go.jp/policy/economy/fta/page1e_000291.html; Ministry of Foreign Affairs (Japan), "RCEP kyotei no keizai loka bunseki" [Analysis of RCEP's Economic Impact], March 19, 2021; and Ministry of Foreign Affairs (Japan), "Waga kuni no keizai renkei kyotei (EPA/ FTA) no torikumi" [Our Country's Efforts in Initiatives Such as Economic Partnerships (EPA/FTA)], March 2021.

[17] Hervé Lemahieu and Alyssa Leng, *Asia Power Index: Key Findings 2020* (Sydney: Lowy Institute, 2020); and "Opinion Poll On Japan," Ministry of Foreign Affairs (Japan), Press Release, March 18, 2020, https://www.mofa.go.jp/press/release/press4e_002784.html.

the Quad.[18] Rather than hedge or seek an escape from U.S.-China strategic competition, Abe successfully designed and implemented a strategy to shape that competition—beginning with Washington.

The distinction from the Trump administration's approach was that Japan sought managed competition with China. Though attacked and isolated by Beijing, Abe attempted from the beginning of his second time in office to restore a predictable power equilibrium in relations with China rather than pursue containment or decoupling. Thus, Abe agreed with Xi to restore the "mutually beneficial relationship based on common strategic interests" that their predecessors Yasuo Fukuda and Hu Jintao had announced in 2008. In 2018, for example, the Japan Bank for International Cooperation (JBIC) negotiated a memorandum of understanding with the China Development Bank to cooperate between the Belt and Road Initiative and the free and open Indo-Pacific strategy—an important gesture even though no concrete follow-through resulted.[19] Japanese companies reported improved market access in China the next year as Abe sought to "bring Japan-China relations to a new level" in his summitry with Xi.[20] In fact, the geopolitical tensions between Japan and China continued beneath the surface. Japanese scrambles of fighter aircraft to intercept Chinese intrusions of Japanese airspace spiked as Abe met with Xi in 2019, and Chinese patrol ships entered the 24-nautical-mile contiguous zone of the Senkaku Islands for an unprecedented 112 days in 2021.[21] Nevertheless, the Sino-Japanese relationship stabilized to some extent as Abe and then Suga sought the right balance between actively countering Chinese coercion and benefiting from China's economic growth.

Weathering and Harnessing the Trump Shock

The election of Trump was far from conducive to such a predictable strategy toward China. The Abe government had found the Obama

---

[18] U.S. Department of State, *A Free and Open Indo-Pacific: Advancing a Shared Vision* (Washington, D.C., November 2019), https://www.state.gov/wp-content/uploads/2019/11/Free-and-Open-Indo-Pacific-4Nov2019.pdf; and Ministry of Foreign Affairs (Japan), "Free and Open Indo-Pacific," April 1, 2021, https://www.mofa.go.jp/policy/page25e_000278.html.

[19] See Ministry of Foreign Affairs (Japan), "Prime Minister Abe Visits China," October 26, 2018, https://www.mofa.go.jp/a_o/c_m1/cn/page3e_000958.html; and Shi Jiangtao, "China-Japan Ties at 'Historic Turning Point' after Shinzo Abe's Visit, but Can the Goodwill Hold?" *South China Morning Post*, October 28, 2018, https://www.scmp.com/news/china/diplomacy/article/2170469/china-japan-ties-historic-turning-point-after-shinzo-abes-visit.

[20] "Abe and Xi Pledge to Elevate Ties to a New Level," *Japan Times*, December 23, 2019.

[21] Ministry of Defense (Japan), *Nippon no boei 2019* [Defense of Japan 2019] (Tokyo, 2019), 274; and "Remote Control: Japan's Evolving Senkaku Strategy," Asia Maritime Transparency Initiative, Center for Strategic and International Studies (CSIS), July 29, 2020, https://amti.csis.org/remote-control-japans-evolving-senkakus-strategy.

administration sometimes too soft on China but recognized in Hillary Clinton a candidate who would stand by alliances and Abe's own balance-of-power logic.[22] Abe had broken protocol by visiting Clinton during the 2016 presidential campaign and then after Trump was elected rushing back to New York to offer a game of golf with her opponent just weeks after he surprised the world by winning the U.S. election.[23] In contrast to European leaders who held Trump in visible disdain, Abe was not going to let the mercurial American president disrupt his strategy for strengthening the U.S.-Japan alliance as a counterbalance to China. Through multiple rounds of golf and more engagement than even British prime minister Theresa May enjoyed (or could endure), Abe dissuaded Trump from his more destructive pledges to abandon allies and cut deals with adversaries. More importantly, Abe and his team won over the more traditional national security hawks that led the senior levels at the NSC, State Department, and Defense Department—officials who embraced Abe's free and open Indo-Pacific strategy, bilateral defense guidelines review, and quality infrastructure initiatives. The U.S. retreat from the TPP and multilateral trade and diplomatic organizations and Trump's ideational feud with Europe all hurt Abe's strategy for countering China's regional and global revisionism. Many around Abe, however, agreed with an anonymous senior adviser to the Japanese prime minister who wrote in 2020 that Japan was better off with Trump than it had been with Obama.[24]

Still, the Trump years proved exhausting for the majority of Japanese people and officials: the number of Japanese who said Japan could trust the United States to do the right thing in Pew polling dropped from 66% during the Obama administration to 25% during the Trump administration, while influential advisers around Abe began openly questioning the reliability of

---

[22] See, for example, "Shasetsu: Nichi-Bei shuno kaidan Ajia no ishizue e ippo wo" [Editorial: U.S.-Japan Summit Meeting: Need to Take a Step toward Asia's Foundation], *Asahi Shimbun*, April 25, 2014.

[23] David Brunnstrom, "Japan PM Stresses Importance of TPP Trade Pact in Meeting with Clinton," Reuters, September 19, 2016, https://www.reuters.com/article/us-japan-trade-clinton-idUSKCN11Q0BK; and Andy Sharp, "Abe Woos Trump with Golf Just Like His Grandfather Did," *Japan Times*, November 19, 2016, https://www.japantimes.co.jp/news/2016/11/19/national/politics-diplomacy/abe-wooed-trump-golf-just-like-grandfather-eisenhower/#.XxSwLm5Fxyw.

[24] Y.A., "The Virtues of a Confrontational China Strategy," *American Interest*, April 10, 2020, https://www.the-american-interest.com/2020/04/10/the-virtues-of-a-confrontational-china-strategy; and CSIS, "Mapping the Future of U.S. China Policy," https://chinasurvey.csis.org. See also William Sposato, "Japan Worries about Four More Years of Trump—and about a Biden Presidency," *Foreign Policy*, November 3, 2020.

the United States as Trump's presidency spiraled to its chaotic conclusion.[25] Though more Japanese strategic experts than Europeans said that Trump would be better for Japan than Biden in 2020 surveys taken by the Center for Strategic and International Studies (CSIS), surveys in Japan still showed that a majority thought Trump's re-election would harm Japan's interests vis-à-vis China.[26]

It is striking, therefore, that Abe's successor, Suga, and Trump's successor, Biden, both sought to strike a note of continuity with the Abe-Trump years on national security policy—as did Suga's successor after one year, Prime Minister Fumio Kishida. Biden announced that the United States would be continuing the free and open Indo-Pacific strategy and elevated Abe's Quad to a summit and the centerpiece of U.S. diplomacy in the region.[27] Suga, the chief cabinet secretary and engineer for Abe's cabinet, emphasized continuity as well in his April 2021 visit to Washington for the first in-person summit of a foreign leader with the new U.S. president.[28] Personalities matter in geopolitics, but in the case of the U.S.-Japan alliance structure prevailed. The bipartisan consensus behind the alliance reinforced this continuity in both countries, with even the progressive rump of the former DPJ (now the Rikken Minshuto, or Constitutional Democratic Party) abandoning Hatoyama's earlier dreams of autonomy from the United States, and the Japanese Communist Party standing as the only Communist party in the world to break with the Chinese

---

[25] Bruce Stokes, "Japanese Divided on Democracy's Success at Home, but Value Voice of the People," Pew Research Center, October 17, 2017, https://www.pewresearch.org/global/2017/10/17/japanese-divided-on-democracys-success-at-home-but-value-voice-of-the-people; and "'Nichi-Bei ryoko' Nihon kyuraku 39% honsha Gyarappu Kyodo yoron chosa" [Yomiuri/Gallup Public Poll: Views Seeing U.S.-Japan Relations as Good Dropped to 39% in Japan], *Yomiuri Shimbun*, December 19, 2018. Japan's Genron NPO found that 50% of Japanese respondents said they trusted the United States less with Trump in office. See "Japanese Public Opinion on U.S. Leadership and the Role of Japan," Genron NPO, July 13, 2017, https://www.genron-npo.net/en/opinion_polls/archives/5359.html. Two core advisers to Abe, Professor Hosoya Yuichi of Keio University and former NSC official Kanehara Katsuhiko, both expressed concern at Trump's squandered leadership in the world. See "Keidai kyoju Hosoya Yuichishi—Anpo kankyoga kyuhen kado no taibei izon dakkyaku wo (posuto korona no Nihon seiji)" [Keio University Professor Hosoya Yuichi: Sudden Change of Security Environment Requires Departure from Prior Dependence on U.S. (Post-Coronavirus Japanese Politics)], *Nikkei*, July 7, 2020.

[26] CSIS, "Mapping the Future of U.S. China Policy"; and Aizawa, "Survey Suggests Growing Concern among Japanese at Prospect of Trump Re-election."

[27] "Remarks by President Biden, Prime Minister Modi of India, Prime Minister Morrison of Australia, and Prime Minister Suga of Japan in the Virtual Quad Leaders Summit," White House, March 12, 2021, https://www.whitehouse.gov/briefing-room/speeches-remarks/2021/03/12/remarks-by-president-biden-prime-minister-modi-of-india-prime-minister-morrison-of-australia-and-prime-minister-suga-of-japan-in-virtual-meeting-of-the-quad.

[28] "U.S.-Japan Joint Leaders' Statement: 'U.S.—Japan Global Partnership for a New Era,'" White House, Press Release, April 16, 2021, https://www.whitehouse.gov/briefing-room/statements-releases/2021/04/16/u-s-japan-joint-leaders-statement-u-s-japan-global-partnership-for-a-new-era; and Prime Minister of Japan and His Cabinet, "Nichibei kyodo kisha kaiken" [Japan-U.S. Joint Press Conference], April 16, 2021, https://www.kantei.go.jp/jp/99_suga/statement/2021/0416kaiken1.html.

Communist Party (CCP) on its one-hundredth anniversary in July 2021.[29] With issues like Okinawa bases and status of forces agreements, alliance management is no easy task under the best of circumstances. But in 2021 the U.S.-Japan alliance was arguably in the best circumstance it had ever enjoyed.

Covid-19: External Clarity and Internal Consternation

The main impact of the Covid-19 pandemic on Japan's external relations was to accelerate distrust of China, though that would likely have happened to some extent already because of China's growing pressure on the Senkakus and Beijing's repressive policies in Hong Kong and Xinjiang. Initially, the Japanese people responded to the outbreak in Wuhan with sympathy and offers of assistance. There was perhaps a moment when the human costs of the virus and the need for international collaboration might have been used by forward-thinking leaders to repair Sino-Japanese relations.[30] However, Beijing's aggressive "wolf warrior" diplomacy and the increasingly vocal criticism of China in the Japanese Diet and media killed that hopeful moment.[31] A large caucus of LDP members moved to block Xi's planned visit to Japan in 2020 (canceled because of the Covid-19 pandemic anyway) and formed a new human rights league that focused initially on Xinjiang and Hong Kong.[32] As the Biden administration ramped up support for Taiwan in the face of growing Chinese military pressure on the island, Suga agreed in Washington to cooperate on security in the Taiwan Strait—the first such summit-level statement since 1969. In subsequent months, prominent Japanese political leaders reiterated Tokyo's determination to support Taiwan

---

[29] "Japan Communist Party Slams China in First Platform Change since 2004," *Japan Times*, January 18, 2020, https://www.japantimes.co.jp/news/2020/01/18/national/politics-diplomacy/japanese-communist-party-china-platform.

[30] For example, see "Chata-ki ni shien bussi, Chugoku no SNS ko, 'iine' hirogaru, shingata haien" [Backup Supplies on Charter Planes, "Like" Spreads on Chinese SNS, Novel Coronavirus], *Asahi Shimbun*, January 30, 2020, https://www.asahi.com/articles/DA3S14347315.html; and "'Bukan ganbare!': Masuku teikyo, hirogaru sien—shingata haien" ["Wuhan, Hang in There!": Providing Mask, Spreading Support—Novel Coronavirus], *Jiji Press*, January 28, 2020, https://financial.jiji.com/magazine_bk/back_number_news.html?number=26.

[31] Jesse Johnson, "Japan Records Most Negative View of China as Unfavorable Opinions Surge, Survey Finds," *Japan Times*, October 6, 2020, https://www.japantimes.co.jp/news/2020/10/06/national/japan-most-negative-view-china-survey.

[32] "LDP Policy Group, Not Party, Requests State to Cancel Xi's Visit," *Asahi Shimbun*, July 8, 2020, http://www.asahi.com/ajw/articles/13526200; and Yukihiro Sakaguchi, "Japan's Ruling Party Torn over Xi Jinping Invitation," *Nikkei Asia*, July 8, 2020, https://asia.nikkei.com/Politics/Japan-s-ruling-party-torn-over-Xi-Jinping-invitation.

through stronger defense cooperation with the United States.[33] Underlying these political statements was a new level of bilateral defense planning based on the 2015 revised defense guidelines and Japan's reinterpretation of Article 9 of the constitution to allow collective self-defense.[34] China's somewhat softer tone toward Japan in the Trump years receded as Beijing fired back at Tokyo for its more active support of Taiwan and criticism of China's human rights abuses.[35]

Technology decoupling from China also intensified, in part as a result of Covid-19. Japan had already expanded strategic investment screening laws in 2015 and in 2018 banned Chinese firms like Huawei from its 5G market while quietly advising Japanese firms through "administrative guidance" to follow new U.S. policies blocking the export of key technologies and components related to artificial intelligence (AI) and 5G.[36] As part of the April 2020 economic stimulus package after Covid-19, the Japanese government set aside over $2 billion to help Japanese companies onshore supply chains and manufacturing back to Japan to create jobs and protect technology.[37] While there was some reason to suspect this was political posturing, given that Japan

---

[33] "Nichi-Bei kyodo seimei, yaku hanseiki buri ni Taiwan ni genkyu, Chugoku wo tsuyoku kensei" [Japan-U.S. Joint Statement Mentions Taiwan for the First Time in about Half a Century: Strongly Containing China], NHK World, April 17, 2021, https://www3.nhk.or.jp/news/html/20210417/k10012980541000.html; and Jesse Johnson, "Senior Japanese Defense Official Says Democracies Must Back Up Taiwan and Stand Up to China," Japan Times, June 29, 2021, https://www.japantimes.co.jp/news/2021/06/29/national/politics-diplomacy/taiwan-nakayama-china-defense.

[34] Demetri Sevastopulo, "U.S. and Japan Conduct War Games amid Rising China-Taiwan Tensions," Financial Times, June 30, 2021, https://www.ft.com/content/54b0db59-a403-493e-b715-7b63c9c39093.

[35] For example, see "Japan-China Summit Meeting and Dinner," Ministry of Foreign Affairs (Japan), June 27, 2019, http://www.mofa.go.jp/a_o/c_m1/cn/page3e_001046.html; and Shannon Tiezzi, "Is the China-Japan Thaw Over?" Diplomat, April 7, 2021, https://thediplomat.com/2021/04/is-the-china-japan-thaw-over.

[36] "Gaishi kisei seifu kanyo tsuyomeru Chūgoku nento ni gijutsu hogo" [Enhanced Government Involvement in the Foreign Exchange Regulations for Protecting Technology with China in Mind], Nikkei, October 9, 2019; and Ministry of Finance (Japan), "Draft Rules and Regulations of the Foreign Exchange and Foreign Trade Act," March 25, 2020. See Ministry of Internal Affairs and Communications (Japan), "Dai 5 sedai ido tsushin shisutemu no donyu no tame no tokutei kichikyoku no kaisetsu keikaku ni kakaru nintei shinsei no uketsuke kekka" [Results of Acceptance of Applications for Authorization of Establishment Plans for Specified Base Stations for Diffusion of 5G Mobile Communications Systems], February 26, 2019, http://www.soumu.go.jp/menu_news/s-news/01kiban14_02000375.html; "Japan to Ban Huawei, ZTE from Govt Contracts-Yomiuri," Reuters, December 7, 2018, https://www.reuters.com/article/japan-china-huawei/japan-to-ban-huawei-zte-from-govt-contracts-yomiuri-idUSL4N1YB6JJ; Isabel Reynolds and Emi Nobuhiro, "China Says Unfair Treatment of Huawei Could Damage Japan Ties," Bloomberg, March 29, 2019, https://www.bloomberg.com/news/articles/2019-03-29/china-says-unfair-treatment-of-huawei-could-damage-japan-ties; and Simon Denyer, "Japan Effectively Bans China's Huawei and ZTE from Government Contracts, Joining U.S.," Washington Post, December 18, 2018.

[37] "Japan to Pay Firms to Leave China, Relocate Production Elsewhere as Part of Coronavirus Stimulus," South China Morning Post, April 8, 2020; Takashi Tsuji and Kazuhiro Furuyama, "Japan Preps First Subsidy to Company Moving Production Out of China," Nikkei Asia, April 21, 2020, https://asia.nikkei.com/Spotlight/Coronavirus/Japan-preps-first-subsidy-to-company-moving-production-out-of-China; and Ministry of Economy, Trade and Industry (Japan), "Reiwa ninendo hosei yosanan no jigyo gaiyo" [Overview of Supplementary Budget for FY2020], PowerPoint presentation, April 2020, 24.

still needed access to China's market and the draw of Chinese tourists after the Covid-19 pandemic, the response to the reshoring opportunity from Japanese business was overwhelming. By July, applications for total funding by Japanese firms were over ten times the available funds, and polls in 2020 showed that 80% of the Japanese public approved of the tightening of sensitive technology exports.[38] The Japan Center for Economic Research found in a 2020 survey of 3,000 Japanese business leaders that 46% (a plurality) favored reducing tie-ups with Chinese firms and 48% supported the Trump administration's aggressive export control policies against China.[39]

However, if the Covid-19 pandemic accelerated support for Taiwan, technology decoupling, and criticism of China on human rights, it also hobbled Japan's strategic focus and policy execution. After an unprecedented seven-plus years in office, Abe's earlier health issues returned with the pressure of responding to the economic and public health crises of the pandemic.[40] Although the transition to Suga was smooth, the former chief cabinet secretary struggled to retain his moniker of "Mr. Fix It" as lockdowns swept Tokyo in 2020 and 2021 and economic output slumped to 1.5% below the 2019 pre-pandemic peak.[41] While an independent commission on Japan's response led by the Asia Pacific Initiative gave the Abe and Suga governments "passing grades" for their performance in contrast to G-7 peer countries, the experts also lamented Japan's poor showing compared with other regional governments like South Korea and Taiwan.[42] Confident in the "Japan model" of broad access to medical services and a nationwide network of public health centers, the Japanese Ministry of Health, Labour and Welfare was unable to break logjams in PCR testing and lost control of data and contact tracing that neighboring South Korea had perfected. As the Asia Pacific Initiative noted in its detailed assessment of Japan's performance, bureaucratic complacency and inflexibility had proved almost as problematic during the pandemic as during the 2011 nuclear disaster at Fukushima.[43]

---

[38] "Korona de seisan kaiki hojokin kyosoritsu 11-bai masuku ya iyakuhin" [As the Coronavirus Promotes Reshoring of Production, Applications for the Government Subsidy Swell to 11 Times the Budget, Many in Mask and Medical Equipment Producers], *Nikkei*, September 8, 2020.

[39] "Japanese Business Rethinks Hi-Tech Deals with China," *Nikkei Asia*, September 3, 2020, https://asia.nikkei.com/Politics/International-relations/US-China-tensions/Japanese-business-rethinks-high-tech-deals-with-China.

[40] Michael J. Green and Nicholas Szechenyi, "Shinzo Abe's Decision to Step Down," CSIS, August 28, 2020, https://www.csis.org/analysis/shinzo-abes-decision-step-down.

[41] "GDP, Korona zen suijun nao toku—kojin shohi 0.8 %zo domari" [GDP Recovery to Pre-Covid Level Still a Distant Goal—Consumer Spending Only Rises by 0.8%], *Nikkei*, August 16, 2021, https://www.nikkei.com/article/DGXZQOUA13ACD0T10C21A8000000.

[42] Asia Pacific Initiative, *The Independent Investigation Commission on the Japanese Government's Response to COVID-19: Report on Best Practices and Lessons Learned* (Tokyo: Asia Pacific Initiative, 2021), 11.

[43] Ibid., 13.

Critics in Japan also noted that the successful top-down political style of Abe and Suga in strategic competition with China—with heavy intervention in bureaucratic personnel decisions—may have paralyzed the ministries' initiative in the complex domestic case of Covid-19.[44] Keen to support domestic manufacturers and fearful of an earlier entrenched anti-vaccination movement in Japan, the Suga government only approved the Moderna and AstraZeneca vaccines for use on May 21, 2021, and Suga had to personally negotiate with the manufacturers while in the United States to ensure speedy delivery.[45] The questions about Japan's supposedly improved crisis-management capabilities provoked by the pandemic were amplified when bureaucratic red tape slowed down Japan's evacuation of Afghan allies after the U.S. withdrawal. Only 15 of over 500 Afghans who had worked for Japan's government or NGOs in the country were evacuated.

Suga's political fortunes were also buffeted by the 2021 Tokyo Summer Olympics. The iconoclastic Soft Bank CEO Masayoshi Son and a growing chorus of Japanese business leaders called for canceling or postponing the Olympics with its estimated $15.6 billion price tag.[46] Citizen activism against the games then mounted, with over 300,000 signatures and polling showing that 80% of the Japanese public was skeptical about hosting the event—even before the Delta variant caused a new lockdown in Tokyo on the eve of the games.[47] The Olympics came off without major embarrassments, and Suga's support rate held at a steady but low 43%, according to center-right *Yomiuri Shimbun* and 33% according to the liberal *Asahi Shimbun*.[48] But that would not last. In the aftermath of the Olympics and lead-up to LDP presidential and national Diet elections, Covid-19 cases surged again to an all-time high of more than 29,700 new confirmed cases on August 28, while Suga struggled to communicate his pandemic strategy effectively to the public.[49] His public support rate visibly plummeted in early September, and rank-and-file LDP

---

[44] Jun Iio, "Korona ni kikanai 'kanryo tanomi' Suga shusho no kukyo no riyu—seisaku kenkyu daigakuin daigaku kyoju io jun" [Relying on Bureaucrats Is Not Effective for Covid: The Reason Why Prime Minister Suga Faces Predicaments—Jun Iio, Professor at the National Graduate Institute for Policy Studies], *Nikkei*, February 22, 2021.

[45] Tetsushi Kajimoto, "Most Japan Firms Say Olympics Should Be Cancelled or Postponed, Poll Shows," Reuters, May 20, 2021, https://www.reuters.com/lifestyle/sports/fretting-about-covid-most-japan-firms-say-olympics-should-be-cancelled-or-2021-05-20; and William Pesek, "Opinion: Why Is Japan Failing So Badly on Vaccinations?" *Washington Post*, May 4, 2021, https://www.washingtonpost.com/opinions/2021/05/04/why-is-japan-failing-so-badly-vaccinations.

[46] Kajimoto, "Most Japan Firms Say Olympics Should Be Cancelled or Postponed, Poll Shows."

[47] "Over 80% of Japanese Oppose Olympics This Summer, Poll Shows," *Japan Times*, May 17, 2021, https://www.japantimes.co.jp/news/2021/05/17/national/tokyo-olympics-cancel-survey.

[48] Sheila A. Smith, "Japan's Difficult Summer," Council on Foreign Relations, May 27, 2021, https://www.cfr.org/blog/japans-difficult-summer.

[49] "Reuters COVID-19 Tracker: Japan," Reuters, September 13, 2021, https://graphics.reuters.com/world-coronavirus-tracker-and-maps/countries-and territories/japan.

members refused to stand behind party elders who had been backing the prime minister. On September 2, 2021, Suga surprised even his close friends by announcing he would not contest the LDP leadership race at the end of the month.

While the contenders to replace Suga in the LDP pledged to continue the strategies begun under Abe—particularly the ultimate winner of the party leadership race, Kishida—there is new concern that Japan might return to the pattern in the late 1990s and late 2000s when strong prime ministers were replaced by a rotating cast of premiers unable to cling to office for more than a year or to gain traction with their counterparts abroad. It remains to be seen whether Covid-19 might ultimately take this toll—not on Japan's strategic trajectory but on its capacity for continued leadership and activism in the Indo-Pacific.

South Korea: Shaken, Not Stirred

The Dilemma of Strategic Ambiguity: Korea's Trajectory before Covid-19

South Korea entered the second decade of the 21st century no less affected by the rise of China than was Japan. But as much as China's increasingly coercive behavior has shaken the ROK, it has not stirred the Korean strategic elite to the same levels of proactive foreign policy strategy as their Japanese counterparts. This is not because of a lack of commitment to an open rules-based order underpinned by U.S. security guarantees and forward presence. On that count, surveys show that Korean and Japanese strategic elites do not differ.[50] However, Korean strategic thinkers are understandably drawn for reasons of national aspiration and peril to the immediate threat north of the Demilitarized Zone (DMZ). Strategic relations with the United States, China, Russia, and Japan are all considered first through the spectrum of how much purchase those relationships give Seoul in deterring and perhaps enticing the dangerous regime in Pyongyang.

Also underpinning Korean views of China and regional security is a fundamentally different assumption about the emerging distribution of power in Asia. As one of South Korea's top Japan scholars notes, geopolitics underpin diverging Japan-ROK relations as much as the two countries' difficult history.[51] Where Japan's free and open Indo-Pacific vision and the Quad all

---

[50] Green and Szechenyi, *Power and Order in Asia*; and CSIS, "Mapping the Future of U.S. China Policy."

[51] Cheol Hee Park, *Strategic Estrangement between South Korea and Japan as a Barrier to Trilateral Cooperation* (Washington, D.C.: Atlantic Council, November 2019); and Andrew Yeo, "South Korea and the Free and Open Indo-Pacific Strategy," CSIS, July 20, 2020, https://www.csis.org/analysis/south-korea-and-free-and-open-indo-pacific-strategy.

indicate recognition that there is a growing multipolarity in Asia that must be harnessed to counter Chinese coercion, Korean strategic thinkers tend to accept the Chinese assertion that the region is moving toward a bipolar power structure between the United States and China.[52] Where Japanese officials and experts urged the United States to reject Xi Jinping's 2013 proposal for a "new model of great-power relations" that would formalize bipolarity and relegate Japan and India to second-tier status, Korean scholars and officials accepted the Chinese formula and sought to position South Korea in the new framework.[53] In Seoul this was a bipartisan perspective taken within both conservative and progressive camps. President Roh Moo-hyun had previewed this mode of thinking with his 2005 proposal that South Korea could be an independent "balancer" in Northeast Asia between Japan and China.[54] President Park Geun-hye's conservative government then downgraded Japan's strategic importance by implicitly accepting Xi's new model of great-power relations in a report to the National Assembly. The report stated that the government would prioritize relations with China and the United States, with Japan and Russia being at the second tier. After fierce Japanese diplomatic protests and some pointed queries from Washington, the Ministry of Foreign Affairs retracted the statement, but it was a "tell" for observers in the region.[55] Park followed the same pattern with promises to host a U.S.-China-ROK trilateral dialogue, which the U.S. State Department handed to CSIS to organize as a Track 1.5 meeting in deference to Tokyo's concerns about the optics.[56] Park then disturbed observers by appearing at Beijing's patriotic and overtly anti-Japanese 70th anniversary celebration of victory in World War II—the only leader of a U.S. ally to do so.[57]

---

[52] For example, see Chaesung Chun, "South Korea's Middle Power Strategy as a Foreign Strategy," *American Studies* 37, no. 2 (2014): 45–80; and Jongryn Mo, "South Korea's Middle Power Diplomacy: A Case of Growing Compatibility between Regional and Global Roles," *International Journal* 71, no. 4 (2017): 587–607.

[53] "Kankoku 'Nihon hazushi' gaiko kaigi ya senryaku Taiwa Bei-Chu nomini dashin Nihon seifu fukaikan" [Korean Diplomacy to Remove Japan, Suggesting Conferences and Strategic Dialogue Only to the United States and China; Japanese Government Showing Annoyance], *Yomiuri Shimbun*, May 14, 2013.

[54] Choe Sang-Hun, "South Korea's 'Balancer' Policy Attacked," *New York Times*, August 9, 2005, https://www.nytimes.com/2005/04/09/world/asia/south-koreas-balancer-policy-attacked.html.

[55] "Paku gaiko yusen juni wa 'Bei Chu tsugini Nichi-Ro' gaisho koho ga kenkai" [For Park Diplomacy, the Order of Priority Is "the US, China, Followed by Japan and Russia," Noted by the Candidate for Foreign Minister], *Yomiuri Shimbun*, March 1, 2013.

[56] Victor Cha, Michael J. Green, and Christopher K. Johnson, "CSIS Experts Participate in Seoul 'Track 1.5' Dialogues," CSIS, July 22, 2013, https://www.csis.org/news/csis-experts-participate-seoul-%E2%80%9Ctrack-15%E2%80%9D-dialogues; and "Bei Chu Kan de anpo kaigi 22nichi kaisai e Kankoku 'Nihon hazushi' de shin wakugumi" [U.S.-China-Korea Security Conference to be Held on the 22nd—Korea to Create a New Framework without Japan], Kyodo News, July 19, 2013.

[57] Shannon Tiezzi, "South Korea's President and China's Military Parade," *Diplomat*, September 3, 2015, https://thediplomat.com/2015/09/south-koreas-president-and-chinas-military-parade.

This strong preference for what Korean scholars and officials call "strategic ambiguity" in Sino-U.S. strategic competition had taken hold in Seoul before Trump and Covid-19 had any impact. To the extent that the ROK governments have sought to shape the external environment beyond the Korean Peninsula, the approach has been far more circumspect than Japan's—or Australia's or India's for that matter. President Lee Myung-bak promoted "global Korea" as he hosted a series of international summits on nuclear safety and high-level aid effectiveness in 2009–10, but his government was hesitant to engage in broader regional shaping strategies with Washington or Tokyo. (He was saved by an Obama administration that was initially uncertain on the same issue.)[58] After Korean companies began shifting supply chains away from China to cheaper and safer destinations like Vietnam in the wake of the 2017 THAAD boycott (following a Japanese pattern from a decade earlier), the government of Moon Jae-in announced its own New Southern Policy to take diplomatic advantage of the increased engagement with Southeast Asia.[59] However, Seoul has resisted both the Trump and Biden administrations' efforts to bring South Korea into the free and open Indo-Pacific framework—which by 2021 included not only Japan and Australia but increasingly India, Canada, and European allies. Instead, the Moon government agreed only to align the U.S. version with South Korea's New Southern Policy on a bilateral basis.[60]

This stubborn adherence to strategic ambiguity should not indicate weakness in the U.S.-ROK bilateral alliance except insofar as it relates to aligning policies on the China challenge. Polls indicate that in Asia, Koreans are topped only by Japanese and Vietnamese in their skepticism of Chinese intentions. Moreover, any veteran of the U.S.-ROK alliance will appreciate the depth of alignment embodied in the bilateral combined forces command (a jointness of military effort to which the U.S.-Japan alliance still aspires).[61]

---

[58] Michael J. Green, "Korea's Middle Power Diplomacy and Asia's Emerging Multilateral Architecture," in *The Korean Pivot: The Study of South Korea as a Global Power*, ed. Victor D. Cha and Marie Dumond (Washington, D.C.: CSIS, 2017), 17–34.

[59] Choe Wongi, *"New Southern Policy": Korea's Newfound Ambition in Search of Strategic Autonomy* (Paris: Ifri, 2021); and Presidential Committee on New Southern Policy of the Republic of Korea (ROK), *New Southern Policy* (Seoul, February 2020), https://apcss.org/wp-content/uploads/2020/02/Republic_of_Korea-New_Southern_Policy_Information_Booklet.pdf.

[60] "Secretary Michael R. Pompeo's Meeting with Korean Foreign Minister Kang Kyung-Wha," Office of the Spokesperson, U.S. Department of State, January 14, 2020, https://2017-2021.state.gov/secretary-michael-r-pompeos-meeting-with-korean-foreign-minister-kang-kyung-wha; and "Joint Statement of the 2021 Republic of Korea–United States Foreign and Defense Ministerial Meeting ('2+2')," Office of the Spokesperson, U.S. Department of State, March 18, 2021, https://www.state.gov/joint-statement-of-the-2021-republic-of-korea-united-states-foreign-and-defense-ministerial-meeting-22.

[61] Laura Silver, Kat Devlin, and Christine Huang, "People Around the Globe Are Divided in Their Opinions of China," Pew Research Center, December 5, 2019, https://www.pewresearch.org/fact-tank/2019/12/05/people-around-the-globe-are-divided-in-their-opinions-of-china.

However, surveys also indicate that despite this deep distrust of Beijing, Koreans broadly view China as the secondary threat for South Korea compared with the North—which is logical, of course.[62] Ironically, Seoul's disinterest in harnessing multipolarity to counter China's hegemonic ambitions may also reflect Koreans' higher confidence in both the power of the U.S. military and the U.S. economy vis-à-vis China.[63] Moreover, while both the Park and Moon administrations trumpeted the opportunity to work with Beijing to curb the North Korea threat, polls show that the Korean public remains deeply skeptical of claims that China will really assist on North-South relations, with fully three-quarters of Koreans justifiably doubting that Beijing will help Seoul with unification.[64] Koreans increasingly recognize that Beijing's support for "independent unification" means unification on terms that China approves, which includes severing the alliance with the United States. Even on economic issues, where South Korea's bilateral trade volume with China surpasses the flow of goods and services to the United States and Japan combined, the reality is that Korean foreign direct investment is much stronger in stock and flow in the U.S. economy and growing at a faster rate than investment in China.[65] As some of us used to put it during the Bush administration, the U.S.-ROK alliance is reminiscent of what Mark Twain said about the music of Richard Wagner—"it's not as bad as it sounds."

Moreover, strategic ambiguity does not mean that South Korea has become pacifist or passive about its own defense amid the shifting power dynamics in Northeast Asia. The Moon administration increased defense spending after relative decline in the conservative Park Geun-hye years and announced an ambitious new Defense Reform 2.0 plan that would create a "smaller but smarter military"—one that will compensate manpower loss due to demographic decline with cutting-edge technologies such as big data, combat drones, and advanced missile defense systems.[66] South Korea moved

---

[62] Karl Friedhoff, "South Koreans See China as More Threat Than Partner, but Not the Most Critical Threat Facing the Country," Chicago Council on Global Affairs, April 6, 2021, https://www.thechicagocouncil.org/research/public-opinion-survey/south-koreans-see-china-more-threat-partner-not-most-critical-threat.

[63] The 2020 CSIS survey on China found Korean strategic thinkers among the most confident in the world that the United States would prevail in a conflict with China. See CSIS, "Mapping the Future of U.S. China Policy." On Korean confidence in the U.S. economy, see J. James Kim et al., *South Korean Caution and Concern about China* (Seoul: Asan Institute for Policy Studies, 2019).

[64] Chung Min Lee, "South Korea Is Caught between China and the United States," Carnegie Endowment for International Peace, October 21, 2020, https://carnegieendowment.org/2020/10/21/south-korea-is-caught-between-china-and-united-states-pub-83019.

[65] "South Korea–U.S. Economic Relations," Congressional Research Service, CRS Report for Congress, RL30566, February 12, 2007.

[66] Sungyoung Jang, "How Will 'Defense Reform 2.0' Change South Korea's Defense?" *Diplomat*, August 27, 2018, https://thediplomat.com/2018/08/how-will-defense-reform-2-0-change-south-koreas-defense; and Seong-ho Sheen, "South Korea's Overdue Defence Reforms," East Asia Forum, May 29, 2019.

forward on developing strike capabilities before Japan with the approval of the Trump and then Biden administrations. And senior political figures and former defense officials have called for redeploying U.S. tactical nuclear weapons on the peninsula or developing Korean alternatives. Such views—held by people such as Chun In-bum, a retired lieutenant general in the South Korean army, and two-time presidential candidate Chung Mong-joon—are consistently supported by a majority of the Korean public, according to polls.[67] These trends stand in contrast to Japan, which has only incrementally increased defense spending and may soon be overtaken by South Korea, as well as Taiwan, where the opposition Kuomintang (KMT) in the Legislative Yuan has hobbled the Tsai government's attempts to increase spending in the face of a military challenge even more daunting than North Korea. In part, Korean enthusiasm for self-defense capabilities reflects a curious alignment of the left and right of the political spectrum. The conservatives favor the military, while the progressives seek greater autonomy from the United States and the transfer of wartime operational control to South Korea (which has not yet been completed under Moon, despite his supporters' enthusiasm).

However, as a result of its policy of strategic ambiguity, Seoul has far less agency in Washington than do Tokyo or Canberra—shaping neither U.S. nor Chinese strategic behavior to any significant extent. At the same time, it must be recognized that Seoul is focused almost entirely on trying to shape U.S. strategy toward North Korea rather than the broader Indo-Pacific. To be sure, the Lee, Park, and Moon governments can all claim some success in this regard. After the unpredictable Roh government, for example, President Obama put his trust in the conservative Lee and Park governments to take the lead on engagement with North Korea while the United States stood back in what some officials called a policy of "strategic patience" toward the North. Nevertheless, the disconnect between Washington and Seoul will grow without greater South Korean focus on the pre-eminent strategic challenge to U.S. leadership in the region.

From Fire and Fury to Love Affairs: The Wild Ride with Trump

The arrival of Donald Trump tested Moon Jae-in's ability to keep a U.S. focus on North Korea—or at least the right kind of focus. Yet in the end, while conservatives in South Korea were alarmed at candidate Trump's

---

[67] Jeff Daniels, "South Koreans Want Their Own Nuclear Weapons but Doing So Risks Triggering a Wider War," CNBC, August 27, 2017, https://www.cnbc.com/2017/08/24/south-koreans-want-their-own-nukes-but-doing-so-risks-wider-war.html; and Anna Fifield, "As North Korea Flexes Its Muscles, Some in South Want Nukes, Too," *Washington Post*, March 20, 2016, https://www.washingtonpost.com/world/asia_pacific/as-north-korea-flexes-its-muscles-the-other-korea-looks-at-nukes-too/2016/03/20/e2b1bb22-eb88-11e5-a9ce-681055c7a05f_story.html.

repeated threat to pull troops out of the country and his demands that South Korea pay an astronomical 400% increase in host nation support under the bilateral Special Measures Agreement, Trump's own affinity for dictators eventually aligned well with the Korean progressives' desire for engagement and confidence-building with the North. When President Trump threatened "fire and fury" and his NSC began planning for a "bloody nose" military strike to dissuade Pyongyang from moving to full capacity for an intercontinental ballistic missile (the Hwasong-14) it had tested in 2017, the Moon government faced an almost existential crisis.[68] Moon's agency was evident when he invited North Korean leader Kim Jong-un's sister Kim Yo-jong as a VIP guest at the 2018 PyeongChang Winter Olympics, brokering a summit that summer between Trump and Kim Jong-un in Singapore.[69] Even though Trump continued wreaking havoc on the alliance over burden-sharing and Kim Jong-un rebuffed Moon's overtures for summitry (except when Moon accompanied Trump on a stroll across the DMZ), the South Korean leader's decisive role in averting war on the peninsula caused his domestic support to soar.[70] Even Moon's obsequious proposal that Trump be nominated for the Nobel Peace Prize did not significantly diminish support for his influence on the U.S. president—something European or Canadian publics would never have tolerated from their leaders.[71]

Just as Biden continued the Trump administration's adherence to Japan's free and open Indo-Pacific framework, the new U.S. president also agreed in the May 22, 2021, summit with Moon in Washington to continue the Singapore agreement reached by Trump and Kim Jong-un, even though there was broad recognition in the administration that Trump's joint statement with Kim was based on Pyongyang's commitment to "denuclearization of the Korean Peninsula" (which essentially meant that the North would denuclearize on the peninsula only in parallel with the United States doing

---

[68] Steven Lee Myers and Choe Sang-Hun, "Trump's 'Fire and Fury' Threat Raises Alarm in Asia," *New York Times*, August 9, 2017, https://www.nytimes.com/2017/08/09/world/asia/north-korea-trump-threat-fire-and-fury.html.

[69] James Masters and Aimee Lewis, "Winter Olympics Opening Ceremony Sees Historic Handshake," CNN, February 9, 2018, https://www.cnn.com/2018/02/09/sport/winter-olympics-opening-ceremony-intl/index.html; and Walter Russell Mead, "Kim Yo Jong's Shattered Olympic Dream," *Wall Street Journal*, February 12, 2018, https://www.wsj.com/articles/kim-yo-jongs-shattered-olympic-dream-1518478897.

[70] Chung Min Lee and Kathryn Botto, *President Moon Jae-in and the Politics of Inter-Korean Détente* (Washington, D.C.: Carnegie Endowment for International Peace, 2018). According to an opinion poll released by KBS in May 2018, Moon garnered an 83% approval rating following his April summit meeting with Kim Jong-un.

[71] Hyonhee Shin, "South Korea President Says Trump Deserves Nobel Peace Prize," Reuters, April 30, 2018, https://www.reuters.com/article/us-northkorea-southkorea-trump/south-korea-president-says-trump-deserves-nobel-peace-prize-idUSKBN1I10OD.

the same off the peninsula).⁷² The Biden administration's commitment to reassuring allies had the ironic effect of reinforcing Trump policies that many in the administration had once criticized. For Moon, however, the U.S. endorsement of continued high-level engagement of the North was a political victory—and ultimately one that cost the White House relatively little since North Korea was unlikely to respond to the U.S. overture for talks without the ardent suitor that Trump had been leading the U.S. negotiations.

Ready for Covid-19 but Not U.S.-China Strategic Competition

The Covid-19 pandemic added to Moon's luster, at least initially. South Korea had stumbled in managing the MERS outbreak in 2018 and undertook major structural reforms to avoid a repeat of the same poor crisis response well before Covid-19 struck. When Covid-19 was first detected in Wuhan, the Korean government responded immediately with widespread testing and contact tracing; close coordination across government, medical professions, and civil society; and quick establishment of screening clinics to inhibit transmission at healthcare institutions. Korean citizens, already aware of the disease risk because of MERS, responded positively to mandates for social distancing and use of face masks.⁷³ Koreans' reliance on scientific experts and disdain for anti-vaccination movements contrasted favorably with the U.S. and Japanese situations, while the South Korean government's open debate and reflection after MERS demonstrated that democracies deliver good governance—an important contrast to Beijing's closed and hyper-defensive response to the pandemic.⁷⁴

Yet pride cometh before the fall. After leading in the Covid-19 battle, South Korea fell even further behind Japan in mass vaccinations. In part this was complacency after initial success at containing the virus, and in part this was the result of bureaucratic intransigence and economic nationalism. The country was slow to approve AstraZeneca and insisted on domestic

---

⁷² Kim Tong-Hyung, "Moon Urges Biden to Learn from Trump's N. Korea Diplomacy," Associated Press, January 18, 2021, https://apnews.com/article/donald-trump-north-korea-seoul-nuclear-weapons-south-korea-1dc2f8c8df7c7916baccb167cf3cc687.

⁷³ Victor Cha, "A Timeline of South Korea's Response to COVID-19," CSIS, March 27, 2020, https://www.csis.org/analysis/timeline-south-koreas-response-covid-19; June-Ho Kim et al., "Emerging COVID-19 success story: South Korea learned the lessons of MERS," Our World in Data, Exemplars in Global Health, March 5, 2021, https://ourworldindata.org/covid-exemplar-south-korea; and Seulki Lee, Jungwon Yeo, and Chongmin Na, "Learning from the Past: Distributed Cognition and Crisis Management Capabilities for Tackling COVID-19," *American Review of Public Administration* 50, no. 6–7 (2020): 729–35.

⁷⁴ Min-Hyu Kim et al., "Assessing the South Korean Model of Emergency Management during the COVID-19 Pandemic," *Asian Studies Review* 44, no. 4 (2020): 567–78. In terms of responsiveness, the government coordinated the collective reaction of public health experts, thereby giving it more flexibility and discretion in the field to trace contacts via digital technologies.

production opportunities for the Korean pharmaceutical industry.[75] Moon's governing Democratic Party was punished for this combination of hubris and mismanagement in two critical mayoral races won by the conservative opposition. Meanwhile, the president's own support plummeted to 32%—thrusting him into the lame duck status he had thus far avoided as a term-limited leader with less than a year left in office.[76] The struggling Korean economy did not help, shrinking by 1% in 2020, the first economic contraction in more than two decades. A year earlier Moon's party had won a historic three-fifths majority in the National Assembly and the conservatives were divided and desperately trying to rebrand themselves with the oddly Marxist-sounding name "People Power Party." Looking ahead to presidential elections in 2022, the odds suddenly seem evenly divided between progressives and conservatives.

In this context, the politics of Covid-19 may shake Korean politics to the point that stirrings about China lead to closer alignment with Washington and perhaps even Tokyo than once seemed likely. Scholars and journalists are increasingly pointing to China's wolf-warrior diplomacy during Covid-19 as the tipping point in Korean strategic thinking on China that the THAAD boycott and Hong Kong crackdown were not.[77] Political criticism of Moon's avoidance of confrontation with China (what one influential Korean scholar anonymously calls "see no evil, hear no evil, speak no evil") has increased in parallel with criticism of his handling of vaccine distribution.

The increasing alignment of leading democracies with the Biden administration on China—particularly in Europe and Canada—has also left South Korea as the regional outlier rather than Japan.[78] And Beijing's nationalistic claims of proprietary ownership in international organizations over Korean staples like kimchi have further inflamed the popular mood.[79] With 80% of the public viewing China as a national security threat and 60% as an economic threat, according to a poll in 2021, the conservatives in South

---

[75] William Gallo, "After Initially Leading World in COVID-19 Battle, Why Is South Korea Among Last Developed Nations to Start Mass Vaccinations?" Voice of America, February 24, 2021, https://www.voanews.com/covid-19-pandemic/after-initially-leading-world-covid-19-battle-why-south-korea-among-last.

[76] Andrew Jeong and Timothy W. Martin, "South Korea's Ruling Party Is Reeling as Conservatives Win Big in Mayoral Polls," *Wall Street Journal*, April 7, 2021, https://www.wsj.com/articles/south-korean-conservatives-are-on-the-rise-a-year-before-presidential-election-11617782132.

[77] Kim Dong-ho, "Getting Over China's Influence," *Korea Joongang Daily*, December 20, 2020, https://koreajoongangdaily.joins.com/2020/12/20/opinion/columns/trade-sanctions-retribution-competitiveness/20201220194100455.html.

[78] Yang Moo-jin, "Balancing Diplomacy, Strategic Ambiguity," *Korea Times*, April 28, 2021, https://www.koreatimes.co.kr/www/opinion/2021/07/790_307938.html.

[79] William Gallo, "In South Korea, Antagonism toward China Is Growing," Voice of America, April 20, 2021, https://www.voanews.com/east-asia-pacific/south-korea-antagonism-toward-china-growing.

Korea ramped up calls for closer alignment against China going into the presidential election in 2022.[80]

This was the context for Moon's unexpected inclusion in the joint statement with Biden in May 2021 that the security of Taiwan was important to South Korea.[81] Like Japan, South Korea has begun shifting high-technology supply chains to the United States. Samsung and other companies, for example, agreed in the 2021 Moon-Biden summit to invest over $50 billion in semiconductor, battery, and AI-related production in the United States.[82] While South Korea did not join Japan or Australia in openly banning Huawei and other Chinese firms from the 5G market, that is becoming the de facto stance of the government.

Whereas Japan's strategy for China was well established and continued through the shocks of Trump and Covid-19, South Korea's China strategy remained a secondary consideration after North Korea. Moon weathered the Trump shock well in that regard, but strategic ambiguity on China has proved increasingly untenable, particularly as Covid-19 has shaken the progressive camp's political standing.

Taiwan: Seeking Resilience without Catastrophe

Xi Jinping and Taiwan's Wake-Up Call

In July 2021, Xi Jinping's one-hundredth anniversary statement on Taiwan (and his pledge to actualize "China's complete reunification") revealed to the world what Taipei has been fearing for years—a growing Chinese confidence that coercion against Taiwan can work.[83] Election interference and constant gray-zone coercion are the new normal for Taipei, beginning with social media attacks on Democratic Progressive Party (DPP) candidate Tsai Ing-wen during the 2020 presidential election in Taiwan, followed in short order by expanded social media attacks designed to undermine Taiwanese citizens'

---

[80] Suh Young Park and Karl Friedhoff, "Ahead of Biden-Moon Summit, South Koreans and Americans Align on China and North Korea," Chicago Council on Global Affairs, May 19, 2021.

[81] The U.S.-ROK joint statement said that "President Biden and President Moon emphasize the importance of preserving peace and stability in the Taiwan Strait." See "U.S.-ROK Leaders' Joint Statement."

[82] Charlie Campbell, "Here's What to Know about the Summit between Joe Biden and Moon Jae-in," *Time*, May 19, 2021, https://time.com/6049665/biden-moon-summit; and Choi Si-young, "Moon, Biden Agree to Bolster Chip Alliance, Lift Missile Ban," *Korea Herald*, May 23, 2021, http://www.koreaherald.com/view.php?ud=20210523000193.

[83] "Full Text of Xi Jinping's Speech on the CCP's 100th Anniversary," July 1, 2021, available at https://asia.nikkei.com/Politics/Full-text-of-Xi-Jinping-s-speech-on-the-CCP-s-100th-anniversary.

faith in democracy writ large.[84] In 2021 the People's Liberation Army (PLA) expanded its incursions across the line of demarcation in the Taiwan Strait with major flights of fighters and bombers toward and around the island, heralded with belligerent YouTube propaganda threats against Taiwan.[85] The repression of Hong Kong's autonomy helped Tsai crush her KMT opponent and further consolidated the view of people on Taiwan that unification with the mainland is unacceptable—at least under the current CCP.[86] Even the KMT, in a desperate bid to recover from the damning example of Beijing's crackdown in Hong Kong, proposed formal diplomatic relations with the United States in a failed gamble to recover before the 2020 election.[87] Taiwan's economic isolation, dependence on Chinese economic growth, and sluggish economic performance might have doomed Tsai and her party were security and democratic values not so prominently at the top of voters' concerns because of Xi.[88]

To be clear, some of the old divisions in Taiwan remain over China. Polls, for example, do not show the same level of distrust of China in Taiwan that one finds in Japan or South Korea. The "green" camp around Tsai's DPP are most distrustful of Beijing, but within the "blue" camp of the KMT there is still residual interest in stronger economic ties with the mainland. The difference from several years ago is the pronounced reaction against unification with the same China that is bullying Taiwan militarily and diplomatically and removing civil liberties from Hong Kong. By 2021, surveys conducted by the

---

[84] "PRC Interference in Taiwan's Elections," CSIS, Washington, D.C., February 11, 2020, https://www.csis.org/events/prc-interference-taiwans-elections; and Joshua Kurlantzick, "How China Is Interfering in Taiwan's Election," Council on Foreign Relations, November 7, 2019, https://www.cfr.org/in-brief/how-china-interfering-taiwans-election.

[85] Ryan Pickrell, "China and Taiwan Are Waging War Online with These Dueling Military Propaganda Videos," Business Insider, February 4, 2019, https://www.businessinsider.com/china-taiwan-wage-war-online-with-dueling-military-propaganda-videos-2019-2.

[86] Lindsay Maizland, "Why China-Taiwan Relations Are So Tense," Council on Foreign Relations, May 10, 2021, https://www.cfr.org/backgrounder/china-taiwan-relations-tension-us-policy; Dennis V. Hickey, "More and More Taiwanese Favor Independence—and Think the U.S. Would Help Fight for It," Diplomat, December 3, 2020, https://thediplomat.com/2020/12/more-and-more-taiwanese-favor-independence-and-think-the-us-would-help-fight-for-it; and Kat Devlin and Christine Huang, "In Taiwan, Views of Mainland China Mostly Negative," Pew Research Center, May 12, 2020, https://www.pewresearch.org/global/2020/05/12/in-taiwan-views-of-mainland-china-mostly-negative.

[87] Nick Aspinwall, "KMT Pushes for Formal U.S.-Taiwan Ties in Course Change for Beijing-Friendly Party," Diplomat, October 9, 2020, https://thediplomat.com/2020/10/kmt-pushes-for-formal-us-taiwan-ties-in-course-change-for-beijing-friendly-party.

[88] Timothy Rich and Madelynn Einhorn, "Taiwanese Public Opinion on China and Cross-Strait Relations: The Challenges for 2021," Jamestown Foundation, China Brief, February 4, 2021, https://jamestown.org/program/taiwanese-public-opinion-on-china-and-cross-strait-relations-the-challenges-for-2021; and Mainland Affairs Council of the Republic of China, "Public's View on Current Cross-Strait Relations," March 25, 2021, https://www.mac.gov.tw/en/cp.aspx?n=88AA6C56524EEE0F.

Mainland Affairs Council found that over 90% of the public disapproved of Beijing's proposed "one country, two systems."[89]

The challenge for Tsai has been that the continuing polarization in Taiwan's politics has hampered closer alignment with the two most powerful democracies Taiwan needs for its security and economic independence from the mainland—the United States and Japan. When Tsai tried to improve relations with Japan in 2018 by removing a ban on food imports from Fukushima Prefecture, where the 2011 nuclear crisis occurred, the Legislative Yuan boxed her into holding a national referendum. After the question on the referendum was manipulated to ask whether citizens favored continuing the ban on "nuclear food" from Japan, it passed by a wide margin, putting a major crimp in Tsai's efforts to strengthen ties with an otherwise deeply sympathetic Japanese people.[90] Tsai later was punished by the KMT for removing a ban on U.S. pork and beef imports in 2020, even though the ban was based on unscientific claims surrounding the dangers of ractopamine.[91] With major political capital being needed to push forward trade talks with the United States and eventual participation in the TPP to wean Taiwan's economy from dependence on China, Tsai was using all her chips in a highly contested domestic political environment. Unlike Japan, which surged to replace the United States' retreat from the TPP and regional economic rulemaking, Taiwan was handicapped by domestic polarization.

Was Taiwan Trump's Pawn?

In this context, Trump emerged as the best and worst of Taipei's hopes for U.S. leadership. On the one hand, he surrounded himself with the most hawkish elements of former Republican administrations who convinced him to receive an unprecedented congratulatory call from Tsai after his election.[92] On the other hand, Trump's disruptive and transactional approach to alliances and his initial affinity for Xi led many Taiwanese commentators to warn that Taiwan could easily become a "pawn" in Trump's bid for a big economic

---

[89] Mainland Affairs Council of the Republic of China, "Public's View on Current Cross-Strait Relations."

[90] Ko Shu-Ling, "Taiwan Ban on Japanese Food Looks Set to Stay," *Japan Times*, December 8, 2020, https://www.japantimes.co.jp/news/2020/12/08/asia-pacific/taiwan-ban-japanese-food.

[91] Sean Lin, "Taiwan to Ease Rules on U.S. Pork, Beef," *Taipei Times*, August 29, 2020, https://www.taipeitimes.com/News/front/archives/2020/08/29/2003742461.

[92] Damian Paletta, Carol E. Lee, and Andrew Browne, "Trump Spoke with Taiwan President in Break With Decades of U.S. Policy," *Wall Street Journal*, December 2, 2016, https://www.wsj.com/articles/donald-trump-spoke-with-taiwan-president-tsai-ing-wen-1480718423.

breakthrough with Beijing.[93] In the end, Xi's own coercive actions so alarmed Washington and the region that Taiwan never became such a "pawn" in a Sino-U.S. rapprochement. Meanwhile, the Trump national security establishment ensured increased arms sales to Taiwan and strengthened defense cooperation with Japan that reinforced Taiwan's own security.[94]

As a result, 2020 surveys by CSIS showed that half of Taiwanese strategic experts thought that Trump would be better for Taiwan in dealing with China than Biden, while surveys in Taiwan showed a majority of the general public wanted Trump to win.[95] As with Japan and South Korea, the incoming Biden administration followed the lead of veteran Asia strategist and now senior coordinator for the Indo-Pacific on the NSC staff, Kurt Campbell, and sent strong signals of continuity on Taiwan policy. The administration dispatched Biden's close friend former senator Chris Dodd and a senior delegation to Taipei in June 2021 to meet personally with Tsai and pledge U.S. support.[96] When Biden then convinced the leaders of Japan, South Korea, and the European Union to flag support for Taiwan in their joint statements, the Taiwanese press recognized that their earlier misgivings about the return of a Democratic administration in Washington were misplaced.[97]

A Democracy Delivers: Taiwan and Covid-19

The Covid-19 pandemic had considerably less bearing on Taiwanese views of China than it did on Japanese and Korean views. Before the wolf-warrior diplomacy of Covid-19, Taiwan was already under relentless pressure from the mainland. But while Covid-19 did not accelerate de-alignment vis-à-vis Beijing, it contributed to Taiwan's own standing internationally

---

[93] J.R. Wu and Jess Macy Yu, "Taiwan Doesn't Want to Become a Pawn between the U.S. and China," *Time*, March 30, 2017, https://time.com/4706354/taiwan-china-us-trump-xi; and Nahal Toosi and Lara Seligman, "Trump Seizes a New Cudgel to Bash China: Taiwan," *Politico*, May 21, 2020, https://www.politico.com/news/2020/05/21/trump-cudgel-china-taiwan-274160.

[94] "Factbox: U.S. Arms Sales to Taiwan in Past Decade," Reuters, June 6, 2019, https://www.reuters.com/article/us-usa-taiwan-china-defence-factbox/factbox-u-s-arms-sales-to-taiwan-in-past-decade-idUSKCN1T717N.

[95] CSIS, "Mapping the Future of U.S. China Policy"; Matthew Smith, "Who Do People in Asia-Pacific Want to Win the U.S. Presidential Election?" YouGov America, October 15, 2020, https://today.yougov.com/topics/politics/articles-reports/2020/10/15/who-do-people-asia-pacific-want-win-us-presidentia; and Ja Ian Chong, "Support for Trump in Hong Kong and Taiwan Is Unsurprising (but Misguided)," *Diplomat*, November 17, 2020, https://thediplomat.com/2020/11/support-for-trump-in-hong-kong-and-taiwan-is-unsurprising-but-misguided.

[96] "President Tsai Meets U.S. Senate Delegation," Office of the President (Taiwan), Press Release, June 6, 2021, https://english.president.gov.tw/NEWS/6128.

[97] "U.S.-Japan Joint Leaders' Statement: 'U.S.-Japan Global Partnership for a New Era,'" White House, Press Release, April 16, 2021, https://www.whitehouse.gov/briefing-room/statements-releases/2021/04/16/u-s-japan-joint-leaders-statement-u-s-japan-global-partnership-for-a-new-era; "U.S.-ROK Leaders' Joint Statement"; and "U.S.-EU Summit Statement," White House, Press Release, June 15, 2021, https://www.whitehouse.gov/briefing-room/statements-releases/2021/06/15/u-s-eu-summit-statement.

and thus its alignment with other democracies. Taiwan's performance was as impressive as South Korea's—motivated in Taiwan's case by the struggle to respond to the SARS outbreak in 2003 and structural reforms under an earlier DPP government that were similar to South Korea's reforms.[98] Even before the World Health Organization (WHO) declared a "public health emergency of international concern" on January 30, 2021, Taiwan had already deployed sufficient personal protective equipment and established a presidential-level task force to contain the outbreak.[99] Mask production in Taiwan was so effective that Taipei was able to distribute excess masks in the United States. As Beijing defied international requests for transparency on the outbreak in Wuhan and blocked Taiwan's participation in the WHO-linked World Health Assembly, Taiwan stood as a paragon of transparency, democracy, and effective crisis management. International opinion pages took note.[100] The accelerated reshoring of supply chains away from China also highlighted the centrality of Taiwan Semiconductor Manufacturing Company to the democracy's competitiveness in AI.[101] The U.S. Congress passed bipartisan legislation enhancing support for Taiwan in the Taipei Act of 2020.[102] In Japan, Abe sent over one million doses of Covid-19 vaccines to Taipei at a time when Japan itself had none to spare and 74% of Japanese said in polls that their country should help with the security of Taiwan. Further, the LDP formed a committee to design closer security ties with Taipei.[103] While all these developments had their origin in China's growing revisionism,

---

[98] Shih-Chung Chen, "Taiwan's Experience in Fighting COVID-19," *Natural Immunology* 22 (2021): 393–94, https://doi.org/10.1038/s41590-021-00908-2.

[99] Wayne Soon, "From SARS to COVID-19: Rethinking Global Health Lessons from Taiwan," *East Asian Science, Technology and Society: An International Journal* 14, no. 4 (2020): 647–55.

[100] "Taiwan's Coronavirus Example," *Wall Street Journal*, April 27, 2020, https://www.wsj.com/articles/taiwans-coronavirus-example-11588026299.

[101] Frank Sun, "How Did TSMC Become Taiwan's Silicon Shield?" *News Lens*, August 7, 2020, https://international.thenewslens.com/article/138922; Debby Wu, "TSMC to Spend $100 Billion Over Three Years to Grow Capacity," Bloomberg, March 31, 2021, https://www.bloomberg.com/news/articles/2021-04-01/tsmc-to-invest-100-billion-over-three-years-to-grow-capacity; and "TSMC Says Has Begun Construction at Its Arizona Chip Factory Site," Reuters, June 1, 2021, https://www.reuters.com/technology/tsmc-says-construction-has-started-arizona-chip-factory-2021-06-01.

[102] "MOFA Thanks U.S. Congress for Legislation Supporting Taiwan," Taiwan Today, December 23, 2020, https://taiwantoday.tw/news.php?unit=2,6,10,15,18&post=191383; and "Pelosi Statement on Passage of TAIPEI Act," Nancy Pelosi Speaker of the House, Press Release, March 4, 2020, https://www.speaker.gov/newsroom/3420-1.

[103] Yusuke Oshima, "The Inside Story of Japan's Donation of 1.24 Million Vaccine Doses to Taiwan," Japan Forward, June 7, 2021, https://japan-forward.com/the-inside-story-of-japans-donation-of-1-24-million-vaccine-doses-to-taiwan; Tetsuo Kotani, "The New Taiwan Clause: Taiwan and the Security of Japan," Japan Institute of International Affairs, June 1, 2021, https://www.jiia.or.jp/en/strategic_comment/2021/06/2021-01.html; and Takuya Mizorogi, "In Support of Taiwan, Japan's Ruling Party Buries Old Rivalries," *Nikkei Asia*, March 5, 2021, https://asia.nikkei.com/Politics/International-relations/In-support-of-Taiwan-Japan-s-ruling-party-buries-old-rivalries.

Taiwan's courageous stand on Covid-19 accelerated the alignment of major democracies toward Taipei at Beijing's expense.

But Is Taiwan Ready for More Coercion?

However, one current that has consistently undermined U.S. support for Taiwan over the past two decades has been Taipei's unwillingness to increase defense spending and focus on the right capabilities to deter Chinese aggression and survive if deterrence fails. From a U.S. political perspective, it is harder to justify accepting more risk for the U.S. military if the people in Taiwan are not willing to do more in their own defense. Tsai's relatively strong political standing and growing public alarm at Beijing's coercion have changed that dynamic somewhat in recent years. Taiwan's Overall Defense Concept and shift toward asymmetrical capabilities were seen in Washington as a step in the right direction.[104] National disaster drills and the procurement of Harpoon anti-ship missiles and Patriot anti-aircraft missiles in recent years also suggest that Taipei is preparing a hedgehog strategy to bristle with weapons systems that would put PLA assets at risk more effectively than the expensive plans for indigenous submarine forces that animated Taiwan's defense establishment in prior years. But the pace of preparation still pales in comparison with the PLA military buildup and the operational tempo around Taiwan.

Tsai's government also suffered from some of the same performance legitimacy problems as Japan and South Korea during the vaccine distribution phase. Perhaps complacent after a stellar initial response—and undercut by a social-media anti-vaccine movement more virulent than Japan's (with polls showing that 40% resisted vaccination in Taiwan)—Taipei waited too long to negotiate terms for vaccines. Consequently, it was only able to secure commitments of 20 million doses by the summer of 2021, which was just short of what was required.[105] Although Taiwan's economy did much better than Japan's and South Korea's in navigating the Covid-19 shock because of expanding demand for semiconductors, the pandemic has exacerbated income inequality within Taiwan. Tsai paid some cost in popular support and was certainly helped by the fact that she had four years before the next presidential election. Nonetheless, her foreign policy strategy continues to

---

[104] Michael J. Green, Richard C. Bush, and Bonnie S. Glaser, "Toward a Stronger U.S.-Taiwan relationship," CSIS, 54–55, October 2020, https://csis-website-prod.s3.amazonaws.com/s3fs-public/publication/201021_Glaser_TaskForce_Toward_A_Stronger_USTaiwan_Relationship_0.pdf.

[105] Michael Zennie and Gladys Tsai, "How a False Sense of Security, and a Little Secret Tea, Broke Down Taiwan's COVID-19 Defenses," *Time*, May 21, 2021, https://time.com/6050316/taiwan-covid-19-outbreak-tea.

resonate with a majority of the Taiwan public, which also wants to see greater strategic (if unofficial) alignment with the United States and Japan.

Conclusion

It should not be surprising that despite the turbulence of the Trump presidency and the Covid-19 pandemic, U.S. alliances and security relationships with the democracies in Northeast Asia have grown stronger amid China's growing assertiveness. Yet turbulence also serves as a stress test, and the pandemic spotlighted weaknesses within Japan, South Korea, and Taiwan that could matter in a security crisis in the region. Though broadly unified around the China challenge and the importance of the U.S.-Japan alliance, Japan revealed continued weaknesses in crisis management and defense spending (highlighted, interestingly, by all three candidates to replace Suga in September 2021). South Korea performed better in terms of crisis management, but revealed a lack of national focus on the China challenge that could complicate a U.S.-ROK alliance viewed by the vast majority of Koreans as essential for national survival. In Taipei, Tsai capitalized on China's repression of Hong Kong and pressure on Taiwan to strengthen national focus, but polarization at home hindered the implementation of her strategy. Yet even as these exogenous shocks pulsed through the institutions in all three places in different ways, one common experience—from Hokkaido to Kaohsiung—was an awakening to the importance of democratic values and the U.S.-led neoliberal order.

This is also what animated Biden's 2020 bid for the presidency and his administration's pledge to return to stable leadership in the Indo-Pacific. The prospects for that goal were diminished somewhat by the continuing lack of a U.S. economic framework for the region, but personal engagement by Biden with Suga and Moon (and his team with Tsai) raised expectations that the United States was now on a more reliable heading. The fact that the White House listened to Tokyo, Taipei, and Seoul and retained aspects of the previous administration's free and open Indo-Pacific strategy and North Korea diplomacy was reassuring to all three leaders. While hyper-partisanship, anti-Asian racism, and vaccine hesitancy in the United States all made the news in Northeast Asia, these pale in comparison with the dangerous trends in China and North Korea. The Biden administration appeared poised to bring U.S. alliances and partnerships through the Covid-19 pandemic and Chinese coercion in stronger shape.

In the summer of 2021, however, a new disruption emerged. The U.S. withdrawal from Afghanistan—though premised in part on the goal of shifting attention and resources toward the Indo-Pacific—sent shockwaves through U.S. alliances in the region. Questions were raised by prominent political leaders and editorial pages about the United States' commitment, competence, and staying power. In fact, surveys in 2020 showed the highest support for defending Japan, South Korea, and Taiwan on record in the United States (and an inverse desire by the American people to get out of Afghanistan), but echoes of the retreat from the Vietnam War proved difficult to silence.[106] This shock to alliances could prove as serious as Covid-19 and should convince the administration to double down on its commitment to all three democracies and the principles of a free and open Indo-Pacific.

This will require a combination of humility and resolve. Washington must do more to listen to allies' and partners' expectations on policy issues ranging from technology decoupling to the democracy summits planned by the White House, which remain heavily transatlantic in implementation and character. In addition to listening better, the administration will need to produce some kind of economic vision for the region to compensate for the vacuum left with the retreat from the TPP. A regional digital or environmental goods trade agreement might be the right start. And since U.S. allies and partners can do the math and see the PLA's growing power projection and nuclear modernization, the administration will have to move aggressively with allies in Congress to implement the increased resources promised in the Pacific Deterrence Initiative. At the same time, the administration must raise the bar of expectations on Japan, South Korea, and Taiwan (especially Japan and Taiwan) with respect to investments in deterrence capabilities for their own forces. This combination of humility and rising expectations may seem like a contradiction, but the essence of good statecraft is managing such contradictions.

Ultimately, the turbulence of the past few years has demonstrated both the wisdom and the resilience of the alliance-centered postwar system that the United States constructed in Asia. But more turbulence lies ahead, whether from China, pandemics, climate change, North Korea, or populism and hyper-nationalism at home. The alliance system is not one that will weatherproof itself without vision and effort from Washington.

---

[106] CSIS, "Mapping the Future of U.S. China Policy." See, for example, Junnosuke Kobara, "Chaotic Afghan Exit Compels Japan to Rethink Reliance on U.S. Security," *Nikkei Asia*, August 20, 2021, https://asia.nikkei.com/Politics/International-relations/Afghanistan-turmoil/Chaotic-Afghan-exit-compels-Japan-to-rethink-reliance-on-US-security.

EXECUTIVE SUMMARY

This chapter assesses Russia's response to the challenges brought on by U.S.-China competition, deglobalization, and the Covid-19 pandemic.

MAIN ARGUMENT

U.S.-China competition has not changed Russia's foreign policy trajectory during the past decade. Instead, the Russian leadership continues to deepen cooperation with Beijing and push back against Washington. Russia has provided China with strategic support but lacks similar capacity to assist technologically or economically in the Sino-U.S. trade war. Challenges to globalization have only marginally influenced Russia's capacity to generate national power due to its limited role in the global economy, which is concentrated in a few sectors such as energy and arms. Finally, the Covid-19 pandemic has impeded efforts to improve demographic trends and initially threatened the Putin regime's legitimacy. The Kremlin, however, has used measures to control the pandemic as an opportunity to consolidate power by pushing through constitutional amendments and cracking down on political opposition.

POLICY IMPLICATIONS

- Although Russia cannot be expected to support the U.S. in its competition with China, Russian support for China has clear limits. Moscow is not ready to endorse Beijing's territorial claims or bid for regional hegemony in East Asia. Russia has been accommodating of China's growing economic and political influence in Central Asia, but Moscow attempts to maintain the upper hand in the security realm. Thus, the prospect of a revisionist Sino-Russian alliance directed against the U.S. and its allies is unlikely.

- Russia will attempt to capitalize on the U.S. preoccupation with China and improve its position globally—in particular in the post-Soviet neighborhood, Europe, and the Middle East.

- Whereas deglobalization has not significantly affected Russia, climate change and international efforts to reduce carbon emissions pose serious challenges to the political-economic model built around Vladimir Putin.

Russia

Russian Foreign Policy in a Time of Rising U.S.-China Competition

Marcin Kaczmarski

The crisis of U.S. leadership and the onset of Sino-U.S. rivalry have generated contradictory assessments in Russia. On the one hand, they have been hailed as evidence of the emergence of a multipolar world order, the creation of which has been Russia's long-term goal in the post–Cold War period. On the other hand, the Russian elite recognizes the worsening of the international situation and the ongoing instability of international politics, putting the blame on the United States' attempt to maintain primacy. Moscow has continued to position itself as a challenger to Washington and has intensified cooperation with Beijing. The U.S.-China rivalry has improved Russia's position in global politics and, coupled with the weakening of U.S. leadership, broadened Russia's room for maneuver in both its vicinity and more distant regions.

Yet this relative success in foreign policy has been accompanied by mounting domestic challenges. Whereas the threats to globalization have affected the Russian economy only to a limited extent, the Covid-19 pandemic has exerted a heavy toll on Russia. All positive demographic trends in recent years have been reversed. While the response to the pandemic facilitated a crackdown on domestic political opposition, the authorities' failure to tackle the public health crisis poses a long-term challenge to the ruling regime.

This chapter is divided into five sections. The first provides background on Russia's foreign policy, its key aims, and its dominant features. The second section focuses on developments in the U.S.-China competition and their significance for Russia's ongoing rivalry with the United States and its closer cooperation with China. The third section discusses the implications of the

---

Marcin Kaczmarski is a Lecturer in Security Studies in the School of Social and Political Sciences at the University of Glasgow. He can be reached at <marcin.kaczmarski@glasgow.ac.uk>.

challenges to globalization and argues that, given Russia's limited place in the global economy, deglobalization has mattered relatively little to its markets. The subsequent section analyzes the impact of the Covid-19 pandemic, which may have long-term effects that undermine the Putin regime's legitimacy and harm Russian demographics for years to come. The final section assesses the implications of these trends for the United States and U.S.-Russia relations.

The Drivers of Russian Foreign Policy

The overarching trajectory of Russia's foreign policy began to take its current shape in the mid-2000s during Vladimir Putin's second presidential term. Material resurgence, the strengthening of the state, and domestic political consolidation fueled Russia's assertiveness in international politics. These processes culminated in Putin's provocative 2007 Munich speech about U.S. dominance in world affairs and the 2008 war with Georgia. The period of the so-called tandemocracy (2008–12) followed, with Putin becoming prime minister and Dmitri Medvedev serving as president, and led to a partial and temporary warming in relations with the West, even though Russia did not alter its foreign policy course in any fundamental manner. This period also marked Russia's deepening cooperation with a rising China. Putin's return to the presidency in 2012 initiated a conservative-nationalist turn in domestic politics, which was reflected in Russia's foreign policy. Moscow increasingly positioned itself as not only a geopolitical but also a normative challenger to the West. The annexation of Crimea in 2014, followed by the military intervention in Syria in 2015, initiated a new phase in Russian foreign policy. Interference in the U.S. presidential election the subsequent year signaled the growing sophistication of Russia's sharp-power instruments. In recent years, Moscow has enlarged its presence in regions such as sub-Saharan Africa and emerged as a key protagonist in the Arctic.

Since Putin's return to the presidency, Russia's foreign policy has become increasingly entangled in domestic politics. Regime survival considerations have shaped Moscow's policy toward the West as well as facilitated an embrace of a rising China. The search for great-power status has helped the Putin regime maintain domestic legitimacy, which was particularly visible during the annexation of Crimea. Parochial interests of powerful individuals close to the Kremlin and state-owned enterprises (SOEs) have weighed in on the policy implementation process. Although Putin has remained the ultimate decision-maker, he often charts broad directions and leaves decisions about concrete policy actions to other actors. Domestic politics constitute both an asset and a liability for Russian foreign policy. The absence of domestic opposition provides stability that catalyzes the decision-making process and increases room for maneuverability in international forums. At the same time, certain foreign policy activities that provoke rivals are driven by a willingness to prioritize popularity at home and mobilize support for the regime. As a consequence, Russia's post-2012 foreign policy has been shaped by a combination of strategic, realpolitik considerations (offensive and defensive), the search for great-power status, and domestic political dynamics.

Whereas the concrete form of Russia's interests has been malleable, depending on specific circumstances, it is possible to reconstruct Moscow's general interests in international politics. In its immediate neighborhood, Russia aims at maintaining political primacy and preventing other powers from establishing a security presence in its vicinity. In Europe, Russia has continuously aimed at limiting the U.S. presence and eroding transatlantic ties. Moscow views bilateral relations with leading European states as the best way to secure its influence. Globally, Russia is challenging U.S. primacy by opting for a multipolar international order in which Moscow would retain its strategic autonomy and participate in global decision-making as a key player.

In terms of national security, the Kremlin's perception of external threats remains tightly linked to domestic stability and its challenges. The United States is the main focus of the regime's feeling of insecurity, not only internationally but also domestically. The Russian elite perceives Washington as responsible for undermining the stability of the international system, and U.S. power projection continues to be interpreted as a means for the United States to effect regime change. To address this challenge, Moscow is prepared to use a number of instruments, ranging from nuclear brinkmanship to election interference.

The assessment of Russia's national power has been a constant challenge for scholars and observers. Looked at from a purely material perspective, Russia has been in long-term decline and has been unable to reverse this course. Despite attempts to modernize its economy, Russia still lags economically far behind the United States, China, and the European Union. During this same period, however, Russia has not only re-emerged as a relevant global player but also demonstrated substantial resilience to external shocks. This capacity to generate national power is the function of Russia's ability to translate economic potential into instruments of power, such as military and sharp-power resources (i.e., disinformation and cyberwarfare potential). Revenue from natural resources constitutes the country's economic foundation. This allows the Putin regime to maintain the social contract and thus domestic political stability, retain the support of the elites by perpetuating patron-client networks, fund foreign policy activities, and modernize the armed forces.[1] Instruments of both hard and sharp power have gained relevance in the last couple of years, becoming key for Russia's power projection. Moreover, Russian soft power has influenced populist and right-wing movements in Europe and beyond.[2]

Following Putin's re-election in 2018, new signs of social discontent began to emerge. The positive effect of the annexation of Crimea died down, and growing popular frustrations were increasingly related to worsening socioeconomic conditions. The decreased standard of living was due to a lack of substantial economic growth and a conservative fiscal policy. As a result, the Kremlin faced growing discontent, ranging from protests after the 2019 local elections in Moscow to the arrest and trial of a popular governor who represented a systemic opposition party in Khabarovsk Krai in the Russian Far East.[3] Attempting to respond to these challenges, the Kremlin resorted to strengthening the technocratic element of its governance process and promoting a new generation of elites. At the same time, the Russian leadership attempted to boost the regime's legitimacy by mobilizing supporters under anti-American and anti-liberal banners.

Yet decarbonization of the world economy, driven by the necessity to counter climate change, has emerged as the most serious long-term challenge for Russia's generation of national power. The European Green Deal threatens to close the EU market to Russian oil and gas in the long term and increases the importance of energy markets in Asia, and China in particular. Natural resources (and especially hydrocarbons), as noted above, constitute the material foundation of the regime and are the engine of Russia's economy. Even though the share of revenue from natural resources has passed its peak, in the late 2010s they still provided around 25% of GDP, almost 40% of the federal budget, and around 65% of export earnings.[4] The most obvious risk relates to the declining demand for Russian natural resources, first and foremost oil, due both to lower overall demand for oil and to Russia losing out to cheaper producers, such as Saudi Arabia. This would, in turn, lead

---

[1] Kathryn E. Stoner, *Russia Resurrected: Its Power and Purpose in a New Global Order* (New York: Oxford University Press, 2021). This work enumerates the economic basis, human capital, hard-power resources, soft-power resources, and sharp-power resources as the basis of Russia's national power.

[2] Vincent Keating and Katarzyna Kaczmarska, "Conservative Soft Power: Liberal Soft Power Bias and the 'Hidden' Attraction of Russia," *Journal of International Relations and Development* 22, no. 1 (2019): 1–27.

[3] Aimar Ventsel, "The Background to the Protests in the Russian Far East," International Centre for Defence and Security, August 27, 2020, https://icds.ee/en/the-background-to-the-protests-in-the-russian-far-east.

[4] James Henderson and Tatiana Mitrova, "Implications of the Global Energy Transition on Russia," in *The Geopolitics of the Global Energy Transition*, ed. Manfred Hafner and Simone Tagliapietra (Cham: Springer, 2020), 100.

to a drastic decrease in budget revenue that could jeopardize the survival of the regime by undermining its legitimacy among both the elites and the general public.

U.S.-China Competition

The U.S.-China competition has broadened Russia's room to maneuver in international politics. After the annexation of Crimea in 2014, Moscow had to rely on Beijing's support to stave off Western political pressure and economic sanctions. The shift in U.S. policy toward China from engagement toward decoupling and neo-containment opened new possibilities for Moscow.[5] Russia is no longer singled out by the United States as its only rival great power. For the Chinese leadership, the value of the partnership with Russia has risen, especially in the political and military-security dimensions. In the United States, meanwhile, the number of voices calling for a "reverse Kissinger" (i.e., pulling Moscow away from Beijing) has grown steadily,[6] even as the 2017 National Security Strategy identified Russia as a competitor on par with China and the U.S. government aimed to punish Russia for interference in the 2016 presidential election.[7] Similar ideas about the need to re-establish dialogue with Russia to counter China have appeared among U.S. allies.[8] As a result, amid escalating U.S.-China competition, Russia appears to have found itself as a swing power, courted by both Washington and Beijing, an ideal situation from the realpolitik perspective.

This is not, however, how the Russian expert community has assessed the implications of the U.S.-China rivalry. Prior to the conflict over Ukraine, most Russian experts regarded the scenario of Sino-U.S. competition as disadvantageous to Moscow's interests, equal to the potential marginalization

---

[5] Michael Mastanduno, "Partner Politics: Russia, China, and the Challenge of Extending U.S. Hegemony after the Cold War," *Security Studies* 28, no. 3 (2019): 479–504.

[6] See, for instance, an anonymous paper prepared by a former U.S. official, "The Longer Telegram: Toward a New American China Strategy," Atlantic Council, January 28, 2021, https://www.atlanticcouncil.org/content-series/atlantic-council-strategy-paper-series/the-longer-telegram; and Simon Tisdall, "Donald Trump Attempting to Play Nixon's 'China Card' in Reverse," *Guardian*, December 12, 2016, https://www.theguardian.com/us-news/2016/dec/12/donald-trump-us-china-relations-taiwan-nixon.

[7] White House, *National Security Strategy of the United States of America* (Washington, D.C., December 2017), https://trumpwhitehouse.archives.gov/wp-content/uploads/2017/12/NSS-Final-12-18-2017-0905.pdf. On election meddling, see, for example, Nathan Layne, "U.S. Imposes Fresh Russia Sanctions for Election Meddling," Reuters, December 19, 2018, https://www.reuters.com/article/us-usa-russia-sanctions-treasury-idUSKCN1OI27F.

[8] "Emmanuel Macron in His Own Words (English)," *Economist*, November 7, 2019, https://www.economist.com/europe/2019/11/07/emmanuel-macron-in-his-own-words-english; and Matthew Dal Santo, "Yes, to Balance China, Let's Bring Russia in from the Cold," Lowy Institute, Interpreter, July 7, 2020, https://www.lowyinstitute.org/the-interpreter/yes-balance-china-bring-russia-in-from-cold.

that might result from the United States and China setting up an informal G-2. Even though some experts continue to favor equidistance between the two powers,[9] the majority seem to prefer closer ties with China as a way of limiting U.S. influence and advancing a multipolar order.[10] They do not see the rivalry as an opportunity for Russia to maneuver between Washington and Beijing. Instead, the emerging U.S.-China cold war is interpreted as being provoked by the United States, whereas China is regarded as interested in slowing down the pace of confrontation.[11] Russian experts do not see a new bipolarity but rather a shift from unipolarity to multipolarity, in which Russia will maintain its relevance and the threat of marginalization in the bipolar world will fade away. These views may be read as a response to a Kremlin policy that has preferred closer ties with China.[12]

Russia's Grand Strategy

Russia's response to U.S.-China competition has been more complex than realists would predict. Rather than striking a balance between its two most important bilateral relationships, Moscow's actions have further eroded relations with the United States and deepened collaboration with China.

Russia-U.S. relations. U.S.-China competition has emerged at a time of crisis in Russia-U.S. relations.[13] Washington's shifting focus toward the Indo-Pacific generally and East Asia specifically means that Moscow could capitalize on diminished U.S. attention toward Europe, post-Soviet states, or the Middle East. Alternatively, Moscow could soften its anti-Americanism and broaden its room for maneuver in relations with China.

Russia's relationship with the United States has been driven by a combination of defensive and offensive strategic considerations, regime survival, and desire for recognition as a great power. In terms of power politics, Moscow has sought to gain an advantage in particular regions and prevent U.S. encroachment on what it has perceived as its sphere of

---

[9] Dmitri Trenin, for instance, argues that Russia should keep its distance from the conflict between China and the United States. See Dmitri Trenin, "Rossija budet nahodit'sja v sostojanii konfrontacii s Zapadom eše dovol'no dlitel'noe vremja" [Russia Will Be in a State of Confrontation with the West for Quite a Long Time], *Kommersant*, June 3, 2021, https://www.kommersant.ru/doc/4838065.

[10] See, for example, Timofei Bordachev, "Kogda sblizheniye Kitaya i Rossii stanet vygodnym ikh protivnikam?" [When Does Sino-Russian Rapprochement Become Beneficial for Their Rivals?], *Rossiya v globalnoi politike* 20, no. 4 (2021), https://globalaffairs.ru/articles/kogda-sblistanet-vygodnym.

[11] See, for example, Vasily Kashin and Ivan Timofeev, "Amerikano-Kitayskiye otnosheniya: K novoy Kholodnoy Voyne?" [U.S.-China Relations: Towards a New Cold War?], Valdai Discussion Club, 2021, https://ru.valdaiclub.com/files/37874.

[12] Ibid.

[13] Andrei P. Tsygankov, *Russia and America: The Asymmetric Rivalry* (Cambridge: Polity, 2019).

influence.[14] With regard to domestic politics, the Kremlin has perceived U.S. policies as threatening the regime's survival and employed anti-Americanism to prop up domestic legitimacy.[15] Finally, Russia's search for great-power status has been largely driven by the pursuit of Washington's recognition of it as an equal.[16]

Russian expectations are sometimes unclear, and the elite's attitude toward the United States retains a contradictory character. On the one hand, Moscow aims to capitalize on the weakening U.S. global position and the damage done to U.S. leadership during Donald Trump's presidency. On the other hand, there is a deepening perception that the United States is working to undermine, if not directly overthrow, the ruling regime. This "doublethink" of strength and vulnerability, especially vis-à-vis Washington, was identified by scholars as part of the dominant worldview of the Russian elite in the late 2000s.[17]

The U.S.-China competition has not changed Moscow's calculus. First, Washington put Russia on par with China as a "strategic competitor." Even if this rhetoric was challenged by some U.S. leaders, including Trump himself, the majority of the U.S. establishment, and Congress in particular, has recognized Russia's actions as detrimental to U.S. interests and countered with new sanctions on Russia on an almost regular basis. Second, the Kremlin has been interpreting U.S. actions through a prism of domestic politics. The United States' support for political opposition in Russia, including Alexei Navalny, and critique of Russia's continuous crackdowns are interpreted by Moscow not only as interference in domestic politics but as encouragement for a color revolution and regime change.[18] The growing number of sanctions against Russia has only reinforced the Russian elite's belief that the United States is trying to contain and punish Russia for any independent action in international politics in order to maintain U.S. global leadership.[19]

---

[14] Alexander Gabuev, "Russian-U.S. Flashpoints in the Post-Soviet Space: The View from Moscow," Carnegie Endowment for International Peace, February 2018, https://carnegieendowment.org/files/Gabuev_Flashpoints_web.pdf.

[15] Michael A. McFaul, "Putin, Putinism, and the Domestic Determinants of Russian Foreign Policy," *International Security* 45, no. 2 (2020): 95–139.

[16] Deborah Welch Larson and Alexei Shevchenko, "Russia Says No: Power, Status, and Emotions in Foreign Policy," *Communist and Post-Communist Studies* 47, no. 3–4 (2014): 269–79.

[17] Andrew Monaghan, "'An Enemy at the Gates' or 'from Victory to Victory'? Russian Foreign Policy," *International Affairs* 84, no. 4 (2008): 717–33.

[18] Andrew Roth, "Putin Rejects Navalny Poisoning Allegations as 'Falsification,'" *Guardian*, December 17, 2020, https://www.theguardian.com/world/2020/dec/17/putin-questions-navalny-poisoning-covid-crisis-annual-press-conference-russian-president-kremlin.

[19] Andrei P. Tsygankov, "The Revisionist Moment: Russia, Trump, and Global Transition," *Problems of Post-Communism* (2020).

Moscow has demonstrated a lack of interest in mending ties with Washington, unless Washington makes substantial concessions, and instead has chosen to capitalize on U.S.-China competition to maximize its gains. Russia has exercised pressure on the United States in two areas in particular: U.S. domestic politics and Europe. Moscow has continued to interfere in U.S. politics via hacking and disinformation campaigns conducted by state and nonstate actors to sow unrest and deepen existing divisions.[20] Russia also has intensified its military buildup across Europe—from the Arctic through Central Europe and from the Black Sea to the Mediterranean.[21] Moscow consistently has opposed U.S. missile defense plans as well. With the sale of S-400 missile systems to Turkey, it has successfully driven a wedge between Turkey and other NATO members, the United States in particular.[22] Russia has also tried to dissuade Washington from pursuing closer ties with Ukraine, especially to prevent weapon sales. The amassing of Russian troops at the border with Ukraine has been interpreted as both a warning signal to and a test of the Biden administration. On top of this, Russian and U.S. interests have clashed in other regional conflicts, with Moscow and Washington supporting opposing sides in Syria and Libya, and the Kremlin promoting formats that exclude its rival like the Russia-Iran-Turkey triangle.

Whereas in Europe Russia has aimed to capitalize on Washington's diminishing attention and the rifts in transatlantic ties generated by Sino-U.S. competition, in Asia Russia faces different obstacles. U.S. attempts to bring India into a loose anti-China camp, coupled with Sino-Indian tensions, have threatened to weaken Russia's ties with India. While Washington has achieved limited success so far, and some moves have even been counterproductive, such as threats to sanction India for purchasing Russian weapons, India's tilt toward the United States, driven by poor relations with China, poses a challenge to Russia's attempt to keep both India and China in its orbit.

The arrival of the Biden administration, as keen on countering China as the Trump administration, has not changed Russia's approach to the

---

[20] NATO Cooperative Cyber Defence Centre of Excellence, *Russia's Strategy in Cyberspace* (Riga: NATO Strategic Communications Centre of Excellence, 2021), https://stratcomcoe.org/cuploads/pfiles/Nato-Cyber-Report_15-06-2021.pdf; and Joe Walsh, "Here Are Some of the Major Hacks the U.S. Blamed on Russia in the Last Year," *Forbes*, June 1, 2021, https://www.forbes.com/sites/joewalsh/2021/06/01/here-are-some-of-the-major-hacks-the-us-blamed-on-russia-in-the-last-year.

[21] Eugene Rumer, Richard Sokolsky, and Paul Stronski, "Russia in the Arctic—A Critical Examination," Carnegie Endowment for International Peace, March 2021, https://carnegieendowment.org/files/Rumer_et_al_Russia_in_the_Arctic.pdf; and Can Kasapoğlu and Sinan Ülgen, "Russia's Ambitious Military-Geostrategic Posture in the Mediterranean," Carnegie Europe, June 10, 2021, https://carnegieeurope.eu/2021/06/10/russia-s-ambitious-military-geostrategic-posture-in-mediterranean-pub-84685.

[22] Mehmet Yegin, "Turkey between NATO and Russia: The Failed Balance," German Institute for International and Security Affairs, SWP Comment, no. 30, June 2019, https://www.swp-berlin.org/publications/products/comments/2019C30_Yegin.pdf.

United States. The relationship seems to have stabilized at a low level, especially after Putin's summit with President Joe Biden in June 2021.[23] However, the outlook remains uncertain.

Deepening cooperation with China. The deterioration of Russia-U.S. relations has coincided with Russia's closer cooperation with the United States' key rival—China. Russia's post–Cold War relationship with China is marked by two turning points. First, Moscow abandoned its cautious policy vis-à-vis Beijing in the aftermath of the 2008–9 global economic crisis and accelerated cooperation. The Kremlin agreed to construct an oil pipeline to China, and key players in oil and liquefied natural gas (LNG), state-owned Rosneft and privately owned Novatek, concluded long-term, multibillion dollar deals with their Chinese counterparts. Moscow allowed arms trade between the two sides to revive, despite previous unease about reverse engineering. Joint armed forces exercises became a regularity, with naval exercises emerging as the second pillar of the security and defense collaboration. In Central Asia, Russia chose policies that accommodated China's growing influence and implicitly promoted a division of labor, with Beijing dominating the energy sector and Russia the security realm.[24]

The second turning point came with the Ukraine crisis, which accelerated Russia's political and economic dependence on China. In a first, Russia provided China with its most advanced fighter jets and anti-missile systems available for export (the Su-35 and S-400, respectively). Russian state-owned energy corporation Gazprom concluded a long-term contract to deliver natural gas to China and embarked on the construction of the Power of Siberia gas pipeline along a route preferred by Beijing.[25] Moscow also actively sought ways to reconcile its Eurasian Economic Union (EAEU) with the Belt and Road Initiative, which had implicitly challenged Russian influence in the post-Soviet space.[26]

Russia's closer relationship with China has been accompanied by a rise in asymmetry between the two states. An imbalance in material power and the ability to project influence abroad have led many observers to perceive

---

[23] Sharyl Cross et al., "The Biden-Putin Summit: An Expert Analysis," Wilson Center, June 21, 2021, https://www.wilsoncenter.org/article/biden-putin-summit-expert-analysis.

[24] Marcin Kaczmarski, *Russia-China Relations in the Post-Crisis International Order* (New York: Routledge, 2015).

[25] Edward C. Chow, "Russia-China Gas Deal and Redeal," Center for Strategic and International Studies, May 11, 2015, https://www.csis.org/analysis/russia-china-gas-deal-and-redeal.

[26] Marcin Kaczmarski, "Russia-China Relations in Central Asia: Why Is There a Surprising Absence of Rivalry?" *Asan Forum*, August 19, 2019, https://theasanforum.org/russia-china-relations-in-central-asia-why-is-there-a-surprising-absence-of-rivalry.

Russia as China's "junior partner."[27] Some have gone further, reducing Russia's role to that of a "resource appendage." While the latter assessment simplifies the complexity of the relationship, the asymmetry between the two states has become an increasingly relevant factor.

Russia's acquiescence to China and readiness to forge closer ties despite the power asymmetry confirm that Moscow is driven by more than just realist assumptions. Instead, its policy toward Beijing is underpinned by a combination of strategic considerations, domestic politics, and status seeking. The deteriorating relationship with the United States is a factor but cannot alone explain the dynamics of the Sino-Russian relationship. Domestic politics have facilitated Russia's accommodation of China's rising power in a number of ways. The growing similarity in political systems, characterized by a high degree of centralized power and a crackdown on dissent, has shaped similar threat assessments. Because the Putin regime has not been challenged by Beijing, China's rising power and influence, while disadvantageous geopolitically for Russia, have not posed a threat to regime survival. Moreover, in some areas, the privileged position of certain domestic individual and corporate actors has enabled them to promote closer cooperation with China.[28] China for its part has skillfully deferred to Russia's great-power status, making sure to diminish rather than emphasize the asymmetry.[29] Personal chemistry between Putin and Xi Jinping has helped prioritize the relationship for both states' elites, leading to the suppression of skeptical voices.[30]

The shift in U.S. policy toward China has paved the way for Moscow to reassert its position vis-à-vis Beijing and choose how and in what ways to support China in its competition with the United States. Ultimately, Russia has increased cooperation and expanded ties with China, even defending it against criticism from the West.[31] In some areas, Moscow's willingness to

---

[27] Alexander Gabuev and Vita Spivak, "The Asymmetrical Russia-China Axis: An Overview," in "Russia and China: Anatomy of a Partnership," ed. Aldo Ferrari and Eleonora Tafuro Ambrosetti, Italian Institute for International Political Studies, May 3, 2019, 37–60.

[28] Alexander Gabuev, "Russia's Policy towards China: Key Players and the Decision-making Process," *Asan Forum*, March 5, 2015, https://theasanforum.org/russias-policy-towards-china-key-players-and-the-decision-making-process.

[29] Deborah Welch Larson, "An Equal Partnership of Unequals: China's and Russia's New Status Relationship," *International Politics* 57, no. 1 (2020): 790–808.

[30] Bo Xu and William M. Reisinger, "Russia's Energy Diplomacy with China: Personalism and Institutionalism in Its Policy-making Process," *Pacific Review* 32, no. 1 (2019): 1–19.

[31] See, for instance, Putin's comments on the West trying to drive a wedge between Russia and China and defense of Chinese policies. "Full Transcript of Exclusive Putin Interview with NBC News' Keir Simmons," NBC News, June 14, 2021, https://www.nbcnews.com/news/world/transcript-nbc-news-exclusive-interview-russia-s-vladimir-putin-n1270649.

cooperate has been constrained by a lack of capacity, specifically economic and technological.

Since 2017, Russia has sent several signals of its readiness to provide China with strategic, political, and military support. The most significant so far were the participation of the Russian Air Force in joint bomber patrols in the vicinity of Japan and South Korea and the first joint naval patrol in the seas surrounding Japan, which suggested that Moscow was considering expanding its security ties with Beijing.[32] Support for China and a readiness to intimidate U.S. allies in Asia seemed to have prevailed over Moscow's desire to maintain close relations with Tokyo and Seoul. Yet the potentially most far-reaching testimony to Russia's readiness to expand cooperation with China was Putin's October 2019 announcement that Russia had begun assisting China in the construction of an early-warning missile system.[33] Though Putin repeated this declaration several months later, no further details emerged and the Chinese side remained silent.[34] If confirmed, this would not only strengthen Chinese nuclear potential vis-à-vis the United States but also send a clear signal of Moscow's readiness to seriously consider a full-fledged alliance with Beijing.

At the same time, the change in joint military exercises, observed since 2018, has testified to Moscow's growing confidence vis-à-vis Beijing. Joint land and maritime exercises have been supplemented with the Chinese troops' participation in Russia's annual strategic exercises. In 2018, three thousand Chinese troops took part in the Vostok 2018 exercise; in 2019, Russian and Chinese armed forces cooperated within the framework of the Tsentr 2019 exercise; and in 2020, the Southern Military District hosted Chinese troops in the Kavkaz 2020 exercise in the Caucasus.

Of these three exercises, the Vostok exercise sent the most potent signal. Exercises in previous years (2010 and 2014) left a certain ambiguity about the potential targets, with many observers interpreting the drills as a warning to Beijing.[35] The invitation of Chinese troops to take part in the largest military

---

[32] Franz-Stefan Gady, "The Significance of the First Ever China-Russia Strategic Bomber Patrol," *Diplomat*, July 25, 2019, https://thediplomat.com/2019/07/the-significance-of-the-first-ever-china-russia-strategic-bomber-patrol; and Justin McCurry, "Japan and South Korea Scramble Jets to Track Russian and Chinese Bomber Patrol," *Guardian*, December 22, 2020, https://www.theguardian.com/world/2020/dec/22/russia-and-china-fly-joint-bomber-patrol-over-the-pacific. On the naval patrol, see "China, Russia Ships Needle through Japan's Southern Chokepoint," *Nikkei Asia*, October 24, 2021, https://asia.nikkei.com/Politics/International-relations/China-Russia-ships-needle-through-Japan-s-southern-chokepoint.

[33] Vladimir Putin, "Valdai Discussion Club Session," President of Russia, October 3, 2019, http://en.kremlin.ru/events/president/news/61719.

[34] Vladimir Putin, "Vladimir Putin's Annual News Conference," President of Russia, December 19, 2019, http://en.kremlin.ru/events/president/news/62366.

[35] Paul N. Schwartz, "The Military Dimension in Sino-Russian Relations," in *Sino-Russian Relations in the 21st Century*, ed. Jo Inge Bekkevold and Bobo Lo (Basel: Springer International Publishing, 2018), 87–111.

exercise since the 1980s deepened Russian-Chinese ties, on the one hand, and projected Russia's bolstered self-confidence, on the other. During subsequent exercises, the profile of Chinese participation has been significantly lower, "hidden" among other invited guests. In 2020, Russia was unable to secure participation of troops from both China and India, as New Delhi decided to withdraw. Although the official reason was the Covid-19 pandemic, India probably did not want to create the impression of normalizing relations with China after violent clashes along their shared border.[36] Likewise, the pattern of naval exercises changed too, with Russia and China increasing the number of exercises with third parties, including trilateral drills with South Africa and Iran in 2019 and a repeat with Iran in 2020. These strategic exercises may be interpreted as a step backward in terms of practical coordination of Russian and Chinese armed forces, especially compared with the land-based Peaceful Mission or naval Joint Sea exercises in previous years.[37] Instead, China's recent participation in Russian strategic exercises seems to prioritize sending political signals, with the practical dimension of military preparedness being of secondary importance.

The majority of Russian signals have not, however, been reciprocated by China. As mentioned, Beijing has remained silent about the prospects of an early-warning system built with Russian assistance. The joint activities conducted in China's neighborhood have not been re-enacted in the regions of Russia's greatest interest—Central Europe or the Black and Baltic Seas. Beijing's wariness to throw its weight behind Moscow's political-military brinkmanship in Europe was recently confirmed during Russia's Zapad 2021 exercise.

The Zapad series of exercises tends to simulate conflict with the West through the use of the full spectrum of Russia's capabilities, including nuclear weapons.[38] Thus, the participation of Chinese troops in Zapad 2021 (in line with their participation in three previous strategic exercises) would have sent a strong signal about Beijing's readiness to elevate its relations with Moscow to the level of a de facto military alliance. China decided, however, against sending such a signal. Rather than joining Russia in the European theater, the People's Liberation Army (PLA) hosted their Russian counterparts in Chinese territory. Russia and China conducted a joint exercise directed at the West

---

[36] Dinakar Peri, "India Decides to Pull Out of Kavkaz 2020 Military Exercise on Russia Due to Chinese Participation," *Hindu*, August 29, 2020, https://www.thehindu.com/news/national/india-decides-to-pull-out-of-kavkaz-2020-military-exercise-on-russia-due-to-chinese-participation/article32475212.ece.

[37] For complete data on all exercises, see Alexey D. Muraviev, "Strategic Reality Check: The Current State of Russia-China Defence Cooperation and the Prospects of a Deepening 'Near Alliance,'" *Australian Journal of Defence and Strategic Studies* 3, no. 1 (2021): 27–48.

[38] Andreas Ventsel et al., "Discourse of Fear in Strategic Narratives: The Case of Russia's Zapad War Games," *Media, War and Conflict* 14, no. 1 (2019): 21–39.

that, according to the Russian media, paralleled Zapad 2021. Even its name, Zapad/Vzaimodeistviye-2021, suggested the link to the Russian exercise. In the exercise, troops from the Russian Eastern Military District arrived in China and joined PLA units.[39] The exercise was regarded as the Sino-Russian demonstration of participation capacity directed at the United States. China's decision to not participate in the main Zapad exercise is evidence of its desire to mitigate potential fears of the Sino-Russian threat among key European states. While there are voices in China calling for more coordinated activities with Russia, Beijing does not seem ready to bankroll Moscow's aggressive moves in Europe.[40]

Surprisingly, U.S.-China competition has not accelerated Russian arms exports to China. Instead, arms sales have stagnated. Since the big contracts on the S-400 and Su-35 were signed in 2014–15, Russia and China have not concluded any new major agreements. Moreover, unconfirmed reports suggest that in 2020 Moscow put on hold the delivery of S-400 missiles to China amid rising tensions between China and India.[41] Another limitation of Russia's cooperation with China is the absence of shifts in both states' attitudes toward each other's territorial claims. Russia has neither secured Chinese support for its annexation of Crimea nor recognized China's territorial claims in the East and South China Seas. Fears of entrapment and an unwillingness to commit resources to the other side's interests—territorial claims and bids for regional hegemony, in particular—seem to be preventing the emergence of a revisionist Sino-Russian alliance.

Russia's readiness and capacity to strategically and militarily support China in the latter's great-power competition with the United States also does not extend to the economic and technological domains—those areas where the rivalry between Washington and Beijing has been most intense.[42] While Sino-Russian technology cooperation embraces a number of areas, such as civilian nuclear energy and aviation, Russia cannot provide China

---

[39] Reid Standish, "China, Russia Showcase Growing Ties with Joint Military Exercises," Radio Free Europe/Radio Liberty, August 9, 2021, https://www.rferl.org/a/china-russia-military-cooperation/31401442.html.

[40] For example, in response to the Lithuanian government's decisions to withdraw from China's 17+1 grouping with Central and Eastern European states and agree to the name change of a Taiwan representative office in Vilnius, Beijing recalled its ambassador and asked Lithuania's representative to return home. The editorial in the English-language version of the *Global Times*, a mouthpiece for the Chinese Communist Party, called for China and Russia "to jointly deal a heavy blow to one or two running dogs of the U.S. to warn other countries." "China, Russia Can Cooperate to Punish Lithuania," *Global Times*, August 11, 2021, https://www.globaltimes.cn/page/202108/1231251.shtml.

[41] Probal Dasgupta, "Why Russia Really Stopped Its S-400 Supply to China," *Print*, November 12, 2020, https://theprint.in/opinion/why-russia-really-stopped-its-s-400-supply-to-china/542583. This news has not been confirmed by either Russian or Chinese sources independently of the Indian news outlets.

[42] Ferial Ara Saeed, "The Sino-American Race for Technology Leadership," War on the Rocks, April 23, 2021, https://warontherocks.com/2021/04/the-sino-american-race-for-technology-leadership.

with cutting-edge technology, and the Russian market is too small in size and too poor in purchasing power to be attractive for Chinese companies that are deprived of access to Western markets.[43] On the contrary, it is Russia that may benefit from Chinese technologies such as artificial intelligence. Space and aerospace are the only sectors where Russia can provide China with tangible assistance. While the two sides have advertised cooperation in space, implementation of ambitious designs remains to be seen.[44] The most promising undertaking in the aerospace industry, a widebody jet codenamed CR929 and designed to compete with Boeing and Airbus, is in the early stages of development. The Sino-Russian joint venture started the construction of the first prototype in 2021, with mass production to begin in 2025.[45]

Apart from strategic and security-oriented cooperation, the Sino-U.S. competition has accelerated normative convergence between Russia and China. Prior to the shift in U.S. policy, Chinese rhetoric directed toward the United States tended to be more benign than that coming from Russia. Faced with U.S. pressure, Beijing has adopted a much harsher attitude, which at times approaches the level of anti-Americanism observed in Russian discourse. While Russia and China have consistently emphasized the right to each state's "own political and economic path," the escalating U.S.-China competition has elevated these declarations of mutual support for sovereignty and noninterference in domestic affairs to new heights. The focus on regime survival and the similarity of both sets of ruling elites' worldviews have reinforced their perception of the West as the main driver behind any domestic opposition. Both states have declared unambiguous support for the other side's domestic actions, be it Russia's crackdown on Navalny and his associates or China's suppression of Hong Kong's autonomy and independent media. Putin has explicitly lent support to China's policies on Xinjiang, with any criticism being dismissed as unacceptable Western interference.[46] Russian representatives drew parallels between protests in Belarus and Hong Kong, seeing both as failed color revolutions.[47] Moscow has also stood by Beijing regarding debates about the origins of the virus

---

[43] For an overview of Sino-Russian technology cooperation, see Christopher Weidacher Hsiung, "China's Technology Cooperation with Russia: Geopolitics, Economics, and Regime Security," *Chinese Journal of International Politics* 14, no. 3 (2021): 447–49.

[44] Pavel Luzin, "Russian-Chinese Cooperation in Space," Jamestown Foundation, Eurasia Daily Monitor, March 31, 2021, https://jamestown.org/program/russian-chinese-cooperation-in-space.

[45] Linnea Ahlgren, "China and Russia Want to Start Building the 1st CR929 This Year," Simple Flying, June 25, 2021, https://simpleflying.com/china-russia-cr929-construction.

[46] "Full Transcript of Exclusive Putin Interview with NBC News' Keir Simmons."

[47] Xie Wenting and Bai Yunyi, "No Armed Conflict Predicted between China and the U.S.; Russia's Position Is Clearly Much Closer to China's: Russian Ambassador," *Global Times*, June 11, 2021, https://www.globaltimes.cn/page/202106/1225982.shtml.

that causes Covid-19, actively supporting Chinese disinformation efforts and echoing Chinese conspiracy theories linking the virus to the United States.[48] This convergence has been particularly acute in global forums, such as the United Nations or G-20. At the same time, Moscow and Beijing have remained divided on other issues such as separatism and globalization.[49]

Strategic support and normative convergence notwithstanding, Russia's approach toward China's rising influence in Asia and regional competition with the United States has oscillated between staying on the sidelines and tacit to open support for Chinese policies. Russia has sought to remain neutral in China's territorial disputes with Moscow's traditional Asian partners, such as India and Vietnam. Even though Moscow supported China's position vis-à-vis the international arbitration with the Philippines in 2016, it has refrained from offering any other kind of support for China's claims in the South China Sea, as noted above.[50] Russia has even pursued political-military and energy cooperation with Vietnam, and Rosneft conducted drillings in Vietnamese territorial waters, an area over which China claims sovereignty as part of its nine-dash line. To not test Beijing's patience, however, Rosneft (a company with a large stake in the Chinese market) handed operations over to another Russian SOE, Zarubezhneft.[51] While maintaining cooperation with Vietnam, Russia was unwilling to risk the position of its key energy company in China.

Moscow has invested considerable effort to remain neutral during Sino-Indian border tensions, even offering services that might help keep communication lines between the two adversaries open.[52] This policy is grounded both in Russia's desire to keep cordial relations with India and in the widespread belief that the Russia-China-India triangle serves as an instrument to balance U.S. primacy. While it is difficult to pinpoint any tangible results of this trilateral cooperation, the Russian elite seems convinced of the necessity to maintain this format.[53] Moscow's determination to overcome Beijing's opposition to India's accession to the Shanghai Cooperation Organisation

---

[48] "Russian Officials, Experts Say Covid-19 Origin Tracing Should Not Be Politicized," Xinhua, July 13, 2021, https://www.globaltimes.cn/page/202107/1230157.shtml.

[49] Marcin Kaczmarski, "Convergence or Divergence? Visions of World Order and the Russian-Chinese Relationship," *European Politics and Society* 20, no. 2 (2018): 207–24.

[50] Andrey Dikarev and Alexander Lukin, "Russia's Approach to South China Sea Territorial Dispute: It's Only Business, Nothing Personal," *Pacific Review* (2021).

[51] Vladimir Afanasiev, "Zarubezhneft to Pick Up Rosneft's Offshore Assets in Vietnam," Upstream, May 7, 2021, https://www.upstreamonline.com/production/zarubezhneft-to-pick-up-rosnefts-offshore-assets-in-vietnam/2-1-1007528.

[52] Artyom Lukin, "How Russia Emerged as Key Mediator in the China-India Dispute," East Asia Forum, October 23, 2020, https://www.eastasiaforum.org/2020/10/23/how-russia-emerged-as-key-mediator-in-the-china-india-dispute.

[53] For instance, the triangle is repeatedly included in all relevant foreign policy and security documents of the Russian Federation.

demonstrates Russia's persistence in keeping China and India on the same side. Yet boiling tensions between them, as well as U.S. courtship of India, make this balancing act increasingly difficult for the Kremlin. Moscow clearly dislikes the U.S.-led cooperation within the Quad and criticizes the concept of the Indo-Pacific region as a U.S. construct aimed at containing China.[54] At the same time, Moscow tries to avoid antagonizing India so as not to push it into the U.S. orbit and seeks to demonstrate the value of the Russian-Indian partnership through various means, such as by providing India with S-400 anti-missile systems. With some of its actions, however, Russia has inadvertently undermined its policy of diversifying ties in Asia.

Russia's Capacity to Generate National Power

The escalation of open U.S.-China competition could improve Russia's economic situation in several ways. Moscow might count on the easing of economic sanctions and pressures from the United States and other Western states eager to prevent further Sino-Russian rapprochement. It might also hope for potential benefits from Russian companies replacing U.S. companies in the Chinese market or attracting Chinese companies debarred from the U.S. market. Yet in both cases, these hopes have so far turned out to be overblown. As discussed in the previous section, there are some sectors in which Russian companies have profited from their U.S. competitors being pushed out of China. In the majority of cases, however, Russia does not have the capacity to fill the gaps that have emerged. Moreover, China's gradual shift toward dual circulation (i.e., greater self-sufficiency and less reliance on overseas markets for long-term development) has made it more difficult for Russia to economically capitalize on the Sino-U.S. rift.[55]

While the Russian economy has been quite resilient to sanctions imposed by the United States and EU following the Crimea conflict, the lifting of at least some of those sanctions would certainly improve its situation. However, U.S.-China competition has not generated enough pressure for the United States to consider reversing sanctions. As a result, the majority have remained in place, even after the change of the U.S. presidency in January 2021. The only major concession made by the Biden administration has been to lift sanctions on the Nord Stream 2 gas pipeline. However, this move had less to do with a general policy shift toward Russia and instead stemmed from Washington's

---

[54] Ian Hill, "Why Is Russia Worried about the Quad?" Australian Strategic Policy Institute, Strategist, July 1, 2021, https://www.aspistrategist.org.au/why-is-russia-worried-about-the-quad.

[55] Kevin Yao, "What We Know about China's 'Dual Circulation' Economic Strategy," Reuters, September 15, 2020, https://www.reuters.com/article/china-economy-transformation-explainer-idUSKBN2600B5.

desire to mend ties with Germany.[56] Meanwhile, the U.S. Congress has continued to impose new sanctions on Russia.

The Chinese side of the Sino-U.S. equation has had a greater potential impact on Russia's capacity to generate national power because of several factors. First, with growth in bilateral trade and investment, Russia's GDP has become increasingly dependent on China's rate of economic growth.[57] Thus, negative trends in the Chinese economy from the U.S.-China trade war increasingly have the potential to harm Russia. Second, after China cut ties with some of its economic partners, Russia was able to step up in some sectors, such as natural resources and agriculture. The fallout from the Sino-U.S. competition has increased Russian food and agricultural exports to China (e.g., soy beans).[58] Likewise, China's disputes with Australia paved the way for Russian companies to increase their coal exports.[59] Moscow even went so far as to support the construction of new railway infrastructure to allow for increased transport of coal to China.[60]

While these inroads into the Chinese market have benefited Russian companies, they have only amplified the existing economic imbalance between the two countries. The persistence of this asymmetry explains Russia's inability to benefit from Sino-U.S. "decoupling" in other, more sophisticated economic areas. Regarding market access, as noted earlier, the size of the Russian market will not compensate for Chinese losses in the U.S. or European markets. Concerning investment opportunities, the Russian market offers only a few options for Chinese investors. With the exception of the energy sector, the scope of participation in projects to construct transportation infrastructure is limited by Moscow's financial constraints. The Russian stock exchange does not provide an alternative platform for Chinese companies forced to delist from U.S. stock exchanges. In sum, Russia is not positioned to fully benefit from the U.S.-China economic rift.

U.S.-China competition has only marginally influenced the energy sector, which is the cornerstone of Sino-Russian economic cooperation and the bedrock of the Russian political economy. Collaboration in the oil sector

---

[56] "Nord Stream 2: Biden Waives U.S. Sanctions on Russian Pipeline," BBC, May 20, 2021, https://www.bbc.com/news/world-us-canada-57180674.

[57] Alexander Gabuev and Temur Umarov, "Will the Pandemic Increase Russia's Economic Dependence on China?" Carnegie Moscow Center, July 8, 2020, https://carnegiemoscow.org/2020/07/08/will-pandemic-increase-russia-s-economic-dependence-on-china-pub-81893.

[58] Tatyana Karabut, "Bob ne vydast" [Bob Won't Give In], *Rossiyskaya gazeta*, April 21, 2021, https://rg.ru/2021/04/21/postavki-rossijskogo-prodovolstviia-v-kitaj-vyrosli-v-poltora-raza.html.

[59] Natalia Skorlygina and Yevegenii Zainullin, "Dayesh na storone ugliya" [Gimme on the Coal Side], *Kommersant*, December 16, 2020, https://www.kommersant.ru/doc/4615746.

[60] "Putin soglasilsiya s ideei postroit' 'novyi BAM' dlya eksporta ugliya" [Putin Agreed with the Idea to Build a "New BAM" for Coal Export], RBC, July 8, 2021, https://www.rbc.ru/rbcfreenews/60e633099a7947bba18b53fa.

flourished well before the Western response to the Crimean crisis, with major pipelines already in place and major contracts signed by 2013. China also began investing in the Russian LNG sector before 2014. Russia's conflict with the West only made a difference in Sino-Russian cooperation on pipeline natural gas. After years of negotiation, Moscow chose to accept Chinese demands concerning the price and the route of a gas pipeline. The Power of Siberia project (opened in 2019) supplies China's east coast cities from newly explored gas fields.[61] The scope of China's participation in Novatek's LNG projects has also broadened, with Chinese companies buying stakes in the Arctic LNG 2 project and Chinese banks providing substantial loans to increase production amid Western sanctions.[62] In addition, despite advances made by China's civilian nuclear energy sector over the last decade, Russian SOE Rosatom secured the contracts for the construction of new units at two nuclear power plants in Jiangsu and Liaoning Provinces.[63]

Nonetheless, energy cooperation has been driven primarily by the activities of domestic players and economic calculations made by both sides rather than in response to U.S. pressure or U.S.-China competition. The case of pipeline gas exports from Russia illustrates this phenomenon. Even in 2024, Russia will still supply less than half the pipeline natural gas purchased by Chinese companies in Central Asia. However, the future of new gas pipelines, such as Power of Siberia 2 (a project crossing a western section of the Sino-Russian border, negotiated since the mid-2000s under the name Altai) and Power of Siberia 3 (a project transiting Mongolian territory), remains uncertain. Regarding Power of Siberia 2, Russia lobbied for the project as a way of putting pressure on the EU. If implemented, the gas to supply the pipeline would originate in Western Siberia (the same area used to supply the EU), giving Moscow substantial leverage over its customers in both the West and East. Although Beijing took part in negotiations, from the Chinese perspective the pipeline would duplicate already existing infrastructure in Central Asia and probably require additional infrastructure to bring gas to the eastern coast. The Power of Siberia 3 pipeline remains more plausible, but the issue of transit is looked at with suspicion by Beijing and may turn out to be an insurmountable obstacle. China's demand for natural gas is predicted to rise along with the country's attempts to limit coal consumption, but Gazprom has to compete with other Central Asian sources and LNG delivery.

---

[61] Chow, "Russia-China Gas Deal and Redeal."

[62] Nastassia Astrasheuskaya, "Russia's Novatek to Sell Stake in Arctic Gas Project to Chinese Partners," *Financial Times*, April 25, 2019, https://www.ft.com/content/f7c32864-676a-11e9-9adc-98bf1d35a056.

[63] "Work Starts on New Tianwan and Xudabao Units," World Nuclear News, May 19, 2021, https://world-nuclear-news.org/Articles/First-concrete-poured-for-new-Tianwan-and-Xudabao.

Moreover, Biden's conciliatory approach toward the Nord Stream 2 pipeline has decreased the relevance of the Chinese market for Gazprom.

Russia's National Security

Contrary to the limited impact of U.S.-China competition on Russia's capacity to generate power, the influence on Russia's national security has been considerable. On the one hand, Russia's strategic environment has improved as the intensifying U.S.-China rivalry has diverted Washington's attention away from Europe and limited the scope of U.S. actions in the European theater. On the other hand, U.S.-China competition has seriously weakened the existing arms control architecture and accelerated the development of the U.S. arsenal in some areas. Even if Russia's lack of compliance contributed directly to U.S. withdrawal from the Intermediate-Range Nuclear Forces (INF) Treaty in February 2019, Washington also cited Beijing's unwillingness to join the regime. Moscow blamed the United States for the breakdown of arms control and consistently denied U.S. accusations that Russia breached the INF Treaty.[64] As a result, Russia must balance the benefits of increased freedom of action in the defense realm with the costs of heightened regional and global instability generated by escalating U.S.-China competition.

The threat assessment espoused by the Russian elite has not undergone any substantial changes because of the U.S.-China rivalry. Rather, anti-American and anti-Western trends that have dominated thinking about Russian security for the last decade have only been reinforced, with Washington being identified as the major source of instability. The new National Security Strategy, signed by Putin on July 2, 2021, represents Russia's first major attempt to assess the dominant developments in international politics.[65] The lack of any reference to the impact of U.S.-China competition on Russia's security environment, however, demonstrates its limited utility. Chapter 2, titled "Russia in the Contemporary World: Tendencies and Possibilities," emphasizes the ongoing transformation toward multipolarity that is accompanied and countered by "attempts of Western states to maintain hegemony."[66] The general assessment is that international security has worsened since the 2015 edition. According to the 2021 National Security Strategy, the number of sources of pressure on Russia have increased, with a proliferation of protectionist instruments and sanctions, as well as the use

---

[64] Shannon Bugos, "U.S. Completes INF Treaty Withdrawal," Arms Control Association, September 2019, https://www.armscontrol.org/act/2019-09/news/us-completes-inf-treaty-withdrawal.

[65] Office of the President of Russia, *Strategiya bezopasnosti Rossiiskoi Federatsii* [National Security Strategy of the Russian Federation] (Moscow, February 2021), http://www.kremlin.ru/acts/bank/47046/page/5.

[66] Ibid., para. 6.

of climate change as a pretext to limit Russian access to export markets and establish control over transportation routes, including in the Arctic.[67]

Faced with growing U.S.-China tensions, Russia has focused on strengthening its strategic deterrence potential. First, it has accelerated work on new armaments that would prevent the U.S. missile defense system from weakening Russia's second-strike capability. These weapons include, among others, Avangard hypersonic glide vehicles and new RS-28 Sarmat intercontinental ballistic missiles.[68] Second, Russia has attempted to exploit the ambiguity of conditions under which it would be ready to use nuclear force. The U.S. withdrawal from the INF Treaty was one of the reasons behind Russia's new nuclear doctrine, which was made public (for the first time) in June 2020.[69] The document, titled "Basic Principles of State Policy of the Russian Federation on Nuclear Deterrence," however, did little to clarify Russia's nuclear policy.[70]

Finally, while pushing the United States to extend the New Strategic Arms Reduction Treaty (New START), Moscow refused to support Washington in pressuring Beijing to join strategic arms control talks. The Trump administration made extension conditional on China joining the treaty and explicitly asked Moscow to apply pressure to Beijing in this regard. But Moscow has consistently resisted and sided with Beijing in opposing any trilateral arms control talks. Russian representatives claimed that they "understood" China's position and expressed no intention to exercise leverage over Beijing. Russian observers then pointed out that the United States should include the UK and France in any multilateral talks and accused Washington of trying to drive a wedge between Russia and China.[71] All the while, Russia continued to push for a bilateral extension to New START and officially submitted a proposal to extend the treaty to the U.S. State Department in December 2019.[72] By generating

---

[67] Office of the President of Russia, *Strategiya bezopasnosti Rossiiskoi Federatsii*, para. 16.

[68] Hans M. Kristensen and Matt Korda, "Russian Nuclear Weapons, 2021," *Bulletin of the Atomic Scientists* 77, no. 2 (2021): 90–108.

[69] Ministry of Foreign Affairs (Russia), "Basic Principles of State Policy of the Russian Federation on Nuclear Deterrence," June 8, 2020, https://www.mid.ru/en/foreign_policy/international_safety/disarmament/-/asset_publisher/rp0fiUBmANaH/content/id/4152094.

[70] Andrzej Wilk and Marek Menkiszak, "Russia on the Information War's Nuclear Frontline," Centre for Eastern Studies, June 4, 2020, https://www.osw.waw.pl/en/publikacje/analyses/2020-06-04/russia-information-wars-nuclear-frontline.

[71] Elena Chernenko, "Obvinenija SŠA ne podkrepleny nikakimi dokazatel'stvami" [The U.S. Accusations Are Not Supported by Evidence], *Kommersant*, June 15, 2020, https://www.kommersant.ru/doc/4378452.

[72] Some Russian scholars suggest ratification is necessary on Russia's part. See Anton Khlopkov and Anastasia Shavrova, "Pyat shagov na puti k prodleniyu DSNV. Osobennosti protsedury v Rossiyskoi Federatsii" [Five Steps towards an Extension of the START Treaty. Features of the Procedure in the Russian Federation], *Rossiya v globalnoi politike* 19, no. 4 (2020), https://globalaffairs.ru/articles/pyat-shagov-na-puti-k-dsnv.

uncertainty about its principles for the use of nuclear weapons, Moscow might have hoped to tilt the calculus in Washington. Russian pundits warned that Moscow "takes a world without arms control seriously and is preparing for it"[73] and recognized the dissolution of the arms control system.[74]

Biden's election as president and his determination to expeditiously extend New START removed this item from the list of contentious bilateral issues between the United States and Russia. Nonetheless, the parameters for future talks on strategic stability and arms control remain uncertain. Russia has maintained an ambiguous attitude to arms control. For one, it responded to Biden's extension offer by shortening the ratification process (required by Russian law) to less than 24 hours. Thus, the extension of New START seemed to signal Moscow's willingness to return to a comprehensive strategic dialogue with the United States. That being said, the new security strategy omits the New START extension and contains no suggestions of Russia's readiness to engage in further dialogue on strategic stability or arms control. Instead, it emphasizes the necessity to maintain nuclear deterrence potential.[75] The joint statement issued by Putin and Biden during their June 2021 summit promises a dialogue on strategic stability but does not offer any suggestions as to how the two sides might reconcile their differences.[76]

Pressures on Russia's Economic Outlook from Challenges to Globalization

Unlike the United States, China, or the EU, Russia does not depend on globalization for economic growth and related geopolitical clout. This has stemmed from its marginal place in the global division of labor, limited participation in global supply chains, and the attitude of the Russian regime toward globalization in general. While political and business elites have benefited from globalization, the Russian economy as a whole has remained in the backwater, with no political push to embrace it. As a result, the challenges to globalization—such as growing protectionism, U.S.-China decoupling, and the gradual replacement of the global trade regime regulated by the World Trade

---

[73] Dmitri Trenin, "Decoding Russia's Official Nuclear Deterrence Paper," Carnegie Moscow Center, June 5, 2020, https://carnegie.ru/commentary/81983.

[74] Vasily Kashin, "Rossiyskaya yadernaya doktrina: Neobkhodimaya prozrachnost" [Russian Nuclear Doctrine: Essential Transparency], *Rossiya v globalnoi politike*, https://globalaffairs.ru/articles/rossijskaya-yadernaya-prozrachnost.

[75] Office of the President of Russia, *Strategiya bezopasnosti*, para. 40.

[76] "U.S.-Russia Presidential Joint Statement on Strategic Stability," June 16, 2021, available at https://www.whitehouse.gov/briefing-room/statements-releases/2021/06/16/u-s-russia-presidential-joint-statement-on-strategic-stability.

Organization (WTO) with regional agreements—have turned out to be less of a problem for Russia than for other major powers. Instead, Western sanctions and volatile prices have constituted its biggest economic challenges.

Russia's Grand Strategy

The shifting attitudes of the Russian ruling elite to globalization can be traced back to the 2008–9 global economic crisis. At the time, Moscow decided to delay its application for WTO membership. Rather than joining the global trading regime, Russia chose to pursue regional economic integration in the form of a customs union with Belarus and Kazakhstan, which evolved into the EAEU. Although Moscow ultimately joined the WTO in 2012, its participation has continued to be half-hearted.[77]

Western sanctions imposed since 2014 have reinforced Russia's views on globalization as a Western-led process skewed to benefit the United States as an instrument of political influence.[78] Russian leaders sought ways to limit potential harm to the economy. The instruments employed have included countersanctions (mostly directed at European food producers), import substitution, tightening control over regional economic integration, de-dollarization (moving away from the U.S. dollar as the main currency used in transactions with external partners), and relatively conservative fiscal policies aimed at maintaining macroeconomic stability.[79] A relatively consistent macroeconomic policy has allowed Russia to withstand the impacts of Western sanctions. Moscow has managed to rebuild its sovereign funds ($180 billion) and substantially increase the Central Bank's reserves to $600 billion.[80] In addition, Russia's sovereign debt remains at a low level (19.3% of GDP in 2020).[81]

The Russian economy thus has turned out to be quite resilient to external economic pressures that accelerated during the Trump administration. Russia's energy exports continue to provide the bulk of revenues and are in most cases regulated by bilateral agreements rather than multilateral

---

[77] Pamela A. Jordan, "Diminishing Returns: Russia's Participation in the World Trade Organization," *Post-Soviet Affairs* 33, no. 6 (2017): 452–71.

[78] Nigel Gould-Davies, "Russia's Sovereign Globalization: Rise, Fall and Future," Chatham House, January 2016, https://www.chathamhouse.org/sites/default/files/publications/research/20160106R ussiasSovereignGlobalizationGouldDaviesFinal.pdf.

[79] Richard Connolly, *Russia's Response to Sanctions: How Western Economic Statecraft Is Reshaping Political Economy in Russia* (New York: Cambridge University Press, 2018).

[80] Ministry of Finance (Russia), https://www.minfin.gov.ru; and "International Reserves of the Russian Federation (End of Period)," Bank of Russia, https://www.cbr.ru/eng/hd_base/mrrf/mrrf_m.

[81] "Russia's Sovereign Rating Resilient to Latest U.S. Sanctions," Fitch Ratings, April 16, 2021, https://www.fitchratings.com/research/sovereigns/russias-sovereign-rating-resilient-to-latest-us-sanctions-16-04-2021.

trade regimes. Since December 2016, Russia has participated in the OPEC+ mechanism, within which participants agree to reduce exploration in order to keep prices sufficiently high. In March 2020, Moscow temporarily left and increased oil exploration but quickly found itself on the losing side as Saudi Arabia suppressed prices by increasing its own exploration.[82] As a result, Moscow returned to the mechanism within a couple of weeks.[83] Likewise, Gazprom has been able to adapt to regulatory frameworks introduced in the EU's gas market. Although sanctions have deprived Russian energy companies of access to most advanced Western technologies and made it more difficult to secure financing for future projects, they have not directly targeted oil and gas exports. Similarly, industries in which Russia has a competitive edge— the civilian nuclear energy and arms manufacturing—are isolated from multilateral regulatory frameworks, and neither sanctions nor the process of deglobalization has harmed Russian exports in either sector.

Russia continues to promote regional cooperation projects in Eurasia, but the slow pace of their implementation suggests that the Russian leadership considers them to be valuable geopolitically to strengthen the country's great-power credentials rather than a response to challenges from deglobalization.[84] The Greater Eurasian Partnership, put forward by Putin in 2016, seems to confirm Russia's relative lack of interest in practical arrangements.[85] The partnership, of which the EAEU is a part, serves mostly to promote Russia's status as a great power and has not gone beyond rhetoric. It is, however, a useful instrument to counter the concept of the Indo-Pacific region. The synchronization of the Belt and Road Initiative and the Greater Eurasian Partnership also reduces possible tensions between Moscow and Beijing, though the practical dimension of the partnership remains limited.[86]

Russia's National Power

From the perspective of Russia, oil prices have remained the single most important factor defining its capacity to generate national power. In this sense, the Russian capacity to generate national power depends not so much on

---

[82] Nikolay Kozhanov, "The Fall of OPEC+ and the Age of Oil Price Wars," Al Jazeera, March 12, 2020, https://www.aljazeera.com/opinions/2020/3/12/the-fall-of-opec-and-the-age-of-oil-price-wars.

[83] Nigel Gould-Davies, "Russia's Failed OPEC Gamble," International Institute for Strategic Studies, April 15, 2020, https://www.iiss.org/blogs/analysis/2020/04/russia-opec-agreement.

[84] Marcin Kaczmarski, "Non-Western Visions of Regionalism: China's New Silk Road and Russia's Eurasian Economic Union," *International Affairs* 93, no. 6 (2017): 1357–76.

[85] David G. Lewis, "Geopolitical Imaginaries in Russian Foreign Policy: The Evolution of 'Greater Eurasia,'" *Europe-Asia Studies* 70, no. 10 (2018): 1612–37.

[86] Gaziza Shakhanova and Jeremy Garlick, "The Belt and Road Initiative and the Eurasian Economic Union: Exploring the 'Greater Eurasian Partnership,'" *Journal of Current Chinese Affairs* 49, no. 1 (2020): 33–57.

globalization as on the global demand for oil and, to a lesser extent, natural gas. Given that Russia has been experiencing increasing external pressures since 2014—in the form of both Western sanctions and a dramatic fall in oil prices—the trend of deglobalization has not caught Moscow by surprise. As noted above, with its exports focused on natural resources and limited inclusion in global value chains, Russia does not rely on globalization as much as other players, such as China, the United States, and the EU. The challenges to globalization are dangerous for Russia mostly in terms of their implications for demand. Russia used the period of higher prices to build its reserves and thus increase its resilience to external economic pressures, from the West in particular.

Russia has tailored existing instruments to withstand additional pressures. For example, it has managed to build resilience to most of the Western sanctions, even if import substitution has often been costly and produced far from desired results. Low-growth seems to be satisfactory to Moscow as long as it brings sufficient revenues and maintains macroeconomic stability. The role of external partners remains limited, even though Chinese assistance has helped with financing key energy projects such as the Yamal LNG joint venture. Russia's flagship pipeline project, Nord Stream 2, was initially delayed as a result of U.S. sanctions and pressures, but Gazprom completed the project in 2021.[87]

In terms of generating military power, Russia modernized a substantial part of its armed forces before the Ukraine crisis. Moreover, domestic political mobilization after 2014 enabled the Kremlin to increase military expenses. Russia's military-industrial complex is capable of providing the majority of required systems and relies on external partners only to a miniscule degree. The military budget peaked in 2016 and, though decreasing since then, remained at 4% of GDP in 2020.[88]

The Impact of the Covid-19 Pandemic on Russia

Russia's actions in response to the Covid-19 pandemic strongly resemble its response to the 2008–9 global financial crisis. In the initial phase, the Kremlin attempted to score points internationally by portraying Russia as safe from the pandemic and offering help to Western nations. In later phases, the

---

[87] Vladimir Soldatkin, "Russia Completes Nord Stream 2 Construction, Gas Flows Yet to Start," Reuters, September 10, 2021, https://www.reuters.com/business/energy/russias-gazprom-says-it-has-completed-nord-stream-2-construction-2021-09-10.

[88] Michael Kofman and Richard Connolly, "Why Russian Military Expenditure Is Much Higher than Commonly Understood (as Is China's)," War on the Rocks, December 16, 2019, https://warontherocks.com/2019/12/why-russian-military-expenditure-is-much-higher-than-commonly-understood-as-is-chinas.

efforts have focused on tackling domestic challenges that might arise from the mismanagement of the pandemic.

Russia's Grand Strategy

The Covid-19 pandemic's overall effect on Russia's trajectory in international politics has been limited so far. Moscow has attempted to elevate its great-power status, increase its soft power, and project influence. The pandemic, however, has neither made Russia more cooperative nor less assertive.

Moscow's first attempts to improve its international image and demonstrate great-power credentials occurred during the early stages of the pandemic in spring 2020 when it sent highly publicized medical assistance to Italy and the United States.[89] These activities turned out to be short-lived once the virus began spreading in Russia itself. Moscow later used production of a Covid-19 vaccine as a means to increase its status. The Russian-made vaccine was the first Covid-19 vaccine to be registered and the government has promoted it as evidence of Russia's scientific potential and credentials as a modern great power. The very name of the vaccine, Sputnik V ("V" for "victory"), suggests the country's ambitions to play the role of the world's savior from the pandemic. To this end, Moscow has engaged in vaccine diplomacy, attempting to improve bilateral relations and demonstrate its upper hand as well as generosity vis-à-vis the West.

Although not yet approved by the World Health Organization, the vaccine has gained approval in over 70 countries, including some EU members. As of September 2021, Russia had sold around 600 million doses, with India, Iran, Argentina, Egypt, the Palestinian Authority, Mexico, Nepal, Peru, Turkey, Vietnam, and Venezuela being among the biggest buyers. Other countries have declared willingness to produce the Sputnik vaccine domestically: South Korea (1,850 billion doses), India (1,150 billion doses), and China (260 million).[90] In addition, Russia has provided a smaller number of doses as humanitarian aid, often as a way to open commercial talks.[91]

Russia's self-promotion as a scientific great power has faced some backlash. A low vaccination rate in Russia of only 32% of the population,

---

[89] Holly Ellyatt, "From Russia with Love? Why the Kremlin's Coronavirus Aid to the West Is Controversial," CNBC, April 7, 2020, https://www.cnbc.com/2020/04/07/why-the-kremlins-coronavirus-aid-to-the-west-is-controversial.html.

[90] Statista, "Sputnik V Doses Bought from Russia 2021, by Country," https://www.statista.com/statistics/1123927/sputnik-v-exports-from-russia-by-country.

[91] Kerry Cullinan and Esther Nakkazi, "Russian and Chinese Bilateral Vaccine Deals & Donations Outmaneuver Europe & United States," Health Policy Watch, March 3, 2021, https://healthpolicy-watch.news/russia-and-chinas-bilateral-vaccine.

bottlenecks in the production of the vaccine, and ongoing uncertainty surrounding the vaccine's efficacy have undermined confidence in Sputnik V.[92] Some partners, such as Ghana and Kenya, have even canceled orders.[93] Russia was also accused by the EU of spreading disinformation related to the pandemic and other vaccines.[94]

Russia's National Power

The pandemic's impact on Russia's capacity to generate national power has been threefold: economic, demographic, and political. From the Kremlin's perspective, the most relevant impact has been in the domestic political sphere. Given the importance of political will as an instrument of Russia's power,[95] the ability to rein in potential rivals and control allies is one of the key determinants of Russia's capacity to generate national power. Initially, the government's weak response to the pandemic appeared to have seriously undermined the regime and Putin's personal legitimacy.[96] Since then, however, the Kremlin has used the opportunities provided by social distancing measures to consolidate power. Major steps taken by Moscow have included the introduction of constitutional amendments and the crackdown on Alexei Navalny and his supporters. The constitutional amendments enable Putin to run for president twice more (and potentially remain in power until 2036), while deferring the question of leadership succession, which had begun to loom over the Russian elite and had the potential to create divisions.[97] Furthermore, the targeting of Navalny has temporarily removed the most able and serious political opposition to the ruling regime. Navalny was poisoned in summer 2020, and upon his return from Germany (where he received medical treatment), he was arrested and tried for violating parole. His imprisonment was followed by crackdowns

---

[92] Grace Kier and Paul Stronski, "Russia's Vaccine Diplomacy Is Mostly Smoke and Mirrors," Carnegie Endowment for International Peace, August 3, 2021, https://carnegieendowment.org/2021/08/03/russia-s-vaccine-diplomacy-is-mostly-smoke-and-mirrors-pub-85074.

[93] Ibid.

[94] Lorne Cook, "EU Report Takes Aim at Russia over Vaccine Fake News," Associated Press, April 28, 2021, https://apnews.com/article/european-union-russia-europe-fake-news-coronavirus-d12316c1e6c21fe2f1a450e8f387dbac.

[95] Stoner, *Russia Resurrected*.

[96] Graeme P. Herd, "Covid-19, Russian Responses, and President Putin's Operational Code," George C. Marshall European Center for Security Studies, Security Insights, no. 50, April 2020, https://www.marshallcenter.org/sites/default/files/files/2020-11/PDF_PUB_SI_50.pdf.

[97] Ben Noble and Nikolay Petrov, "From Constitution to Law: Implementing the 2020 Russian Constitutional Changes," *Russian Politics* 6, no. 1 (2021): 130–52.

on his organization, the Anti-Corruption Foundation, which was labeled as an "extremist organization" and effectively disbanded.[98]

The economic effects of the Covid-19 pandemic have been unexpectedly mild, especially when compared with the impact on other states. The biggest challenge for Russia was a slump in oil demand, which in turn led to a sharp decrease in prices, but the global economy's revival has lifted prices and allowed Moscow to rebuild its coffers. Russia's GDP contracted in 2020 by only 3%, and growth is expected to reach 3% in 2021 and 2022.[99]

The demographic effects of the pandemic are among the most difficult to assess. According to official data, as of November 2021, Covid-19 cases had reached 8.4 million and reported deaths were 245,000. However, external observers have questioned official data provided by the Russian government.[100] Based on a statistical analysis to determine "excess deaths" compared with a typical year, the real death rate from the virus may be four times what the state has reported. As of September 2021, total excess fatalities in Russia since March 2020 had reached more than 750,000.[101] The pandemic has aggravated several long-term trends in human life indicators and reversed the previous efforts of the Kremlin to stop demographic decline. The decrease in population was the biggest since 2005, while the number of births fell to its lowest level in the last two decades. As a result, Russia's population declined to 146.2 million, the lowest point since 2014.[102]

Implications for the United States and U.S.-Russia Relations

The Russian ruling elite continues to perceive the United States both as a declining hegemon that is struggling to maintain its dominant position and as the major threat to Russia's role in international politics. U.S. competition with China has not altered this dominant way of thinking. Moscow has been

---

[98] Jan Matti Dollbaum, Morvan Lallouet, and Ben Noble, *Navalny: Putin's Nemesis, Russia's Future?* (London: Hurst Publishers, 2021); and "Crackdown on Navalny Allies," Bell, January 31, 2021, https://thebell.io/en/crackdown-on-navalny-allies.

[99] "Russia's Economic Recovery Gathers Pace, Says New World Bank Report," World Bank, Press Release, May 26, 2021, https://www.worldbank.org/en/news/press-release/2021/05/26/russia-s-economic-recovery-gathers-pace-says-new-world-bank-report.

[100] "Coronavirus in Russia: The Latest News: Nov. 3," *Moscow Times*, https://www.themoscowtimes.com/2021/11/05/coronavirus-in-russia-the-latest-news-nov-5-a69117.

[101] Polina Ivanova, John Burn-Murdoch, and Oliver Barnes, "Russia Excess Deaths Soar amid Jab Hesitancy," *Financial Times*, November 3, 2021, https://www.ft.com/content/f1a270c3-3870-46ad-99e8-45b5d8f127e0.

[102] Jadwiga Rogoża, "The Pandemic Takes Its Toll: Russia's Demographic Crisis," Centre for Eastern Studies, February 16, 2021, https://www.osw.waw.pl/en/publikacje/analyses/2021-02-16/pandemic-takes-its-toll-russias-demographic-crisis.

unwilling to make any concessions that would pave the way for mending ties or improving relations with Washington. Instead, Russia has chosen to strengthen its ties with China and provide Beijing with strategic and political support.

Russian policy complicates U.S. strategy both globally and toward China. Globally, Russia can be expected to seek benefits from U.S.-China competition, first and foremost by counting on and exploiting the United States' inability to fully address two strategic challenges simultaneously: one in Europe and one in Asia. While a scenario where Russia openly supports China in a confrontation with the United States appears to be far-fetched, a rise in pressure on U.S. allies in Europe is highly plausible. Moscow will opportunistically capitalize on Washington's diminished attention to regions such as the post-Soviet environs, the Black Sea, and the Middle East. With regard to China, Moscow can be expected to extend political support and demonstrate cordial relations with Beijing, including in the security and defense realms. Joint exercises will amplify political signals sent to Washington by Beijing, and any further Russian arms transfers or support for the construction of early-warning missile systems will strengthen China's military potential. As the case of the New START negotiations demonstrated, Washington will find it more difficult to convince Beijing of the benefits of arms control if Russia backs China's intransigence. The Sino-Russian strategic partnership helps secure China's backyard, allowing the country to concentrate on its rivalry with the United States.

The bottom line is that the United States cannot count on any form of Russian support in its competition with China. Any potential rift emerging between China and Russia is highly implausible. Russia has been careful not to send signals suggesting the possibility of anti-Chinese policy, while China in turn tends to downplay its advantage and demonstrate respect for Russia's equal status, despite the growing asymmetry between the two countries.[103] Under such circumstances, even the U.S. attempts to make Russia "neutral" in the U.S.-China competition may turn out to be futile.

Still, the United States can diminish the value of Russia's support for China by shifting the weight of Sino-U.S. competition to those areas in which Moscow is either unwilling or unable to provide strategic assistance to China. Russia will not throw its full weight behind China because the two have not established a revisionist alliance, one in which both states would

---

[103] See, for example, China's silence on its military presence in Tajikistan, close to the border with Afghanistan. See "Tajikistan: Secret Chinese Base Becomes Slightly Less Secret," Eurasianet, September 23, 2020, https://eurasianet.org/tajikistan-secret-chinese-base-becomes-slightly-less-secret; and Stephen Blank, "China's Military Base in Tajikistan: What Does It Mean?" Central Asia-Caucasus Analyst, April 18, 2019, https://www.cacianalyst.org/publications/analytical-articles/item/13569-chinas-military-base-in-tajikistan-what-does-it-mean?.html.

support each other's most aggressive foreign policy actions and commit to mutual defense. As noted earlier, for example, Russia is unwilling to support China's territorial claims—either in the South and East China Seas or vis-à-vis India. Moscow does not want Chinese hegemony in East Asia or Eurasia and wants to maintain close relations with states such as Vietnam. Closer Russia-India relations might slow down Russia's cooperation with China and thus indirectly benefit Washington. At the very least, any U.S. attempts to punish New Delhi for closer ties to Moscow will ultimately be counterproductive, alienating India while doing little harm to Russia.

In the Sino-U.S. technological race and trade war, Moscow does not have sufficient capacity to partner with Beijing. Apart from certain technologies helpful in space exploration, Russian capabilities in the high-tech sector are limited. Nor will Russia be able to compensate China for any economic losses incurred through loss of access to the U.S. or European markets. The Sino-Russian partnership matters solely for classical power-political games and multilateral diplomacy in the United Nations. Its potential in nontraditional areas of great-power competition is much smaller and thus less relevant.

In its policy toward Russia, the United States might capitalize on China's unwillingness to back Russia's political-military brinkmanship in Europe. While China may be willing to join Russia in targeting individual European states seen as "U.S. clients" (as in the case of Lithuania), it continues to demonstrate restraint toward Europe as a whole.

The options for improvement in U.S.-Russia relations remain limited. Finding common rules in cyberspace requires trust that is absent. The list of sixteen critical infrastructure areas presented by Biden to Putin during their June 2021 summit may invite Russia to test U.S. resolve rather than deter competition. Likewise, progress in arms control will be difficult to achieve without substantial concessions made by the United States. For Russia, the most contentious issue since the early 2000s has been the U.S. missile defense program. While Moscow ultimately agreed to New START back in 2010 without receiving any concessions from Washington, opening a dialogue on a replacement treaty in five years may be extremely difficult. The fact that the Russian elite still craves U.S. recognition of Russia's great-power status may provide a certain degree of flexibility for the United States. What is most problematic is that the expected forms of this recognition are often difficult to disentangle, as Russia awaits not only symbolic but also substantial concessions.

Finally, Russian domestic politics creates a substantial obstacle to more stable U.S.-Russia relations. Tensions with the United States, including over sanctions, provide an excellent scapegoat for any failures of Putin's leadership and serve as an instrument to mobilize his conservative base.

Any improvement of bilateral relations would make it more difficult for the Kremlin to play this anti-American card. The usefulness of this strategy has only increased amid the economic difficulties and challenges to the legitimacy generated by the regime's mismanagement of the Covid-19 pandemic.

EXECUTIVE SUMMARY

This chapter contends that India has taken intensified U.S.-China competition as an opportunity to push forward in its quest to become a leading power in Asian and global affairs—a goal that mostly aligns with current U.S. interests.

MAIN ARGUMENT

A shared interest in limiting China's rise has elevated the defense and strategic partnership between Washington and New Delhi and enhanced India's geopolitical stature as a hub of strategic coordination in the Indo-Pacific. Although the Covid-19 pandemic will depress its medium-term trajectory and exacerbate preexisting challenges, India may yet resume its robust rise with deft policymaking. India is partly pursuing this goal by trying to take advantage of risks to globalization, such as the quest for supply chain resilience among Indo-Pacific countries. Ultimately, however, India's interests are its own and unlikely to bend significantly in the direction of U.S. interests, absent a shared threat or joint opportunity.

POLICY IMPLICATIONS

- Washington can expect India's support in U.S.-China competition, but India will also leverage the current situation to achieve its national interests, which will occasionally clash with those of the U.S. This should not be cause for U.S.-India discord but rather the basis for managing expectations.

- The pandemic will delay but not derail India's rise if the government can devise a mix of long-term policies focused on growth, employment, and human development. To this end, the U.S. can further develop partnerships in India's health sector.

- India's efforts at economic self-reliance are an opportunity for the U.S. and its allies to diversify supply chains in the Indo-Pacific. Investing in India's long-term potential to become a manufacturing powerhouse can only benefit countries looking to reduce their dependence on China.

India

Leveraging Uncertainty: India's Response to U.S.-China Competition

Rohan Mukherjee

With the world's second-largest population, third-largest economy (in terms of purchasing power parity), third-largest military budget, and a relatively small but survivable nuclear arsenal, India is vital to the future of Asian and global geopolitics. Although India is not a permanent member of the UN Security Council, its role in the co-management of the U.S.-led international order has grown steadily over the last decade in terms of its own activity as well as recognition by other states. With the emergence of the Indo-Pacific as the defining geopolitical concept and strategic space of the 21st century, understanding India's approach to the international order and to U.S.-China competition has taken on great significance in regional capitals and beyond.

The three drivers of change central to this volume—U.S.-China competition, the Covid-19 pandemic, and risks to globalization—do not affect India's grand strategy in equal measure. The most important driver for India has been the increased intensity of U.S.-China competition. Covid-19, a more recent phenomenon, will have near- to medium-term effects on India's ability to maintain the economic basis of its power potential. Perhaps the least impactful driver of the three is the risks to globalization created by the rise of populism in the West, the trade war between the United States and China, and the efforts by the United States and its allies to reduce their economic dependence on China. Although both India's imports from and trade deficit with China have steadily grown over the last two decades, Indian firms

---

Rohan Mukherjee is an Assistant Professor of Political Science at Yale-NUS College in Singapore. He can be reached at <rohan.mukherjee@yale-nus.edu.sg>.

The author would like to thank Darlene Onuorah for providing research assistance.

are keenly attuned to the advantages of doing business with their Chinese counterparts. As a result, the Indian government is unlikely to push too hard in the direction of reducing trade dependence or decoupling supply chains so long as Beijing does not directly threaten India's national security and territorial integrity.

This chapter will examine the impacts of the three drivers on India's national power and trajectory and its security environment. It will also discuss how India has responded to these changes and what the overall picture means for the United States. The main findings are threefold. First, U.S.-China competition has had a positive effect on India's power and trajectory. While India may not always agree or align with U.S. interests in the international order, there is sufficient friction in the India-China relationship to ensure that India's self-interest will de facto align with U.S. interests. Second, although Covid-19 will decelerate India's growth and flatten its trajectory somewhat, India may return to its robust trajectory of a decade ago if the government can enact further reforms aimed at speeding up human development while lightening the burden of regulation on households and private enterprise. Finally, India stands to gain as countries learning from the pandemic start to diversify their economic ties to reduce dependence on a single country (most often China). Some of the current risks to globalization thus present an opportunity for India to ramp up manufacturing in key sectors where China is losing global market share.

These findings should produce cautious optimism in the United States, which has so far calibrated its relationship with India in a way that balances the imperatives of strategic partnership with India's quest for strategic autonomy and great-power status. Bilateral relations today are at a historical peak, and Indian leaders have never been more comfortable with U.S. power and leadership in the Indo-Pacific. At the same time, India can be expected to relentlessly pursue its own national interests, often to the exclusion of U.S. interests. This means that while India can be counted on to resist China's rise, Washington will have limited influence on where, when, and how New Delhi does so. This equilibrium, while not ideal for the United States, is certainly not bad, especially in the context of India's growing partnerships with Japan, Australia, the Quad grouping, and the Association of Southeast Asian Nations (ASEAN) countries.

U.S.-China Competition and India's Grand Strategy

The last five years have seen an intensification of U.S.-China competition worldwide, a trend that has been developing for a long time but was kicked into higher gear by the Trump administration. India's evolving relations with both China and the United States play into New Delhi's assessments of, and response to, this growing competition.

The Souring of India-China Relations

After decades of tension, including a war and numerous standoffs along their disputed border, India-China relations took a turn for the better toward the end of the Cold War. At that time, both countries agreed to compartmentalize the dispute for the sake of making progress on other aspects of their relationship. Starting in the early 1990s, India and China began several rounds of dialogue, concluding a series of agreements designed to maintain peace along the border and implement confidence-building measures pending the eventual resolution of the dispute. The boundary remained mostly peaceful until the early 2010s, when Indian officials and media began reporting numerous incursions by Chinese soldiers into territory claimed by India.[1]

Against this backdrop, in 2017 the construction of a Chinese road on the Doklam plateau, a region disputed by China and Bhutan near the trijunction of their respective borders with India, became a flashpoint. When Indian troops crossed the international border to enter the plateau and face off against Chinese troops, a 73-day standoff ensued and was only resolved through diplomacy, followed by two summits between Prime Minister Narendra Modi and President Xi Jinping at Wuhan in 2018 and Mamallapuram in 2019. Both were aimed at moving beyond the crisis and focusing on areas of cooperation such as trade and tourism.

In the spring of 2020, as Covid-19 was spreading, India discovered incursions by large numbers of Chinese troops at various points along the disputed boundary near the Indian territory of Ladakh. Indian and Chinese patrols in the area were soon entangled in numerous physical altercations, culminating in the Galwan Valley skirmish of June 2020 and the deaths of twenty Indian soldiers and an indeterminate number of Chinese soldiers.[2] This episode turned the tide of Indian elite and public opinion firmly against China. In stark contrast to India's prior position that the boundary dispute could be bracketed from the rest of the bilateral relationship, India's foreign

---

[1] Saurabh Shukla, "Growing Intrusion by the Chinese Army on the LAC Has Set the Alarm Bells Ringing in South Block. Can the Indian Army Maintain Restraint?" *India Today*, October 16, 2012, https://www.indiatoday.in/india/north/story/sino-indian-border-dispute-chinese-army-intrusions-118767-2012-10-16.

[2] Snehesh Alex Philip, "4, 9 or 14? Even China 'Isn't Sure' How Many PLA Soldiers Died in Galwan Valley," *Print*, March 1, 2021, https://theprint.in/defence/4-9-or-14-even-china-isnt-sure-how-many-pla-soldiers-died-in-galwan-valley/613372.

minister stated publicly that the border crisis had "significantly damaged" the relationship and that things could not be "business as usual" without peace.³

The border issue is not the only bone that India has to pick with China. Beijing's steadfast support for India's rival Pakistan, for example, has long been a source of tension. New Delhi's frustration has been aggravated by the expansion of the Belt and Road Initiative (BRI) into South Asia, particularly in the form of the China-Pakistan Economic Corridor, which runs through parts of Kashmir.⁴ Linked to this concern is a feeling of strategic encirclement in New Delhi. In recent years, China's naval footprint has expanded in the Indian Ocean and Beijing has poured billions of dollars into large-scale infrastructure projects and other investments in Nepal, Bangladesh, Sri Lanka, and Maldives.

The U.S. withdrawal from Afghanistan and the return of Taliban rule have further complicated India's neighborhood. Given Pakistan's long-standing relationship with the Taliban, Indian observers remain concerned about the potential for Kabul to be turned against Indian interests due to Islamabad's influence. Adding to India's difficulties on this front, China has aligned with Pakistan in cultivating the Taliban, thus extending its strategic reach to yet another of India's neighbors—one that was until recently predisposed toward India due to the U.S. influence on its government.⁵ Despite these developments, however, China's alignment with the Taliban will remain incomplete.⁶ China's treatment of its Muslim Uighur population, which the Taliban has for now studiously ignored, could become a sore point in the future. More importantly, as Chinese nationals are increasingly the targets of terrorist attacks in Pakistan, Beijing will seek to pressure both the Pakistani establishment and the Taliban to curb their ties to extremist groups operating in both countries. China remains concerned about Uighur separatists who enjoy safe haven in Afghanistan and may in the future use the country as a base for planning and launching attacks on Chinese territory and interests.⁷

Finally, New Delhi has been frustrated by Beijing's actions in international institutions, which have been inimical to India's interests and pursuit of great-

---

³ Anirban Bhaumik, "Business Cannot Be as Usual with China Unless PLA Restores Status Quo: India," *Deccan Herald*, September 4, 2020, https://www.deccanherald.com/national/business-cannot-be-as-usual-with-china-unless-pla-restores-status-quo-india-882574.html.

⁴ Soyen Park, "Why India Boycotted the Belt and Road Forum," East Asia Forum, June 13, 2017, https://www.eastasiaforum.org/2017/06/13/why-india-boycotted-the-belt-and-road-forum.

⁵ Tsukasa Hadano, "China Extends Hand to Taliban for Rebuilding with Eye on Xinjiang," *Nikkei Asia*, August 27, 2021, https://asia.nikkei.com/Politics/International-relations/Afghanistan-turmoil/China-extends-hand-to-Taliban-for-rebuilding-with-eye-on-Xinjiang.

⁶ Derek Grossman, "China and Pakistan See Eye to Eye on the Taliban—Almost," *Foreign Policy*, September 20, 2021.

⁷ "China Wary about Taliban Commitments on Uyghur Separatist Group ETIM," ANI News, September 19, 2021, https://www.business-standard.com/article/international/china-wary-about-taliban-commitments-on-uyghur-separatist-group-etim-121091900017_1.html.

power status. For example, China consistently has blocked India's attempts to list Pakistan-based Masood Azhar, founding leader of terrorist group Jaish-e-Mohammed (JeM) and architect of numerous terrorist attacks on Indian soil, as a global terrorist at the United Nations. It was only in May 2019, after a major terrorist attack by JeM in Indian Kashmir, that China finally dropped its opposition.[8] Beijing has also repeatedly blocked Indian efforts to join key international institutions such as the Nuclear Suppliers Group and the UN Security Council (as a permanent member).

The above issues all combine to create a growing sense among the Indian elite that China represents the greatest obstacle to India's long-term security, prosperity, and status in the international order.[9] This assessment has led India to develop stronger ties with the United States over the last two decades.

The Blossoming of India-U.S. Relations

The United States was early to recognize India as a vital bulwark in the coming competition with China. From the George W. Bush presidency onward, Washington has focused on cultivating India as a strategic partner and bolstering its hard-power capabilities in order to create a credible counterweight to China.[10] In July 2005, President Bush and Prime Minister Manmohan Singh issued a historic joint statement resolving to "transform the relationship between their countries and establish a global partnership." The centerpiece of this agreement was the official recognition of India as a "responsible state with advanced nuclear technology" that deserved "the same benefits and advantages as other such states."[11] This document laid the foundation for what came to be known as the U.S.-India nuclear deal, which went into effect in October 2008. President Barack Obama's visit to New Delhi in January 2015 resulted in the U.S.-India Joint Strategic Vision for the Asia-Pacific and Indian Ocean Region.[12] While previous bilateral statements contained allusions to international security and stability, this was the first

---

[8] Sarah Zheng, "Why China Dropped Its Opposition to UN Blacklisting of Pakistan-Based Terror Chief Masood Azhar," *South China Morning Post*, May 2, 2019, https://www.scmp.com/news/china/diplomacy/article/3008614/why-china-dropped-its-opposition-un-blacklisting-pakistan.

[9] Rajesh Rajagopalan, "Countering China Is Now a Priority for Both India and U.S. but Only One Needs the Other," *Print*, October 28, 2020, https://theprint.in/opinion/countering-china-is-now-a-priority-for-both-india-and-us-but-only-one-needs-the-other/532106.

[10] T.V. Paul and Erik Underwood, "Theorizing India-U.S.-China Strategic Triangle," *India Review* 18, no. 4 (2019): 348–67.

[11] "Joint Statement by President George W. Bush and Prime Minister Manmohan Singh," White House, Press Release, July 18, 2005, https://2001-2009.state.gov/p/sca/rls/pr/2005/49763.htm.

[12] "U.S.-India Joint Strategic Vision for the Asia-Pacific and Indian Ocean Region," White House, Press Release, January 25, 2015, https://obamawhitehouse.archives.gov/the-press-office/2015/01/25/us-india-joint-strategic-vision-asia-pacific-and-indian-ocean-region.

that went beyond bilateral cooperation and focused concretely on regional issues in the Asia-Pacific. More than previous agreements, its language echoed official U.S. rhetoric on regional connectivity, economic integration, freedom of navigation, and support for democracy and human rights.

India was among a handful of countries that reacted adroitly to the election of President Donald Trump. Less than ten days after the 2016 U.S. presidential election, Foreign Secretary S. Jaishankar visited the United States and met with members of Trump's transition team and the outgoing administration.[13] Meanwhile, with less than six weeks left in office, the Obama administration designated India a "major defense partner," which the Department of Defense described as "a status unique to India [that] institutionalizes the progress made to facilitate defense trade and technology sharing with India to a level at par with that of the United States' closest allies and partners."[14]

For Indian leaders, the writing on the wall was increasingly clear even prior to the Trump presidency: the aftermath of the global financial crisis, a shifting global balance of power, and a weak U.S. response (the "rebalance to Asia") foreshadowed fundamental changes in the international order, of which the Trump presidency was but a symptom. The post–Cold War unipolar moment was beginning to dissipate in terms of both military and normative power, creating space for India to push forward in its path to great-power status. Modi thus sought to cultivate a strong personal relationship with Trump—the "Howdy Modi" rally in Houston in 2019 and the "Namaste Trump" rally in Ahmedabad in 2020 were unusual even for Modi's personalized style of dealing with foreign leaders—while the Indian establishment accelerated institutionalized cooperation. Between 2016 and 2020, India and the United States concluded three foundational agreements that enable mutual logistical support, the use of proprietary U.S. communications technologies, and intelligence sharing between the two militaries. Although these agreements were in the works for years, their conclusion in quick succession signaled a desire to fast-track military coordination and enhance India's power-projection capabilities. Moreover, in September 2018, India and the United States inaugurated an annual "2+2" meeting of their respective foreign and defense ministers, thus elevating their strategic coordination to the highest levels. In February 2020, at the

---

[13] "India's Foreign Secretary Meets Trump's Transition Team during U.S. Visit," Press Trust of India, November 24, 2016, available at https://www.livemint.com/Politics/2drK8H9XKtyfP2QdTw7GaN/Indias-foreign-secretary-meets-Trumps-transition-team-duri.html.

[14] "Joint India-United States Statement on the Visit of Secretary of Defense Carter to India," U.S. Department of Defense, Press Release, December 8, 2016, https://www.defense.gov/Newsroom/Releases/Release/Article/1024228/joint-india-united-states-statement-on-the-visit-of-secretary-of-defense-carter.

Namaste Trump rally, Modi described the United States as India's largest trading partner, the country with which India has the most extensive R&D partnerships, and the country with which the Indian Army conducts the most military exercises.[15]

By and large, the Trump presidency was a strategic gift to India. Washington proved willing and capable of taking the economic and diplomatic fight to China while also censuring Pakistan for its reliance on terrorist networks to achieve strategic ends vis-à-vis India (with disastrous results for other Asian countries as well). Secretary of State Rex Tillerson criticized China for "at times undermining the international, rules-based order even as countries like India operate within a framework that protects other nations' sovereignty."[16] Trump himself accused Islamabad of giving Washington "nothing but lies and deceit" in return for billions of dollars in military and economic assistance.[17] Indian officialdom felt further vindicated in its consistent accusations against Pakistan for sponsoring terrorism when the Pentagon canceled hundreds of millions of dollars of military aid to Pakistan due to its lack of support for U.S. strategy in South Asia.[18] In other areas, too, Trump proved an unwitting agent of Indian interests. In the realm of international cooperation, for example, the U.S. withdrawal from the Paris Agreement enabled India to take on a leadership role in international climate change negotiations, and the U.S. withdrawal from the Trans-Pacific Partnership (TPP) derailed a trade agreement that India had long been wary of on intellectual property rights grounds.[19]

India as a Leading Power

Indian foreign policy is by no means defined by India-U.S. and India-China relations alone. Since the turn of the century, India has actively sought to diversify its external partnerships in an effort to build up its economic and military power. To this end, it has cultivated or deepened partnerships with

---

[15] "English Rendering of PM's Closing Remarks at the Namaste Trump Event in Ahmedabad, Gujarat," Prime Minister's Office (India), February 24, 2020, https://pib.gov.in/Pressreleaseshare.aspx?PRID=1604181.

[16] Rex Tillerson, "Defining Our Relationship with India for the Next Century" (remarks at the Center for Strategic and International Studies, Washington, D.C., October 18, 2017), https://www.csis.org/events/defining-our-relationship-india-next-century-address-us-secretary-state-rex-tillerson.

[17] Shaiq Hussain and Annie Gowen, "'No More!' Trump Tweets to Pakistan, Accusing It of 'Lies & Deceit,'" *Washington Post*, January 1, 2018.

[18] Elizabeth Roche, "U.S. Scraps $300 Million in Military Aid to Pakistan," *Mint*, September 3, 2018, https://www.livemint.com/Politics/EpG1dTWxZbcZklinPKHPIN/US-moves-to-scrap-300-million-in-military-aid-to-Pakistan.html.

[19] Patralekha Chatterjee, "A Fine Line: TPP and India," Gateway House, March 3, 2016, https://www.gatewayhouse.in/the-tpp-and-india-a-fine-line.

a diverse set of countries, including Iran, Saudi Arabia, Israel, the United Arab Emirates, Russia, the European Union, Japan, Australia, and Vietnam, to name a few.[20] Of note in the Indo-Pacific are India's burgeoning ties with Japan and Australia. Starting with Prime Minister Yoshiro Mori's historic visit to New Delhi in 2000, India-Japan relations have grown significantly in a short period of time. The basic bargain that both countries appear to have struck is simple: Japan invests billions of dollars in India's economic potential through concessional loans and grants aimed largely at developing an infrastructural base to accelerate industrial production (in which Japanese firms increasingly participate); in return, India acts as an alternative to China as a destination for Japanese investment and lends its diplomatic weight to Japan's increasingly precarious position in Northeast Asia through policy coordination, military exercises, and institutionalized cooperation at bilateral, trilateral, and multilateral levels.[21]

India's souring relations with China have shaped the nature and pace of India-Japan engagement as well. For example, although New Delhi had stopped inviting Japan to participate in the annual India-U.S. Malabar naval exercise (when hosted in Indian waters) after Japan's participation in 2007 elicited sharp protest from Beijing, in 2015 New Delhi as host took the initiative to invite Japan to rejoin the exercise, and Japan has remained a participant ever since. India and Japan have also concluded agreements on the peaceful use of nuclear energy, the transfer of defense equipment and technology, the sharing of classified military information, and the exchange of supplies and services between militaries during joint exercises, humanitarian operations, and mutual port visits.

Although Australia is neither a major trading partner nor a major source of FDI for India, the noneconomic aspects of the bilateral relationship have developed steadily over the last decade. In 2014, for example, the two countries announced a bilateral framework for security cooperation that institutionalized an annual summit of prime ministers and dialogues between ministers and senior officials on a range of issues, including defense, counterterrorism, nuclear energy cooperation, disaster management, and collaboration in multilateral forums.[22] In the years since then, both sides have engaged in numerous strategic dialogues, information exchanges, naval

---

[20] Ian Hall, "Multialignment and Indian Foreign Policy under Narendra Modi," *Round Table* 105, no. 3 (May 2016): 8.

[21] Rohan Mukherjee, "India and Japan's Grand Bargain in the Context of China's Rise," in *India's Great Power Politics: Managing China's Rise*, ed. Jo Inge Bekkevold and S. Kalyanaraman (New Delhi: Routledge, 2020), 247–61.

[22] "Framework for Security Cooperation between Australia and India 2014," November 18, 2014, https://www.dfat.gov.au/geo/india/Pages/framework-for-security-cooperation-between-australia-and-india-2014.

exercises (such as the AUSINDEX naval exercises), and training programs for military personnel. As in the case of Japan-India relations, albeit somewhat belatedly, India's relations with Australia have kicked into a higher gear as Sino-Indian relations have deteriorated. During the Ladakh crisis in June 2020, Prime Ministers Narendra Modi and Scott Morrison upgraded the relationship to a comprehensive strategic partnership that included the signing of a mutual logistics support agreement to enable greater interoperability between the two militaries and the establishment of a 2+2 dialogue of foreign and defense ministers.[23] In November 2020, after a hiatus of thirteen years, Australia rejoined the Malabar naval exercise alongside India, the United States, and Japan.

India's expanding bilateral relations with the United States, Japan, and Australia have enabled the re-emergence of the Quad as a viable coalition to compete with and counterbalance China's growing footprint in the Indo-Pacific. Initially raised in 2007 by Prime Minister Shinzo Abe, the idea was soon shelved as India and Australia developed cold feet in the face of Beijing's strenuous objections.[24] Nonetheless, the four powers steadily deepened their bilateral and trilateral relationships in subsequent years, growing into an informal "Quad without the Quad."[25] Given that the United States, Japan, and Australia were already treaty allies and had a preexisting trilateral partnership, India's integration as a strategic partner of this alliance network was essential for the Quad's continued viability.

The Quad re-emerged as a formal entity—again at Japan's initiative—on the sidelines of the ASEAN Summit in Manila in 2017 and has developed more institutional heft and purpose since then. Although India was initially reticent about high-level official engagement under the Quad, this calculation changed after the Galwan Valley skirmish in mid-2020. The four leaders met in a virtual summit in March 2021 and unveiled a broad-based plan to compete for influence with China in the Indo-Pacific on the basis of cooperation on Covid-19 vaccine production and distribution, climate change mitigation, and critical and emerging technologies. These plans fit well with India's desire to compete with China without drawing Beijing into an outright conflict. The nonmilitary aspects of the Quad also help assuage the concerns of smaller

---

[23] "Australia and India Sign Defence Arrangement," Department of Defence (Australia), Press Release, June 4, 2020, https://www.minister.defence.gov.au/minister/lreynolds/media-releases/australia-and-india-sign-defence-arrangement.

[24] "No Four-Way Security Pact Including India—Australian Minister," BBC News, July 11, 2007; and "India Not Part of Any 'So Called Contain China' Effort: PM," Press Trust of India, January 10, 2008, available at https://www.outlookindia.com/newswire/story/india-not-part-of-any-so-called-contain-china-effort-pm/534142.

[25] David Brewster, "The Australia-India Security Declaration: The Quadrilateral Redux?" *Security Challenges* 6, no. 1 (2010): 6.

states in South and Southeast Asia over the rise of militarized great-power conflict in their respective regions.

For India, the deepening of these bilateral, trilateral, and multilateral relationships is part of a larger effort to play a "leading role" in the international order.[26] This goal, first articulated by Modi and Jaishankar in 2015, seeks to transform India from a simple "balancing force" that other powers court and factor into their strategies into a state that proactively shapes outcomes in the international order to achieve its own national interests.[27] To this end, Modi has taken the initiative to build on the work of his predecessors and continue developing relations with the United States and its allies. But for Indian officials becoming a leading power is about more than strategic dialogues and military exercises. As described by Jaishankar, it entails "a willingness to shoulder greater global responsibilities."[28] From New Delhi's perspective, these responsibilities include areas of multilateral activity in which India has traditionally been a major contributor: humanitarian assistance and disaster relief, peacekeeping, maritime safety and security, and "active participation in important global negotiations."[29]

India's desire to play a leading role in world politics was well-planned given the trends in U.S.-China relations. As noted above, Indian leaders displayed alacrity in adjusting to global changes that caught other powers flat-footed. The official and unofficial withdrawal of the United States from various institutional aspects of the international order was a major feature of the Trump presidency. As the world reeled after the U.S. withdrawal from the TPP and the Paris Agreement, and as the Trump administration sought to slowly cut off funding to various UN organs, India reiterated its commitment to the United Nations and doubled down on the Paris Agreement. During his visit to the annual UN General Assembly meeting in September 2019, for the first time Modi convened dialogues with leaders of the Pacific Small Island Developing States and the Caribbean Community and announced plans for India to partner with these groups to tackle the problem of rising sea levels.[30]

Seen through this lens, it is unsurprising that India was keen on the Quad's vaccine initiative. Of late, when Indian leaders have spotted gaps and opportunities in the international order, they have sought to provide the

---

[26] "PM to Heads of Indian Missions," Government of India, Press Release, February 7, 2015, https://pib.gov.in/newsite/PrintRelease.aspx?relid=115241">.

[27] Ibid.

[28] "IISS Fullerton Lecture by Dr. S. Jaishankar, Foreign Secretary in Singapore," Ministry of External Affairs (India), July 20, 2015, https://mea.gov.in/Speeches-Statements.htm?dtl/25493/IISS_Fullerton_Lecture_by_Foreign_Secretary_in_Singapore.

[29] Ibid.

[30] Ministry of External Affairs (India), "India and United Nations," June 1, 2020, https://mea.gov.in/Portal/ForeignRelation/India_UN_2020.pdf.

necessary leadership to address global problems. This approach is once again suitable for a world in which the United States' capacity to single-handedly uphold various parts of the international order is eroding and China has risen as a potential challenger that does not so much seek to overturn the order as to control it and reap its benefits.

India's Assessment of U.S.-China Competition

The respective trajectories of bilateral relations with the United States and China may suggest that India has every incentive to be firmly aligned with the United States against a rising China. Indian leaders, however, do not share this assessment. China is a major trading partner for India, and Chinese funding, though not a comparatively large source of FDI, has poured into high-impact sectors such as technology, automobiles, and infrastructure.[31] China's economic heft means that New Delhi cannot afford to alienate Beijing. More broadly, in contrast with the Cold War, the very notion of rival blocs in some sort of superpower competition is difficult to operationalize when one considers the level of economic interdependence between China, on the one hand, and the United States and its allies, on the other.[32] Despite all the talk of economic decoupling between the West and China, a mid-2021 survey of member firms of the Singaporean-German Chamber of Industry and Commerce showed that the majority do not think long-term decoupling is feasible given the complexity of global value chains.[33]

This mix of security threats and economic opportunities presented by China makes external balancing through treaty alliances impractical. Instead, India has chosen internal balancing through the material benefits of its partnerships while also working to improve relations with China whenever possible in order to maintain strong economic ties. This approach equips India with the hard power required to stand firm in crises with China while seeking reconciliation outside of crises (for example, through the two high-profile summits at Wuhan and Mamallapuram that followed the Doklam crisis). Following this pattern, India's stance toward China has hardened during the ongoing crisis in Ladakh, especially after the deaths of Indian soldiers at Galwan Valley. In response, New Delhi has promulgated new rules restricting Chinese FDI to a handful of sectors, canceled government contracts given to

---

[31] Soumya Bhowmick, "Chinese Investments in Indian Startups: Trends and Controversies," Observer Research Foundation, June 5, 2021, https://www.orfonline.org/expert-speak/chinese-investments-in-indian-startups-trends-and-controversies.

[32] Tanvi Madan, "Not Your Mother's Cold War: India's Options in U.S.-China Competition," *Washington Quarterly* 43, no. 4 (2020): 41–62.

[33] Robin Hoenig, "Supply Chains Under Tension," Singaporean-German Chamber of Industry and Commerce, June 2021.

Chinese state-owned enterprises, and banned almost 60 Chinese apps from being used in India.

It is telling, however, that most of these punitive actions were aimed at Chinese investments that do not widely affect the Indian economy. When it came to trade, in the first half of 2021, India reported a record increase among China's major trading partners (62.7%) compared to the same period of the prior year.[34] In fact, India's trade with China was higher in the first half of 2021 than in the first half of 2019 before the Covid-19 pandemic.[35] While this trend may be the short-term effect of the unprecedented need for medical imports due to the second wave of the pandemic that hit India in early 2021, it still highlights the degree to which "business as usual" is a difficult equilibrium to deviate from, no matter what frictions may exist along the Sino-Indian border. Indian diplomats have in the past been cautious to point out that bilateral differences over issues such as BRI would not compromise the trading relationship between the countries.[36] Given the economic compulsions involved, it would not be surprising to eventually see India soften its stance toward China and once again seek reconciliation if the current crisis is resolved.

The India-U.S. relationship is also not without its share of problems. The United States' traditional reliance on Pakistan, particularly with regard to great-power intervention in Afghanistan—be it the Soviet occupation of the 1980s or the U.S. war on terrorism—has limited the extent to which U.S. and Indian interests can align. The same can be said for India's traditional relationships with U.S. adversaries such as Iran and Russia—the latter still being India's most important source of operational defense equipment.[37] The United States and India have locked horns on trade and immigration, particularly under the Trump administration (discussed below), and these problems are unlikely to dissipate soon. When it comes to international institutions, U.S. support for India playing a leadership role in the top ranks of institutions such as the UN Security Council, International Monetary Fund, World Bank, and others has often been little more than rhetorical. It is unsurprising, therefore, that India is the second-largest shareholder in the China-sponsored Asian Infrastructure Investment Bank—an organization shunned by the United States that creates an alternative venue for rising

---

[34] Ananth Krishnan, "India's Trade with China Soared 62% in H1," *Hindu*, July 13, 2021, https://www.thehindu.com/business/indias-trade-with-china-soared-62-in-h1/article35310753.ece.

[35] Ibid.

[36] "India's Boycott of BRI Not to Affect Trade Ties with China: Indian Envoy," Press Trust of India, May 3, 2019, available at https://economictimes.indiatimes.com/news/economy/foreign-trade/indias-boycott-of-bri-not-to-affect-trade-ties-with-china-indian-envoy/articleshow/69162769.cms.

[37] Sameer Lalwani et al., "The Influence of Arms: Explaining the Durability of India–Russia Alignment," *Journal of Indo-Pacific Affairs* 4, no. 1 (2021): 2–41.

powers to achieve the prestige of institutional leadership. At the level of the international order, efforts by the United States and its allies to hold onto their privileged positions do not sit well with India's great-power ambitions. Indeed, in a historic address to the U.S. Congress in June 2016, Modi pointedly observed that "the effectiveness of [U.S.-India] cooperation would increase if international institutions framed with the mindset of the 20th century were to reflect the realities of today."[38]

Given its ambitions and interests, India remains wary of both Chinese coercion and overweening U.S. power, while also being keenly attuned to the advantages offered by both countries. In his recent book, *The India Way*, Jaishankar repeatedly invoked the importance of "leveraging" the current moment of heightened U.S.-China competition: "India has little choice but to pursue a mix of multiple approaches…. Much of that would revolve around the West and Russia. But China, now the world's second largest economy, can hardly be disregarded in any calculation. Leveraging them all may not be easy but still no less necessary for that."[39] Elsewhere in the book he observed: "Even with neighbours with whom there are serious issues, there should be hope that the price of a pragmatic settlement will be less than the costs of a difficult relationship."[40] In this vein, India is likely to remain an independent actor in the current state of the world, seeking advantage wherever possible. India's independence on this front is linked to its desire to play a leading role in a world that Indian leaders see as increasingly multipolar, and desirably so.[41] Multipolarity for India signifies a world in which power is more widely distributed than it was during the Cold War and its immediate aftermath, and in which no single country or group of countries can maintain a grip on the core institutions of international cooperation. This sort of international order is arguably the most hospitable for India to pursue its own rise to great-power status. Accordingly, Indian leaders welcome the current period of transition away from unipolarity as a moment in which to press their country's case for leadership in the international order.

India's view of U.S.-China competition is thus embedded in a broader commitment to both regional and global multipolarity. Not only would India prefer Asia to be multipolar as a way of containing China; it would also prefer the world to be multipolar as a way of keeping the United States

---

[38] "Text of the Prime Minister's Address to the Joint Session of U.S. Congress," *Hindu*, June 8, 2016, https://www.thehindu.com/news/resources/Text-of-the-Prime-Ministers-address-to-the-Joint-Session-of-U.S.-Congress/article14391856.ece.

[39] S. Jaishankar, *The India Way: Strategies for an Uncertain World* (Noida: HarperCollins Publishers India, 2021).

[40] Ibid.

[41] Elizabeth Roche, "India Supports Multipolar World Order: Shringla," *Mint*, June 23, 2021, https://www.livemint.com/news/world/india-supports-multipolar-world-order-shringla-11624450754028.html.

from becoming globally preponderant as it was briefly after the end of World War II and the Cold War. Competition between Washington and Beijing achieves both these goals. In the minds of Indian leaders, so long as they can be flexible and firm at the right moments, India can benefit from the intensification of U.S.-China competition. This calculation is clearest when one considers one of India's greatest fears with regard to U.S.-China relations: that the two great powers would somehow arrive at an understanding and seek to co-manage the international order. Prior to the Trump presidency, the possibility of a G-2 condominium between the United States and China cast a shadow over the U.S.-India relationship, threatening to compromise Indian interests for the sake of accommodation between the two great powers.[42] The state of U.S.-China relations today suggests that India no longer has any cause to fear this particular outcome.

The Trump presidency was a welcome change for India due to Washington's newfound willingness to both challenge China and pressure Pakistan.[43] Not only did the Trump administration openly call China a revisionist power,[44] it also undertook to challenge China in several domains. Ashley Tellis has identified five efforts to this end: resisting China's attempts to geopolitically dominate the Indo-Pacific, opposing China's unfair economic practices, stymieing Beijing's efforts to create alternative standards for new technologies, confronting China's quest for global technological dominance, and neutralizing advances in China's military capabilities.[45] These can be broadly grouped into three overlapping categories: military power, geopolitics, and economics, with the issue of technology cutting across all three. India's national power and trajectory have mostly benefited from U.S.-China competition in these domains. The following two subsections focus on military power and geopolitics. Economic issues are discussed later in a separate section on the risks to globalization.

The Impact on India's Military Power

In military terms, China's growing power and presence in South Asia would have posed much harder problems for India than they do now in the

---

[42] Tanvi Madan, "The U.S.-India Relationship and China," in "The Second Modi-Obama Summit," Brookings Institution, January 2015, 13.

[43] Rohan Mukherjee, "Chaos as Opportunity: The United States and World Order in India's Grand Strategy," *Contemporary Politics* 26, no. 4 (2020): 420–38.

[44] White House, *National Security Strategy of the United States of America* (Washington, D.C., December 2017), 25, https://trumpwhitehouse.archives.gov/wp-content/uploads/2017/12/NSS-Final-12-18-2017-0905.pdf.

[45] Ashley J. Tellis, "The Return of U.S.-China Strategic Competition," in *Strategic Asia 2020: U.S.-China Competition*, ed. Ashley J. Tellis, Alison Szalwinski, and Michael Wills (Washington, D.C.: National Bureau of Asian Research, 2020), 3–43.

shadow of an increased U.S. commitment to the Indo-Pacific. U.S. investment in a strategic partnership with India has opened up significant new sources of defense imports, not just from the United States but also from U.S. allies such as Israel and France. This has allowed India to both access high-end technologies such as unmanned aerial vehicles, precision munitions, radar, and fourth-generation aircraft and reduce its dependence on Russian imports.[46] Data on arms transfers suggest that India's diversification efforts began bearing fruit after 2012, when Russia's share of India's defense imports stood at 87% and the share of the United States and its allies at 12%. In the eight years since then, Russia's average annual share is down to 56%, while the United States and its allies have increased their share to 43%. In 2019 and 2020, Russia accounted for only 38% and 35% of Indian arms imports, while the United States and its allies accounted for 61% and 65%, respectively.[47]

Many advanced military technologies were out of reach for India prior to the early 2000s. In the time frame leading up to the nuclear deal, Washington removed India-specific export restrictions on dual-use technologies—a category that can include, among other technologies, missile and guidance systems, which are valuable for advanced conventional capabilities. The restrictions had been in place ever since India's first nuclear test in 1974.[48] The 2008 waiver for India in the Nuclear Suppliers Group sponsored by the United States further expanded New Delhi's access to global defense commerce. In a straightforward sense, therefore, the increased willingness of the United States and its allies to supply India's military needs has strengthened India's deterrence and warfighting capabilities in any potential contingencies involving China. The intensification of U.S.-China competition has further strengthened India's international standing, with Washington either mulling or creating exemptions for India's dealings with U.S. adversaries, such as Russia through the purchase of the S-400 missile platform and Iran through investment in the Chabahar port.[49] In both cases, the United States has been quick to sanction other states involved in similar deals with these countries.

---

[46] Niha Dagia, "Bilateral Bond between Pakistan and Russia Deepening," *Diplomat*, June 23, 2021, https://thediplomat.com/2021/06/bilateral-bond-between-pakistan-and-russia-deepening.

[47] U.S. allies in this calculation are Australia, Canada, France, Germany, Israel, Italy, the Netherlands, South Korea, and the United Kingdom. Stockholm International Peace Research Institute (SIPRI), SIPRI Arms Transfer Database, https://www.sipri.org/databases/armstransfers.

[48] Matthew Hoey, "India's Quest for Dual-Use Technology," *Bulletin of the Atomic Scientists* 65, no. 5 (2009).

[49] "U.S. Gave 'Narrow Exemption' to India from Sanctions on Chabahar for Afghanistan's Humanitarian Assistance," ANI News, December 19, 2019, available at https://www.business-standard.com/article/news-ani/us-gave-narrow-exemption-to-india-from-sanctions-on-chabahar-for-afghanistan-s-humanitarian-assistance-119121900257_1.html; and Manu Pubby, "No Blanket Waiver on S-400, Urge India to Avoid Russian Deals: U.S.," *Economic Times*, February 3, 2021, https://economictimes.indiatimes.com/news/defence/no-blanket-waiver-on-s-400-urge-india-to-avoid-russian-deals-us/articleshow/80655707.cms?from=mdr.

A downside of this burgeoning defense relationship with the United States and its allies is the potential for India's growing military power to trigger security dilemmas with Pakistan or China. For example, in 2010, Pakistan and China were quick to conclude their own agreement on civilian nuclear cooperation on the heels of the India-U.S. agreement.[50] Similarly, although not directly linked to U.S. arms transfers, India's enhanced ability to access, patrol, and reconnoiter border areas may have triggered Chinese concerns about a shrinking window of opportunity to turn facts on the ground in the favor of the People's Liberation Army (PLA), leading to the most recent military standoff between India and China.[51] To the extent that military equipment purchased from the United States and its allies enables India to project force in greater quantity or with more reliable accuracy—such as the use of Israeli guided munitions in the 2019 airstrike by the Indian Air Force at Balakot in Pakistan—India's rivals may feel compelled to respond with arms buildups of their own. While evidence of arms racing or a deterioration in India's security environment as a direct result of security dilemmas is scant, this mechanism of strategic competition cannot be ruled out.

The Impact on India's Geopolitical Stature

As noted above, India has benefited from deeper strategic partnerships with the United States and its key allies in the Indo-Pacific such as Australia and Japan. No doubt India has done a great deal to cultivate these partnerships, but a one-sided effort would have been inadequate in the absence of a growing commitment on the part of the United States to treat the Indo-Pacific as the preeminent theater of great-power competition in the 21st century. Strategic partnerships with the United States and its allies benefit India in at least three ways. First, they involve government-to-government coordination at various levels and across multiple domains, from education and science and technology research to military exercises and humanitarian assistance. These relationships benefit all parties by creating opportunities for collaboration and policy coordination in strategic sectors such as energy, counterterrorism, and maritime security, to name a few. Ultimately, the interoperability of not just militaries but civilian bureaucracies with an eye to specific regional challenges is a major benefit to India as well as its strategic partners. This ensures open channels of communication and points of contact between like-minded governments in any potential future crisis scenarios involving China.

---

[50] Sharad Joshi, "The China-Pakistan Nuclear Deal: A Realpolitique Fait Accompli," Nuclear Threat Initiative, December 11, 2011, https://www.nti.org/analysis/articles/china-pakistan-nuclear-deal-realpolitique-fait-accompli-1.

[51] Taylor M. Fravel, "Why Are China and India Skirmishing at Their Border? Here's 4 Things to Know," *Washington Post*, June 2, 2020.

Second, the institutionalization of relationships—in a 2+2 format of defense and foreign ministers, in trilaterals such as the India-Japan-U.S. summit, and ultimately via the Quad—adds considerable substance to India's position within a coalition aimed at competing with China and keeping its rise within limits acceptable to Indo-Pacific countries. Over the last two decades, India has actively sought to deepen its respective bilateral partnerships with the United States, Japan, and Australia, among other countries. More recently, India has increased its support for the Quad as a viable coalition of democratic major powers seeking to uphold key principles such as the freedom of navigation, noncoercion, sovereignty, and territorial integrity in the Indo-Pacific. This ideational aspect of the U.S. commitment to the region often goes unnoticed but is arguably critical as a fundamental normative challenge to countervailing notions of a Sinocentric regional order.[52]

Third, and finally, India's increasing alignment with the United States and its allies serves as an important signal to China (as well as Pakistan) of India's growing importance as a geopolitical pole in a potentially multipolar Asia. A resident power that can manage multiple partnerships and coordinate coalitions aimed at countering China's rise becomes a force to reckon with. This is where the geopolitical weight of the Quad rather than pure capability aggregation becomes a vital factor. The stronger the bonds between India and other Quad members, and indeed other states in the Indo-Pacific such as the members of ASEAN, the greater the collective diplomatic weight that can be brought to bear on key issues such as the freedom of navigation and overflight. Social opprobrium can be a powerful influence in international politics, and most states find resisting its pressures difficult if they are sustained over time.[53] More cynically, the tighter a coalition, the harder it is to pick its members apart. Therefore, the political weight of configurations such as the Quad and Quad Plus (involving like-minded countries such as Vietnam and South Korea) is an asset for India, which seeks all possible means by which to manage its increasingly antagonistic relationship with China. Having the backing of significant states in China's periphery can greatly strengthen India's hand in a future negotiation or crisis.

Given India's penchant for strategic autonomy and allergy toward formal alliances, the flexibility of the partnership with the United States has allowed India to achieve its geopolitical goals without being encumbered by excessive obligations to other capitals. The Trump administration's insistence that U.S. allies and partners should do more to provide for their own security did not disadvantage India. If anything, it created openings for New Delhi

---

[52] Tellis, "The Return of U.S.-China Competition," 26.

[53] Alastair Iain Johnston, *Social States: China in International Institutions, 1980–2000* (Princeton: Princeton University Press, 2008).

to overtly take the initiative in securing its borders and responding to provocations, all the while knowing that Washington was in India's corner, providing support when necessary. For example, the absence of overt U.S. diplomatic intervention in India's respective crises with China at Doklam in 2017 and with Pakistan at Pulwama/Balakot in 2019 was evidence of a healthy strategic partnership that enabled India to make its own decisions while receiving intelligence and diplomatic support from the United States behind the scenes.[54] In this sense, the United States' willingness to challenge China in the Indo-Pacific has not come at significant cost to India—unlike Japan, which faced uncomfortable questions from the Trump administration over its contribution to the U.S.-Japan alliance.[55]

A nascent area in which U.S.-China competition may benefit India is that of geoeconomics in India's neighborhood. As noted above, since the early 2000s, China has made sustained inroads into South Asia, less through trade (barring India) and more through capital. Chinese state-owned enterprises have funded large-scale infrastructure projects in all of India's neighboring countries, and consequently Beijing has become a major political actor in the region. South Asian states that have traditionally chafed under India's power have benefited from these developments. They are now able to rely on China to reduce Indian influence, while relying on India to ensure that China does not demand too much in return for its investments. Three countries neighboring India—Pakistan, Bangladesh, and Myanmar—alone account for 63% of China's arms exports in the last decade.[56] China's growing strategic footprint in South Asia therefore has both economic and security implications.

India has sought to counter this influence through a mix of economic statecraft and an underlying threat of coercion if countries in its orbit start to feel China's gravitational pull too strongly. As U.S.-China competition has stepped up, the United States and its allies have announced their desire to participate on the economic side of things through various initiatives, such as the Asia-Africa Growth Corridor jointly announced by Japan and India in 2017, the U.S. BUILD (Better Utilization of Investments Leading to Development) Act of 2018 that established a new vehicle for channeling development finance to low- and lower-middle-income countries, and the G-7's Build Back Better World initiative of 2021, which is designed to focus

---

[54] See Debarshi Dasgupta, "Indian Elephant Fit for a Marathon—Not a Sprint—in Taking On China," *Straits Times*, July 19, 2021, https://www.straitstimes.com/opinion/indian-elephant-fit-for-a-marathon-not-a-sprint-in-taking-on-china.

[55] Paul O'Shea and Sebastian Maslow, "'Making the Alliance Even Greater': (Mis-)managing U.S.-Japan Relations in the Age of Trump," *Asian Security* (2020): 1–21, https://doi.org/10.1080/14799855.2020.1838486.

[56] Calculated from SIPRI Arms Transfer Database.

on infrastructure in similar settings. At this moment, however, these plans remain in their early stages, and it is unclear whether they signal commitments of new funding or simply an effort to channel existing sources of private, public, and nonprofit funding in a more concerted effort to compete with China's BRI. Moreover, the U.S.-backed initiatives are intended to compete with BRI's global footprint, and to that extent it is also unclear how much of an impact they will have on South Asia in particular. Nonetheless, this area of cooperation between India and advanced Western economies is likely to grow and become more complex in the near future.

A downside of India's growing geopolitical ties to the United States has been the rise of a narrative from Beijing that paints India as a U.S. puppet being manipulated into weakening China on its western flank.[57] This view overlooks the many bilateral conflicts of interest between India and China that have contributed to India autonomously seeking alignment with the United States and other countries. Nonetheless, while empirically inaccurate, Beijing's rhetoric signals a potential deterioration in India's security environment with China. It is worth noting that the last time China used similar rhetoric was at the height of Sino-Indian tensions in the 1960s, when Chinese leaders labeled India a "running dog of imperialism."[58] Present trends suggest that Beijing may use India's closeness to the United States and active membership in the Quad as a pretext for aggressive actions aimed at achieving ulterior gains, such as territory along the disputed border.

In sum, the intensification of U.S.-China competition has largely been positive for India's military power and geopolitical stature. India has tried to leverage the increasingly competitive environment to diversify its strategic and defense relationships and build up its military power. Although their respective interests are not always aligned and can often be in conflict, both India and the United States have developed a mutual understanding and robust strategic partnership that is likely to get stronger over time.

The Covid-19 Pandemic and India's Grand Strategy

The impact of Covid-19 on India's national trajectory and power is primarily economic. The pandemic acted as both a supply shock and a demand shock. On the one hand, supply chains throughout the country came

---

[57] Christopher K. Colley, "China's Ongoing Debates about India and the United States," Wilson Center, Asia Dispatches, June 30, 2020, https://www.wilsoncenter.org/blog-post/chinas-ongoing-debates-about-india-and-united-states; and "Confronting China for U.S. Worst Strategy for India," *Global Times*, June 29, 2021.

[58] Anton Harder, "Defining Independence in Cold War Asia: Sino-Indian Relations, 1949–1962" (PhD diss., Department of International History, London School of Economics and Political Science, May 2015), 249.

to a grinding halt due to lockdowns and the spread of the virus. On the other hand, demand steeply declined for the same reasons. This double effect caused businesses—especially small and medium-sized enterprises—to struggle to meet overhead costs due to a paucity of both revenue and labor.[59] The impact of the pandemic on business balance sheets and household incomes will be felt for many years to come. New Delhi responded to the crisis through multiple rounds of stimulus funding, tax relief, loan waivers, employment insurance, and liquidity measures (for banks).[60] As India's second wave in spring 2021 exposed the glaring inadequacies of the public healthcare system, the government announced its plan to double healthcare spending from the 2019 level of 1.29% of GDP.[61]

The short-term effects of the pandemic are already evident in the contraction of India's economy.[62] Equally evident is the impact on India's official spending priorities. The increase in health spending coupled with economic contraction and lower tax revenue has meant lower shares in the government budget for other sectors. India's defense budget, which had been steadily rising over the last decade and maintained a consistent share of approximately 16.4% of overall government spending, fell to 13.7% of total spending in 2021.[63] The silver lining was that capital expenditures—the funds available for acquisition and modernization of military equipment—were at 27% of the total defense budget in 2021. This figure continued the reversal, since 2019, of a long-term decline in the share of capital expenditures in the defense budget, which was typically dominated by salaries and pensions.[64] The pandemic thus did not affect India's efforts to rationalize personnel costs in order to make more room for capital outlays. Indeed, India's ongoing standoff with China in Ladakh has made defense acquisitions a top priority. Soon after the Galwan Valley clash, the Ministry of Defence approved expenditure

---

[59] EY, "Managing the Impact of Covid-19 on India's Supply Chains—Now, Next and Beyond," July 2020.

[60] "Government and Institution Measures in Response to Covid-19," KPMG, December 2, 2020, https://home.kpmg/xx/en/home/insights/2020/04/india-government-and-institution-measures-in-response-to-covid.html.

[61] Puja Mehra, "India's Economy Needs Big Dose of Health Spending," Mint, April 8, 2020, https://www.livemint.com/news/india/india-s-economy-needs-big-dose-of-health-spending-11586365603651.html; and Anshula Raj, "Budget 2021: 'Increase Healthcare Expenditure from 1.2% to 2.5% of GDP,'" Business India, February 1, 2021, https://www.businesstoday.in/business/expectations/story/increase-healthcare-expenditure-from-12-to-25-of-gdp-286233-2021-02-01.

[62] "India's March Quarter GDP at 1.6%, FY21 Growth Revised to -7.3%," India Today, May 31, 2021, https://www.indiatoday.in/business/story/india-s-march-quarter-gdp-grows-1-6-fy21-growth-revised-to-7-3-1809144-2021-05-31.

[63] "Demand for Grants 2021–22 Analysis," PRS Legislative Research, February 12, 2021, https://prsindia.org/budgets/parliament/demand-for-grants-2021-22-analysis-telecommunications.

[64] Ibid.

worth $5.5 billion toward upgrading and acquiring fighter aircraft, artillery pieces and rounds, combat vehicles, cruise missiles, and anti-tank missiles.[65]

While there is no doubt that India's public health priorities will impinge on the resources available for defense preparedness in the near term, the effects are likely to diminish over time as the Indian economy recovers and an ever-larger share of the population is vaccinated. India thus faces a window of vulnerability in which its adversaries might attempt to make territorial gains or weaken the country through other means, though such attempts will be costly for the adversary given India's commitment to defending its borders.[66]

It is possible that the pandemic itself may have negatively affected India's security environment by providing an opportunity to the PLA to make its moves along the border while India and other countries were distracted. However, there is little evidence to suggest that the PLA decided to use the pandemic as cover for its actions. Rather, it is more likely that actions planned earlier, in late 2019, could only be implemented in the spring of 2020 due to the inhospitable conditions of winter in the high Himalayas. India's completion of a major road-building project near the border in April 2019 and a new law converting the Ladakh region into a territory directly governed by the central government (as opposed to a state government) in October 2019 are more likely as proximate causes of the crisis.[67] The deep causes of the crisis are related to China's grand strategy and perception of India as an upstart nation emboldened by the United States.[68] These two factors have given rise to Chinese apprehensions about India's ability to exert greater administrative and tactical control along the border, likely leading the PLA to preemptively occupy disputed territories as a *fait accompli*.

In the medium term, the pandemic may exacerbate the economic challenges India already faces. According to World Bank data, from a high

---

[65] Vivek Raghuvanshi, "India Accelerates Weapons Purchases in Wake of Border Clash with China," *DefenseNews*, July 6, 2020, https://www.defensenews.com/global/asia-pacific/2020/07/06/india-accelerates-weapons-purchases-in-wake-of-border-clash-with-china.

[66] In June 2021, India moved another 50,000 troops to the Ladakh border, raising the total number of Indian troops in the region to 200,000. "India Shifts 50,000 Additional Troops to China Border in Historic Move," Bloomberg, June 28, 2021, available at https://www.business-standard.com/article/current-affairs/india-shifts-50-000-additional-troops-to-china-border-in-historic-move-121062801542_1.html.

[67] Ajay Banerjee, "India Completes Vital Ladakh Road," *Tribune*, April 22, 2019, https://www.tribuneindia.com/news/archive/nation/india-completes-vital-ladakh-road-762332; Sutirtho Patranobis, "India Building Border Infra, Deploying Military Root Cause of Tension: China," *Hindustan Times*, October 13, 2020, https://www.hindustantimes.com/world-news/india-building-border-infra-deploying-military-root-cause-of-tension-china/story-HJIhvB3dUAsTYB8IdDO7cK.html; and Zeba Siddiqui and Fayaz Bukhari, "India, China Clash Over Kashmir as It Loses Special Status and Is Divided," Reuters, October 31, 2019, https://www.reuters.com/article/us-india-kashmir/india-china-clash-over-kashmir-as-it-loses-special-status-and-is-divided-idUSKBN1XA0M9.

[68] Yun Sun, "China's Strategic Assessment of the Ladakh Clash," War on the Rocks, June 19, 2020, https://warontherocks.com/2020/06/chinas-strategic-assessment-of-the-ladakh-clash.

of 8.5% in financial year 2010–11, India's GDP growth rate was already down to 6.8% by 2017–18 and dropped further to 6.5% in 2018-19.[69] Manufacturing, the sector in which India has tried to become more competitive, declined in terms of value added as a share of GDP from 17.1% in 2008–9 to 14.9% in 2018–19. During the same period, R&D expenditure as a share of GDP—an indicator of technological innovation—declined from 0.9% to 0.6%, labor force participation for those aged 15 and above declined from 55.7% to 49.4%, and net inflows of FDI as a share of GDP declined from 3.6% to 1.6%. Meanwhile, two-thirds of the population remains rural, the income tax base is only 1% of the entire population, and annual growth in human development as measured by the United Nation's Human Development Index slowed down between 2010 and 2019 compared to the previous two decades.[70] Although economic growth is expected to rebound after the pandemic, it will need to climb higher than immediate pre-pandemic levels if India is to sustain its steady rise.

There are some positive signs that India may be able to get back on track in the medium term. Infrastructure provision in terms of electricity supply, railways, and surfaced roads has continued to steadily rise; industrial production (including mining, manufacturing, and electricity generation) has been increasing; foreign exchange reserves are at an all-time high; gross domestic saving and investment are at historically high levels (though not as high as the period between 2005 and 2012); the fiscal deficit as a share of GDP fell from 5.9% in 2011–12 to 3.4% in 2018–19; the inflation rate declined from 10.9% in 2009 to 3.7% in 2019; and employment in the formal sector is at historic highs and rising faster than before.[71]

The overall picture suggests that India's economy was already slowing down prior to the pandemic—in part due to depressed economic activity resulting from successive poorly implemented national policies such as currency demonetization in 2016 and a goods and services tax in 2017—and the government will need to pay particular attention to growth and employment in the short term while prioritizing human development in the

---

[69] World Bank, World Development Indicators, "GDP Growth (Annual %)," https://data.worldbank.org/indicator/ny.gdp.mktp.kd.zg.

[70] Samrat Sharma, "Only 1% of India Pays Income Tax, Govt Shows Proof; Tax Evasion Still a Major Roadblock," *Financial Express*, September 21, 2020, https://www.financialexpress.com/economy/only-1-of-india-pays-income-tax-govt-shows-proof-tax-evasion-still-a-major-roadblock/2088141; and UN Development Programme, *Human Development Report 2020* (New York: UNDP, 2020), 348, http://hdr.undp.org/sites/default/files/hdr2020.pdf.

[71] Ministry of Finance (India), *Economic Survey 2020–21*, vol. 2 (New Delhi, January 2021), Tables A26, A44–49, A53, A58, A84, https://www.indiabudget.gov.in/economicsurvey/doc/echapter_vol2.pdf; World Bank, World Development Indicators; and "Formal Employment Rises from 17.9% to 22.8% in 6 Years: Economic Survey," *India Today*, January 31, 2020, https://www.indiatoday.in/budget-2019/story/formal-employment-rises-from-17-9-to-22-8-in-6-years-economic-survey-1641990-2020-01-31.

long term. The positive side of the ledger suggests that the state can return to past growth levels through a mix of policies that prioritize infrastructure and social spending while reducing the burden of regulation on households and private enterprise. Covid-19 will dent the government's ability to undertake decisive reforms in the short term, but the longer-term challenges India faces have little to do with the pandemic itself.

India's response to the pandemic has been to focus, as all other nations have, on domestic management and recovery. At the same time, India's desire to become a leading power was on display as the government embarked in January 2021 on an ambitious program of health diplomacy by distributing drugs, personal protection equipment, and vaccines to a large number of countries around the world.[72] According to government data at the time of writing, India supplied 66.4 million doses of vaccines, of which 16% were given as grants (mostly to neighboring countries), 54% on a commercial basis, and 30% as part of India's commitment to the World Health Organization's COVAX initiative.[73] By April 2021, in the throes of its second wave, India had to suspend vaccine exports in order to cater to its own population.[74] Although this certainly dented India's image in the eyes of expectant countries in dire need of vaccines, the reputational effects are unlikely to outlast the export ban, especially at a time when national public health trumping global concerns is an entirely unexceptional practice among major powers such as the United States and the European Union.[75]

In sum, while the Covid-19 pandemic will affect India's ability to generate national power in the medium term, it is possible for India to regain its economic vitality so long as the deeper economic problems facing the country are addressed. The necessity of managing with lower shares of the public budget may in fact provide the impetus needed to continue reforming defense procurement and utilization, especially in ways that might further increase the share of capital expenditures. India has also taken the pandemic as an opportunity to burnish its credentials for global leadership through the

---

[72] "Yearender 2020: Health Diplomacy Dominates India's Foreign Policy amidst Covid-19," ANI News, December 29, 2020, available at https://economictimes.indiatimes.com/news/politics-and-nation/yearender-2020-health-diplomacy-dominates-indias-foreign-policy-amidst-covid-19/articleshow/80013768.cms.

[73] For government data on vaccine supplies, see "Made-in-India Covid19 Vaccine Supplies So Far (in Lakhs)," Ministry of External Affairs (India), https://www.mea.gov.in/vaccine-supply.htm.

[74] "Coronavirus: India Temporarily Halts Oxford-AstraZeneca Vaccine Exports," BBC News, March 24, 2021, https://www.bbc.com/news/world-asia-india-56513371.

[75] "American Export Controls Threaten to Hinder Global Vaccine Production," Economist, April 24, 2021, https://www.economist.com/science-and-technology/2021/04/22/american-export-controls-threaten-to-hinder-global-vaccine-production; and "Coronavirus: WHO Criticises EU over Vaccine Export Controls," BBC News, January 30, 2021, https://www.bbc.com/news/world-europe-55860540.

provision of drugs, health equipment, and vaccines, both on a bilateral basis and through multilateral coalitions such as the Quad.

Risks to Globalization and India's Grand Strategy

The risks to globalization in an era of intensified U.S.-China competition suggest a mixed picture in terms of their impact on India's national power and trajectory. On the positive side of the ledger, China's rise as the world's factory in the 21st century has made it a major trading partner for India and a competitor with the United States for Indian markets. As **Figure 1** shows, China has risen from only 0.1% of India's overall merchandise trade in 1990 to account for 12.1%, just slightly ahead of the United States, whose share has fallen from a peak of 14.7% in 1993 to 11.8% in 2020.[76]

India has benefited from this trade competition due in part to the fact that the United States and China serve different aspects of India's trading needs. The United States is by far India's largest export market and China is conversely India's largest source of imports. India also benefits from the comparative advantages of the U.S. and Chinese economies. From 2016 to 2020, India's top imports from China included cellular phones, data processors, electronics components, and integrated circuits, whereas top imports from the United States included diamonds, petroleum oils, gold, turbo jets, and coal.[77] Thus, although they compete in a broader sense for overall market share, U.S. and Chinese firms are not in direct competition in the most valuable categories of trade with India. As an importing nation, however, India has benefited from the emergence of China as a major producer of electronics and computers.

The major difference between India's trading relationships with the United States and China lies in the balance of trade. As **Figure 2** shows, barring 2008, the year of the global financial crisis, India has maintained a trade surplus with the United States, which grew annually from 2009 to 2014 and has hovered around $20 billion per annum ever since. By contrast, India has experienced a steadily worsening trade deficit with China, rising from $2 billion in 2003 to a peak of $59 billion in 2016.[78]

These trade imbalances have been problematic in two respects. First, India's consistent and large trade surpluses with the United States became a target of the Trump administration's protectionist trade policy. In early 2018, Washington imposed tariffs on 14% of imports from India and New Delhi

---

[76] UN Comtrade, UN Comtrade Database, https://comtrade.un.org.

[77] Ibid.

[78] Ibid.

FIGURE 1   Trade with China and the United States as a share of India's total trade

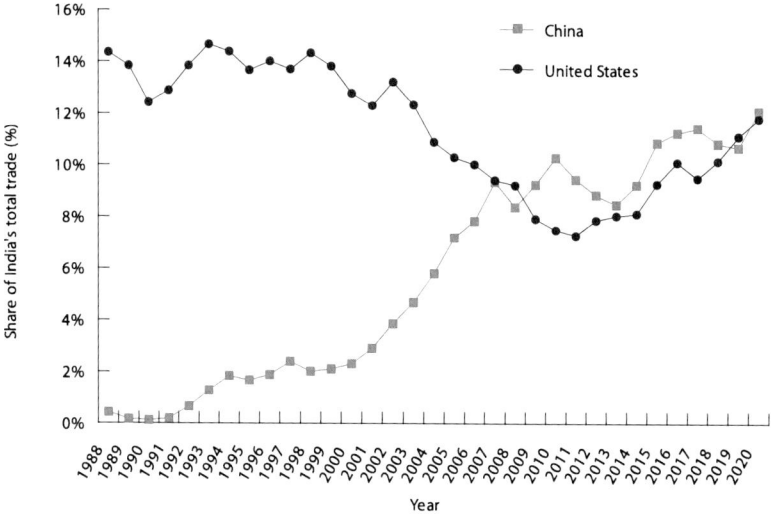

SOURCE: UN Comtrade, UN Comtrade Database.

FIGURE 2   India's balance of trade with the United States and China

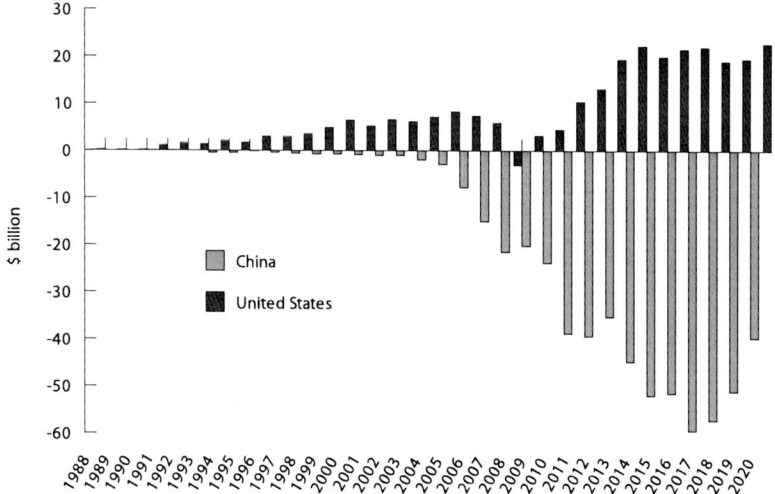

SOURCE: UN Comtrade, UN Comtrade Database.

countered with its own tariffs, leading to what one analyst dubbed a "mini-trade war" compared to the much bigger stakes in the U.S.-China contest.[79] In mid-2019, Washington revoked India's preferential trading status under the Generalized System of Preferences (GSP). A subsequent attempt by Trump and Modi to strike a side agreement on trade floundered on issues of market access, intellectual property, and tariffs—all traditional concerns that the United States has harbored regarding India but rarely taken punitive action to address.[80] Thus, although the tariff spiral between the United States and China has led firms to look to India as an alternative market,[81] these gains have been somewhat offset by the sweeping nature of U.S. protectionism, which may well be extended by the Biden administration.[82]

Indeed, in the brief period for which we have data, it is unclear whether India has benefited significantly from the U.S.-China trade war. Given that the United States announced its first round of tariffs against China in January 2018, and given that the Covid-19 pandemic began in early 2020, we can only look at the change in trade patterns from 2018 to 2019 to get a picture of potential trade substitution toward India. If we look at goods where China lost substantial market share in U.S. imports between these two years—defined as a drop of at least ten percentage points—and compare that list with goods where India gained market share by at least ten percentage points, there is prima facie evidence of trade substitution. These goods include soybean oil, chemicals of certain varieties, iron tubes, synthetic precious stones, slate, carpets, woven fabrics, and silk yarn. In all these categories, India gained commensurately to what China lost as a share of U.S. imports.[83] However, the monetary gain to India in these product categories was only approximately $340 million, or 10% of the overall increase in imports to the United States from India in 2019 compared to the previous year.[84] While one cannot decisively say that the U.S.-China trade war caused this increase, and while this is only evidence from the first year of the trade war, it provides some indication of possible future economic gains to India from U.S.-China

---

[79] Chad P. Bown, "Trump's Mini-Trade War with India," Peterson Institute for International Economics, July 8, 2019, https://www.piie.com/blogs/trade-and-investment-policy-watch/trumps-mini-trade-war-india.

[80] "Donald Trump in India: Key Deals Signed on Defence but Not on Trade," BBC News, February 25, 2020, https://www.bbc.com/news/world-asia-india-51625503.

[81] Stella Soon, "India Could Be a Winner in the U.S.-China Trade War," CNBC, September 18, 2019, https://www.cnbc.com/2019/09/19/india-could-be-a-winner-in-the-us-china-trade-war.html.

[82] "Biden Reinvigorates Tariff War Against India with Retaliation Against Digital Tax," Indo-Asian News Agency, June 7, 2021, available at https://economictimes.indiatimes.com/news/economy/foreign-trade/biden-reinvigorates-tariff-war-against-india-with-retaliation-against-digital-tax/articleshow/83289565.cms.

[83] Calculated from UN Comtrade.

[84] Ibid.

competition. These gains may increase substantially if Indian firms are able to compete successfully in sectors where Chinese firms are losing market share.

The second challenge of India's trading relationships is the country's ballooning trade deficit with China, which has raised concerns about overdependence on a single country for imports in certain sectors.[85] This worry is compounded by increasing tensions between India and China, which raise the specter of economic coercion, as do the security risks surrounding China's efforts to promote alternative technical standards for new technologies such as 5G. Given its relatively low investment in R&D as a share of GDP, India has not been at the forefront of technological innovation compared to technological superpowers such as the United States and China. Nonetheless, as a large-scale adopter of new technologies, India does have a vital stake in who shapes their development and implementation. Given China's dominance as a source of telecommunications and consumer electronics, analysts have also warned of the operational security risks of allowing Chinese firms and investors unfettered access to the Indian market.[86]

As it did for several other countries, the Covid-19 pandemic served as a moment of introspection regarding India's dependence on China-centric supply chains, and the Ladakh crisis has further heightened Indian concerns. The resulting policy momentum has dovetailed with U.S. efforts to create more secure and resilient supply chains in the Indo-Pacific. In March 2020, India announced a Production Linked Incentive scheme that provides subsidies to companies able to expand their manufacturing base in India and hit certain production targets.[87] The program has been rolled out in select sectors that see high domestic as well as foreign demand such as electronics, pharmaceuticals, telecommunications, processed foods, solar cells, automobiles, textiles, and steel. The effects are already visible in the electronics sector, with large cellular-phone components manufacturers moving their production lines to India.[88]

In September 2020, as Japan expanded its subsidy program to help Japanese firms develop supply chains outside China, Modi, in public remarks

---

[85] Bonny Lin et al., *Regional Responses to U.S.-China Competition in the Indo-Pacific: Study Overview and Conclusions* (Santa Monica: RAND Corporation, 2020), 42–43.

[86] Smita Purushottam, "Chinese Threat to Cybersecurity: Why India Needs a Comprehensive & Concrete Action Plan for National Security and Economic Health," *Financial Express*, October 27, 2018, https://www.financialexpress.com/opinion/chinese-threat-to-cybersecurity-why-india-needs-a-comprehensive-concrete-action-plan-for-national-security-and-economic-health/1363012.

[87] Sandeep Soni, "Production-Linked Incentive: What Is Modi Govt's Pet PLI Scheme, Who Is Eligible, Which Sectors Have It?" *Financial Express*, May 31, 2021, https://www.financialexpress.com/industry/sme/production-linked-incentive-what-is-modi-govts-pet-pli-scheme-who-is-eligible-which-sectors-have-it/2262391.

[88] Stephanie Findlay, "Manufacturers Look to India to Tap Market and Diversify Supply Chains," *Financial Times*, December 2, 2020, https://www.ft.com/content/8d3b89fc-007f-4299-a519-a8bd81a7360b.

to the U.S.-India Strategic Partnership Forum, argued that the pandemic had made clear the importance of developing supply chains based not just on cost considerations but also on "trust."[89] In April 2021, India, Japan, and Australia announced a joint initiative to develop supply chain resilience in the Indo-Pacific.[90] The Indian government's efforts to link up with global value chains in key sectors have already begun to pay off, as FDI in computer hardware and software in India jumped from $7.7 billion in 2020 to $26.2 billion in 2021 (due to pandemic-related demand).[91] Although India has seized the opportunity to diversify supply chains in the current geopolitical climate, the success of this strategy will also depend on competition from other countries looking to attract supply chains to their own jurisdictions. Given their greater proximity and cultural similarity, countries such as Vietnam, Malaysia, and Singapore have already snapped up a great deal of the business leaving China.[92]

As the above discussion suggests, India could in theory gain from risks to globalization such as rising protectionism in major economies and attempts by the West and China to decouple supply chains and promote competing standards for new technologies. The ideal strategy for a country such as India would be to boost exports as a way of engineering economic growth, particularly as an element of post-pandemic recovery efforts.[93] Exports require market access overseas, which in turn requires quid pro quo agreements to allow foreign firms access to Indian markets. Events, however, have not matched economic theory. Until 2017, India's average most favored nation (MFN) tariff—i.e., the average tariff for World Trade Organization members with which India does not have preferential trading agreements—hovered around 13%, down from 125% in 1991.[94] In 2018, partly due to the mini-trade war with the United States, India's average tariff rate shot up to

---

[89] Kiran Sharma and Takako Gakuto, "Modi Calls for 'Trustworthy' Supply Chains in Alternative to China," *Nikkei Asia*, September 4, 2020, https://asia.nikkei.com/Economy/Modi-calls-for-trustworthy-supply-chains-in-alternative-to-China.

[90] Asit Ranjan Mishra, "India, Japan and Australia Unveil Supply Chain Initiative," *Mint*, April 28, 2021, https://www.livemint.com/news/world/india-japan-australia-launch-supply-chain-initiative-to-counter-china-11619532624451.html.

[91] "Amount of Foreign Direct Investment (FDI) Equity Inflows for Computer Hardware and Software Sector in India from Financial Year 2015 to 2021," Statista, https://www.statista.com/statistics/711501/india-fdi-equity-inflow-amount-for-computer-hardware-and-software-sector.

[92] Sophia Lewis, "Does India Benefit from a Sino-U.S. Trade Conflict?" Observer Research Foundation, September 19, 2020, https://www.orfonline.org/expert-speak/does-india-benefit-sino-us-trade-conflict; and see also "QIMA Q2 2021 Barometer: As Businesses Leave 'Crisis Mode' Behind, Diversification Continues While Ethical Compliance and Quality Take a Hit," QIMA, 2021.

[93] Shoumitro Chatterjee and Arvind Subramanian, "India's Inward (Re)Turn: Is it Warranted? Will it Work?" Ashoka Center for Economic Policy, Policy Paper, October 2020, 20.

[94] Ibid., 5.

17.5%, and in 2020 it was at 17.9%.[95] Therefore, India has been unable to buck the global protectionist trend and may not be well-placed to "export its way out of the pandemic."[96]

Overall, India remains a relatively protectionist economy. Out of 138 countries for which data was available in 2019, India ranked in the 90th percentile of average MFN tariffs (the United States, following Trump's tariffs, and China were in the 56th and 41st percentiles, respectively).[97] In the Global Trade Alert database of liberalizing and harmful state interventions in international trade since 2008, India ranks 3rd after the United States and Germany (out of 120 countries) in terms of the net harm done to the international trading system when measured by number of interventions. China, by comparison, ranks 37th.[98] The only mitigating factor is India's relatively small share of global trade—2.36% in 2019, making it the thirteenth-largest trading nation by this metric, behind Canada, Italy, Singapore, South Korea, Hong Kong, and others—which limits the damage India's protectionism can do to the world compared to similar policies by the United States and China.[99]

The Modi government's emphasis on self-reliance, enshrined officially in the Atmanirbhar Bharat Abhiyan (Self-Reliant India Campaign) since the onset of the pandemic, also paints a mixed picture of economic openness. On the one hand, the government has consistently denied that self-reliance entails protectionism, and sectors such as defense, railways, construction, insurance, retail, and aviation have been liberalized to allow greater FDI since the Bharatiya Janata Party (BJP) first came to power in 2014.[100] On the other hand, in more recent years, liberalizing gains in some sectors such as defense have been partially reversed, while new tariffs have been introduced in other sectors such as consumer goods. It is often noted that while India signed eleven free trade agreements between 2004 and 2014, none have been signed since. In a particularly high-profile moment of self-reliance, in November

---

[95] Chatterjee and Subramanian, "India's Inward (Re)Turn," 5.

[96] Ibid., 20.

[97] World Bank, World Development Indicators.

[98] Global Trade Alert, "Global Dynamics," https://www.globaltradealert.org/global_dynamics/day-to_0921/flow_all.

[99] World Bank, World Development Indicators.

[100] Jacobo Silva Parada, "Financial Liberalization during the Modi Government: Political and Economic Implications," *India Review* 20, no. 1 (2021): 29–67.

2019 India abandoned the Regional Comprehensive Economic Partnership (RCEP) negotiations after seven years of involvement.[101]

Nonetheless, while self-reliance has dampened India's openness to trade, it has simultaneously led to a spike in FDI flows into India as the government rolls out incentives to both build India's manufacturing capacity and develop supply chains that are not overly dependent on China. Despite the pandemic, India drew its highest ever annual FDI figure of $81.72 billion in the 2020–21 fiscal year.[102] This high-tariff, high-FDI approach may be sustainable so long as the burden of tariffs largely falls on goods and services that are not essential for sectors attracting FDI to continue growing—which will be no easy task to achieve.

In sum, the risks to globalization such as the global protectionist turn and decoupling of supply chains have had mixed results for India. The United States' emphasis on fairer trade competition with China and India has both helped and hurt India, and these effects are likely to persist under the Biden administration. The efforts by the United States and its allies to create supply chain resilience in the Indo-Pacific have benefited India, albeit at the cost of government subsidies designed to connect with global value chains. India's overall response to the changing global scenario has been to raise tariffs substantially while also boosting FDI. The success of this strategy will depend on the skillful distribution of FDI incentives and tariffs across economic sectors, as well as on the state of play in competitor countries such as Vietnam, Malaysia, and Singapore.

Ultimately, however, India's potential gains from diversification are still marginal in the context of China's immense market power in both trade and investment. As recent trade data shows, while India may be able to tackle its trade deficit with China to some extent, dependence on China is unavoidable. Even in the realm of investment, New Delhi hinted in February 2021 that it may relax the restrictions on Chinese FDI imposed at the height of the Ladakh crisis in 2020 in nonsensitive sectors such as manufacturing, automobiles, and services.[103]

---

[101] Asit Ranjan Mishra, "Wary of FTAs, India May Be Turning Trade Protectionist," *Mint*, December 16, 2020, https://www.livemint.com/budget/news/wary-of-ftas-india-may-be-turning-trade-protectionist-11608087352854.html; and Prachi Priya and Aniruddha Ghosh, "India's Out of RCEP: What's Next for the Country and Free Trade?" *Diplomat*, December 15, 2020, https://thediplomat.com/2020/12/indias-out-of-rcep-whats-next-for-the-country-and-free-trade.

[102] Shreya Nandi, "India's Total FDI Inflow Rises 38% Year-on-Year to $6.24 Billion in April," *Business Standard*, June 23, 2021, https://www.business-standard.com/article/economy-policy/india-s-total-fdi-inflow-rises-38-on-year-to-6-24-billion-in-april-121062301664_1.html.

[103] Shrimi Choudhary, "China FDI Proposals for Up to 25% Equity May Get Automatic Approval," *Business Standard*, February 24, 2021, https://www.business-standard.com/article/economy-policy/automatic-approval-likely-for-china-fdi-proposals-up-to-25-equity-121022400084_1.html. No policy change has been announced at the time of writing.

Implications for the United States

Relations between the United States and India have never been better. India is far more comfortable today with the exercise of U.S. leadership and power in the Indo-Pacific than ever before. Both countries have also developed habits and institutions of continued and deep cooperation that no longer depend on individuals. While the presence or absence of particular political leaders and bureaucrats on the scene may affect the pace of engagement between the two governments, the broader trajectory of cooperation is now well-established. Nonetheless, U.S. policymakers must keep in mind the limits of what is possible in the strategic partnership with India relative to the traditional relationships the United States has enjoyed with treaty allies in the Indo-Pacific. The analysis presented in this chapter suggests three broad lessons for U.S. policy.

First, India is likely to express stronger alignment with U.S. interests and initiatives in the Indo-Pacific in times of tension or crisis with China. Put differently, India's interests are its own and may not always align with those of the United States. Outside of crises, India is likely to seek to better relations with China for economic reasons and to broaden the constituency of states that support India's aspirations for great-power status in the international order. This tendency is reinforced by the friction that still exists in the U.S.-India relationship over trade and immigration, historically salient strategic partners (Pakistan, Iran, and Russia, in particular), and the lack of genuine support among successive U.S. administrations for an official leadership role for India in prominent international institutions. As U.S.-China competition intensifies, Washington can expect strong support from India in return for continued investment in India's hard-power capabilities and tacit material and diplomatic support in New Delhi's confrontations with Beijing. Washington can also expect that India will do its best to "leverage" the current situation—to borrow India's foreign minister's turn of phrase—to achieve its national interests, which will occasionally clash with those of the United States. This should not be cause for discord in the U.S.-India partnership but rather the basis for managing expectations.

Second, the pandemic is likely to delay but not derail India's rise if the government can devise a mix of policies focused on growth, employment, and human development. Reasonably strong economic fundamentals, a large military, and growing geopolitical partnerships in the Indo-Pacific will ensure that India remains a central player in the future of both the region and the international order writ large. To facilitate this role, the United States can further develop partnerships in India's health sector. Although India's pharmaceutical and drug industry is highly developed, the pandemic has made foreign investment in areas such as hospital infrastructure, medical education, technological innovation, and medical devices a priority.[104] Rural health and healthcare in second- and third-tier cities, in particular, are areas in which U.S. firms can find mutually beneficial growth opportunities in India.

Third, and finally, India's efforts at self-reliance are an opportunity for the United States and its allies to proceed with their agenda of diversifying supply chains in the Indo-Pacific. Investing in India's long-term potential to become a manufacturing powerhouse can only benefit countries looking to reduce their dependence on China. The investment focus of India's self-reliance campaign, therefore, offers opportunities for U.S. firms to benefit from entering economic sectors that will enjoy the Indian government's support in the coming years. At the same time, continued bilateral differences on trade in the areas of market access, intellectual property, and unfair competition will need to be resolved if India and the United States are to truly find a more harmonious mode of economic cooperation. The United States may need to consider bracketing agricultural market access, a domestic political minefield in India, for the sake of liberalization in other areas, including rolling back the various tariffs and counter-tariffs in place since 2018. A preferential trade agreement that can secure the slow and gradual liberalization of Indian agriculture in exchange for lower tariffs and a negotiated return to GSP status for key Indian exports might offer a way for both sides to achieve their economic goals.

India remains a powerful economic and military actor in the Indo-Pacific whose interests have become strongly aligned with those of the United States over the last two decades. Like the United States in a different era, India is also a rising nation with great-power ambitions and a strong independent streak in its foreign policy. If there is one overarching drawback in India-U.S. relations at the moment, it is their transactional nature. It is unlikely that the alignment between India and the United States would be as strong in the absence of China's rising power and ambition. While a transactional partnership suits both countries in the short term, a longer view suggests that India's trajectory and ambition may eventually conflict with U.S. interests. This outcome can still be managed if the United States today proactively addresses India's desire to be a leading power. The more the United States does to recognize India's claims to this status—for example, by endorsing its equal membership in the highest ranks of the international order—the more the ground can be laid for a long-term understanding between a relatively declining unipolar power and a rising power in an increasingly multipolar world. Such a mutual understanding would carry the potential of not only setting limits on China's rise but securing the future of the international order itself.

---

[104] "Healthcare," FDI India, https://www.fdi.finance/sectors/healthcare.

EXECUTIVE SUMMARY

This chapter examines the impact of great-power competition, the Covid-19 pandemic, and economic decoupling on Southeast Asia, with a focus on Indonesia, the Philippines, and Vietnam.

MAIN ARGUMENT

Southeast Asia has become the epicenter of the U.S.-China competition in the Indo-Pacific—a situation that poses many challenges but also presents some opportunities. While the predominant narratives from the region suggest that countries reject the binary choice imposed by either great power, the strategies of individual countries and the intensity with which they exercise their own agency have been significantly different. Moreover, their capacity to respond to the rapidly deteriorating geopolitical circumstances has been weakened by the devastating effects of Covid-19. As variants wreak havoc, the region faces a broad economic recession for the first time in decades. Southeast Asian nations will be in greater need of economic stimulus and will value economic engagement even more than they already do. The ongoing decoupling in the U.S.-China trade relationship, along with the conspicuous absence of the U.S. from regional trade pacts and the lack of an economic pillar to its Indo-Pacific strategy, will further affect the perception of U.S. engagement in the region.

POLICY IMPLICATIONS

- The alignment politics in Southeast Asia are dictated by national interests rather than regional solidarity or even alliance commitments.
- The diversity and fluidity of the policies of Indonesia, the Philippines, and Vietnam demonstrate the region's complexity and fast-changing landscape. The U.S. needs to invest more in understanding regional dynamics and avoid the tendency to lump countries together as one strategic unit.
- The U.S. cannot rely only on its security agenda but must increase its diplomatic presence by filling key posts. Without a broader message, U.S. initiatives will continue to face skepticism, if not distrust, from regional countries.

Southeast Asia in Great-Power Competition: Between Asserting Agency and Muddling Through

Huong Le Thu

Southeast Asia has emerged as the epicenter of U.S.-China great-power competition. This position poses multiple challenges for the region but also presents some opportunities. While there is an increasing diversity of strategies that regional countries are adopting to face that new reality, they share concerns about the escalating U.S.-China competition and its repercussions for the stability, security, and prosperity of the region. The prevailing preference for the whole region is to maintain positive relationships with both major powers and, as much as and as long as possible, avoid having to take sides. However, as the great-power competition intensifies on many fronts, there is less room for Southeast Asian nations to hedge.

Already before the outbreak of the Covid-19 pandemic, the Southeast Asian reaction to the U.S. vision for the regional order—the free and open Indo-Pacific strategy—had been mixed, if not unpopular. President Donald Trump's foreign policy posed challenges to the preferences of the Association of Southeast Asian Nations (ASEAN) members, where patient engagement, preventive diplomacy, and extensive consultations are valued. Trump's trade policies were especially concerning. In particular, his withdrawal from the Trans-Pacific Partnership (TPP) was disappointing and symbolized the absence of a U.S. economic strategy in the region. More importantly, his unpredictable, and sometimes irresponsible, conduct caused many nations to worry that the competition with China might spiral out of control and erupt

---

Huong Le Thu is a Senior Fellow in the Defence and Strategy Program at the Australian Strategic Policy Institute (ASPI). She can be reached at <huonglethu@aspi.org.au>.

into confrontation. Trump skipped most of the regional forums, and when cabinet officials did visit the region, they preached about China's misconduct and called for Southeast Asia to stand up to Beijing—something that few were prepared to do, even if they were bound by an alliance with the United States. In sum, the United States' standing within the ASEAN region, with the notable exception of Vietnam, suffered significantly during the Trump presidency, despite growing distrust of China.

Amid this escalation of Sino-U.S. rivalry, the Covid-19 pandemic was a shock to the system for many Southeast Asian states. It has exposed the region's political vulnerabilities and continues to threaten economic growth. Although the pandemic has unfolded in a very uneven way, its transnational effects pose challenges to the region as a whole. The lockdowns and disruptions have sent the developing economies into simultaneous recessions for the first time in decades. In particular, the Delta variant outbreak has hit those countries that had previously dealt with the pandemic relatively well, putting the entire region under mounting public health, economic, and political strain.

This chapter examines the impact of great-power competition, the Covid-19 pandemic, and economic decoupling on Southeast Asia. While considering the impact of great-power competition on the region as a whole, it focuses on three countries: Indonesia, the Philippines, and Vietnam. Aside from being the largest countries in terms of population in the region, with comparatively more strategic weight, they have displayed more consequential shifts in their alignment orientation. This is not to say that Singapore, Thailand, Malaysia, or other regional countries are in any way less important, but rather that their security outlooks have had a more stable trajectory. By contrast, the Philippines' embrace of China under President Rodrigo Duterte was polar opposite to the country's foreign relations under his predecessor and resulted in a significant disruption of the balance in the South China Sea. Indonesia, as the region's most populous country, remains crucial for any broader consideration of Southeast Asia, and its growing closeness with China is very consequential. Vietnam, in recent years, has worked increasingly closely with the United States on defense and security. After considering the security implications of U.S.-China relations for Southeast Asia, the chapter's focus turns to the economic and political effects of the Covid-19 pandemic on these three countries and the implications for their ability to navigate external challenges. Finally, the chapter assesses the potential impact of the U.S.-China decoupling on the individual countries under examination and the region's economic future.

The Impact of Sino-U.S. Competition on the Regional Landscape

The Escalation of Great-Power Competition during the Trump Administration

Prior to the Covid-19 pandemic, Washington and Beijing were already on a collision course over trade, influence, and values. The Sino-U.S. bilateral relationship has further deteriorated since the outbreak of the pandemic, leading many to worry that the world is facing another cold war. Smaller and middle-sized countries find themselves in an even more challenging space, where hedging and maintaining positive relationships with both major powers are more challenging.[1]

During the Trump administration, Washington's framing of the competition with Beijing as one that pits democracies against autocracies was an obstacle for the success of the free and open Indo-Pacific strategy in Southeast Asia.[2] The ideational component of this strategy championed the importance of democratic values against revisionist and authoritarian powers. It received limited support and did not resonate with many regional states. While Southeast Asia is home to some of the world's largest democracies, it also has strongly entrenched authoritarian tendencies, which had seen a resurgence even before the pandemic. The United States' two treaty allies, Thailand and the Philippines, are ruled, respectively, by a military junta that assumed power in 2014 through a coup and an ultra-populist leader (sometimes called the Trump of Asia). As a result, a democratic agenda will be a hard sell even among the United States' longest-standing and closest partners in the region. For that same reason, authoritarianism is not seen as an obstacle to good relations with China but, in fact, may be a driver of closer ties. China could shield regional countries from Western criticism over governance and human rights concerns.

In general, the response from ASEAN to the Trump administration's free and open Indo-Pacific vision was to push back against the paradigm of great-power competition whereby smaller states are compelled to choose between Washington and Beijing. At the 2018 ASEAN Summit, however, Singapore's prime minister Lee Hsien Loong acknowledged that making such a choice might eventually be unavoidable: "Circumstances may come where ASEAN

---

[1] Kuik Cheng-Chwee, "Hedging in Post-Pandemic Asia: What, How, and Why?" *ASAN Forum*, June 6, 2020, https://theasanforum.org/hedging-in-post-pandemic-asia-what-how-and-why.

[2] Huong Le Thu, "Three Traps of Building the Indo-Pacific Narrative," Pacific Forum, June 22, 2018, https://pacforum.org/publication/pacnet-43-three-traps-in-building-the-indo-pacific-narrative-thus-far.

could have to choose one over the other."³ His speech alluded to the growing sense of decoupling between the United States and China.

The "making a choice" narrative reflects the region's anxiety about growing great-power competition and its resistance to the return of bipolarity.⁴ While Beijing has a track record of pushing binary choices, the debate has shifted the attention onto the United States. In Southeast Asia, in particular, it now appears that Washington is the great power imposing a choice. A concrete example is the Huawei ban declared by the United States.⁵ Though supported by some of the closest U.S. allies, the ban intensified regional anxieties about a potential technology "iron curtain." While the security concerns over Huawei's technology may be justified, for many countries in Southeast Asia, a ban would mean that the future technology ecosystems would evolve in separation, competition, and possibly exclusion of each other. Being forced to choose would have consequences for regional economies—not only for their roles in the global supply chain but for technology transfers and movements of people and ideas.

Huawei technology and equipment have been prevalent on the Southeast Asian market for over two decades.⁶ Vietnam was the first regional country to avoid using Huawei in its 5G network, instead developing a network in cooperation with Nokia and Ericson and its own domestic companies Viettel and MobiFone. Yet it never formally banned Huawei from its market. Singapore and later Malaysia also launched their respective 5G networks without Huawei, but they also did not endorse the ban. Others in the region have opted for using Huawei technology, including Indonesia and the two U.S. allies (Thailand and the Philippines), showing that Washington's China strategy is not guaranteed to gain regional support.

Visits to the region by Vice President Mike Pence and Secretary of State Mike Pompeo reinforced the Trump administration's message about China's assertive behavior, risky lending through its Belt and Road Initiative (BRI), and challenges to the rules-based order in general, while promoting

---

³ Michelle Jamrisko, Jason Koutsoukis, and Toluse Olorunnipa, "Singapore PM Says ASEAN May Need to Choose Between U.S. and China," Bloomberg, November 15, 2018, https://www.bloomberg.com/news/articles/2018-11-15/singapore-fears-asean-may-need-to-choose-between-u-s-china.

⁴ Huong Le Thu, "Southeast Asian Narratives about U.S.-China Competition (Part 2): You've Got to Be in It to Win It," Australian Strategic Policy Institute (ASPI), Strategist, November 18, 2019, https://www.aspistrategist.org.au/southeast-asian-narratives-about-us-china-competition-part-2-youve-got-to-be-in-it-to-win-it; and Huong Le Thu, "Southeast Asians Hope for Neutrality, Prepare for a Choice," Pacific Forum, November 20, 2018.

⁵ Sean Keane, "Huawei Ban Timeline: Detained CFO Makes Deal with U.S. Justice Department," CNET, September 30, 2021, https://www.cnet.com/tech/services-and-software/huawei-ban-timeline-chinese-company-settles-patent-lawsuits-verizon.

⁶ Huong Le Thu, "A Collision of Cybersecurity and Geopolitics: Why Southeast Asia Is Wary of a Huawei Ban," Global Asia 14, no. 3 (2019), https://www.globalasia.org/v14no3/cover/a-collision-of-cybersecurity-and-geopolitics-why-southeast-asia-is-wary-of-a-huawei-ban_huong-le-thu.

the free and open Indo-Pacific strategy as an alternative to a Sino-centric regional order. The manner in which this message was conveyed was rather unpopular in the region. For example, the head of policy planning in the State Department described China as the United States' first ever "non-Caucasian" competitor.[7] Even if the wording may have been quickly clarified, it offended regional countries. Later, in a speech at the 2020 Munich Security Conference, Secretary Pompeo stated that "the West is winning," arguing that the values of democracy and freedom that won the Cold War 30 years ago would continue to prevail today.[8] While this message was understandably better received in Europe, the allusion to East-West antagonism was counterproductive to U.S. diplomacy elsewhere, especially in Southeast Asia given the predominantly postcolonial polities.

Increasingly, the Southeast Asian states have grown worried that for the United States the Indo-Pacific is "all about China," and that Southeast Asia matters only insofar as it is useful in Washington's efforts to compete with Beijing. The "Outlook on the Indo-Pacific" released at the ASEAN Summit in Bangkok in July 2019 is another example of this divergence in views.[9] The ASEAN member states achieved a rare consensus in rejecting the notion of the Indo-Pacific as a single region, instead seeing the Asia–Pacific and the Indian Ocean as two connected but distinct regions. This, in fact, is how the United States viewed the region until the free and open Indo-Pacific strategy. Collectively, the ASEAN states also pushed back on the framing of zero-sum competition over the region and instead advocated for regional cooperation grounded in a commitment to ASEAN centrality.[10]

Southeast Asian countries are certainly not unfamiliar with great-power competition. During the Cold War, for example, the divide was stark as the group stood on opposite sides of the Communist-capitalist divide. The result was the formation of the pro-Western, anti-Communist ASEAN grouping between Thailand, the Philippines, Indonesia, Malaysia, and Singapore.[11] After the end of the Cold War, ASEAN expanded its membership to include former adversaries and competitors from mainland Southeast Asia, including most notably Communist Vietnam. Since then, ASEAN has transformed itself into

---

[7] Tara Francis Chan, "State Department Official on China Threat: For First Time U.S. Has 'Great Power Competitor That Is Not Caucasian,'" *Newsweek*, May 2, 2019, https://www.newsweek.com/china-threat-state-department-race-caucasian-1413202.

[8] "Secretary Pompeo Remarks at the Munich Security Conference," U.S. Mission to the European Union, https://useu.usmission.gov/secretary-pompeo-remarks-at-the-munich-security-conference.

[9] ASEAN, "ASEAN Outlook on the Indo-Pacific," June 2019, https://asean.org/wp-content/uploads/2019/06/ASEAN-Outlook-on-the-Indo-Pacific_FINAL_22062019.pdf.

[10] Ibid.

[11] Ang Cheng Guan, *Southeast Asia's Cold War: An Interpretive History* (Honolulu: Hawaii University Press, 2018).

a convening venue for major-power politics. In the process, Southeast Asian states have perfected their hedging strategies by avoiding commitments to any outside power in order to maximize their influence while minimizing the gap between themselves and the major powers. This has been a relatively successful model for the past few decades, and regional states have been able to expand their dialogue partners beyond the Asia-Pacific. Within the multiple institutions created by the so-called ASEAN-centered regional architecture, smaller and major powers are considered equals. Member states have prided themselves on the fact that ASEAN, through its summits, has become a fulcrum of regional (and even, aspirationally, global) politics.

This historical context is important to bear in mind because it explains why the great-power competition and U.S.-China decoupling are so unsettling for ASEAN. It may also explain Washington's frustration over regional countries' current responses. Whereas during the Cold War most of the key ASEAN countries were on the same page as the United States when it came to containing the spread of Communism, any solidarity with resisting authoritarianism would be hard to find these days. Similarly, it is no surprise that ASEAN has grown uncomfortable with the intensified U.S.-China competition that challenges its position as a "convening power" and risks taking away ASEAN's central role that it gained in the post–Cold War era.

Trump's departure from multilateralism and his strategy of competition with China challenged ASEAN precisely on those levels. Regional skepticism of the emphasis on great-power competition in the free and open Indo-Pacific strategy was only reinforced by Trump's lack of attention to Southeast Asia. In the first year of his presidency, he attended the 2017 APEC Summit in Da Nang, Vietnam. He also was supposed to attend the Manila-chaired East Asia Summit in the following days, but after arriving in Manila, he skipped the meeting and returned home early. For the remaining years of his presidency, Trump missed all the regional forums, sending the vice president, secretaries, and even under-secretaries in his place.[12] This was, in the eyes of the Southeast Asian leaders, a major offense and a testimony to the growing narrative of U.S. neglect. Trump's unconventional diplomatic style frequently outraged and even offended the long-time allies, not only in Asia but also in Europe. The absence of the United States' leadership in regional meetings was very clearly reflected in public perceptions of the United States' waning engagement in Southeast Asia. Other than trips to the region for summits with Kim Jong-un in Singapore and Vietnam, Trump did not make an effort to visit after the 2017 ASEAN Summit. As the informal leader of ASEAN, Indonesia, in

---

[12] "Trump Snubs Meeting with ASEAN Leaders in Bangkok," Al Jazeera, October 30, 2019, https://www.aljazeera.com/news/2019/10/30/trump-snubs-meeting-with-asean-leaders-in-bangkok.

particular, remains resentful that no U.S. presidential visits occurred during the Trump administration.

The Biden Administration and the Promise of Change

The region's confidence in the United States' leadership was at a low point when President Joe Biden took office in January 2021. A significant shift in Southeast Asian views correlated with changes in U.S. leadership and policies under President Trump. The ISEAS–Yusof Ishak Institute regional elite survey showed that the perception of the United States diminished significantly during the Trump presidency. In 2017, 56% of surveyed Southeast Asians thought that the United States' engagement with the region had either decreased or significantly decreased. In 2019, 68% thought so, and that rose to 77% in the survey published in January 2020. Even more telling is the region's views on which country will hold the most power in the future: 72% responded that China will be the most influential economic power in Southeast Asia, whereas around 8% thought the same of the United States. On the question of which country is the most influential strategic political power, around 52% answered China, while just under 28% picked the United States.[13] Perhaps even more damaging were the survey's findings about views on the United States' role in the region. In 2019, over 73% of respondents saw China as having the most economic influence in Southeast Asia, compared with only around 8% who thought the same about the United States. This is despite the fact that U.S. FDI in the region remains higher than that of China.[14]

When Biden won the 2020 U.S. presidential election, most of the United States' international partners, including those in Southeast Asia, felt relief. Biden promised the return of a more engaged United States, one committed to multilateralism and diplomacy. The new attitudes toward the United States in the region were reflected in the ISEAS–Yusof Ishak Institute survey from early 2021, as it was conducted from late November 2020 to early January 2021. Views on the United States improved from the previous iterations, signaling significant optimism toward the Biden presidency, particularly with the return of many familiar Asia hands on his team. For example, compared with 2020 answers, significantly more respondents "welcomed U.S. growing regional political and strategic influence" (from 52% to 63%). Similarly, confidence in the United States taking leadership in championing free trade grew from

---

[13] See the various annual "The State of Southeast Asia" survey reports conducted by the ISEAS–Yusof Ishak Institute, available at https://www.iseas.edu.sg/category/articles-commentaries/state-of-southeast-asia-survey.

[14] It is worth noting, however, that the vast majority of U.S. FDI is directed to Singapore, rather than being evenly spread across the region. This possibly contributes to the relatively negative regional perception of U.S. influence.

a regional median of 14.5% in 2020 to 22.5% in the 2021 survey. Confidence in the U.S. leadership in upholding the rules-based order and international law grew from 24.3% in 2020 to 28.6% in 2021.[15] While the survey took place before Biden took office, it signaled more optimism in his leadership than in his predecessor.

Yet the Biden administration had a slow start in adjusting course in Southeast Asia. It took six months for the administration to begin engaging with the region, and U.S. partners increasingly voiced their impatience.[16] Meanwhile, China's diplomats and leaders have continued their physical visits to the region throughout the pandemic and even hosted an in-person meeting with ASEAN foreign ministers in Chongqing in June 2021.[17]

The Biden administration thus has been relatively slow to fill the diplomatic void it inherited. At the time of writing, there were still several vacant ambassadorial posts in Southeast Asia. Singapore—arguably the most important security partner for the United States in the region—did not have an ambassador for nearly five years, and only in December 2021 was Jonathan Kaplan appointed for the role.[18] The ambassadorships in both U.S. treaty allies in the region, Thailand and the Philippines, remain vacant at the time of writing. Marc Knapper was appointed ambassador to Vietnam in April 2021 but is yet to assume the role at the time of writing. Moreover, no envoy has been appointed to this year's ASEAN chair, Brunei, or the ASEAN Secretariat itself.

By comparison, less than two months into his term, Biden convened a virtual summit with his Quad counterparts from Australia, India, and Japan. The Quad has had an uneasy relationship with ASEAN, with some member countries viewing the Quad as a challenge to ASEAN centrality and worrying about its objective of containing China.[19] The virtual summit signaled to ASEAN leaders that the Quad is the first and most visible foreign policy priority for the Biden administration. The administration also held meetings during its first year with the G-7, NATO, and the leaders of Japan, South

---

[15] Sharon Seah et al., "The State of Southeast Asia: 2021 Survey Report," ISEAS–Yusof Ishak Institute, February 2021, https://www.iseas.edu.sg/articles-commentaries/state-of-southeast-asia-survey/the-state-of-southeast-asia-2021-survey-report.

[16] Richard Heydarian, "Why Biden Has Been a Disappointment to Southeast Asia So Far," *South China Morning Post*, June 8, 2021, https://www.scmp.com/comment/opinion/article/3136344/why-biden-has-been-disappointment-southeast-asia-so-far.

[17] "ASEAN and China Celebrate 30th Anniversary of Relations in Chongqing," Department of Foreign Affairs (Philippines), June 9, 2021, https://dfa.gov.ph/dfa-news/dfa-releasesupdate/29071-asean-and-china-celebrate-30th-anniversary-of-relations-in-chongqing.

[18] Charissa Yong, "Jonathan Kaplan Sworn in as U.S. Ambassador to Singapore," *Straits Times*, December 1, 2021, https://www.straitstimes.com/world/united-states/jonathan-kaplan-sworn-in-as-us-ambassador-to-singapore.

[19] Huong Le Thu, "Southeast Asian Perceptions of the Quadrilateral Security Dialogue," ASPI, October 2018, https://www.aspi.org.au/report/southeast-asian-perceptions-quadrilateral-security-dialogue.

Korea, and Russia, along with a second (in-person) Quad summit at the White House in September. A new trilateral defense cooperation partnership with Australia and the United Kingdom—AUKUS—was announced in September as well.[20]

The first trip to Southeast Asia by a Biden administration cabinet official, Defense Secretary Lloyd Austin, occurred in late July and held considerable symbolic significance. While his visit to Singapore, Vietnam, and the Philippines was successful on each leg, countries not included on the itinerary voiced dissatisfaction.[21] Vice President Kamala Harris's trip to Singapore and Vietnam just weeks after Austin's tour proved that Southeast Asia's importance is increasing in Washington.[22] At the same time, the omission of Indonesia and Thailand from both trips has helped perpetuate the ongoing narrative of neglect and reinforced the perception of the United States as a noncommittal power.[23] The regional leaders still await impatiently for engagement from the U.S. president himself. Countries anticipated whether Biden would attend the regional ASEAN-led summit and were concerned the presence of Myanmar's military junta leader who took power by force earlier in February—Min Aung Hlaing—would deter him. As it turned out, Min Aung Hlaing was not invited by the ASEAN leaders to the summits because he did not comply with ASEAN's conditions for de-escalating the crisis in Myanmar.[24] Biden attended virtually the U.S.-ASEAN and East Asia Summit meetings in late October 2021. The meetings were stronger on courtesy than substance, but they were well-received since it was the first time in years that the United States was represented at the presidential level.

Geopolitics Wait for No One

While recognizing that great-power competition will continue under Biden, most Southeast Asian states see rising tension and militarization as unfavorable. This remains one of the main points of contention. The pandemic has not slowed down China, but instead there has been more Chinese activity in the South China Sea, renewed tensions on the Sino-Indian border, and

---

[20] "Joint Leaders Statement on AUKUS," White House, Press Release, September 15, 2021, https://www.whitehouse.gov/briefing-room/statements-releases/2021/09/15/joint-leaders-statement-on-aukus.

[21] "Snubbed Again, Joe?" *Jakarta Post*, August 3, 2021, https://www.thejakartapost.com/academia/2021/08/02/snubbed-again-joe.html.

[22] Carla Babb, "Vietnam Announces U.S. VP Harris Visit," Voice of America, July 29, 2021, https://www.voanews.com/usa/vietnam-announces-us-vp-harris-visit.

[23] Le Thu, "Southeast Asian Narratives."

[24] Ain Bandial, "ASEAN Excludes Myanmar Junta from the Summit in Rare Move," Reuters, October 17, 2021, https://www.reuters.com/world/asia-pacific/asean-chair-brunei-confirms-junta-leader-not-invited-summit-2021-10-16.

much more provocative posturing in the Taiwan Strait. None of these hotspots are new; what is new, however, is the intensity and severity of their impact.

During the pandemic, China has taken advantage of the fact that most countries have been preoccupied with Covid-19. The People's Liberation Army Navy, for example, has ramped up the pace and scope of its exercises, many of which enter the territorial waters of Southeast Asian states with competing claims. China now regularly utilizes military outposts built in the disputed waters of the South China Sea, frequently violating regional countries' exclusive economic zones (EEZs), territorial waters, and air space. As a result, the United States has maintained its naval presence in the region, and recently European partners (including France, the UK, and Germany) have sent their warships as well.[25] While such support from the United States and other Western powers might embolden the Southeast Asian claimants in rejecting China's dominance and control over the disputed waters, it also heightens anxiety about the militarization of the region. The growing military presence elevates tensions and increases the risk for mistakes and miscalculations. This has led many ASEAN states to express their concerns that the region is becoming the battleground for great-power competition.[26]

Even as China's military buildup continues to threaten the region, few countries are willing to speak up on this point. Vietnam is the one country that has consistently done so each time that China's military exercises have encroached on its maritime or air space. By contrast, Indonesia for most of the time has been relatively reluctant to criticize Beijing's behavior, even when similar incursions happen in its claimed Natuna Sea. Chinese ships have also on several occasions sailed nearby the Indonesian-claimed Natuna Islands and even interfered with offshore drilling operations.[27] Despite Duterte's conciliatory approach, the Philippines likewise was not spared from China's maritime coercion, as in the intense standoff between some 230 Chinese vessels in the Philippines' claimed EEZ that occurred in mid-2021.[28]

---

[25] Ben Blanchard, "U.S. Navy Says Carrier Group Operating S. China Sea," *Reuters*, June 14, 2021, https://www.reuters.com/world/china/us-navy-says-carrier-group-operating-schina-sea-2021-06-15; and Giulio Pugliese, "Europe's Naval Engagement in the South China Sea," Istituto Affari Internazionali, May 2021, https://www.iai.it/en/pubblicazioni/europes-naval-engagement-south-china-sea.

[26] Elizabeth Becker, "Southeast Asia Is Ground Zero in the New U.S.-China Conflict—and Beijing Is Winning," *Foreign Policy*, August 29, 2020, https://foreignpolicy.com/2020/08/29/southeast-asia-china-book.

[27] John McBeth, "Indonesia, China Go Toe-to-Toe in Gas-Rich Natunas," *Asia Times*, September 28, 2021, https://asiatimes.com/2021/09/indonesia-china-go-toe-to-toe-in-gas-rich-natunas.

[28] Karen Lema, "Philippines Flags 'Incursions' by Nearly 300 Chinese Militia Boats," *Reuters*, May 12, 2021, https://www.reuters.com/world/asia-pacific/philippines-flags-incursions-by-nearly-300-chinese-militia-boats-2021-05-12.

Nonetheless, there are some indications that regional states are becoming more willing to challenge China over its activities in the South China Sea. Even Indonesia—in a rare assertion—publicly opposed Beijing's claims. On June 4, 2020, Foreign Minister Retno Marsudi said at a press conference that Jakarta objected to China's so-called nine-dash line and historic rights.[29] By late 2020, Vietnam, Malaysia, Philippines, and Indonesia, along with outside states such as the United States, Australia, and Japan in 2021, had all issued notes verbales to the United Nations explicitly rejecting China's maritime claims.[30]

The Strategies of Indonesia, the Philippines, and Vietnam

Individually, the responses from Indonesia, the Philippines, and Vietnam to Sino-U.S. competition have diverged and reflected their respective national strategies. They have been shaped by individual countries' historical experience, ongoing disputes, and the relationships that their respective political elites have been able to form with either great power. Indonesia is traditionally a nonaligned state that prioritizes strategic autonomy over alliance politics. In this light, as U.S.-China competition intensifies, Indonesia might be expected to refuse to commit to either side in its security policies and insist instead on maintaining a "strategic equilibrium." But in reality, Sino-Indonesian ties have strengthened significantly during the presidency of Joko Widodo (also known as Jokowi), particularly in terms of economic and diplomatic relations. Under Jokowi, Indonesia's focus on infrastructure development has found potent synergy with China's BRI. In 2017, for example, China became Indonesia's second-largest investor, including in key projects like the Jakarta-Bandung high-speed railway. In 2018, Beijing announced infrastructure investments worth $84.4 billion over the coming six years.[31] Notwithstanding issues associated with quality, timeliness, growing costs post-bid, and environmental and societal concerns, BRI is still popular among the Indonesian elite.

Yet bilateral relations are not perfect. China's maritime ambitions have clashed with Indonesia's claims in the Natuna Sea and even challenged Jokowi's Maritime Fulcrum—a strategy for Indonesia to seize global maritime

---

[29] Huong Le Thu, "China's Feverish Overreach Wasted an Opportunity Offered by Covid-19," ASPI, June 26, 2020, https://www.aspi.org.au/opinion/chinas-feverish-overreach-wasted-opportunity-offered-covid-19.

[30] United Nations, "Note Verbale," September 16, 2020, https://www.un.org/depts/los/clcs_new/submissions_files/mys_12_12_2019/2020_09_16_GBR_NV_UN_001.pdf.

[31] Murray Hiebert, *Under Beijing's Shadow: Southeast Asia's China Challenge* (Washington, D.C.: Center for Strategic and International Studies, 2020).

power that he announced in his first term but soon largely abandoned.[32] Indonesia remains a credible maritime and diplomatic power in Southeast Asia for China to reckon with. Yet Jokowi has chosen to be very selective in responding to Beijing's maritime challenges, doing so only when they directly affect the Natuna Islands and making a distinction between the Natunas and the South China Sea. Domestically, moderating historical anti-Chinese sentiments that have in the past led to bloody riots and ethnic unrest has been a consideration as well.[33]

Overall, China's economic power seems to have made other considerations, such as maritime disputes or concerns over the mistreatment of Muslim minorities in Xinjiang, secondary. On top of that, the United States' diplomatic negligence has further reinforced Jakarta's views and made it increasingly inclined to criticize Western and external powers. For example, Indonesian diplomats have criticized U.S. freedom of navigation operations as contributing to "militarization" in the South China Sea (even as they have hesitated to say the same about China's buildup of capabilities on the artificial islands) and accused the Quad of containment of China and overshadowing ASEAN centrality.[34] Likewise, in response to the AUKUS deal for nuclear-powered submarines, Indonesia's Ministry of Foreign Affairs statement expressed concern about an "arms race" and called on Australia to restrain itself from militarization.[35] Around the same time in September 2021, Chinese harassment of Indonesian vessels in the Natuna Sea did not meet with such a strong diplomatic response. Nor did the Indonesian political elites express concern over China's hypersonic missile tests or growing nuclear arsenal.[36]

The Philippines—one of the United States' two treaty allies in Southeast Asia—has been bound by the Mutual Defense Treaty since 1951. However, the long-standing and multifaceted relationship has plummeted to unprecedented lows during Duterte's term. Duterte came into power just weeks before the

---

[32] "Understanding the Cause of Declining Maritime Fulcrum Agenda Performance," Airlangga University, December 30, 2020, https://www.unair.ac.id/site/article/read/3278/understanding-the-cause-of-declining-maritime-fulcrum-agenda-performance.html.

[33] Leo Suryadinata, "Anti-Ethnic Chinese Groups in Indonesia Likely to Strike Again," *ISEAS Perspectives*, February 3, 2020, https://www.iseas.edu.sg/wp-content/uploads/pdfs/ISEAS_Perspective_2020_8.pdf.

[34] Daniel Moss, "Indonesia Calls for U.S.-China to 'Restrain Themselves,' Lashes U.S. 'Power Projection' after Spratly Sail-by," *South China Morning Post*, October 28, 2015, http://www.scmp.com/news/china/diplomacy-defence/article/1873456/indonesia-calls-us-china-restrain-themselves-lashes-us?page=all; and Le Thu, "Southeast Asian Perceptions of the Quadrilateral Security Dialogue."

[35] Ministry of Foreign Affairs (Indonesia), "Statement on Australia's Nuclear-Powered Submarines Program," September 17, 2021, https://kemlu.go.id/portal/en/read/2937/siaran_pers/statement-on-australias-nuclear-powered-submarines-program.

[36] Paul McLeary, "Pentagon Predicts 5 Times Increase in China's Nuclear Weapons over Next 10 Years," *Politico*, November 3, 2021, https://www.politico.com/news/2021/11/03/pentagon-china-nuclear-weapons-519048.

Permanent Court of Arbitration ruled in Manila's favor in the dispute that his predecessor Benigno Aquino III brought against China's claims in the South China Sea. Since assuming the presidency, Duterte has advocated for a more independent foreign policy, which means "less America, more China."[37] He made five trips to Beijing in the first four years of his presidency, more than any of his predecessors, but has yet to visit the United States. Following the arbitral tribunal's ruling, Duterte opted not to pursue the matter, effectively undermining the decision.[38] Instead, he bet on improving relations with Beijing, mainly in the hope of attracting Chinese investment through BRI. Early in Duterte's presidency, China promised tens of billions of dollars in infrastructure investment. Nearly five years later, these promises remain unfulfilled, and the prospects of a fair joint-exploration deal with China in the South China Sea also seem unlikely.[39] Internally, Philippine policy circles remain divided. Many elites from the defense, foreign policy, and legal establishment do not agree with Duterte's conciliatory South China Sea policy, and Foreign Secretary Teodoro Locsin has publicly expressed opinions at odds with Duterte's statements.

Duterte's politics have moved the Philippines further away from the United States in many respects. His domestic popularity has benefited to some degree from stoking anti-American sentiments.[40] Most significantly, he announced the abrogation of the Visiting Forces Agreement (VFA)—an agreement that provides the legal framework for U.S. forces to be stationed on rotation in the Philippines and has been in place for over twenty years.[41] Although Duterte ultimately did not follow through on this threat, the episode could leave a lasting effect on trust in Washington. As the presidential election looms in 2022, in the short and medium term, Manila's alignment politics may continue to be unstable.

---

[37] Camille Elemia, "America's Oldest Ally in Asia Turns towards Asia," *Axios*, May 24, 2020, https://www.axios.com/us-philippines-alliance-china-duterte-trump-vfa-fe9462e1-1bcd-421c-aa59-cdd7adb1241c.html.

[38] "The South China Sea Arbitration (The Republic of the Philippines v. the People's Republic of China)," Permanent Court of Arbitration, Press Release, July 12, 2016, https://pca-cpa.org/en/news/pca-press-release-the-south-china-sea-arbitration-the-republic-of-the-philippines-v-the-peoples-republic-of-china; and Pia Ranada, "Duterte 'Ignoring' Arbitral Ruling to Make Way for Joint Exploration," *Rappler*, September 10, 2019, https://www.rappler.com/nation/duterte-ignoring-arbitral-ruling-make-way-joint-exploration-west-philippine-sea.

[39] Richard Javad Heydarian, "Duterte's China Gambit Fails to Deliver the Goods," *Asia Times*, September 30, 2020, https://asiatimes.com/2020/09/dutertes-china-gambit-fails-to-deliver-the-goods.

[40] Jon Emont, "The Limits of Rodrigo Duterte's Anti-Americanism," *Atlantic*, November 1, 2016, https://www.theatlantic.com/international/archive/2016/11/rodrigo-duterte-philippines-china-united-states/506108.

[41] Sofia Tomacruz, "Despite Risks, Duterte Orders Locsin to Terminate VFA," *Rappler*, February 7, 2020, https://www.rappler.com/nation/duterte-orders-locsin-terminate-vfa-february-2020.

Vietnam has pursued a defense policy that rejects alliances and prioritizes self-reliance.[42] At the same time, it has invested in deepening and expanding international partnerships, including with the United States. Increasingly, the United States is important for balancing China's dominance, and hence Hanoi has grown to steadily support and proactively engage with the United States' presence in the region. Vietnam is an outlier among the ASEAN states in welcoming the efforts from international partners in the South China Sea and rejecting Beijing's argument that the disputes should be confined to the small group of claimants and ASEAN. As the ISEAS–Yusof Ishak Institute surveys have shown, Vietnamese elites consistently are more optimistic and confident about the United States and its role in the region, while showing deeper distrust toward China than their peers in most other ASEAN countries. Similarly, Vietnam stood out among its Southeast Asian peers for its positive views on both the free and open Indo-Pacific strategy and the Quad. It even took part in the Quad Plus dialogue in 2020, along with South Korea and New Zealand.[43]

One factor that pulls Hanoi closer to Washington is its growing concerns about China. The complex Sino-Vietnamese relationship has been strained by a series of coercive Chinese activities within Vietnam's EEZ, complicating its oil and gas explorations. China has also frequently challenged Vietnam through military exercises from the artificial outposts China built in the South China Sea. Unlike most other regional countries, Vietnam considers calling out Beijing's coercive activities as part of a counter-coercion strategy. In fact, following the Philippines' turn under Duterte, it has become the most vocal defender of the maritime order in Southeast Asia. Although Vietnam participates in BRI, it is significantly more vigilant than Indonesia and the Philippines about potential strings attached to Chinese funding.[44]

Vietnam's concerns are not limited to the South China Sea, however, but span issues such as the Mekong, transnational governance of natural resources, and technology. In other words, Vietnam is concerned about China's overall intentions. Consequently, Hanoi's and Washington's outlooks for the region are growing increasingly like-minded. In recent years, Vietnam has become, along with Singapore, one of the countries that is most actively engaged in working to preserve the United States' attention and commitment

---

[42] Huong Le Thu, "Vietnam's Persistent Foreign Policy Dilemma: Caught between Self-Reliance and Proactive Integration," *Asia Policy* 13, no. 4 (2018): 123–44.

[43] Le Thu, "Southeast Asian Perceptions of the Quadrilateral Security Dialogue"; and Dat Nguyen, "U.S.-Led Trade Network Could Strengthen Vietnam's Place in Global Supply Chains," *VnExpress*, May 24, 2020, https://e.vnexpress.net/news/business/economy/us-led-trade-network-could-strengthen-vietnam-s-place-in-global-supply-chains-4103610.html.

[44] Pham Sy Thang and Alice Ba, "Vietnam's Cautious Response to the Belt and Road Initiative: The Imperatives of Domestic Legitimation," *Asian Perspectives* 45, no. 2 (2021).

to the region.⁴⁵ This trend will likely continue during the Biden administration. Judging from the Interim National Security Strategic Guidance, in which Vietnam is listed next to Singapore as a priority partner in Southeast Asia, the United States has recognized the strategic value of Vietnam.⁴⁶

The Covid-19 Pandemic as a Vector of Great-Power Competition

The full impact of the pandemic on Southeast Asia is yet to be fully understood. What already is clear, however, is that the disparities between regional countries and within each society are likely to deepen. The repercussions of Covid-19 are in many ways already undoing the regional efforts that ASEAN has been pursuing for decades. The region is characterized by diverse national interests, and security outlooks will likely be even more divergent in the post-pandemic era. Yet, one common concern stands out: the Covid-19 pandemic. The vast majority of Southeast Asians think that Covid-19 presents the single most dangerous threat for the entire region. According to the 2021 ISEAS–Yusof Ishak Institute survey, the three top challenges to the region are Covid-19 (73% of respondents from all ten ASEAN nations), followed by unemployment (63%) and income inequality (41%).⁴⁷ All three concerns are related to the pandemic and the impact it has on the economy and people's livelihoods.

Beyond the immediate public health crisis, the Covid-19 pandemic is a crisis of governance. The diverse impact of the pandemic across countries reflects the region's dissimilar political systems and unequal levels of resilience. For the first eighteen months of the pandemic, Vietnam, which has been one of the most effective globally, has showcased the Communist government's control and strategic thinking. Indonesia and the Philippines, on the other hand, struggled to contain the spread of the virus, and they remain in a state of protracted national emergency. With their state capacity constrained, Jakarta and Manila tend to show even less engagement with external security and regional issues. The Delta variant outbreak was more of an "equalizer" in that it spared no country in the region. The highly contagious variant was immune to strict lockdowns and was further exacerbated by slow vaccine rollouts and vaccine shortages.

---

⁴⁵ Huong Le Thu, "Strongest in the Region?" La Trobe University, June 2020, https://www.latrobe.edu.au/news/announcements/2020/strongest-in-the-region.

⁴⁶ Joseph R. Biden Jr., *Interim National Security Strategic Guidance* (Washington, D.C., March 2021), https://www.whitehouse.gov/wp-content/uploads/2021/03/NSC-1v2.pdf.

⁴⁷ Seah et al., "The State of Southeast Asia: 2021 Survey Report."

Defense Risks

In the security domain, a number of activities have been reduced for the sake of limiting the spread of Covid-19. This is not limited to the movement of citizens, economic activities, and diplomatic visits, but also includes defense and military drills. Many large-scale multinational exercises were canceled, postponed, or reduced in size in 2020, including the ASEAN Multilateral Naval Exercise, International Maritime Review, International Fleet Review, Balikatan War Games, Exercise Pitch Black, Bersama Shield, and Exercise Milan. Other major exercises were reduced in scale or were concluded prematurely, such as Cobra Gold, Rim of the Pacific, Pacific Pathway Program, and Exercise Hanuman Guardian 20.[48] At the time of writing, it is unclear to what extent these exercises will remain discontinued or reduced, given the severity of the Covid-19 variants in regional countries.

In addition to the detrimental effect on capacity building in the region, the Covid-19 pandemic has imposed material constraints on the defense industry. To respond to Covid-19, many countries have rolled out stimulus packages to boost their economies and help their citizens. The full economic costs of the pandemic have yet to truly unfold, but for most of Southeast Asia, the consequences will likely be severe. Large portions of regional states' economies depend on tourism, manufacturing, services, and remittances—all sectors that have been harmed by Covid-19. The pandemic has sent many countries into recession, including those with the highest continuous growth rates like Indonesia and the Philippines.[49] Vietnam resisted that trend in 2020, but the third quarter of 2021 reflected the largest slowdown due to the Delta outbreak.[50] Reduced economic capacity will mean stringent expenditure cuts, potentially affecting defense procurement plans (see **Table 1** for an overview of current plans across Southeast Asia).

Reduced military spending across many countries in the region could leave them more vulnerable to the power imbalance with neighboring China.[51] For some, economic hardship will mean downscaling military purchases. For example, early in the pandemic, Thailand withdrew from agreements to acquire approximately $290 million worth of landing ships from China in order to purchase protective medical equipment and help

---

[48] Data compiled by the author with assistance from Olivia Truesdale and Joanna Nawrotkiewicz.

[49] "Asian Development Outlook (ADO) 2021 Update: Transforming Agriculture in Asia," Asian Development Bank, September 2021, https://www.adb.org/outlook.

[50] Tomoya Onishi, "Vietnam's GDP Shrinks 6.17% in Q3, Hurt by Pandemic Lockdowns," *Nikkei Asia*, September 29, 2021, https://asia.nikkei.com/Economy/Vietnam-s-GDP-shrinks-6.17-in-Q3-hurt-by-pandemic-lockdowns.

[51] Huong Le Thu, "The COVID-19 Pandemic and Geopolitics in Southeast Asia," Asia Society Australia, January 27, 2021, https://southeastasiacovid.asiasociety.org/the-covid-19-pandemic-and-geopolitics-in-southeast-asia.

TABLE 1   Overview of defense procurement plans in Southeast Asia

Country	Procurement type	Contracted entity/country	Value ($ million)
Indonesia	Type 209/1400 submarines	Daewoo Shipbuilding and Marine Engineering, South Korea	1,020
Indonesia	BT-3F amphibious vehicles	Concern Tractor Plants, Russia	289
Indonesia	ScanEagle reconnaissance drones and Bell 412 helicopter upgrades	United States	35
Indonesia	Utility and attack helicopters	United States	2,000
Indonesia	Sniper advanced targeting pod and other airborne sensors	Lockheed Martin, United States	To be announced
Indonesia	Iver Huitfeldt frigate	Denmark	720
Malaysia	Helicopters	To be announced	146
Malaysia	Medium-range anti-tank guided missiles	To be announced	To be announced
Philippines	Heavy-lift helicopters	Russia	2,521
Philippines	AH-64E Apache and AH-1Z attack helicopters and equipment	United States	1,950
Philippines	ATMOS 2000 self-propelled gun system	Elbit Systems, Israel	47
Philippines	Offshore patrol vessel	OCEA, France	100
Singapore	Purpose-built vessels	To be announced	To be announced
Thailand	30-mm naval gun mountings	MSI Defence Systems, UK	5
Thailand	KAI T-50TH trainers	Korea Aerospace Industries, South Korea	78
Thailand	Sniper advanced targeting pod and other airborne sensors	Lockheed Martin, United States	To be announced
Vietnam	Yak-130 combat training jets	Russia	350

SOURCE: Compiled with assistance from Joanna Nawrotkiewicz.

support cash payments to citizens in need.[52] Thailand and Indonesia have already announced cuts of more than $500 million each, and Malaysia, the Philippines, and even Vietnam face similar pressure.[53]

By contrast, China's military spending—colossal in comparison to its Southeast Asian neighbors—increased by 6.6% in 2020.[54] The post-pandemic period is likely to further widen the gap in capabilities between China and Southeast Asia, leaving the region more vulnerable to the threat of force and less able to defend its sovereignty.

Vaccine Diplomacy

Both of the great powers have suffered significant reputational damage in Southeast Asia as a result of their handling of the pandemic, and both have missed opportunities to display high-quality leadership. Soon after the global outbreak of Covid-19, Trump turned his attention toward seeking the origins of the virus, pointing at China. This politicized narrative, with its deliberate racial connotations, was not well-received in Southeast Asia, where a number of countries are sensitive to their own domestic ethnic relations.

Thus, rather than defusing Sino-U.S. tensions and promoting international cooperation and multilateral efforts involving the two rivals, the pandemic has become another vector of great-power competition. Although such competition initially focused on the distribution of masks and other personal protective equipment, it has since shifted to vaccine diplomacy once vaccines became available. China was faster to roll out Covid-19 vaccines to Southeast Asia. Yet, as with many other Chinese endeavors, whether infrastructure construction or technology, the issue of quality emerged as a major factor for China's vaccine diplomacy. In a similar pattern to the infrastructure and technology stories, countries that have alternatives to Sinovac and Sinopharm and can afford them are likely to choose other options. But China's products have had advantages with accessibility, availability, and affordability, particularly in developing Asia, as well as Africa.[55] Despite some concerns over the efficacy of Chinese-produced vaccines in Thailand and even

---

[52] Asaree Thatrakulpanich, "Defmin Withdraws 6.1 Billion Baht Ship Proposal after Criticism," *Khaosod English*, March 31, 2020, https://www.khaosodenglish.com/politics/2020/03/31/navy-proposes-buying-a-6-1-billion-baht-ship-amid-epidemic.

[53] "Downward Trend: Southeast Asian Countries Cut Defense Spending," Associated Press, May 26, 2020, available at https://www.defensenews.com/global/asia-pacific/2020/05/26/downward-trend-southeast-asian-countries-cut-defense-spending.

[54] Mike Yeo, "China Announces $178.2 Billion Military Budget," *DefenseNews*, May 22, 2020, https://www.defensenews.com/global/asia-pacific/2020/05/22/china-announces-1782-billion-military-budget.

[55] Le Thu, "A Collision of Cybersecurity"; and "Production, Politics, and Propaganda: How Beijing Has Shaped the International Covid Immunization Drive," *Nikkei Asia*, October 12, 2021, https://asia.nikkei.com/static/vdata/chinavaccine-1.

in Indonesia, countries continue to resort to Sinovac and Sinopharm to fulfill their populations' vaccination needs.

In contrast, U.S. vaccine diplomacy has been slower but steadier. The donation of U.S. vaccines to Southeast Asia arrived a few months later than Chinese vaccines and in the beginning in smaller quantities. At the time of writing, the United States has donated over 111 million doses around the world, 21% of which were directed to Southeast Asian countries. Indonesia and the Philippines have received the largest share (8 million doses each), while Vietnam received 6 million doses.[56] The United States, along with the other three Quad countries, committed to a vaccine partnership at their virtual summit in March. Under this agreement, Washington pledged $100 million toward immunization of the Indo-Pacific, including Southeast Asia.[57] But this vaccine initiative was put on hold after India—which was supposed to be the main vaccine manufacturer—was hit hard by the Delta variant and had to redirect vaccine doses for domestic use. The September Quad summit further reinforced the leaders' commitment to the vaccine partnership, much of which is targeting Southeast Asia and the Pacific.[58]

One of the best examples of how vaccine diplomacy has factored into the geopolitics of Southeast Asia is Duterte's change of heart regarding the VFA. Secretary of Defense Austin's visit to Manila in late July 2021 resulted in Duterte withdrawing his earlier decision on the abrogation of the VFA. "I conceded the continuance of the Visiting Forces Agreement, in gratitude," he was reported to have said in explaining his change of mind.[59]

To be sure, Duterte had toyed with the decision previously, extending the cooling period three times. China's assertive behavior, including stationing over two hundred ships (its maritime militia) in the Philippines' waters around Whitsun Reef, which Manila calls Julian Felipe Reef, was an effective reminder of why the alliance with the United States still is important for

---

[56] "Fact Sheet: President Biden Announces Major Milestone in Administration's Global Vaccination Efforts: More than 100 Million U.S. Covid-19 Vaccine Doses Donated and Shipped Abroad," White House, August 3, 2021, https://www.whitehouse.gov/briefing-room/statements-releases/2021/08/03/fact-sheet-president-biden-announces-major-milestone-in-administrations-global-vaccination-efforts-more-than-100-million-u-s-covid-19-vaccine-doses-donated-and-shipped-abroad.

[57] "Quad Summit Fact Sheet," Prime Minister of Australia, https://www.pm.gov.au/sites/default/files/files/quad-summit-fact%20Sheet.pdf.

[58] "QUAD Country Covid-19 Response in Indo-Pacific Region," USAID, https://share.usaid.gov/views/QUADCountryCOVID-19ResponseDashboard/Indo-PacificRegionOverview?%3AshowAppBanner=false&%3Adisplay_count=n&%3AshowVizHome=n&%3Aorigin=viz_share_link&%3AisGuestRedirectFromVizportal=y&%3Aembed=y.

[59] Pia Ranada, "Duterte Says U.S. Vaccine Donations Led Him to Keep VFA," Rappler, August 3, 2021, https://www.rappler.com/nation/duterte-says-united-states-vaccine-donations-decision-keep-vfa.

national security.[60] The decision thus follows Duterte's unsuccessful strategy of appeasing China to avoid tensions in the South China Sea (the West Philippines Sea), as Beijing continued to advance its strategic plans for the disputed waters. It is also possible that Duterte had never intended to really end the VFA but put on a show for political purposes. As the Philippine general election approaches in 2022, relations with the United States and China will emerge in the context of election politics, as they have in the past. As such, it is not inconceivable that the VFA, or other aspects of the alliance, will resurface again.

These important caveats notwithstanding, Duterte's public message remains important. He was reported to have used the VFA as a bargaining chip for more U.S. vaccine donations in December 2020.[61] The statement following the decision to continue the VFA in late July directly links national security with the Covid-19 pandemic. It suggests that whichever country is assisting the Philippines in these difficult times with vaccines will be a closer security partner and expresses gratitude and trust, which arguably is the goal of "vaccine diplomacy."

The Impact of Economic Decoupling on Southeast Asia

The Repercussions of Decoupling

Changes to global supply chains may have already been underway to some degree because of the U.S.-China trade war, but the push to diversify production is being further propelled by the pandemic. As explained earlier, Southeast Asian countries have a shared interest in not choosing sides and reject being forced into making binary choices. Individually, however, their responses and strategies toward the great-power competition have been varied in the trade domain, with some countries more concerned about the decoupling (particularly Singapore) and others gaining from the new opportunities presented by efforts to diversify global supply chains (particularly Vietnam). In late 2020, ASEAN countries managed to finalize the world's largest trade pact, the Regional Comprehensive Economic Partnership (RCEP), with Australia, China, Japan, New Zealand, and South Korea.[62] The RCEP is an important accomplishment in the larger regional economic

---

[60] "Philippines Accuses Beijing of 'Provocative Action' after 220 Chinese Vessels Encroach on South China Sea Reef," Associated Press, available at https://www.abc.net.au/news/2021-03-22/philippines-chinese-boats-south-china-sea/100020278.

[61] Lian Buan, "Duterte Dangles VFA for U.S.-Made Vaccine: 'No Vaccine, Get Out,'" Rappler, December 26, 2020, https://www.rappler.com/nation/duterte-dangles-vfa-us-made-vaccine-december-2020.

[62] "RCEP: Asia-Pacific Nations Sign World's Biggest Trade Pact," Al Jazeera, November 15, 2020, https://www.aljazeera.com/economy/2020/11/15/rcep-15-asia-pacific-nations-set-worlds-biggest-trade-pact.

architecture and may become even more significant in the post-Covid-19 economic recovery. It also represents a diplomatic gap between the region's still-strong embrace of trade and the opposition to globalization in other parts of the world, including the United States.

The rationale behind decoupling was to prevent China from taking advantage of the U.S. market, particularly those sectors considered to be of critical security relevance, such as semiconductors, aviation, medical devices, and chemical industries, among others. Pulling apart two economies that had become closely integrated through decades of exchange is undoubtedly costly for the United States and China, but decoupling also will have significant repercussions for smaller economies, including those of Southeast Asia. In particular, higher tariffs will affect developing economies.

Within Southeast Asia, most countries view the U.S.-China trade war as highly detrimental to economic and political stability. Not surprisingly, the state most dependent on trade (Singapore) is most concerned, but even Vietnam (which is among the biggest winners) is concerned about the long-term repercussions for the global economy and financial markets.[63] Vietnam has become one of the more popular destinations for the relocation of businesses and manufacturing factories that moved out of China.[64] It is an appealing destination for companies because of its proximity to China, stable macroeconomic conditions, political predictability, and cheaper but educated and younger workforce.

Vietnam's initial success has empowered the Communist Party of Vietnam to set ambitious goals for economic development. As a result, at the 13th Party Congress in early 2021, leaders set their sights on developing Vietnam into a middle-income country by 2030 and a high-income country by 2045.[65] The targeted growth rate was set at the same level as its previous growth rate of between 6% and 7%, much of which was predicated on manufacturing growth.[66] In 2016, the United States had a trade deficit with Vietnam worth $32 billion. Despite the Trump administration's concerns about the bilateral trade imbalance, both imports and exports kept growing.

---

[63] Warren Shoulberg, "Vietnam Is Becoming the Big Winner in the China Trade Wars," *Forbes*, October 16, 2019, https://www.forbes.com/sites/warrenshoulberg/2019/10/16/us-finally-succeeds-in-vietnam-as-more-companies-move-sourcing-there.

[64] Lien Hoang, "Global Manufacturers Are Flocking to Vietnam. Is It Ready?" *Nikkei Asia*, November 11, 2020, https://asia.nikkei.com/Economy/Trade/Global-manufacturers-are-flocking-to-Vietnam.-Is-it-ready.

[65] Duc Minh, "Party Sets Ambitious Agenda but Not Matching Targets: Economist," *VnExpress*, February 2, 2021, https://e.vnexpress.net/news/business/economy/party-sets-ambitious-agenda-but-not-matching-targets-economist-4229804.html.

[66] Huong Le Thu, "Vietnam Picks Control Over Reform at 13th National Party Congress," *Foreign Policy*, February 10, 2021, https://foreignpolicy.com/2021/02/10/vietnam-communist-party-congress-reform-coronavirus-economy.

The U.S. trade deficit had deepened to $69.7 billion by the end of 2020.[67] To prevent the trade imbalance from becoming an issue in bilateral relations, Prime Minister Nguyen Xuan Phuc traveled to Washington and signed $15–$17 billion worth of deals on the exchange of technological goods and services, which President Trump described as a win-win outcome.[68] But the imbalance remained a thorn in bilateral relations for the remainder of his term.

Under the Biden administration this imbalance was resolved in July 2021 when the Office of the U.S. Trade Representative released a satisfactory resolution in its investigation of Vietnam's alleged currency manipulation.[69] This development has set the Biden administration on positive footing with an increasingly important partner in Southeast Asia, as a signal to other partners that the United States under Biden is more reasonable and more inclined to set aside disputes for the sake of the larger strategic picture.

The impact of the U.S.-China decoupling has been less clear in Indonesia and the Philippines. This can be appreciated by comparing trade-to-GDP ratios: for Vietnam, before the pandemic it was 206% (second only to Singapore at 326%), whereas the ratios for the Philippines and Indonesia were 65% and 41%, respectively.[70] Unlike Vietnam, these two countries have not gained more prominence in the global supply chain and have not seen significant relocation of manufacturing from China. The Philippine economy, for example, relies more heavily on services and exports of labor force, both of which have been affected far more by the pandemic than decoupling. Although Indonesia's manufacturing sector is a significant portion of its economy, it is not among the sectors that have been targeted in the decoupling of U.S.-China trade. Like the Philippines, the Indonesian economy has been hit much harder by the pandemic. Indonesia was the first country in Southeast Asia to face a recession in late 2020—for the first time in decades. The pandemic has caused massive unemployment and resulted

---

[67] "Trade in Goods with Vietnam," U.S. Census Bureau, https://www.census.gov/foreign-trade/balance/c5520.html.

[68] David Lawder and David Brunnstrom, "Vietnam to Sign Deals for Up to $17 Billion in U.S. Goods, Services: Prime Minister," Reuters, May 30, 2017, https://www.reuters.com/article/us-usa-trade-vietnam-idUSKBN18R02N.

[69] "USTR Releases Determination on Action and Ongoing Monitoring Following U.S.-Vietnam Agreement on Vietnam's Currency Practices," Office of the U.S. Trade Representative, Press Release, July 23, 2021, https://ustr.gov/about-us/policy-offices/press-office/press-releases/2021/july/ustr-releases-determination-action-and-ongoing-monitoring-following-us-vietnam-agreement-vietnams.

[70] World Bank, World Development Indicators. With the exception of trade-to-GDP ratio, measures on "global integration" are in the billions of U.S. dollars.

in millions of what some call the "new Covid poor."[71] Indonesia's gains from the rising prices of commodities, however, offset some of the lagging in the manufacturing sector.[72]

Economic Outlook for Southeast Asia

The real effects of decoupling on the region, like the overall impact of the Covid-19 pandemic, are yet to be fully determined. For some countries, like Indonesia and the Philippines, the shocks may be secondary, whereas for Vietnam (as well as Singapore) the impact will be felt more instantaneously. How countries recover from Covid-induced economic disruptions are the main and immediate concern. Southeast Asian economies will likely be in need of additional stimulus packages, including foreign investment, and have already been in talks with China about future infrastructure projects under BRI.[73]

Any potential frameworks that provide economic relief should be pursued. Trade agreements like the RCEP for all ASEAN economies and five dialogue partners[74] or the Comprehensive and Progressive Agreement for Trans-Pacific Partnership (CPTPP)—only Vietnam, Singapore, Malaysia, and Brunei from Southeast Asia—present other multilateral opportunities for expanding markets for exports. Both bilateral and multilateral efforts will be needed for the region's fast and sustainable recovery and are likely to determine future economic influence, further interconnectedness, and rules-setting advantages. The U.S. Indo-Pacific strategy currently lacks an economic pillar of engagement and the United States is conspicuously missing from regional trade agreement. Yet, the economy is one area that the Southeast Asian countries, regardless of political and strategic differences, consider the most relevant to their future, including in the security domain.

---

[71] Puja Dutta, Deepali Khanni, and Nicola Nixon, "The New Poor: ASEAN Tackles the Challenge of Rising Inequalities," *Diplomat*, December 17, 2020, https://thediplomat.com/2020/12/the-new-poor-asean-tackles-the-challenge-of-rising-inequalities.

[72] Trinh Nguyen, "How Indonesia Can Rev Up Its Faltering Economic Growth," Carnegie Endowment for International Peace, August 19, 2020, https://carnegieendowment.org/2020/08/19/how-indonesia-can-rev-up-its-faltering-economic-growth-pub-82477.

[73] C.K. Tan, "ASEAN Needs More Belt and Road Money, Say Ministers," *Nikkei Asia*, September 1, 2021, https://asia.nikkei.com/Spotlight/Belt-and-Road/ASEAN-needs-more-Belt-and-Road-money-say-ministers.

[74] Australia, China, Japan, New Zealand, and South Korea; India opted out at the last minute.

Conclusion

Soon after Covid-19 spread around the world, many concluded that it would not so much change geopolitics as accelerate existing trends, including the intensifying great-power competition between the United States and China.[75] While that competition has sharpened throughout the pandemic, Covid-19 has proved to be not merely an accelerator but a true disruptor that will continue to test and stress both the organization of the world system and the major actors in the system. The pandemic thus should be treated as a warlike event that has the ability to reshuffle the regional power order and derail multilateral goals. Amid the ongoing systematic great-power competition, the results of a new balance of power are rather unpredictable.

For countries in Southeast Asia, the pandemic has weakened their state capacity, challenged political legitimacy, and even distracted some from external threats. An important factor in the changing balance of power is that the regional alignment politics are likely to become much more nuanced. Rather than countries being either aligned or nonaligned, most are likely to fall somewhere on the spectrum between those positions. The United States needs to be prepared for and work with that fluidity.

To this end, the Biden administration urgently needs to understand that for Southeast Asia economic and security issues are not separate but integral. The absence of an economic pillar to the Indo-Pacific strategy is a major obstacle to its success. Most Southeast Asian countries will be interested in economic recovery first and foremost. Given that the region has moved on to ratify the RCEP, and (to a degree) the CPTPP, the United States risks being left out of the process of rebuilding the economic order. Post-pandemic Southeast Asia will be more vulnerable and more prone to external shocks and influences than before. It will likely be less resilient and more reliant on external economic stimuli. When the Asian financial crisis happened in 1997, it was China that stepped in and helped Thailand, Indonesia, and other affected economies.[76] Thailand to this day remembers that its U.S. ally was not there for it in its time of need. The effect of the financial crisis was the growth of China's interdependence and influence in the region. The United States must learn from the past and be fully involved and consistently present in Southeast Asia's post-pandemic recovery. Only a stable, strong, and resilient Southeast Asia can resist China's, or any other external country's, dominance.

---

[75] Joseph S. Nye Jr., "No, the Coronavirus Will Not Change the Global Order," *Foreign Policy*, April 16, 2020, https://foreignpolicy.com/2020/04/16/coronavirus-pandemic-china-united-states-power-competition.

[76] Kensuke Tanaka, "China's Ties with Southeast Asia: From Green Shoots to Sustained Economy," Economic Research Institute for ASEAN and East Asia, Policy Brief, January 2011, https://www.eria.org/ERIA-PB-2011-02.pdf.

Given its history of nonalignment, Indonesia will resist overtly siding with or becoming a client state of China or any other power. But it is likely to continue to grow closer to China in the coming years—certainly leading up to the 2024 general elections. Vietnam will weigh options to the best of its ability, rejecting China's claims in the South China Sea and exposing Beijing's efforts to control these waters. To this end, it will pursue options and arrangements to strengthen its own capacity while actively cooperating with international actors. But Hanoi's willingness to confront China will likely be concentrated on the maritime domain. The Philippines is arguably the most uncertain actor of all. After Duterte took office and completely went against his predecessor's policy in the West Philippines Sea, the balance of power in the South China Sea was disrupted. Duterte's "appeasement" of China weakened international law, prevented Southeast Asian claimants from working closer together, and allowed China to disregard the 2016 ruling while expanding its presence in the disputed waters. Both China and the United States are likely to be issues in the country's 2022 general election. Domestic issues, particularly those related to the economy, will be a deciding factor. The United States needs to find resources to support the Philippines during this time, especially its social security system and its electoral integrity.

Committed relations with the three countries focused on in this chapter can yield the positive results of deepened strategic and economic cooperation and should be continued. But to improve Southeast Asian views of the United States more broadly, Washington needs to expend more resources and effort in this diverse region. Importantly, this increased interest needs to be demonstrated at the top levels of leadership. One of the most effective ways of doing so is to make more frequent visits to the region and ideally to more countries to avoid the perception of "snubbing" anyone. While Covid-19 constraints are likely to continue to limit travel at the presidential and even secretary levels, the Biden administration should consider hosting the ASEAN leaders in the United States at a special U.S.-ASEAN summit, akin to the one that Obama hosted in Sunnylands in 2016.[77] The 2016 summit was widely considered a diplomatic success and a strong endorsement of ASEAN's central role in U.S. foreign policy. By hosting another summit, Biden could convey the United States' commitment to ASEAN centrality more directly than has been done thus far and help rebuild confidence in U.S. leadership.[78]

---

[77] "Joint Statement of the U.S.-ASEAN Special Leaders' Summit: Sunnylands Declaration," White House, Press Release, February 16, 2016, https://obamawhitehouse.archives.gov/the-press-office/2016/02/16/joint-statement-us-asean-special-leaders-summit-sunnylands-declaration.

[78] Huong Le Thu, "Biden Must Change the Narrative of Neglect in Southeast Asia," *Foreign Policy*, July 9, 2021, https://foreignpolicy.com/2021/07/09/southeast-asia-biden-asean-centrality.

EXECUTIVE SUMMARY

This chapter examines the effects of strategic competition, primarily between the U.S. and China, on the national trajectories and economic and security policies of states in Oceania.

MAIN ARGUMENT

States in Oceania are facing increasingly acute questions about how to balance their security and economic relationships. U.S.-China strategic competition is shaping to varying degrees how these states recalibrate their relationships with great powers while maintaining relative autonomy in their economic, foreign, and security policies. Strategic competition also forms the backdrop for Oceania's complex intraregional politics. While Australia, New Zealand, and the Pacific Island states are all members of the Pacific Islands Forum, an increasing tendency toward subregionalism, exacerbated by the continued presence of colonial powers and diplomatic competition between China and Taiwan, threatens the forum's solidarity. However, the effects of and responses to broader strategic dynamics are not uniform across this diverse region.

POLICY IMPLICATIONS

- China's statecraft has been inconsistent across Oceania, as have regional responses. While Australia views China as a security competitor, other states have engaged with it through projects such as the Belt and Road Initiative.

- Australia previously avoided explicitly choosing sides, but China's coercive tactics and the announcement of the AUKUS security partnership indicate that it has chosen the U.S. While New Zealand is keen to maintain autonomy, it is now, albeit reluctantly, more closely aligning with the U.S. Most Pacific Island states will likely continue using structural dynamics for leverage. Yet how long they can balance their complex relationships remains unclear.

- The U.S. must rebuild trust in its role as a preferred regional partner. The Biden administration's commitment to tackle climate change is a start but should be augmented by wider commitments to regional priorities.

Oceania

Strategic Competition in Oceania

Rebecca Strating and Joanne Wallis

The strategic context in Oceania can be summed up by paraphrasing a famous idiom: much of Oceania is not interested in strategic competition, but strategic competitors are interested in Oceania. During the Trump administration, strategic and economic competition between the United States and China became more explicit, and Oceania became viewed as a stage on which these new security and economic rivalries would be played out. Great-power competition has exacerbated tensions in the economic and security policies of Australia and New Zealand, given the combination of their strong security ties with the United States and trade reliance on China. Trump's "America first" policies generated uncertainty about Washington's leadership and presence in the region, as well as its commitments to partners and allies. Particularly among the Pacific Island states, the United States' withdrawal from the 2015 Paris Agreement undermined their confidence in U.S. leadership to address climate change and issues of sustainability, perceived by the region as an existential security challenge. China began to fill the regional strategic vacuum left by the Trump administration through increased trade with these states and the implementation of its Belt and Road Initiative (BRI). Yet, despite concerns about individual Trump-era policies—including its subversion of the World Trade Organization (WTO)—there appears to be no lasting damage in U.S. bilateral relations with Australia and New Zealand, which remain principally concerned with China's rise and its implications for global and regional order.

Rebecca Strating is the Executive Director of La Trobe Asia and an Associate Professor in Politics and International Relations in the Department of Politics, Media and Philosophy at La Trobe University. She can be reached at <b.strating@latrobe.edu.au>.

Joanne Wallis is Professor of International Security in the Department of Politics and International Relations at the University of Adelaide. She can be reached at <joanne.wallis@adelaide.edu.au>.

Strategic and economic competition, however, is complicated by the multifaceted and interrelated security challenges facing Oceania. Adding even more complexity is the diversity of the region, which ranges from Australia, with a population of 25,787,000 and a GDP of US$1.3 trillion, to Tokelau, with a population of 1,499 and a GDP of US$14 million. While a range of challenges confront this diverse region, including deglobalization, trade decoupling, climate change, and the Covid-19 pandemic, this chapter is primarily concerned with assessing how strategic competition is affecting the security and economic trajectories of Oceania's states. More than any other factor, strategic competition—primarily, although not exclusively—between the United States and China is nudging states in Oceania to reconsider their long-held policy positions.

In this chapter, we find that strategic competition is shaping the security and economic outlooks of Oceanic states across three vectors. First, they are facing increasingly acute questions about how to balance their security and economic relationships, with most being dependent on the United States or its allies for security and China for prosperity. Second, Oceanic states are recalibrating to varying degrees how they manage their relationships with great powers, particularly their preference for maintaining relatively autonomous foreign and security policies. Third, strategic competition is forcing them to reconsider their intraregional policies and relations with each other.

This chapter argues that while Oceania's states would prefer not to make a strategic choice, as competition in the broader Indo-Pacific intensifies, they are being increasingly pushed to choose. This has strategic implications for their relationships both with the United States and with each other. While Oceanic states have many shared interests, such as in the domain of maritime security, they hold differing perspectives on key issues such as BRI and climate change. Australia has made its intent to side with the United States clear, and New Zealand is likely to reluctantly follow, but it is less clear on which side, if any, the different Pacific Island states may fall. This reflects that Australia's defense is deeply embedded with the United States, particularly following the September 2021 announcement of the AUKUS defense partnership between Australia, the United Kingdom, and the United States. While New Zealand has slightly more room to take a semi-independent approach because it formally falls outside the U.S. security guarantee, it will likely support the United States in practice so long as it relies on the U.S.-maintained regional order. In contrast, many Pacific Island states, even though they are much smaller, perceive that they can play the United States and China against each other. Whether they can continue to exercise this agency if strategic competition escalates is an open question.

This chapter is divided into four sections. The first section explains why Oceania matters for the United States, examining the importance of Australia, New Zealand, and the Pacific Island states, and then outlines how Washington is working with these states to advance collective interests. The second section then analyzes the national trajectories of Oceania's states, focusing on their attempts to balance their security and economic interests with their preference for autonomy in foreign and security policies. In the final two sections, we consider how these trajectories are playing out for the states' security and economic policies, respectively.

Why Does Oceania Matter for the United States?

Oceania is a geographic region consisting of Australia, New Zealand, and Pacific Island countries located primarily in the southern, central, and western Pacific Ocean (see **Figure 1** for a map of the region). Pacific Island countries are conventionally divided into subregions: Melanesia (Papua New Guinea, or PNG; Solomon Islands; Fiji; Vanuatu; and New Caledonia), Micronesia (Federated States of Micronesia, Palau, Marshall Islands, Kiribati, and Nauru), and Polynesia (American Samoa, Cook Islands, French Polynesia, Hawaii, Niue, Samoa, Tokelau, Tonga, Tuvalu, and Wallis and Futuna). While the term is commonly used in the United States, and occasionally in the Pacific Islands, "Oceania" is rarely used in Australia or New Zealand.

In U.S. analyses, Oceania implies that island states of the Pacific Ocean, Australia, and New Zealand are part of a single region. In contrast, the Australian government presents itself as an Indo-Pacific nation and since 2013 has officially framed its zone of strategic interest as the region "connecting the Indian and Pacific Oceans through Southeast Asia."[1] However, its core national interests remain in its "inner ring" (i.e., the Pacific Islands and maritime Southeast Asia) and, to a lesser extent, its "outer ring" (i.e., the Indo-Pacific and the wider world). Australia's "nearer region," which includes PNG, other Pacific Island countries, and Timor-Leste, is of fundamental importance and characterized as Australia's "part of the world."[2] New Zealand focuses on the "Asia-Pacific" but describes itself as "a Pacific nation" that is "both in and of the Pacific," with its "security and well-being…intrinsically bound to the peace and stability of the region."[3] Pacific Island states often emphasize regional solidarity as represented by membership in the Pacific Islands Forum (PIF).

---

[1] Department of Defence (Australia), *2013 Defence White Paper* (Canberra, May 2013), 7.

[2] Scott Morrison, "Australia and the Pacific: A New Chapter," Prime Minister of Australia, November 8, 2018, https://www.pm.gov.au/media/address-australia-and-pacific-new-chapter.

[3] Ministry of Defence (New Zealand), *Advancing Pacific Partnerships 2019* (Wellington, October 2019).

FIGURE 1 Oceania

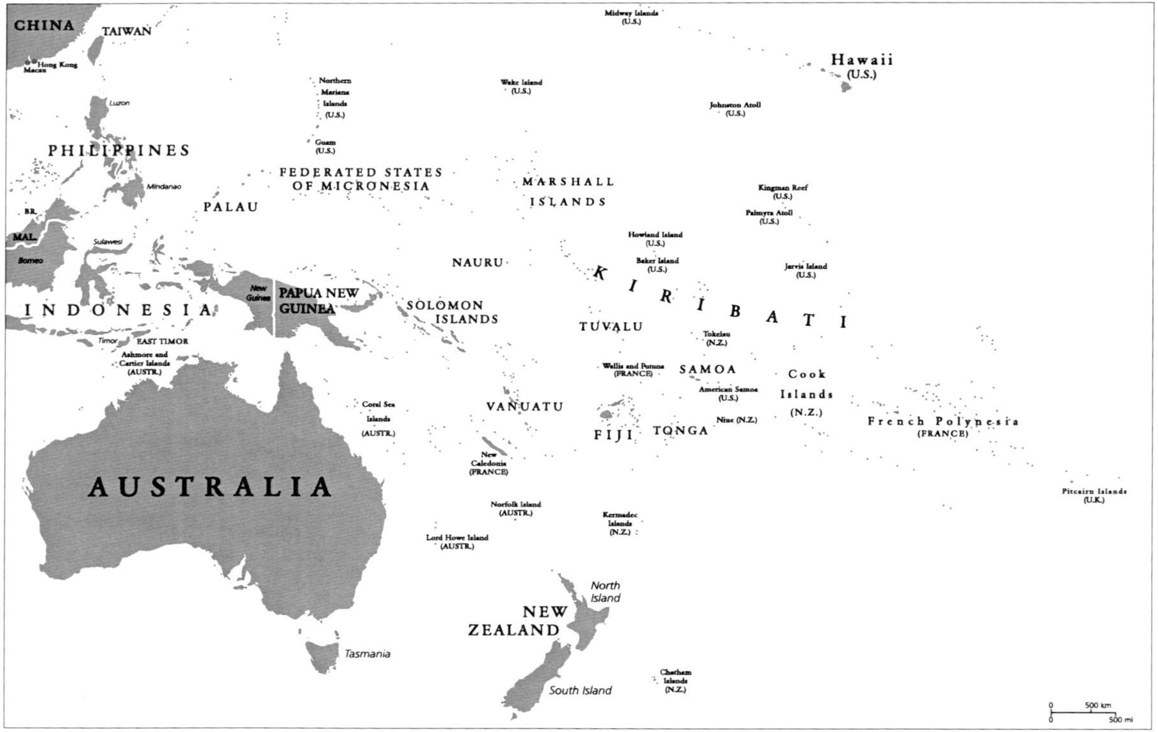

Yet, even though Australia and New Zealand are members of the PIF, the island states seldom characterize them as sharing similar strategic concerns.

Australia

After the Cold War, the United States largely treated Australia (an ally) and New Zealand (a partner) as its proxies in Oceania. But as strategic competition in the broader Indo-Pacific has sharpened over the last five years, U.S. attention to the region has increased. Australia, in particular, is viewed as a "canary in the coal mine" concerning China's efforts to use economic statecraft to influence middle-power states and create a wedge between the United States and its allies. Of the 27 countries affected by China's economic trade coercion between 2010 and 2020, Australia had the highest number of recorded cases (17).[4] Pacific Island states and territories are also seen as potential strategic footholds, with concerns that China's militarization of the South China Sea may migrate to the western and southern Pacific. From a U.S. perspective, the security dynamics playing out in Oceania may reflect broader concerns about China's influence on small and middle powers, the intention and efficacy of BRI, and the effects that changing balance-of-power dynamics have on the international rules-based order.

By virtue of its geography, Australia is an increasingly important ally for the United States that links the Indian and Pacific Oceans and serves as a sanctuary from China's anti-access/area-denial capabilities. Australia is also relatively close to Southeast Asia and key strategic waterways such as the South China Sea. Indeed, its geography was significant during World War II, when it acted as an "unsinkable aircraft carrier" by hosting 250,000 U.S. troops.[5] As competition in the maritime domain grows, Australia's liminality between the Pacific, Southern, and Indian Oceans means that it provides a good location for U.S. security activities. Along with New Zealand, Australia is also a gateway to Antarctica, a region in which strategic competition is intensifying.

Canberra is deeply committed to relations with the United States. It views the alliance as essential for its security, and both public and political opinion are almost uniformly in favor. The defense relationship was reaffirmed in the 1996 Joint Security Declaration (i.e., the Sydney Statement), and its importance is emphasized in every Australian defense white paper. The relationship was further strengthened by the 2021 AUKUS trilateral security partnership to

---

[4] Fergus Hanson, Emilia Currey, and Tracy Beattie, "The Chinese Communist Party's Coercive Diplomacy," Australian Strategic Policy Institute, September 1, 2020, https://www.aspi.org.au/report/chinese-communist-partys-coercive-diplomacy.

[5] "Americans in Australia," State Library Victoria, http://ergo.slv.vic.gov.au/explore-history/australia-wwii/home-wii/americans-australia.

"deepen cooperation on a range of security and defense capabilities" between Australia, the UK, and the United States.[6] Indeed, Australia has often been characterized as a "dependent" ally, and the alliance has allowed Australia to spend much less than it would otherwise need to on defense.

The two countries also have significant military interoperability. Australia's *2016 Defence White Paper* emphasizes acquisition of military capabilities that will enable its forces to cooperate closely with their U.S. counterparts.[7] To that end, Australia has ordered 12 Boeing EA-18G Growlers, 72 Lockheed Martin F-35 joint strike fighters, and 15 Boeing P-8 Poseidon maritime surveillance and patrol aircraft. In 2020 the government's military spending package of AU$270 billion outlined AU$800 million for AGM-158C long-range anti-ship missiles from the United States.[8] This spending, coupled with the AUKUS announcement that Australia would acquire nuclear-powered submarines, has helped Canberra demonstrate that it is sharing the strategic burden and answer criticisms of alliance "free-riding" pronounced during the Trump administration.

Today, Australia hosts several joint facilities that form the basis of a close intelligence relationship with the United States. The Australian Signals Directorate station at Joint Defence Facility Pine Gap is one of the United States' most important covert surveillance bases outside its own territory. With the Northwest Cape facilities, Pine Gap aids U.S. surveillance of East Asia, including China. Since 2011, Australia has also hosted U.S. Marines for training and operations as part of the United States Force Posture Initiatives, with the aim of enhancing military cooperation and regional security through capacity building, interoperability, and warfighting for combined and joint operations.[9] This was expanded in 2014 to include the rotation of the U.S. Air Force, and in February 2020 a $1.1 billion upgrade to the Tindal air force base in northern Australia was announced in order to provide access for U.S. war planes. At the 2021 Australia-U.S. Ministerial Consultations, the allies agreed to "significantly enhance" force posture cooperation, including greater logistics, sustainment, and maintenance of U.S. vessels

---

[6] Scott Morrison, "Joint Leaders Statement on AUKUS," Prime Minister of Australia, September 16, 2021, https://www.pm.gov.au/media/joint-leaders-statement-aukus.

[7] Department of Defence (Australia), *2016 Defence White Paper* (Canberra, February 2016).

[8] Department of Defence (Australia), "$270 Billion Boost to Defence Capability," July 2, 2020, https://news.defence.gov.au/capability/270-billion-boost-defence-capability.

[9] Department of Defence (Australia), "Marine Rotational Force—Darwin," https://www.defence.gov.au/initiatives/usfpi/Home/MRF-D.asp.

in Australia, highlighting Australia's increasing geopolitical importance to the United States.[10]

New Zealand

As with Australia, New Zealand's geographic isolation has been largely a strategic advantage. Yet, despite alignment under the 1951 Australia, New Zealand, United States (ANZUS) Treaty, New Zealand has had a cooler relationship with the United States, partly owing to Wellington's pursuit of an "independent foreign policy." This distance was enhanced in 1986 when the United States suspended its alliance obligations to assist New Zealand if it is attacked after Wellington refused to allow a U.S. vessel to visit. This refusal arose because no assurance was made that the vessel was not carrying nuclear weapons, which contradicted New Zealand's anti-nuclear policy. Following this, New Zealand was no longer given access to U.S. military intelligence and hardware, exchange visits and military exercises stopped, and the U.S. Congress threatened economic sanctions.

Relations began improving in 2001 after New Zealand sent special forces to assist military operations in Afghanistan, and over the last decade the United States and New Zealand have made a concerted attempt to rebuild their diplomatic and defense ties. The 2010 Wellington Declaration declared the countries "strategic partners" and recognized that they share an interest in "maintaining peace, prosperity, and stability" advanced through "practical cooperation in the Pacific region."[11] Two years later, the Washington Declaration focused on high-level dialogue and "deployable capabilities" in areas such as maritime security, humanitarian assistance and disaster relief (HADR), and multilateral cooperation.[12] Subsequently, the United States reinstated almost all military cooperation, including resuming military

---

[10] "The Australia-U.S. Ministerial Consultations Joint Statement: An Unbreakable Alliance for Peace and Prosperity," September 17, 2021, https://www.foreignminister.gov.au/minister/marise-payne/media-release/australia-us-ministerial-consultations-joint-statement-unbreakable-alliance-peace-and-prosperity.

[11] "Wellington Declaration on a New Strategic Partnership between New Zealand and the United States," U.S. State Department, Press Release, November 4, 2010, https://2009-2017.state.gov/r/pa/prs/ps/2010/11/150401.htm.

[12] "Washington Declaration on Defense Cooperation between the Department of Defense of the United States of America and the Ministry of Defence of New Zealand and the New Zealand Defence Force," U.S. Department of Defense and Ministry of Defence (New Zealand), June 2012, http://media.nzherald.co.nz/webcontent/document/pdf/201225/washington%20declaration%20on%20defense%20cooperation.pdf.

exercises in 2010. In 2021, the Biden and Ardern administrations referred to the relationship as a "close partnership."[13]

The Biden administration has signaled its intent to build a coalition of maritime democracies in the broader region. As reflected in the AUKUS security partnership, the United States sees Australia as central to its plan to bring its alliances and partnerships together in a "networked security architecture" in the Indo-Pacific.[14] Australia is also a member of the Quad, along with the United States, Japan, and India, while New Zealand is a key partner and member of the Quad Plus grouping. Furthermore, as parties to the multilateral UKUSA Agreement, New Zealand and Australia belong to the Five Eyes intelligence partnership that cooperates on signal intelligence along with the United States, Canada, and the UK.

Pacific Island States

The United States perceives that Pacific Island states and territories play a critical role in helping to "preserve a free and open Indo-Pacific region."[15] This is particularly the case with respect to the Freely Associated States (Federated States of Micronesia, Marshall Islands, and Palau) and U.S. territories (Guam and the Northern Mariana Islands). The U.S. arrangements with these entities give the United States unfettered military access to their territory, territorial waters, and exclusive economic zones (EEZs). In fact, the Freely Associated States have been described as a "power-projection superhighway running through the heart of the North Pacific into Asia, connecting U.S. military forces in Hawaii to those in theater, particularly to forward-operating positions on the U.S. territory of Guam."[16] This highlights how the Pacific Islands region is vital to maintaining sea lines of communication with Southeast Asia, Australia, and New Zealand and providing a strategic buffer and route for U.S. power projection. The region is likewise critical to potential U.S. adversaries' capacity to project naval power in the Pacific Ocean, as demonstrated by Japan's advance during World War II.

Kwajalein Atoll in the Marshall Islands hosts the Ronald Reagan Ballistic Missile Defense Test Site and the U.S. Space Force's Space Fence program.

---

[13] "Minister of Foreign Affairs Nanaia Mahuta's Call with U.S. Secretary of State Antony J. Blinken," Ministry of Foreign Affairs and Trade (New Zealand), January 30, 2021, https://www.mfat.govt.nz/en/media-and-resources/news/minister-foreign-affairs-nanaia-mahuta-call-us-secretary-state-blinken-readout-30-jan-2021.

[14] U.S. Department of Defense, *Indo-Pacific Strategy Report: Preparedness, Partnerships, and Promoting a Networked Region* (Washington, D.C., June 2019), 44, https://media.defense.gov/2019/Jul/01/2002152311/-1/-1/1/department-of-defense-indo-pacific-strategy-report-2019.pdf.

[15] Ibid., 40.

[16] Derek Grossman et al., *America's Pacific Island Allies: The Freely Associated States and Chinese Influence* (Santa Monica: RAND Corporation, 2019), 1.

Along with U.S. military presence in Hawaii and Guam, these bases are supplemented by fixed or rotational forces in Australia, PNG, and Palau. This may expand further under the Pacific Deterrence Initiative outlined in the 2021 U.S. defense budget, which could include a tactical multi-mission over-the-horizon radar in Palau and a revamped Guam Defense System.

The U.S.-China Economic and Security Review Commission has cautioned that China's influence "could threaten the U.S. Compact of Free Association agreements with Palau, the Marshall Islands, and the Federated States of Micronesia over the long term."[17] Accordingly, in 2019 the United States articulated a Pacific Pledge of the Indo-Pacific Strategy to enhance its relationships in the region.[18] Senior U.S. officials have visited the region more regularly—e.g., Vice President Mike Pence attended the 2018 Asia-Pacific Economic Cooperation (APEC) Summit in PNG and Defense Secretary Mark Esper visited Palau and Guam in 2020—and the United States has more actively engaged in multilateral diplomacy, including high-level representation at the PIF in 2019. The United States has also increased its military deployments, such as by expanding its base in Guam and its Shiprider fisheries-monitoring program.[19] In October 2020, the then president of Palau, Tommy Remengesau, invited the United States to establish a permanent military presence facilitated by the Compact of Free Association (though Washington has not yet responded at the time of writing). The United States has also increased its aid, trade, and investment ties.

While Australia and New Zealand differ in their policies—particularly with respect to climate change—as natural allies they tend to work together in Oceania. Both have been keen to re-anchor the United States to the region. At the 2019 Australia-U.S. Ministerial Consultations, U.S. and Australian leaders pledged to "strengthen their cooperation with Pacific Island partners," which they reaffirmed in 2021.[20] Cognizant that the United States and others perceive that Australia has a "special responsibility" in the Pacific Islands, and reflecting concerns that its influence in the region was declining, then prime minister Malcolm Turnbull in 2017 committed Australia to stepping

---

[17] Ethan Meick, Michelle Ker, and Han May Chan, "China's Engagement in the Pacific Islands: Implications for the United States," U.S.-China Economic and Security Review Commission, June 14, 2018, 1, https://www.uscc.gov/sites/default/files/Research/China-Pacific%20Islands%20Staff%20Report.pdf.

[18] U.S. Department of State, "U.S. Engagement in the Pacific Islands: UN General Assembly Update," October 3, 2019, https://au.usembassy.gov/u-s-engagement-in-the-pacific-islands-un-general-assembly-update.

[19] The Shiprider program involves bilateral agreements that allow the defense and law-enforcement officials of partner Pacific Island states to embark on U.S. Coast Guard and U.S. Navy vessels to observe, board, and search vessels suspected of violating laws or regulations within their EEZs or on the high seas.

[20] "The Australia-U.S. Ministerial Consultations Joint Statement."

up its engagement in the Pacific.[21] This was also driven by concerns about BRI lending and the presence of the Chinese company Huawei in the region. In 2018, Prime Minister Scott Morrison said this "Pacific step-up" would include initiatives focused on enhancing development, security, and diplomatic and people-to-people links.[22] A dedicated cross-agency Office of the Pacific has overseen implementation of the step-up, which has increased infrastructure funding, including AU$2 billion to an Australian Infrastructure Financing Facility for the Pacific and an extra AU$1 billion to the Export Finance and Insurance Corporation. Major infrastructure projects such as the Coral Sea Cable System connecting PNG and Solomon Islands to Australia have sought to prevent Huawei from gaining a foothold in the region, though PNG has contracted the Chinese company to construct its domestic internet cable.[23]

Australia's step-up has a strong security dimension, partly driven by a desire to increase U.S. engagement in the region but also focused on countering China's growing presence. Australia has committed to maintaining a larger military presence, including through partnering with the United States to redevelop Lombrum naval base on Manus Island in PNG. It has also created the Australia Pacific Security College at Australian National University in Canberra to strengthen the capacity of Pacific Island security officials. Furthermore, in October 2020 the government announced that the Pacific Fusion Centre, which had been installed in Canberra on an interim basis to promote regional domain awareness, would be permanently established in Vanuatu.[24] Australia has agreed to redevelop Fiji's Blackrock Peacekeeping and Humanitarian Assistance and Disaster Relief Camp. There has been a palpable shift in Canberra to emphasize Pacific Island states' security priorities, particularly those identified in the PIF's 2018 Boe Declaration on Regional Security, to which Australia is a signatory. Australia is the main provider of HADR and is the top provider of official development assistance

---

[21] Malcolm Turnbull, "Pacific Islands Forum in Samoa," Prime Minister of Australia, September 6, 2017, https://pmtranscripts.pmc.gov.au/release/transcript-41165; and Malcolm Turnbull, "Remarks at Pacific Island Forum—Micronesia," Prime Minister of Australia, September 9, 2016, https://www.malcolmturnbull.com.au/media/remarks-at-pacific-island-forum-micronesia.

[22] Scott Morrison, "Australia and the Pacific: A New Chapter," Prime Minister of Australia, November 8, 2018, https://www.pm.gov.au/media/address-australia-and-pacific-new-chapter.

[23] Department of Foreign Affairs and Trade (Australia), "Strengthening Our Pacific Partnerships," https://www.dfat.gov.au/geo/pacific/engagement/Pages/strengthening-our-pacific-partnerships.

[24] Marisa Payne and Marc Ati, "Pacific Fusion Centre to Be Established in Vanuatu," Minister of Foreign Affairs (Australia), October 19, 2020, https://www.foreignminister.gov.au/minister/marise-payne/media-release/pacific-fusion-centre-be-established-vanuatu.

to Pacific Island states.²⁵ It also has conducted interventions to respond to political instability, including in Bougainville (1997–2003), Solomon Islands (2003–13), and Nauru (2005–10).

As the other regional power perceived to have a special role in the Pacific Islands, New Zealand in 2018 announced a "Pacific reset" to deepen its regional involvement. This reset has included an enhanced aid program, increased diplomatic posts, significant defense policy shifts, and a continuation of labor mobility programs.²⁶ New Zealand identifies as part of the same geographic region and cultural sphere as Pacific Island states, and the fact that one in five New Zealanders has Māori or Pasifika heritage has reinforced the country's "identity as a Pacific nation at all levels of social, cultural, and political involvement."²⁷ New Zealand also has constitutional arrangements with several Polynesian states, some level of control over the foreign affairs of Cook Islands and Niue, and even greater control over Tokelau. Notably, three referendums have been held in Tokelau in which voters have overwhelmingly opted to remain linked to New Zealand.

In 2018, an annual Pacific security trilateral dialogue between Australia, New Zealand, and the United States was established to identify issues of shared concern and complementary capability. In the same year, New Zealand asked the United States to engage more in the region,²⁸ as "foundational democratic values" were "increasingly being challenged in the Pacific."²⁹ The United States is collaborating with Australia, New Zealand, and Japan in the PNG Electrification Partnership to increase the proportion of PNG's population connected to the electrical grid from 13% to 70% by 2030.³⁰ The Better Utilization of Investments Leading to Development (BUILD) Act passed in late 2018 by the U.S. Congress may also allow the United States to use infrastructure financing as a tool of influence. This capability may be

---

²⁵ Joanne Wallis et al., "Mapping Security Cooperation in the Pacific Islands," Australian National University, Department of Pacific Affairs, June 10, 2021; and "ODA to Oceania—Summary," Organisation for Economic Co-operation and Development (OECD), https://www.oecd.org/dac/financing-sustainable-development/development-finance-topics/Oceania-Development-Aid-at-a-Glance-2021.pdf.

²⁶ Winston Peters, "'Shifting the Dial,' Eyes Wide Open, Pacific Reset" (address delivered at the Lowy Institute, Sydney, March 1, 2018), https://www.lowyinstitute.org/publications/winston-peters-new-zealand-pacific.

²⁷ Parliament of Australia, "A Pacific Engaged: Australia's Relations with Papua New Guinea and the Island States of the South-West Pacific," 2003, 231.

²⁸ Winston Peters, "Pacific Partnerships" (address at Georgetown University, Washington D.C., December 15, 2018), https://www.beehive.govt.nz/speech/pacific-partnerships-georgetown-address-washington-dc.

²⁹ Winston Peters (speech to U.S.-NZ Council, Washington, D.C., October 25, 2019), https://www.beehive.govt.nz/speech/us-nz-council-speech.

³⁰ "The Papua New Guinea Electrification Partnership," November 18, 2018, https://www.mofa.go.jp/mofaj/files/000420447.pdf.

enhanced by the Build Back Better World partnership that the United States announced with other G-7 leaders at their 2021 summit, at which Australia was an observer. Congress is also considering the Boosting Long-term U.S. Engagement in the Pacific Act (BLUE Pacific Act) and the Honoring Our Commitment to Elevate America's Neighbor Islands and Allies Act (Honoring OCEANIA Act), both of which seek to enhance the United States' diplomatic, development, and security role in the region. Australia reportedly assisted in writing these bills.[31]

National Trajectories

Strategic competition is an important causal factor affecting the national trajectories and security outlooks of the Oceanic states. One of the biggest challenges for regional states is the frequent misalignment of their security and economic interests, with most looking to the United States and its partners for security (or at least for the stability of the rules-based order) and China for economic prosperity. Trade dependence on China has rendered many Oceanic states vulnerable to Beijing's geoeconomic statecraft, including the strategic implications of BRI, ongoing dependence on the Chinese market in key industries, gray-zone tactics in the maritime domain, and the swath of economic sanctions applied to Australia starting in 2020.

The Oceanic states are responding differently to these pressures. Australia has emphasized the importance of the rules-based order in the Indo-Pacific. While New Zealand has historically tended toward strategic ambiguity, this approach is changing. Pacific Island leaders, such as former PIF secretary general Dame Meg Taylor, have attempted to neutralize narratives of strategic competition by rejecting "the terms of the dilemma which presents the Pacific with a choice between a China alternative and our traditional partners."[32] Regionally, Pacific Island states have emphasized their nontraditional security interests and the Blue Pacific narrative of strategic autonomy vis-à-vis not just China but also the United States, Australia, New Zealand, and other countries. While rumors of potential defense alignments frequently follow announcements that Pacific Island states have signed on for BRI, nothing substantive has materialized. In fact, several Micronesian states have sought to expand their defense relationships with the United States, with Palau and the

---

[31] Alan Tidwell, "U.S. Congress Moves to Prioritise the Pacific," Australian Strategic Policy Institute, Strategist, June 10, 2021, https://www.aspistrategist.org.au/us-congress-moves-to-prioritise-the-pacific.

[32] Dame Meg Taylor, "The China Alternative: Changing Regional Order in the Pacific Islands" (address to the Pacific Islands Forum, Port Vila, February 8, 2019), https://www.forumsec.org/2019/02/12/keynote-address-by-dame-meg-taylor-secretary-general-the-china-alternative-changing-regional-order-in-the-pacific-islands.

Federated States of Micronesia agreeing to host new U.S. bases. Furthermore, several Melanesian states have sought to enhance their security relationships with Australia. Australia signed a security treaty with Solomon Islands in 2017, a *vuvale* (friendship) partnership with Fiji in 2019, and a comprehensive strategic and economic partnership with PNG in 2020.[33] In January 2019, Australia and Vanuatu announced that they would begin negotiations on a bilateral security treaty.[34]

Australia

While the U.S. alliance remains at the core of Australia's defense and security planning, China has been its biggest trading partner since 2007, mainly due to strong Chinese demand for Australian resources such as iron ore and coal. Given this trend, Australia agreed to a comprehensive strategic partnership and a free trade agreement with China in 2014. Until 2020, Australian leaders adopted a pragmatic approach, arguing that Australia does not have to choose because "it is in no one's interest in the Indo-Pacific to see an inevitably more competitive U.S.-China relationship become adversarial."[35] Australia's relationship with China, however, has deteriorated significantly in recent years. One important cause is Beijing's attempts to influence Australian domestic policy through foreign interference campaigns and economic coercion. But the worsening relationship is also partly due to China's strategic assertiveness in Taiwan and the South China Sea, mounting evidence of ethnic cleansing and cultural genocide in Xinjiang, and the rollback of freedoms in Hong Kong. As a result, pragmatism has replaced sovereign resilience as the central tenet of Australian foreign and strategic policy, with a view to the gray-zone security threats presented by China, particularly interference in domestic political, economic, and cyber arenas. Australia has been increasingly willing to publicly push back against China and seek to bandwagon more explicitly with the United States. In 2018, Australia adopted legislation aimed at countering foreign interference

---

[33] "Solomon Islands: Bilateral Security Treaty," Department of Foreign Affairs and Trade (Australia), August 14, 2017, https://www.dfat.gov.au/geo/solomon-islands/Pages/Bilateral-security-treaty; "Fiji-Australia Vuvale Partnership," Department of Foreign Affairs and Trade (Australia), September 16, 2019, https://www.dfat.gov.au/sites/default/files/fiji-australia-vuvale-partnership.pdf; and "Papua New Guinea–Australia Comprehensive Strategic and Economic Partnership," Prime Minister of Australia, August 5, 2020, https://www.pm.gov.au/media/papua-new-guinea-australia-comprehensive-strategic-and-economic-partnership.

[34] "Joint Statement with the Prime Minister of Vanuatu," Prime Minister of Australia, January 16, 2019, https://www.pm.gov.au/media/joint-statement-prime-minister-vanuatu.

[35] Scott Morrison, "Where We Live" (Asialink Bloomberg Address, Sydney, June 26, 2019), https://www.pm.gov.au/media/where-we-live-asialink-bloomberg-address.

and was the first state to ban Huawei from its 5G network.[36] In 2020, it called for an inquiry into the origins of the virus that causes Covid-19, revoked the visas of certain Chinese nationals accused of foreign interference on national security grounds, and canceled the state of Victoria's memorandum of understanding with China under BRI as part of the sweeping 2020 Foreign Arrangements Scheme. Australia has since joined the United States (and the UK and Canada) in condemning China's actions in Hong Kong, emerged as one of most vocal critics of China's human rights abuses toward the ethnic minority Uighur population, and improved its nonofficial ties to Taiwan. Australia's *2020 Defence Strategic Update* was consequently explicit about "China's active pursuit of greater influence in the Indo-Pacific" and the "potential for actions, such as the establishment of military bases, which could undermine stability."[37]

Chinese officials responded to this activism with a list of fourteen grievances against Australia. Australian prime minister Scott Morrison allegedly used this list at the 2021 G-7 summit to convince leaders of the need to take a tougher stance toward China. Yet, despite Australia's stronger stance, there are concerns that Australia has no real strategy beyond continued reliance on the U.S. alliance, and doubts linger about the United States' commitment as the predominant security provider in the Indo-Pacific. During the Trump administration, anxiety that the America-first policy could result in the erosion of the U.S.-led alliance system in Asia was particularly potent. These doubts played on a "fear of abandonment" by "great and powerful friends" that has long haunted Australia's strategic imagination.[38] Yet, by committing to the AUKUS strategic partnership, including the joint development of nuclear-powered submarines, Australia appears to have banished its doubts, at least for the time being.

Australia's emphasis on the importance of the rules-based order had been partly aimed at avoiding taking sides in a strategic competition. Yet the country's use of the term has evolved to be more sharply critical of perceived revisionism by China and more explicitly in favor of an order based on U.S. leadership. Accordingly, Australia increasingly frames its preferred rules-based order in terms of political values such as liberalism and democracy. The *2017 Foreign Policy White Paper* prioritized Australia's relationships with other

---

[36] Australian Government, *National Security Legislation Amendment (Espionage and Foreign Interference) Act 2018*, no. 67, June 29, 2018; Australian Government, *Foreign Influence Transparency Scheme Act 2018*, no. 63, June 29, 2018; and Australian Government, *Security of Critical Infrastructure Act 2018*, no. 29, April 11, 2018.

[37] Department of Defence (Australia), *2020 Defence Strategic Update* (Canberra, July 2020), 11, https://www1.defence.gov.au/sites/default/files/2020-11/2020_Defence_Strategic_Update.pdf.

[38] Allan Gyngell, *Fear of Abandonment: Australia in the World since 1942* (Melbourne: La Trobe University Press, 2017).

Indo-Pacific democracies, and in a June 2021 speech Morrison emphasized that Australia "must continue to demonstrate that liberal democracies work."[39] Australian leaders also explicitly refer to "shared democratic values" when discussing partners such as the United States, India, Japan, and New Zealand. The pillars of Australia's Indo-Pacific concept are peaceful resolution of disputes in accordance with international law, free and open markets and inclusive economic integration, freedom of navigation and overflight, and support for a rules-based order led by the United States.[40] Declaratory policy leaves little doubt that Australia's vision of the U.S.-led rules-based order is also liberal in character, which is echoed in Australia's use of the "Indo-Pacific" regional nomenclature.

Australia has also turned to minilateral groupings to pursue its strategic interests. These include the Quad and trilateral partnerships (Australia-U.S.-Japan, Australia-India-Japan, and Australia-India-Indonesia). In March 2021, the Quad held its first summit. While these groupings are dialogues rather than formal institutions, they are increasingly important forums for strategic coordination. However, they are not without risk. Quad members have differing strategic geographies, threat perceptions, and relationships with China and therefore cannot necessarily be relied on to perceive or respond to a threat in the same, or even a coordinated, way. If the Quad and other strategic partnerships become increasingly focused on defense and security issues, including joint military exercises, they may be misperceived as quasi-military alliances. This poses the risk that partners could find themselves making ambiguous political and military commitments that unintentionally draw them into future conflict. Of more concern, China could interpret their actions as threatening, thereby exacerbating its strategic vulnerability.[41]

New Zealand

In a similar effort to avoid taking sides in developing strategic competition, New Zealand also emphasizes the rules-based order as a foreign and defense policy priority. New Zealand has long gravitated toward multilateralism, primarily due to its status as a "small" and "principled" state rather than a great or middle power with more latitude to act bilaterally.

---

[39] Scott Morrison, "Like-Minded Countries Must Build Our Own Sovereign Capability and Resilience," *Australian*, August 28, 2021.

[40] See, for example, Frances Adamson, "The Indo-Pacific: Australia's Perspective," Secretary of the Department of Foreign Affairs and Trade (Australia), April 29, 2019, https://www.dfat.gov.au/news/speeches/Pages/the-indo-pacific-australias-perspective.

[41] Joanne Wallis, "Is It Time for Australia to Adopt a 'Free and Open' Middle-Power Foreign Policy?" *Asia Policy* 15, no. 4 (2020): 7–20.

Indeed, in her first foreign policy speech as prime minster, Jacinda Ardern pledged that New Zealand's approach would be characterized by "speaking up for what we believe in, standing up when our values are challenged, and working tirelessly to draw in partners with shared views."[42] Ardern has specifically emphasized the role of multilateralism in combating climate change, arguing in 2018 that "not since the inception of the United Nations has there been a greater example of the importance of collective action and multilateralism, than climate change."[43]

New Zealand also has a long-standing emphasis on an independent foreign policy that is grounded in "doubts that the great powers can be relied on to protect and advance this multilateral order ahead of their own selfish interests."[44] This means that while New Zealand aligns closely with the United States on some issues, it does not on others and thus has been reluctant to take positions that are explicitly oppositional to China. For example, the Five Eyes intelligence-sharing partnership is increasingly being presented as a broader strategic, and potentially economic, partnership. While New Zealand's declaratory policy highlights the importance of close engagement with its Five Eyes partners, in 2021, Foreign Minister Nanaia Mahuta warned against using the partnership to pressure China, stating that New Zealand is "uncomfortable with expanding the remit of the Five Eyes Relationship."[45] After China unilaterally declared an air defense identification zone in the East China Sea in 2013, New Zealand declined to join Australia, the United States, Japan, and other regional states in protesting the declaration.

New Zealand's rhetoric on China has emerged as a source of tension with Australia, which intensified when Mahuta suggested in December 2020 that New Zealand could be a mediator between Australia and China.[46] New Zealand's trade minister Damien O'Connor also suggested that Australia

---

[42] Jacinda Ardern (speech to New Zealand Institute of International Affairs, Wellington, February 27, 2018), https://www.beehive.govt.nz/speech/speech-new-zealand-institute-international-affairs-2.

[43] Jacinda Ardern, "New Zealand National Statement to United Nations General Assembly" (New York, September 28, 2018), https://www.beehive.govt.nz/speech/new-zealand-national-statement-united-nations-general-assembly.

[44] Robert Ayson, "New Zealand and the Great Irresponsibles: Coping with Russia, China and the U.S.," *Australian Journal of International Affairs* 74, no. 4 (2020): 456; and Malcolm McKinnon, *Independence and Foreign Policy: New Zealand in the World since 1935* (Auckland: Auckland University Press, 1993).

[45] Stephen Dziedzic, "New Zealand 'Uncomfortable with Expanding the Remit' of Five Eyes, Says Foreign Minister," ABC News (Australia), April 19, 2021, https://www.abc.net.au/news/2021-04-19/new-zealand-five-eyes-intelligence-sharing-china-australia/100078834.

[46] Praveen Menon, "New Zealand Says Willing to Be Arbitrator in Australia-China Spat," Reuters, December 15, 2020, https://www.reuters.com/article/newwzealand-politics-mahuta-idUSKBN28P0GC.

should speak with "more diplomacy" and "respect" toward China,[47] generating condemnation within Australian foreign policy circles. In May 2021, Prime Minister Ardern's government refrained from using "genocide" to describe China's abuses against its Uighur population.[48] Yet, while the *Strategic Defence Policy Statement 2018* remained hopeful that China would contribute to the rules-based order, it also suggested that New Zealand was willing to take a harder line on Chinese activism, particularly in the East and South China Seas.[49]

While New Zealand at times may appear soft on China, Ardern has promised that her government will stand up for New Zealand's values internationally, and it has been more willing to call out Beijing's irresponsibility than previous governments. Ardern's tougher stance has been aided by the willingness of her cabinet officials to challenge China, supported by elements of the public service and broader public opinion. As China's behavior in Xinjiang and the South and East China Seas has become more problematic, the Ardern government has gained more room to be critical. In 2018, the Government Communications Security Bureau rejected a proposal from a local company, Spark, to use Huawei equipment in its bid for the statewide 5G internet upgrade due to security risks, although it was reluctant to implement an outright ban on the Chinese telecom company.[50] New Zealand has also taken steps to regulate foreign investment, including banning foreign buyers from acquiring existing homes.[51] In addition, it signed a joint letter to the UN Human Rights Council expressing concern about China's detention practices in 2019, signed a separate letter about China's practices in Xinjiang in 2020, and condemned China for hacking Microsoft in 2021.[52]

Over the past decade, New Zealand–U.S. security relations have moved beyond historical disagreements on nuclear policy. New Zealand's

---

[47] Anthony Galloway, "NZ Trade Minister Suggests Australia Should Speak with 'More Diplomacy' in Dealings with China," *Sydney Morning Herald*, January 28, 2021, https://www.smh.com.au/politics/federal/nz-trade-minister-suggests-australia-should-speak-with-more-diplomacy-in-dealings-with-china-20210128-p56xex.html.

[48] Tess McClure, "New Zealand Draws Back from Calling Chinese Abuses of Uyghurs Genocide," *Guardian*, May 4, 2021, https://www.theguardian.com/world/2021/may/04/new-zealand-draws-back-from-calling-chinese-abuses-of-uyghurs-genocide.

[49] Ministry of Defence (New Zealand), *Strategic Defence Policy Statement 2018* (Wellington, July 2018), 20, https://defence.govt.nz/assets/Uploads/8958486b29/Strategic-Defence-Policy-Statement-2018.pdf.

[50] "Minister: GCSB Decision about Risk Assessment, Not China," Radio New Zealand, November 29, 2018, https://www.rnz.co.nz/news/political/377048/minister-gcsb-decision-about-risk-assessment-not-china.

[51] Parliament of New Zealand, *Overseas Investment Amendment Act 2018*, no. 25, August 22, 2018, https://www.legislation.govt.nz/act/public/2018/0025/latest/DLM7512906.html.

[52] Max Walden, "Australia Joins UK, Japan in Expressing Concern over China's Treatment of Uyghurs, Hong Kong," ABC News (Australia), June 30, 2020, https://www.abc.net.au/news/2020-07-01/australia-statement-condemn-china-over-hong-kong-uyghur-abuses/12409268.

Defence White Paper 2016 described its engagement with the United States as having "reached a depth and breadth not seen in 30 years."[53] Bilateral and multilateral military-to-military exercises have increased since the Wellington Declaration. In 2016, the USS *Sampson* visited New Zealand to provide HADR to communities affected by the Kaikoura earthquake in the first bilateral ship visit in more than 30 years. The visit was viewed as a confirmation of a de facto alliance.[54] New Zealand now participates in the U.S.-led Rim of the Pacific (RIMPAC) exercise that promotes interoperability among participating navies. The recent procurement of the Boeing P-8A aircraft was partly justified as a means for New Zealand to carry out operations independently and in concert with partners such as the United States.[55] The two countries coordinate capacity-building efforts to prevent illegal, unreported, and unregulated fishing in Pacific Island states' EEZs; participate in joint HADR exercises in the region; and partner on Antarctic scientific operations (driven by concerns about China's rising influence in the area). There are also two U.S. military bases in New Zealand. Moreover, the Biden and Ardern administrations share interests in pressing for greater climate action on the international stage, in contrast with Australia's Morrison government.

While New Zealand has moved closer to the United States on security, its rhetoric continues to express a preference for independence. Foreign Minister Mahuta's first two major foreign policy speeches in 2021 suggested a cautious approach to strategic competition.[56] Reflecting this, until recently New Zealand resisted using the term "Indo-Pacific," given its connotation of a U.S.-led rules-based order. In 2018, New Zealand began to refer to the region as the Indo-Pacific, but only in some circumstances and with the caveat that it would only participate in Indo-Pacific initiatives when "principles of inclusivity and openness applied."[57] This has been characterized as New

---

[53] Ministry of Defence (New Zealand), *Defence White Paper 2016* (Wellington, June 2016), https://www.defence.govt.nz/publications/publication/defence-white-paper-2016.

[54] Benjamin Schaare, Christopher Doyle, and Murray Hiebert, "In from the Cold: U.S.-New Zealand Ties Returning to Normal," National Bureau of Asian Research, Special Report, no. 49, December 10, 2014, https://www.nbr.org/publication/in-from-the-cold-u-s-new-zealand-ties-returning-to-normal.

[55] Ministry of Defence (New Zealand), *Defence Capability Plan 2019* (Wellington, June 2019), https://www.defence.govt.nz/publications/publication/defence-capability-plan-2019.

[56] Nanaia Mahuta, "Inaugural Foreign Policy Speech to Diplomatic Corps," Ministry of Foreign Affairs (New Zealand), February 4, 2021, https://www.beehive.govt.nz/speech/inaugural-foreign-policy-speech-diplomatic-corps; and Nanaia Mahuta, "He Taniwha he tipua, he tipua he Taniwha—The Dragon and the Taniwha," Ministry of Foreign Affairs (New Zealand), April 19, 2021, https://www.beehive.govt.nz/speech/%E2%80%9Che-taniwha-he-tipua-he-tipua-he-taniwha-dragon-and-taniwha%E2%80%9D.

[57] Robert Ayson, "New Zealand: A Re-elected Government with Less Appetite for Geopolitics," in *CSCAP Regional Security Outlook 2021*, ed. Ron Huisken (Canberra: Council for Security Cooperation in the Asia Pacific, 2020), 3.

Zealand "avoiding new groupings that were established deliberately to exclude others in the Asia-Pacific region, especially China."[58] However, in 2020, in the context of responding to the Covid-19 pandemic, New Zealand began to participate in talks with "coalitions of the trusted" such as Australia, the United States, India, Japan, and Vietnam, which have been described as looking "remarkably like a Quad Plus affair."[59]

Pacific Island States

The national trajectories of the Pacific Island states have been shaped by U.S.-China strategic competition within the region and the broader Indo-Pacific, but this competition has generated differing responses. For example, in the 2018 Boe Declaration, PIF member states recognized the "dynamic geopolitical environment leading to an increasingly crowded and complex region" and committed their governments to "pursue our collective security interests."[60] However, island state leaders do not necessarily share the same perspectives on the geopolitical environment. Palau, the Marshall Islands, and the Federated States of Micronesia have the Compacts of Free Association with the United States, providing them considerable economic support and immigration access in exchange for U.S. defense access and protection. The Cook Islands and Niue have similar relationships with New Zealand. Furthermore, the region still includes several colonies. American Samoa, the Northern Mariana Islands, and Guam are U.S. territories; New Caledonia, French Polynesia, and Wallis and Futuna are French overseas collectivities; Tokelau is held by New Zealand; and the Pitcairn Islands is a British overseas territory.

In their Blue Pacific narratives, Pacific Island states have emphasized their strategic autonomy in coping with increased competition. Due to its already apparent impact on sea-level rise and the frequency and destructiveness of natural disasters, climate change is instead framed as the most significant challenge shaping their national trajectories and "the single greatest threat to the livelihoods, security and wellbeing of the peoples of the Pacific."[61]

China has gradually developed its diplomatic and economic presence in the Pacific Islands over the last 40 years, primarily in the context of its

---

[58] Ayson, "New Zealand," 3.

[59] Ibid., 3.

[60] Pacific Islands Forum, "Boe Declaration on Regional Security," September 5, 2018, https://www.forumsec.org/2018/09/05/boe-declaration-on-regional-security.

[61] "Pacific Islands Forum Statement for the High-Level Open Debate of the UN Security Council on 'Climate and Security,'" Permanent Mission of Tuvalu to the United Nations, July 24, 2020, https://www.un.int/tuvalu/statements_speeches/pacific-islands-forum-statement-high-level-open-debate-un-security-council-.

competition with Taiwan for diplomatic recognition. In 2019, Beijing persuaded Solomon Islands and Kiribati to switch their diplomatic recognition to China, reducing the number of Pacific Island states that have diplomatic relations with Taiwan to four (Nauru, Palau, Marshall Islands, and Tuvalu). This competition for diplomatic recognition and the related alleged corruption of local politicians have political ramifications. Although there is no evidence that either Chinese or Taiwanese actors actively incited post-election riots in Solomon Islands and Tonga in 2006, their perceived corruption of local politicians and officials exacerbated existing grievances.[62] There are signs that the competition is again heating up, with reports of a physical altercation between Chinese and Taiwanese diplomats in Fiji in October 2020.[63]

The United States, Australia, and New Zealand are concerned that the upsurge in Chinese diplomacy—President Xi Jinping, for example, visited Fiji in November 2014 and attended the APEC summit in PNG in 2018, where he held a side meeting with the Pacific Island states with which China has relationships—may give China a strategic edge. In April 2018, China was reportedly in talks to build a military base in Vanuatu, though both governments denied these reports. In September 2019 a Chinese company had sought to lease the small island of Tulagi in Solomon Islands, home to a former Japanese naval base, though Solomon Islands vetoed the lease.[64] China has also offered to develop Kiribati's transshipment hubs and fish processing plants in the strategically useful Line and Phoenix group and integrate BRI into its twenty-year vision development plan. China's 2014–15 *Blue Book of Oceania* specifically notes that the Pacific Ocean is the only sea route between China, on the one hand, and South America, Antarctica, Australia, and New Zealand, on the other, as well as its "second and third island chains of defense."[65] Although there is no precise definition of these chains, most include the Micronesian subregion in the second island chain and Melanesia

---

[62] Jon Fraenkel, *The Manipulation of Custom: From Uprising to Intervention in the Solomon Islands* (Wellington: Victoria University Press, 2004); and Matthew G. Allen, *Greed and Grievance: Ex-Militants' Perspectives on the Conflict in Solomon Islands, 1998–2003* (Honolulu: University of Hawaii Press, 2013).

[63] Ben Doherty et al., "Taiwan Official in Hospital after Alleged 'Violent Attack' by Chinese Diplomats in Fiji," *Guardian*, October 19, 2020, https://www.theguardian.com/world/2020/oct/19/taiwan-official-in-hospital-after-alleged-violent-attack-by-chinese-diplomats-in-fiji.

[64] "Solomons' Government Vetoes Chinese Attempt to Lease an Island," *Guardian*, October 25, 2019, https://www.theguardian.com/world/2019/oct/25/solomons-government-vetoes-chinese-attempt-to-lease-an-island.

[65] Chang Sen Yu, "The Pacific Islands in China's Strategy for the 21st Century," in *2014–2015 Dayangzhou lanpi shu* [2014–2015 Blue Book of Oceania], ed. Chang Sen Yu, 2nd ed. (Beijing: Social Sciences Academic Press, 2015). See also Graeme Smith and Denghua Zhang, "China's Blue Book of Oceania," Australian National University, Department of Pacific Affairs, 2015, http://dpa.bellschool.anu.edu.au/sites/default/files/publications/attachments/2016-07/ib2015.70_smith_and_zhang.pdf.

and part of Polynesia in the third.⁶⁶ Kiribati's reversal to recognize China is likely to result in the satellite-tracking station that China built there in 1997 being updated and returned to operation. Beijing had mothballed the station when Kiribati recognized Taiwan in 2003.⁶⁷

According to former PIF secretary general Dame Meg Taylor, "if there is one word that might resonate amongst all Forum members when it comes to China, that word is access. Access to markets, technology, financing, infrastructure. Access to a viable future."⁶⁸ Several Pacific Island leaders have expressed disquiet about the increased focus of Australia, the United States, and other partners on strategic competition in Oceania. In 2018, Samoan prime minister Tuilaepa Sailele Malielegaoi described it as a "form of strategic manipulation" because the "big powers are doggedly pursuing strategies to widen and extend their reach and inculcating a far reaching sense of insecurity."⁶⁹ Pacific Island leaders are particularly concerned about the implication that their states will inevitably have to make a strategic choice.⁷⁰

Nonetheless, some Pacific Island states have shrewdly exploited strategic competition to pursue their own priorities, including greater aid, concessional loans, military assistance, and international influence. Even Taylor has suggested that "perhaps the time is now right to leverage the geopolitical interests and opportunities that are available to us to advocate for and secure our maritime interests into perpetuity."⁷¹ There have been efforts by Pacific Island states to use regional groupings to respond to strategic competition. PIF leaders, for example, adopted the Framework for Pacific Regionalism in 2015 to strengthen the forum's ability to act as a platform for regional dialogue. Since 2017, they have adopted the Blue Pacific concept to describe "a long-term Forum foreign policy commitment to act as one 'Blue Continent.'"⁷²

---

⁶⁶ Andrew S. Erickson and Joel Wuthnow, "Barriers, Springboards and Benchmarks: China Conceptualizes the Pacific 'Island Chains,'" *China Quarterly* 225 (2016): 1–22.

⁶⁷ Michelle Nichols, "China Restores Ties with Kiribati, Site of Space Tracking Station," Reuters, September 27, 2019, https://www.reuters.com/article/us-china-kiribati-idUSKBN1WC2KB.

⁶⁸ Taylor, "The China Alternative."

⁶⁹ Tuilaepa Sailele Malielegaoi (address delivered at the Lowy Institute, Sydney, August 30, 2018), https://www.lowyinstitute.org/publications/speech-hon-prime-minister-tuilaepa-sailele-malielegaoi-pacific-perspectives-new.

⁷⁰ Taylor, "The China Alternative."

⁷¹ Dame Meg Taylor, "Introductory Statement by the Secretary General to the Pacific Islands Forum at the Regional Conference on Securing the Limits of the Blue Pacific: Legal Options and Institutional Responses to the Impacts of Sea Level Rise on Maritime Zones, in the Context of International Law," Pacific Islands Forum, September 9, 2020, https://www.forumsec.org/2020/09/09/introductory-statement-by-the-secretary-general-to-the-pacific-islands-forum-at-the-regional-conference-on-securing-the-limits-of-the-blue-pacific-legal-options-and-institutional-responses-to-the-imp.

⁷² Pacific Islands Forum, "Forty-Eighth Pacific Islands Forum: Forum Communiqué," September 8, 2017, https://www.forumsec.org/wp-content/uploads/2018/02/Final_48-PIF-Communique_2017_14Sep17.pdf.

The 2019 PIF communiqué set out "Blue Pacific principles" that emphasize among other things "regional priorities," a "partnership approach," and "collective outcomes and impact."[73] Taylor has argued that the Blue Pacific concept should encourage Pacific Island states to exercise "stronger strategic autonomy," understand "the strategic value of our region," and "maintain our solidarity in the face of those who seek to divide us."[74]

The three subregions have also created the Melanesian Spearhead Group (formed in 1988, institutionalized in 2007), the Polynesian Leaders Group (formed in 2011), and the Micronesian Presidents' Summit (formed in 1994). As the oldest, the Melanesian Spearhead Group is the most formal of the three. It has a secretariat building in Port Vila, Vanuatu, that was funded by China, and its members have agreed to create a free trade area and a scheme for the movement of skilled labor, though neither has yet borne fruit. Almost every independent head of state in the Pacific Islands attends the annual PIF leaders' meetings, which suggests that the forum remains the region's preeminent political and security organization. Still, the subregional groupings are changing the PIF's dynamics. In October 2020, Micronesian Presidents' Summit leaders agreed to suspend their participation in the PIF if their preferred candidate, Gerald Zackios, the Marshall Islands' ambassador to the United States, was not appointed the next PIF secretary general. They also agreed to establish a secretariat in Nauru.[75] At the special PIF leaders' meeting in February 2021, Zackios was narrowly defeated by former Cook Islands prime minister Henry Puna, motivating Micronesian leaders to express a collective intent to withdraw from the PIF. As the PIF agreement provides a twelve-month waiting period between when an intention to withdraw is announced and when it takes effect, there is a significant diplomatic effort across the region to encourage Micronesian states to remain in the forum.

Pacific Island states historically used the PIF as the basis for the Pacific Group at the United Nations. Since post-coup Fiji was suspended from the PIF in 2009 (a suspension that was lifted in 2014), they have consolidated into the Pacific Small Island Developing States grouping without Australia and New Zealand. A more active "new Pacific diplomacy" has boosted the Pacific Island states' international influence and contributed to the passage of the first UN climate change resolution in 2009, the insertion of stand-alone Sustainable

---

[73] Pacific Islands Forum, "Fiftieth Pacific Islands Forum: Forum Communiqué," August 16, 2019, https://www.forumsec.org/wp-content/uploads/2019/08/50th-Pacific-Islands-Forum-Communique.pdf.

[74] Dame Meg Taylor (keynote address to the Pacific Islands Forum, Canberra, September 8, 2018), https://www.forumsec.org/2018/09/10/keynote-address-by-secretary-general-meg-taylor-to-the-2018-state-of-the-pacific-conference.

[75] Bernadette Carreon, "Micronesian Nations to Withdraw from Forum If Concerns Not Heeded," Radio New Zealand, October 4, 2020, https://www.rnz.co.nz/international/pacific-news/427562/micronesian-nations-to-withdraw-from-forum-if-concerns-not-heeded.

Development Goals on oceans and climate change in 2015, the renaming of the Asia Group to the Group of Asia and the Pacific Small Island Developing States (or Asia-Pacific Group for short), and the election of Pacific Islanders to key positions.[76] For example, Fijian diplomat Peter Thomson was elected as president of the UN General Assembly in 2016, and Fiji's ambassador to the United Nations, Nazhat Shameem Khan, was elected as president of the UN Human Rights Council in January 2021.

National Security

Australia

The consequences of strategic competition for national security have been most significant in Australia. Since the release of the *2016 Defence White Paper*, the security outlook for Australia has deteriorated considerably. Its *2020 Strategic Defence Update* references gray-zone tactics, military bases, and new weapons that challenge Australia's capabilities, suggesting that its security posture is driven by threat perception shaped primarily by China's rising influence.[77] Australia's Indo-Pacific concept views the maritime domain as a theater of increasing strategic competition and norm contestation, which has had implications for defense planning and procurement. The 2020 Force Structure Plan promises a capability investment of AU$75 billion to maritime security, although the AUKUS announcement has complicated these projections because the cost of acquiring nuclear-powered submarines is not yet clear.[78] Massive shipbuilding plans to acquire or upgrade up to 23 different classes of maritime vessels had been projected to cost AU$50 billion over the next decade.[79] Indeed, Australia's defense budget grew by 9% in 2020 to AU$42.7 billion during the first year of the pandemic.[80]

Australia has also sought to augment its defense capabilities by emphasizing its alliance with the United States, but there is concern that hosting joint military facilities could make Australia a target during a U.S.-China conflict, even if it is not an active party. This highlights Australia's

---

[76] For further discussion, see Greg Fry and Sandra Tarte, eds., *The New Pacific Diplomacy* (Canberra: Australia National University Press, 2015).

[77] Department of Defence (Australia), *2020 Defence Strategic Update*.

[78] Ibid., 37.

[79] Department of Defence (Australia), "Growing Our Shipbuilding Enterprise and Creating More Opportunities for Australian Industry," July 1, 2020, https://www.minister.defence.gov.au/minister/melissa-price/media-releases/growing-our-shipbuilding-enterprise-and-creating-more.

[80] Marcus Hellyer, "The Cost of Defence 2020–2021. Part 2: ASPI 2020–2021 Defence Budget Brief," Australian Strategic Policy Initiative, October 22, 2020, https://www.aspi.org.au/report/cost-defence-2020-2021-part-2-aspi-defence-budget-brief.

apprehension that the geographic scope of the ANZUS Treaty—the "Pacific area"—could see the country entrapped and its military resolve tested if U.S. forces in Japan, South Korea, around Taiwan, or in the South China Sea are attacked. Canberra has consistently resisted engaging in alliance activities that will potentially provoke Beijing or make it a target in an increasingly competitive region. This is despite pressure applied by U.S. officials for Canberra to conduct freedom of navigation operations in the maritime domain.

Australia has therefore sought support beyond the alliance from like-minded partners in the region. The *2017 Foreign Policy White Paper* singles out Japan, Indonesia, India, and South Korea as "central to this agenda."[81] Japan-Australia relations have become increasingly institutionalized, and efforts at security cooperation have advanced under the umbrella of their 2014 special strategic partnership. For example, the previously thorny issue of a visiting forces agreement appears on the road to resolution. In November 2020, the two countries agreed in principle to their troops conducting training and joint operations in each other's territories.[82] Earlier, in June 2020, the India-Australia relationship was also enhanced by a comprehensive strategic partnership, augmented with bilateral and trilateral dialogues and joint exercises. Both bilateral relationships are viewed as key pillars of Australia's Indo-Pacific concept to deepen security and economic engagement and counterbalance China.

New Zealand

While it prefers to characterize itself as independent and autonomous, New Zealand unequivocally states that it "has no better friend than Australia."[83] This reflects the fact that Australia is New Zealand's only formal ally. Much like the Australia-U.S. arm of ANZUS, their alliance is not without problems, with Australia concerned that New Zealand lacks both sufficient resolve to contain China and a commitment to carry its share of the strategic burden. As a small state, New Zealand has less to spend on defense: Australia has 59,000 permanent defense force personnel, whereas New Zealand has only 9,000.[84] Likewise, New Zealand devotes approximately 1% of its GDP

---

[81] Department of Foreign Affairs and Trade (Australia), *2017 Foreign Policy White Paper* (Canberra, November 2017), 4.

[82] Kiyoshi Takenaka and Ju-min Park, "Japan, Australia Reach Security Pact amid Fears over Disputed South China Sea," Reuters, November 17, 2020, https://www.reuters.com/article/us-japan-australia-idUSKBN27X131.

[83] Ministry of Defence (New Zealand), *Strategic Defence Policy Statement 2018*, 14, 24.

[84] Joanne Wallis and Anna Powles, "Australia and New Zealand in the Pacific: Ambiguous Allies?" *Centre of Gravity* 43 (2018): 4.

to defense, less than Australia's 2%.[85] The sophistication of New Zealand's defense technologies and capabilities has also been left behind, and Australia is able to conduct more air and maritime operations in the Pacific Islands than its neighbor. This situation has been partially corrected over the last few years. New Zealand has invested in P-8 Poseidon aircraft to replace its aging P-3 Orion maritime surveillance capability and in C-130Js to replace C-130 Hercules transport aircraft.[86] However, with New Zealand incurring significant debt during the Covid-19 pandemic, further defense acquisitions are unlikely, at least in the short term. The total defense budget for 2021–22 will be $3.7 billion, an increase of nearly 11% over the 2020–21 budget, which had decreased by about 7% from 2019–20 due to budget cuts caused by the pandemic.[87]

Pacific Island States

Maritime security is a shared interest in Oceania. The United States, France, and Australia possess the world's three largest EEZs, assisted in all cases by international legal entitlements generated in the Pacific Ocean. The United Nations Convention on the Law of the Sea (UNCLOS) also provides territorially small Pacific Island states with vast maritime zones: they have rights to over 30,569,000 square kilometers (km^2) of EEZ area,[88] far exceeding their combined landmass of 552,789 km^2 (84% of which is PNG).[89] New Zealand's EEZ is over 4 million km^2, but its territorial landmass is only 268,021 km^2, with an extended continental shelf claim adding 1.7 million km^2 more area.[90] Oceanic states of course depend significantly on maritime trade: over 99% of New Zealand's and Australia's trade by volume is seaborne. Maritime resources are also vital to the economies of Pacific Island states, many of which depend on fisheries to provide revenue from licenses and access agreements, employment, and an important source of food.

The United States, Australia, New Zealand, and France coordinate via the Quadrilateral Defense Coordination Group to provide maritime surveillance

---

[85] Wallis and Powles, "Australia and New Zealand in the Pacific."

[86] Ayson, "New Zealand," 2.

[87] Jon Grevatt, "New Zealand's Defence Budget Returns to Growth," Janes, May 21, 2021, https://www.janes.com/defence-news/news-detail/new-zealands-defence-budget-returns-to-growth.

[88] Quentin Hanich, Clive Schofield, and Peter Cozens, "Oceans of Opportunity? The Limits of Maritime Claims in the Western and Central Pacific Region," in *Navigating Pacific Fisheries: Legal and Policy Trends in the Implementation of International Fisheries Instruments in the Western and Central Pacific Region*, ed. Quentin Hanich and Martin Tsamenyi (Wollongong: Oceans Publications, 2009), 21.

[89] Quentin Hanich and Martin Tsamenyi, "Managing Fisheries and Corruption in the Pacific Islands Region," *Marine Policy* 33, no. 2 (2009): 386–92.

[90] Ministry of Foreign Affairs and Trade (New Zealand), "Our Maritime Zones and Boundaries," https://www.mfat.govt.nz/en/environment/oceans-and-fisheries/our-maritime-zones-and-boundaries.

support to Pacific Island states. The key pillar of Australian maritime security in Oceania is the Pacific Maritime Security Program,[91] which exists within its Defence Cooperation Program. The Pacific Maritime Security Program aims to enhance the Pacific Islands' sovereign capabilities to combat transnational maritime crimes such as illegal, unreported, and unregulated fishing and the trafficking of drugs, humans, and illegal weapons. The program commits Australia to spending US$2 billion in the region over the next 30 years to replace Pacific patrol boats, support integrated regional aerial surveillance, and strengthen regional coordination efforts.[92] From 2018 to 2023, Canberra will give 21 Guardian-class patrol boats to twelve Pacific Island states to replace vessels gifted between 1987 and 1997. New Zealand's *Maritime Strategic Update 2020* also aims to support initiatives under the Pacific Maritime Security Program.[93] The 2019 New Zealand Defence Capability Plan seeks to enhance maritime awareness capability by adding, among other capabilities, new P-8A maritime patrol aircraft, satellite surveillance, and unmanned aerial vehicles, budgeted to cost NZ$300–NZ$600 million.[94] In 2020, New Zealand released its new maritime security strategy, setting out a multi-agency approach to establish a whole-of-nation system that enables "comprehensive and sustainable *kaitiakitanga* (guardianship) of our maritime domain."[95] While not explicitly naming China, the strategy document emphasizes the presence of "malicious and negligent actors" undermining international maritime rules.[96]

The preoccupation of Australia and New Zealand with strategic competition has consequences for Pacific Island states. For example, part of the United States' response to the perception that China is gaining strategic influence in the Pacific Islands has been to encourage Taiwan's role in the region. Taiwan has historically had the most significant presence in the Micronesian subregion, where the United States' closest relationships and greatest geostrategic interests in the Pacific Islands are found. In October 2019, Taiwan and the United States organized the first Pacific Islands Dialogue in Taipei, which included representatives of Pacific Island states that recognize Taiwan with the aim of shoring up their support. At that meeting, Taiwanese officials warned that taking diplomatic recognition

---

[91] Department of Defence (Australia), "Pacific Maritime Security Program," in *Defence Annual Report 2017-2018* (Canberra, 2017), https://www.defence.gov.au/annualreports/17-18/features/maritime.asp.

[92] Ibid.

[93] Ministry of Transport (New Zealand), *Maritime Security Strategy 2020* (Wellington, December 2020), https://www.transport.govt.nz/assets/Uploads/Report/MaritimeSecurityStrategy.pdf.

[94] Department of Defence (New Zealand), *Defence Capability Plan 2019*, 29.

[95] Ministry of Transport (New Zealand), *Maritime Security Strategy 2020*.

[96] Ibid., 4.

away from Taipei risked encouraging Chinese aggression, with Minister of Foreign Affairs Joseph Wu warning that Taiwan does not "want to see the Pacific turned into another South China Sea."[97] Sandra Oudkirk, the U.S. deputy assistant secretary of state for Australia, New Zealand, and the Pacific Islands, spoke in support of Taiwan's regional role, which she described as a "force for good in the Pacific."[98]

However, U.S. activism on Taiwan's diplomatic relationships in the Pacific Islands could exacerbate domestic political instability. This is most notable in Solomon Islands, where a secessionist movement in Malaita intersected with strategic competition and access to commercial opportunities. After the decision by Solomon Islands to switch recognition to China, there were protests in Malaita, the most populous province, accompanied by allegations of government corruption. The Malaita provincial government had reportedly received aid directly from Taiwan. Fueling an already combustible situation between Malaita and the central government, the United States directed US$25 million (of a total US$200 million) of regional aid directly to Malaita but denied that it was connected to geostrategic competition.[99]

Events in Malaita show that escalating strategic competition risks exacerbating security and developmental challenges in the Pacific Islands. Pressing security challenges include the unresolved political future of Bougainville (after the November 2019 referendum overwhelmingly favored independence from PNG), secessionist movements in Rongelap (Marshall Islands), and an independence referendum in Chuuk (Federated States of Micronesia). Moreover, historical patterns of uneven development, disrupted land tenure, destructive resource extraction, corruption, climate change (including increasing HADR demands), transnational crime, and incomplete decolonization (e.g., the Indonesian claim over West Papua or the French territories of New Caledonia and French Polynesia) must also be dealt with.

Indeed, while Pacific Island states are cognizant of the implications of strategic competition, they are primarily focused on nontraditional security challenges. The most significant existential threat facing many of these countries is climate change, which is reflected in the discourses of leaders and regional institutions, including in the 50th Pacific Islands Forum communiqué in 2019, which declared that "escalating climate change related impacts, coupled with the intensification of geostrategic competition, is

---

[97] Lawrence Chung, "U.S. and Taiwan Hold Forum to Shore Up Support for Taipei in Pacific," *South China Morning Post*, October 7, 2019, https://www.scmp.com/news/china/diplomacy/article/3031891/us-and-taiwan-hold-forum-shore-support-taipei-pacific.

[98] Ibid.

[99] Evan Wasuka, "U.S. Pumps $25M into Solomon Islands' Rebel Province," ABC Radio (Australia), October 15, 2020, https://www.abc.net.au/radio-australia/programs/pacificbeat/us-pumps-us$25m-into-solomon-islands-rebel-province/12769230.

exacerbating the region's vulnerabilities."[100] The effects of climate change are already evident: Cyclone Pam devastated Vanuatu in 2015, Cyclone Winston caused significant damage in Fiji in 2016, and Cyclone Harold caused death and destruction across Vanuatu, Solomon Islands, Fiji, and Tonga in April 2020. Cyclone Harold compounded the challenges already posed by the Covid-19 pandemic, with government services being stretched to respond to two simultaneous crises. The challenges posed by closed internal and external borders were particularly acute, making it difficult for both domestic and international assistance to reach affected communities.

Kiribati, Marshall Islands, Tokelau, and Tuvalu are either wholly or almost entirely made up of low-elevation atolls and reef features. These features are at risk of inundation due to sea-level rise, with implications for their habitability and the maritime entitlements these states may claim under UNCLOS. Under the current principles of ambulatory baselines, if the territory used to determine the normal baseline of a state disappears, so does its maritime jurisdiction. Pacific Island states, in partnership with Australia and the Pacific Community, have been working since the early 2000s to clarify, declare, and potentially fix the extent of their maritime jurisdictions through the Pacific Islands Regional Maritime Boundaries Project. They have also been negotiating the delimitation of the estimated 48 maritime boundaries between them, with 13 remaining to be confirmed.[101]

New Zealand has likewise taken a strong stance on climate change, which Prime Minister Ardern has described as "my generation's nuclear-free moment."[102] By contrast, Australia has been reluctant to take serious policy action and is perceived to have stymied stronger collective action within the PIF. At the 2019 PIF leaders' meeting, Australia reportedly refused to support the Tuvalu Declaration made by small Pacific Island states that called for an end to the use of coal in electricity generation. The Australian government's emphasis on spending, rather than domestic action, to address climate change disappointed Pacific leaders. Tuvaluan prime minister Enele Sopoaga commented that "no matter how much money you put on the table, it doesn't give you the excuse…not to do the right thing."[103]

---

[100] Pacific Islands Forum, "Fiftieth Pacific Islands Forum: Forum Communiqué."

[101] "The Status of Pacific Regional Maritime Boundaries as of July 2020," Pacific Community, September 9, 2020, https://www.spc.int/updates/blog/2020/09/the-status-of-pacific-regional-maritime-boundaries-as-of-july-2020.

[102] Jacinda Ardern, "Labour's Next Steps to Reduce Climate Emissions," New Zealand Labour Party, October 7, 2020, https://www.labour.org.nz/release-labours-next-steps-to-reduce-climate-emissions.

[103] Quoted in Melissa Clarke, "Tuvalu's PM Says +Australia's Climate Funding for Pacific 'Not an Excuse' to Avoid Emissions Cuts," ABC News (Australia), August 13, 2019, https://www.abc.net.au/news/2019-08-13/australias-climate-funding-pacific-islands-forum-tuvalu/11408930.

Australia's climate change inaction not only threatens its credibility as a regional partner but also has re-emerged as an issue in its relationships with the Biden administration and other like-minded governments. Ahead of the April 2021 Leaders' Summit on Climate, a senior U.S. official told reporters that Australia's existing policies are "insufficient" for achieving net-zero emissions by 2050. Similarly, the UK denied Australian leaders a speaking role at the Climate Ambition Summit 2020. While Canberra's perceived domestic political imperatives have upstaged vital environmental and international interests for decades, climate advocates hope that international pressure led by the United States may ultimately force a shift in priorities.

Economic Considerations

As previously described, strategic competition is putting pressure on states in Oceania to reconcile the emerging contradictions between their security and economic relationships. This pressure has been exacerbated by the impact of the Covid-19 pandemic. During 2020, Oceania was a relative Covid-19 success story, with less than one thousand deaths reported in Australia (out of 25.5 million), 26 in New Zealand (out of 4.8 million), 173 in PNG (out of 9 million), and 7 in Fiji (out of 900,000).[104] However, the economic costs of the pandemic have been devastating, even before the Delta variant increased infection rates across Australia, Fiji, PNG, and French Polynesia in 2021. Closed international borders have largely protected populations from the virus but have decimated the tourism industries on which most Oceanic states rely.

These effects have been most pronounced in the Pacific Islands, where tourism contributes over 40% of GDP and up to 50% of employment opportunities.[105] The collapse of the private tourism sector has in turn caused a fall in government revenue, foreign reserves, and cash balances and led to the loss of incomes and livelihoods. Other significant sources of revenue, such as remittances, have also declined significantly, as many temporary visa holders and permanent residents from the Pacific Islands in Australia, New Zealand, and the United States have lost their jobs. Remittances were predicted to drop by at least 20% during the pandemic, likely having a higher impact on rural villages that rely on overseas workers for money.[106] Australia committed an

---

[104] "WHO Coronavirus (COVID-19) Dashboard," World Health Organization, https://covid19.who.int. Data as of June 25, 2021.

[105] "Pacific Islands Threatened by Covid-19," International Monetary Fund, May 27, 2020, https://www.imf.org/en/News/Articles/2020/05/27/na-05272020-pacific-islands-threatened-by-covid-19

[106] Ibid.

additional AU$500 million to help ensure that Pacific Island states are able to achieve full immunization coverage, shared vaccines, supported health security initiatives, invested AU$130 million in the COVAX initiative, and is working through the Quad on a vaccine partnership program.[107]

Australia

Australia's economy faces two major pressures of its own: Covid-19 and the trade war with China. In 2020, Australia exported US$100.1 billion to China, compared to US$30.3 billion to its next largest export destination, Japan. A similar pattern was evident with imports, with US$61.1 billion coming from China in 2020. The next largest source was the United States at US$25.1 billion.[108] Consequently, debates in Australia about trade diversification have intensified, particularly as the impact of the pandemic has laid bare the country's vulnerabilities to supply chain disruption and generated a belief that its economic reliance on China adversely affects sovereign decision-making capabilities.[109] This concern was exacerbated by worsening Australia-China relations during 2020. In response to Australia's unilateral call for an inquiry into Covid-19's origins, China announced an 80% tariff on Australian barley and throughout the year placed additional tariffs on meat, seafood, wine, and cotton.[110] In 2021, Australia lodged a complaint with the WTO in response to antidumping and countervailing measures on barley and wine.[111]

While it is difficult to separate the impact of sanctions from the pandemic, Chinese sanctions are estimated to have cost Australia US$3 billion in lost exports.[112] Nevertheless, it appears that the net effect on Australian exports to China has so far been minimal. In 2020, goods exported totaled AU$145 billion, only 2% less than exports in 2019. There are several reasons for this outcome. First, China's sanctions have not yet targeted the most

---

[107] "Vaccine Access and Health Security Initiative," Indo-Pacific Centre for Health Security, https://indopacifichealthsecurity.dfat.gov.au/vaccine-access.

[108] "International Trade in Goods and Services Based on UN Comtrade Data," Department for International Trade and Department for Business, Energy and Industrial Strategy (United Kingdom), https://dit-trade-vis.azurewebsites.net/?reporter=36&type=C&year=2019&flow=2.

[109] Scott Morrison, "A World Order That Favours Freedom" (address to the Perth USAsia Centre, Perth, June 9, 2021), https://www.pm.gov.au/media/address-perth-usasia-centre-perth-wa.

[110] Kath Sullivan, "China's List of Sanctions and Tariffs on Australian Trade Is Growing. Here's What Has Been Hit So Far," ABC News (Australia), December 16, 2020, https://www.abc.net.au/news/2020-12-17/australian-trade-tension-sanctions-china-growing-commodities/12984218.

[111] Ibid.

[112] "China Trade Row Has Cost Australia $3 Billion in Lost Exports," Bloomberg, January 21, 2021, https://www.bloomberg.com/news/articles/2021-01-21/china-trade-row-has-cost-australia-3-billion-in-lost-exports.

significant industry in the economic relationship: iron ore. Iron ore remains the largest source of Australia's export revenue, and over 80% still goes to China (constituting 60% of its total iron ore imports).[113] The value of these exports offsets losses in other industries. Second, restrictions only began in May 2020, which may also distort the overall effect of China's trade sanctions on the Australian economy. For example, in the targeted industries, Australian exports to China in 2019 totaled AU$25 billion; yet from November 2020 to January 2021, the annualized value of these exports was around AU$5.5 billion.[114] Third, Australian exports to the rest of the world increased by more than exports to China declined. This is due to the highly competitive nature of Australian exporters and challenges in ramping up global supply to capture Australia's market share. Australia was able to diversify trade away from China in the targeted industries, although this has not been evident in key export industries. Iron ore trade remains mutually beneficial to both countries. There is some evidence, however, that China is seeking to diversify its sources of iron ore.[115]

New Zealand

A major reason that New Zealand has attempted to maintain a more neutral position in the emerging strategic competition is its economic reliance on China. Indeed, New Zealand once proudly celebrated achieving "five firsts" with China: (1) the first Western state to conclude a bilateral agreement with China in 1997 that assisted China's accession to the WTO, (2) the first Western state to recognize China as a market economy in 2004, (3) the first Western state to enter into free trade agreement negotiations with China in 2004, (4) the first to conclude that agreement in 2008, and (5) the first to negotiate an upgrade to that agreement in 2017 (concluded in 2021).[116] New Zealand also

---

[113] Ian Verrender, "Why Iron Ore Has Been Out of Bounds in China's Trade War with Australia—for Now," ABC News (Australia), August 30, 2020, https://www.abc.net.au/news/2020-08-31/why-iron-ore-has-been-out-of-bounds-in-the-china-trade-war/12611498; and Weizhen Tan, "China Should Consider Alternatives for Australian Iron Ore as Trade Tensions Simmer, Analyst Says," CNBC, December 15, 2020, https://www.cnbc.com/2020/12/16/as-china-australia-trade-tensions-rise-beijing-needs-iron-ore-alternative.html.

[114] Roland Rajah, "The Big Bark but Small Bite of China's Trade Coercion," Lowy Institute, Interpreter, April 8, 2021, https://www.lowyinstitute.org/the-interpreter/big-bark-small-bite-china-s-trade-coercion.

[115] "China Puts Australia on Notice with Push to Diversify Iron Ore," Bloomberg, May 18, 2021, https://www.bloomberg.com/news/articles/2021-05-18/china-puts-australia-on-notice-with-push-to-diversify-iron-ore.

[116] Reuben Steff and Francesca Dodd-Parr, "Examining the Immanent Dilemma of Small States in the Asia-Pacific: The Strategic Triangle between New Zealand, the U.S. and China," *Pacific Review* 32, no. 1 (2019): 90–112.

signed a nonbinding memorandum of understanding on BRI in 2017 and was the first developed country to join the Asian Infrastructure Investment Bank.

New Zealand's trade portfolio is highly tilted toward China and has become more so over the last five years. While China was New Zealand's largest destination for exports in 2015 at US$6 billion, US$5.9 billion went to Australia and US$4 billion to the United States. By 2020, the situation had changed, with US$10.8 billion of New Zealand's exports going to China, US$5.3 billion to Australia, and US$4.2 billion to the United States. The situation is repeated with imports. In 2015, the largest source was China (US$7.1 billion), followed by Australia (US$4.3 billion) and the United States (US$4.3 billion). The gap grew by 2020, with China providing US$8.4 billion of imports, Australia US$4.5 billion, and the United States US$3.6 billion.[117] During the Covid-19 pandemic, export demand fell among all of New Zealand's top trading partners except China. Exports to China amounted to 30.2% of total exports from April 2020 to April 2021, an increase from 23% in 2019.[118] Foreign Affairs Minister Mahuta publicly urged exporters to consider trade diversification, pointing to Australia's experience with Chinese economic coercion: "If they are close to an eye of the storm or in the eye of the storm, we've got to legitimately ask ourselves—it may only be a matter of time before the storm gets closer to us."[119]

Cognizant of the risks of economic reliance on China, both Australia and New Zealand have attempted to diversify trade through multilateral trade liberalization. Both have taken a leading role in the Comprehensive and Progressive Agreement for Trans-Pacific Partnership (CPTPP) that was agreed to in 2017 as a replacement for the Trans-Pacific Partnership (TPP). New Zealand was a member of its precursor, the Trans-Pacific Strategic Economic Partnership, alongside Singapore, Brunei, and Chile. Australia and New Zealand are also part of the Regional Comprehensive Economic Partnership comprising fifteen Indo-Pacific states (several of which are also signatories to the CPTPP).

Pacific Island States

Many Pacific Island states face a similar challenge of economic dependence on China. Chinese state-owned corporations have commenced major logging projects and developed fisheries across the region, as well as

---

[117] "International Trade in Goods and Services Based on UN Comtrade Data."

[118] "China Top Trade Partner in 2019," Stats NZ, March 2, 2020, https://www.stats.govt.nz/news/china-top-trade-partner-for-2019.

[119] Tracey Withers, "New Zealand Eyes Risks in China's Warm Trade Embrace," Bloomberg, May 26, 2021, https://www.bloomberg.com/news/newsletters/2021-05-26/supply-chains-latest-new-zealand-rethinks-close-china-trade-ties

run the massive Ramu nickel and cobalt mine and the Frieda River copper mine in PNG. China has also emerged as a major export partner for many Pacific Island states. For example, US$2.82 billion of PNG's exports went to China in 2019, whereas only US$2.85 billion went to Australia.[120] Solomon Islands sent US$415 million of exports to China in 2019, while sending only US$57.4 million to its next biggest export destination, Italy.[121]

Reflecting its increasing reliance on geoeconomics to support its geostrategy, China has also emerged as a major donor to the Pacific Islands. However, its aid program to these states is still significantly smaller than that of Australia (and to a lesser extent New Zealand), and now appears to be declining in real terms. After committing US$290 million in 2018 and US$1 billion in 2019, Beijing committed only US$4.2 million in 2020.[122] China has made greater inroads in financing infrastructure and holds approximately 12% of all regional debt.[123] Nine Pacific Island states—Cook Islands, Federated States of Micronesia, Fiji, Niue, PNG, Samoa, Solomon Islands, Tonga, and Vanuatu—have signed on to BRI, raising concerns that China will use debt as leverage to gain a strategic foothold in the Pacific. However, while almost half the Pacific Island states are classified by the International Monetary Fund and Asian Development Bank as being at high risk of debt distress, this is not due to Chinese lending, which amounts to less than half the total debt of any state in the region except Tonga.[124] Although this undermines the "debt-trap diplomacy" argument, the significant scale of Chinese lending does raise questions about debt sustainability. The United States and Australia have expressed concern that the obligations that Pacific Island states assume under BRI may impinge their sovereignty, and New Zealand has warned China that "there is a substantial difference between financing loans and contributing to greater ODA investment."[125] But aid and loans under BRI may be as much about creating economic opportunities for Chinese companies amid oversupply and economic stagnation at home as increasing China's influence.

---

[120] Observatory of Economic Complexity (OEC), "Papua New Guinea," https://oec.world/en/profile/country/png.

[121] OEC, "Solomon Islands," https://oec.world/en/profile/country/slb.

[122] Lowy Institute, Pacific Aid Map, https://pacificaidmap.lowyinstitute.org/graphingtool. Note that not all donors have reported data for 2019 and 2020.

[123] Rohan Fox and Matthew Dornan, "China in the Pacific: Is China Engaged in 'Debt-trap Diplomacy?'" Australian National University, Development Policy Centre, November 8, 2018, https://devpolicy.org/is-china-engaged-in-debt-trap-diplomacy-20181108.

[124] Ibid.

[125] Mahuta, "He Taniwha He Tipua, He Tipua He Taniwha."

Conclusion

The explicit strategic competition between the United States and China that emerged during the Trump administration is one of Oceania's biggest challenges, as it is causing the security and economic interests of Oceanic states to diverge. While Trump's America-first policies provoked uncertainty about the United States' intentions in the region and concerns about moves such as the withdrawal from the TPP, there appears to be no lasting damage in U.S. bilateral relations with Australia or New Zealand, and the Biden administration has reassured allies and partners that U.S. diplomacy is "back to normal." In response to the deep structural changes in the international system, Canberra has adopted an alliance-centered approach, while Wellington has attempted strategic ambiguity while moving further into Washington's orbit. Several Micronesian states have also sought to expand their defense relationships with the United States, with Palau and the Federated States of Micronesia agreeing to host new U.S. bases. Except for Australia, Oceanic states have mostly signed on to BRI, albeit with varying levels of enthusiasm. While there are concerns that Pacific Island states' participation in BRI is a sign they are tilting toward Beijing, as well as rumors of defense alignments with China, nothing substantial has materialized. In reality, the Pacific Islands continue to emphasize agency and autonomy and have sought to leverage the strategic competition to their advantage.

Australia's security outlook is shaped by concerns about China's rising military power and assertiveness and its potential to disrupt the U.S.-led rules-based order that has served Australian security and economic interests so well. While claims about the effects of foreign interference and coercion on Australia's democracy and economy tend to be overstated in public discussions, Beijing's actions have compelled Canberra to move away from the pragmatic approach that has defined its China policy since the early 1970s and toward a strategy that prioritizes both sovereign resilience and a U.S. alliance. This was most clearly highlighted by the September 2021 announcement of the AUKUS security partnership with the United States and the UK. The debates about Australia choosing a side now appear redundant. What remains are the challenges of developing a workable China policy, delineating parameters for engagement if great-power conflict emerges in East Asia, and negotiating the increasingly fraught issue of climate change.

In line with a small-state conception of foreign policy, New Zealand uses strategic ambiguity to maximize maneuverability and continues to avoid explicitly choosing sides. But while New Zealand is known to advance an independent foreign policy, it relies on its alliance with Australia for security and remains a close friend and de facto ally of the United States. Its attitude toward China is mixed. Wellington recognizes a need to engage Beijing economically but is growing increasingly wary of the challenges it poses to the rules-based order.

For Pacific Island states, climate change threatens the habitability and livability of all islands and thus is viewed as the biggest existential security challenge. While New Zealand has taken a strong stance on climate change, domestic politics in Australia have constrained substantive policy action. This has implications for diplomatic relations with the Biden administration, which has increased public pressure on Australia to set more ambitious targets, as well as with other Oceanic states. Oceania is a maritime region, and along with nonconventional security challenges such as illegal, unreported, and unregulated fishing, climate change is threatening the sea-based entitlements and jurisdictions of Pacific Island states. Many of these states have economies that rely heavily on maritime resources. Maritime security has been a strong basis for intraregional cooperation, including with the United States and France, and this is likely to continue. However, Australia's climate inaction continues to make it an outlier in Oceania and undermine its credibility as a regional leader.[126]

The United States and Australia, and to a lesser extent New Zealand, should acknowledge that their perception that strategic competition will inevitably require strategic choices is not necessarily shared by all Pacific Island states (although several Micronesian states arguably support this view). Regardless of how realistic it is for many Pacific Island states to indefinitely avoid strategic choices, the United States, Australia, and New Zealand will have the most success advancing their regional relationships—and consequently their strategic priorities—if they are perceived to be committed partners that genuinely support the interests of Pacific Island states. The United States' and New Zealand's commitments to addressing climate change, a priority for most Pacific Island states, go some way to achieving this. While Australia has now committed to a net-zero target by 2050—at least partly a consequence of international pressure, including from the United States—its recalcitrance on climate change has undermined the credibility of its claimed commitment to the region. The development and articulation of a clear pathway to achieving the new target will be necessary for reducing this credibility gap. The United States also needs to do more to rebuild trust with Pacific Island states after the damage done both during the Trump administration and, before that, by a tendency to announce but not follow-through on initiatives in the region. Large-scale military investments will be important in the event of open conflict (although any submarines developed under AUKUS will not be

---

[126] Wesley Morgan, "Oceans Apart: Considering the Indo-Pacific and the Blue Pacific," *Security Challenges* 16, no. 1 (2020): 44–64.

available for several decades), but in a region that faces multifaceted human security challenges and where relationships are vital, strategic competition in Oceania is more likely to be decided by the lower-key, but equally important, everyday work of development and diplomacy.

About the Contributors

Michael J. Green is Director of Asian Studies and Chair in Modern and Contemporary Japanese Politics and Foreign Policy at the School of Foreign Service at Georgetown University and Senior Vice President for Asia and Japan Chair at the Center for Strategic and International Studies. He previously served in government as special assistant to the president for National Security Affairs and senior director for Asia on the National Security Council staff. His recent publications on Asia include *By More Than Providence: Grand Strategy and American Power in the Asia Pacific Since 1783* (2017) and *Line of Advantage: Japan's Grand Strategy in the Era of Abe Shinzo* (2021). He serves on the boards of the Asia Foundation and Radio Free Asia and the advisory board of the Center for a New American Security. He received his undergraduate degree from Kenyon College and his master's and doctoral degrees from the Johns Hopkins University School of Advanced International Studies.

Marcin Kaczmarski is a Lecturer in Security Studies in the School of Social and Political Sciences at the University of Glasgow. His research focuses on Russia-China relations, Russia's foreign and security policy, comparative regionalism, and the role of rising powers in international politics. Dr. Kaczmarski is the author of *Russia-China Relations in the Post-Crisis International Order* and has published articles in leading academic journals, including *Survival, International Affairs, International Politics,* and *Europe-Asia Studies*. He was a visiting scholar at the Chengchi University in Taiwan, the Slavic-Eurasian Research Center in Japan, the Aleksanteri Institute in Finland, the Kennan Institute in Washington, D.C., and the Shanghai International Studies University in China. Prior to joining the University of Glasgow, Dr. Kaczmarski combined research and teaching at the University of Warsaw with policy-oriented analysis for the Finnish Institute of International Affairs in Helsinki and the Centre for Eastern Studies in Warsaw.

Huong Le Thu is a Senior Fellow in the Defence and Strategy Program at the Australian Strategic Policy Institute (ASPI). At ASPI, she leads projects on Southeast Asia, including on regional alignment politics, Southeast Asian perceptions of great-power competition, regional dispute management, and ASEAN regionalism. Prior to joining ASPI, Dr. Le Thu taught at the Australian National University and held research positions at the ISEAS–Yusof Ishak Institute in Singapore and the Institute of International Relations at the National Chengchi University in Taiwan. She has worked and lived in Kuala Lumpur, Jakarta, and Seoul, among other cities. In 2020, she was awarded an inaugural Asia EDGE fellowship at the National Bureau of Asian Research (NBR). Dr. Le Thu frequently comments in global media and has written for *Asian Security*, *Asia-Pacific Review*, *Asia Policy*, Oxford University Press, *Foreign Policy*, the *Financial Times*, the *Washington Post*, the *New York Times*, the *Los Angeles Times*, *Nikkei Asia*, the *Australian Financial Review*, the *Straits Times*, *Japan Times*, and *Taipei Times*, among others. Dr. Le Thu received her PhD from the National Chengchi University in Taiwan and holds a master's in international studies from Jagiellonian University in Poland. She speaks five languages and has published in four.

Rohan Mukherjee is an Assistant Professor of Political Science at Yale-NUS College in Singapore. His research focuses on the grand strategies of rising powers and their impact on international security and order, with an empirical specialization in South Asia and East Asia. His book, *Ascending Order: Rising Powers and the Politics of Status in International Institutions*, is forthcoming with Cambridge University Press. His work has been published in journals such as *International Affairs*, *Asian Security*, *Contemporary Politics*, *Survival*, *Global Governance*, *International Relations of the Asia-Pacific*, *India Review*, and *International Journal*, as well as in edited volumes from academic presses such as Oxford, Cambridge, Stanford, University of North Carolina, and Brookings. Dr. Mukherjee has co-edited a policy-focused volume with Oxford University Press that brings together top scholars and analysts across generations from Japan and India to chart the future course of bilateral relations. He received his PhD from the Department of Politics at Princeton University and an MPA in international development from Princeton University's School of Public and International Affairs. He has also been a Stanton Nuclear Security Fellow at the MIT Security Studies Program and a nonresident visiting fellow at the United Nations University in Tokyo.

Rebecca Strating is the Executive Director of La Trobe Asia and an Associate Professor in Politics and International Relations in the Department of Politics, Media and Philosophy at La Trobe University. Her research focuses on Australian foreign policy and maritime disputes in the Indo-Pacific. She has published over twenty peer-reviewed articles and three monographs, with the most recent being *Defending the Maritime Rules-Based Order: Regional Responses to the South China Sea Disputes* (2020). In 2019, Dr. Strating was awarded an Asian Studies visiting fellowship to the East-West Center in Washington, D.C. She has been a visiting affiliate fellow at the ISEAS–Yusof Ishak Institute in Singapore and a visiting affiliate at Georgetown University, and she is currently a non-visiting fellow at the Perth USAsia Centre. Dr. Strating was awarded the Boyer Prize for best article published in the *Australian Journal of International Affairs* in 2017. She received her PhD in politics from Monash University.

Alison Szalwinski is Vice President of Research at the National Bureau of Asian Research (NBR). She provides executive leadership to NBR's policy research agenda and oversees research teams in Seattle and Washington, D.C. She is the author of numerous articles and reports and a co-editor of six volumes in the *Strategic Asia* series along with Ashley J. Tellis and Michael Wills. Prior to joining NBR, Ms. Szalwinski spent time at the U.S. Department of State and the Center for Strategic and International Studies. Her research interests include U.S. policy toward Asia, especially U.S.-China relations and the importance of great-power competition for U.S. alliances in the region. She holds a BA in foreign affairs and history from the University of Virginia and an MA in Asian studies from Georgetown University's Edmund A. Walsh School of Foreign Service.

Ashley J. Tellis is the Tata Chair for Strategic Affairs and a Senior Fellow at the Carnegie Endowment for International Peace. He has also served as Research Director of the Strategic Asia Program at the National Bureau of Asian Research (NBR) and co-editor of the program's annual volume since 2004. While on assignment to the U.S. Department of State as senior adviser to the undersecretary of state for political affairs, Dr. Tellis was intimately involved in negotiating the civil nuclear agreement with India. Previously, he was commissioned into the Foreign Service and served as senior adviser to the ambassador at the U.S. embassy in New Delhi. He also served on the U.S. National Security Council staff as special assistant to President George W. Bush and senior director for strategic planning and Southwest Asia. Prior to his government service, Dr. Tellis was a senior policy analyst at the RAND Corporation and professor of policy analysis at the RAND Graduate School. He is the author of *India's Emerging Nuclear Posture* (2001) and co-author of *Interpreting China's Grand Strategy: Past, Present, and Future* (2000). He holds a PhD in political science from the University of Chicago.

Joanne Wallis is Professor of International Security in the Department of Politics and International Relations at the University of Adelaide. She is the author or editor of seven books, including *Constitution Making during State Building* (2014) and *Pacific Power? Australia's Strategy in the Pacific Islands* (2017). Dr. Wallis is the chief investigator on two Australian Research Council Discovery projects that analyze Australian interventions in the Pacific Islands and the operation of the Australia–New Zealand alliance. She is also the chief investigator on an Australian Department of Defence Strategic Policy Grant that studies the potential of a networked security architecture in the Pacific Islands. Dr. Wallis co-edits the journal *Peacebuilding*, is on the international advisory board of the *Round Table*, and serves on the editorial boards of the *Australian Journal of International Affairs* and *Global Studies Quarterly*. She completed her PhD at the University of Cambridge as a Poynton Cambridge Australia scholar and then spent over eight years with the Strategic and Defense Studies Centre at the Australian National University. Prior to that, she was a lawyer at Allens Arthur Robinson (now Allens Linklaters).

Michael Wills is Executive Vice President at the National Bureau of Asian Research (NBR). He manages all aspects of NBR's financial and business operations, serves as secretary to the Board of Directors, and is a member of the *Asia Policy* journal's editorial advisory committee. His research expertise includes geopolitics, international security, and the international relations of Asia, with a particular interest in China's relations with Southeast Asia. Mr. Wills is co-editor of twelve *Strategic Asia* volumes (with Ashley Tellis and, since 2015, Alison Szalwinski) as well as *New Security Challenges in Asia* (2013, with Robert M. Hathaway). Before joining NBR, he worked at the Cambodia Development Resource Institute in Phnom Penh, and prior to that with Control Risks Group, an international political and security risk management firm, in London. He holds a BA (Honors) in Chinese studies from the University of Oxford.

Suisheng Zhao is Professor and Director of the Center for China-U.S. Cooperation in the Josef Korbel School of International Studies at the University of Denver. He was previously a postdoctoral Campbell National Fellow at Stanford University's Hoover Institution, associate professor of political science and international studies at Washington College in Maryland, and associate professor of government and East Asian politics at Colby College in Maine. Dr. Zhao is the founder and editor of the *Journal of Contemporary China* and the author and editor of more than two dozen books and several dozen articles on Chinese nationalism, Chinese politics and political economy, Chinese foreign policy, U.S.-China relations, cross-strait relations, and East Asian regional issues. His forthcoming book is tentatively titled *The Dragon Roars Back: Transformational Leaders and Dynamics of Chinese Foreign Policy* (2022). He received his PhD in political science from the University of California, San Diego.

About Strategic Asia

The **Strategic Asia Program** at the National Bureau of Asian Research (NBR) is a major ongoing research initiative that draws together top Asia studies specialists and international relations experts to assess the changing strategic environment in the Asia-Pacific. The program combines the rigor of academic analysis with the practicality of contemporary policy analyses by incorporating economic, military, political, and demographic data and by focusing on the trends, strategies, and perceptions that drive geopolitical dynamics in the region. The program's integrated set of products and activities includes:

- an annual edited volume written by leading specialists
- an executive brief tailored for public- and private-sector decision-makers and strategic planners
- briefings and presentations for government, business, and academia that are designed to foster in-depth discussions revolving around major public policy issues

Special briefings are held for key committees of Congress and the executive branch, other government agencies, and the intelligence community. The principal audiences for the program's research findings are the U.S. policymaking and research communities, the media, the business community, and academia.

Previous Strategic Asia Volumes

Now in its twentieth year, the *Strategic Asia* series has addressed how Asia functions as a zone of strategic interaction and contends with an uncertain balance of power.

> *Strategic Asia 2020: U.S.-China Competition for Global Influence* offered a forward-looking assessment of how the rivalry between China and the United States is playing out around the globe and drew implications for U.S. policymakers.

Strategic Asia 2019: China's Expanding Strategic Ambitions assessed Chinese ambitions in a range of geographic and functional areas and presented policy options for the United States and its partners to address the challenges posed by a rising China.

Strategic Asia 2017–18: Power, Ideas, and Military Strategy in the Asia-Pacific identified how Asia's major powers have developed military strategies to address their most significant challenges.

Strategic Asia 2016–17: Understanding Strategic Cultures in the Asia-Pacific explored the strategic cultures of the region's major powers and explained how they inform decision-making about the pursuit of strategic objectives and national power.

Strategic Asia 2015–16: Foundations of National Power in the Asia-Pacific examined how the region's major powers are building their national power as geopolitical competition intensifies.

Strategic Asia 2014–15: U.S. Alliances and Partnerships at the Center of Global Power analyzed the trajectories of U.S. alliance and partner relationships in the Asia-Pacific in light of the region's shifting strategic landscape.

Strategic Asia 2013–14: Asia in the Second Nuclear Age examined the role of nuclear weapons in the grand strategies of key Asian states and assessed the impact of these capabilities—both established and latent—on regional and international stability.

Strategic Asia 2012–13: China's Military Challenge assessed China's growing military capabilities and explored their impact on the Asia-Pacific region.

Strategic Asia 2011–12: Asia Responds to Its Rising Powers—China and India explored how key Asian states have responded to the rise of China and India, drawing implications for U.S. interests and leadership in the Asia-Pacific.

Strategic Asia 2010–11: Asia's Rising Power and America's Continued Purpose provided a continent-wide net assessment of the core trends and issues affecting the region by examining Asia's performance in nine key functional areas.

Strategic Asia 2009–10: Economic Meltdown and Geopolitical Stability analyzed the impact of the global economic crisis on key Asian states and explored the strategic implications for the United States.

Strategic Asia 2008–09: Challenges and Choices examined the impact of geopolitical developments on Asia's transformation over the previous eight years and assessed the major strategic choices on Asia facing the incoming U.S. administration.

Strategic Asia 2007–08: Domestic Political Change and Grand Strategy examined internal and external drivers of grand strategy on Asian foreign policymaking.

Strategic Asia 2006–07: Trade, Interdependence, and Security addressed how changing trade relationships affect the balance of power and security in the region.

Strategic Asia 2005–06: Military Modernization in an Era of Uncertainty appraised the progress of Asian military modernization programs.

Strategic Asia 2004–05: Confronting Terrorism in the Pursuit of Power explored the effect of the U.S.-led war on terrorism on the strategic transformations underway in Asia.

Strategic Asia 2003–04: Fragility and Crisis examined the fragile balance of power in Asia, drawing out the key domestic political and economic trends in Asian states supporting or undermining this tenuous equilibrium.

Strategic Asia 2002–03: Asian Aftershocks drew on the baseline established in the 2001–02 volume to analyze changes in Asian states' grand strategies and relationships in the aftermath of the September 11 terrorist attacks.

Strategic Asia 2001–02: Power and Purpose established a baseline assessment for understanding the strategies and interactions of the major states within the region.

Research and Management Team

The Strategic Asia research team consists of leading international relations and security specialists from universities and research institutions across the United States and around the world. A new research team is selected each year. To date, more than 150 scholars have written for the program. The research team for 2021–22 is led by Ashley J. Tellis (Carnegie Endowment for International Peace), Alison Szalwinski (NBR), and Michael Wills (NBR). Aaron Friedberg (Princeton University, and Strategic Asia's founding research director) and Richard Ellings (NBR, and Strategic Asia's founding program director) serve as senior advisors to the program.

Attribution

Readers of *Strategic Asia* and visitors to the Strategic Asia website may use data, charts, graphs, and quotes from these sources without requesting permission from NBR on the condition that they cite NBR and the appropriate primary source in any published work. No report, chapter, separate study, extensive text, or any other substantial part of the Strategic Asia Program's products may be reproduced without the written permission of NBR. To request permission, please write to publications@nbr.org.

Index

Afghanistan, 43, 45, 76, 91–92, 130, 193

Africa, 96, 178

Antarctica, 191, 206

Arctic, 96, 102, 112, 114

Asian financial crisis, 184

Asian Infrastructure Investment Bank (AIIB), 138, 218

Asia-Pacific Economic Cooperation (APEC), 10, 195, 206

Association of Southeast Asian Nations (ASEAN), 128, 135, 143, 163–69, 170–71, 174–75, 180–81, 184–85

Australia, 23, 134–35, 186–87, 189, 191, 195–96, 199–201, 209–10, 212, 214, 216–17, 220

Australia, New Zealand, United States (ANZUS) Security Treaty, 186, 193, 210

Australia, United Kingdom, United States, (AUKUS), 169, 172, 188, 191–92, 194, 200, 209, 215, 220

Australia-China, 111, 191, 199, 209, 212, 216–17

Australia-India, 134–35, 170, 201, 210

Australia-Japan, 201

Australia–New Zealand, 187, 201–2, 210–11, 218

Australia–United States, 187, 191–92, 196, 199, 200–201, 209, 220–21

Belt and Road Initiative (BRI), 53, 54, 103, 130, 186–88, 191, 196, 198, 200, 206, 208, 218–20

BRICS (Brazil, Russia, India, China, South Africa), 54

Canada, 79, 84, 194, 200

Central Asia, 112, 116–17

China, 23–24, 27–28, 31–32, 85–86; China dream, 37, 39–40; demographics, 57–58; domestic politics, 38, 50, 56–60, 108; economy, 13, 38–39, 49–50, 57–60; grand strategy, 41, 130; great-power status, 5, 14, 43, 59, 60; nationalism, 38, 57, 67; one-China policy, 55; People's Liberation Army (PLA), 38, 54, 106–7; regional security, 54–55, 201, 206; rise, 18, 39, 40–42, 45, 130; territorial disputes, 53, 55–56, 58, 64, 67, 70, 107, 123, 130, 147; values, 45, 47, 52, 61

China-Australia (*see* Australia-China)

China-India: economic relations, 127–28, 137–38, 144, 150–51, 153; geopolitical and strategic relations, 102, 106, 129, 137–38, 157; historical relations, 129; security relations, 102, 106, 123, 129, 135, 147; trade, 127–28, 137–38, 150–51

China-Japan: geopolitical and strategic relations, 68, 70–71, 73–74; territorial disputes, 58, 64, 67, 70

China–New Zealand, 202–3, 212, 217–18
China–North Korea, 42–43
China-Pakistan, 130
China-Russia, 96, 103–10, 112, 117, 122–23; economic relations, 103, 107–8, 110; geopolitical and strategic relations, 54, 94, 96, 103–10, 122; security relations, 103–7; social and cultural relations, 104; trade, 103–4
China–South Korea, 43, 77–79, 85
China-Taiwan, 33, 44, 55, 73–74, 85, 88, 186, 199
China–United States: economic relations, 10–12, 14–15, 22, 49, 57, 111, 152, 181; geopolitical and strategic relations, 4, 6, 12–13, 26, 34, 36, 38, 41–44, 49, 51, 57, 59–61, 99, 108, 111, 113–14, 163, 186, 188, 199, 205; historical relations, 43; security relations, 34, 55, 113–14; trade, 13–15, 25, 34, 42–43, 50, 57, 94, 152, 181
Chinese Communist Party (CCP), 45, 52, 56–58
climate change, 44, 61, 98, 114, 133, 188, 202, 213–15, 220–21
Cold War, 8–9, 27, 37, 42, 59, 60, 165
Comprehensive and Progressive Agreement for Trans-Pacific Partnership (CPTPP), 69, 183–84, 218
Covid-19 pandemic, 5–6, 28–30, 38, 41, 43, 47–48, 50–53, 58–60, 65–67, 73–77, 83–85, 88–91, 94, 108–9, 118–21, 123, 127, 138, 145–49, 175–76, 178–79, 184, 200, 205, 211, 214–16

demographics, 14, 32, 58, 80, 95, 121

East China Sea, 55, 64, 67, 123
energy, 103, 105, 111–13, 117–18, 121
Europe, 97–98, 102, 106, 110, 112, 117, 119, 123

European Union, 51, 110, 117
extended deterrence, 5, 8, 27

Fiji, 196, 199, 206, 208–9, 214
Five Eyes, 194, 202
free and open Indo-Pacific strategy, 64, 69–72, 163, 165, 194, 204
freedom of navigation operations, 132, 143, 172, 210

G-7, 54, 198, 200
global financial crisis, 5, 17, 29, 116, 132
globalization, 6–19, 37–38, 47–49, 58, 94, 115–18, 127–28, 150–56, 181, 188
Guam, 55, 194–95

Hong Kong, 42, 44, 52, 58, 64, 86, 108, 199–200
human rights, 42, 199–200, 203
humanitarian assistance and disaster relief (HADR), 193, 196, 204, 213

India: diplomacy, 132, 134, 136, 142, 149; economy, 127–28, 137–38, 145–56, 158; foreign policy, 131, 133–36; grand strategy, 132, 136; military strategy, 128, 132, 135, 139, 141–42; strategic culture, 128, 132–33, 136–37, 139–40, 158
India-Australia (*see* Australia-India)
India-Japan, 134
India-Pakistan, 130, 133, 142
India-Russia, 102, 106, 109, 110, 123, 141
India–United States: economic relations, 150–51, 158; geopolitical and strategic relations, 102, 128, 131–33, 138, 141–44, 157–58; security relations, 102, 131–33, 141–143; trade, 150–51, 158

Indonesia, 170–72, 179, 182–83

Intermediate-Range Nuclear Forces (INF) Treaty, 113, 114

international economic system, 7, 11–12, 23–24, 30

Japan: domestic politics, 67–68, 73, 75–77; economy, 67, 69, 74–75; foreign policy, 68–72, 134; military strategy, 68; multilateralism, 69, 135; Self-Defense Forces, 68; strategic culture, 68–69, 72; territorial disputes, 64, 67, 70; trade, 69

Japan-Australia (*see* Australia-Japan)

Japan-China (*see* China-Japan)

Japan-India (*see* India-Japan)

Japan–United States, 68, 71–74

Japan-Taiwan, 73–74, 87

Korea (*see* North Korea and South Korea)

Korean Peninsula, 64

liberalism, 4, 7–8, 11, 13, 59–60

Malaysia, 164–65, 178

Micronesia, 205–6, 208

Middle East, 100, 122

multilateralism, 69, 89, 143

multipolarity, 9, 38, 47, 59, 61, 78, 95, 97, 100, 113, 117–18, 139, 186

Myanmar (Burma), 169

nationalism, 4, 13, 18–32, 36, 38, 57, 67, 83

New Zealand, 23, 186–87, 189, 193–94, 197, 201–5, 210–11, 214, 217–18, 220

New Zealand–Australia (*see* Australia–New Zealand)

New Zealand–China (*see* China–New Zealand)

nontraditional security, 123, 198

North Atlantic Treaty Organization (NATO), 102

North Korea, 25, 42–43, 65, 80–82, 91

North Korea–China (*see* China–North Korea)

North Korea–South Korea, 77, 80–83

Northeast Asia, 31, 62–92, 134

nuclear energy, 107

nuclear weapons, 81, 106, 115

Oceania, 23–24, 28, 32, 187–222

Pacific Islands, 55, 186, 189, 191, 194–95, 205–9, 211–15, 218–20; diplomatic relations, 191, 205, 207–9; economic relations, 191, 205, 215, 217–19; security relations, 55, 205, 212; recognition of Taiwan, 206–7

Pacific Islands Forum (PIF), 189, 191, 195–96, 198, 205, 207–8, 214

Pakistan, 130–31, 133, 142

Pakistan-China (*see* China-Pakistan)

Pakistan-India (*see* India-Pakistan)

Papua New Guinea (PNG), 195–96, 199, 215, 219

Philippines, 56, 172–73, 179–80, 182

Quad, 66, 69, 72, 78, 110, 135, 143, 194, 201, 205, 211, 216

Regional Comprehensive Economic Partnership (RCEP), 60, 156, 180–81

Russia: arms transfer, 102–3, 109–10; demographics, 95, 121; domestic politics, 96, 98, 101, 104, 108, 116, 120–21, 123–24; economy, 97–99, 110, 115–18, 121, 123; energy, 98, 110, 111, 117, 121; foreign policy, 96–97, 119–20; grand strategy, 100–101, 116, 118–20; great-power status, 97, 101, 111, 117, 123; military, 96, 102, 105–6, 118; missiles, 102–3, 109–10, 114, 122–23; nuclear weapons, 105; regional security, 97, 113; resources, 98, 110–11; Russian Far East, 112; territorial disputes, 107

Russia-China (*see* China-Russia)

Russia-India (*see* India-Russia)

Russia–United States, 8, 97, 99–103, 108, 110, 113–16, 121–24

Senkaku/Diaoyu Islands, 64, 67, 70, 73

Shanghai Cooperation Organisation (SCO), 109

Singapore, 163–64, 168–69, 174, 181, 183

Solomon Islands, 197, 199, 206, 213–14

South Asia, 130, 133, 140–41, 144–45

South China Sea, 38, 55–56, 109, 123, 170–71, 191

South Korea: domestic politics, 77, 78, 81, 83–85; economy, 84–85; foreign policy, 78–79, 81–82, 85; security, 80–81; strategic culture, 77–81, 83

South Korea–China (*see* China–South Korea)

South Korea–North Korea (*see* North Korea–South Korea)

South Korea–United States, 77–82, 85

Southeast Asia, 10, 23, 28, 31, 69, 79, 136, 161–85, 189, 191, 194

Soviet Union, 7–9

Taiwan, 46–47, 86–90, 206, 212–13

Taiwan-China (*see* China-Taiwan)

Taiwan-Japan (*see* Japan-Taiwan)

Taiwan–United States, 44, 87–88, 90, 212–13

Terminal High Altitude Air Defense (THAAD), 64, 79, 84

Thailand, 162, 168–69, 177–78, 184

Tibet, 42, 44

Trans-Pacific Partnership (TPP), 21, 35, 71, 87, 133, 161, 218, 220

Ukraine, 99, 102–3

United Kingdom (UK), 169–70, 188, 192, 194, 215, 220

United Nations, 46, 123, 171, 208–9

United Nations Convention on the Law of the Sea (UNCLOS), 211, 214

United States, 3–4, 15–18, 20–21, 25, 32, 48, 65–66, 69, 71–72, 82–83, 88, 91–92, 131–33, 136, 140, 166; economy, 8, 14, 15, 17, 22, 32–33, 35, 47, 60; foreign policy, 3–4, 16–17, 22, 24–26, 33, 35, 60, 91–92, 161, 222; governance, 6, 9, 29–30, 33, 35, 44–47, 186; great-power status, 9, 59–60; isolationism, 20, 35, 48, 99, 200, 220; liberalism, 4, 59–60; nationalism, 19–32; rebalancing strategy, 26–28; security, 8, 48; strategic culture, 29–30

United States–Australia (*see* Australia–United States)

United States–China (*see* China–United States)

United States–India (*see* India–United States)

United States–Japan (*see* Japan–United States)

United States–Russia (*see* Russia–United States)

United States–South Korea (*see* South Korea–United States)

United States–Taiwan (*see* Taiwan–United States)

Vietnam, 162, 166, 169, 171, 174–75, 181–83

World Bank, 7
World Health Organization (WHO), 46–47, 51–52, 89, 119, 149
World Trade Organization (WTO), 11, 115–16, 187, 216–17
World War II, 7, 11, 44–45, 60, 191, 194

Xinjiang, 42, 44, 108, 199–200, 203